ENEMIES OF ALL

ENEMIES OF ALL

The Rise and Fall of the Golden Age of Piracy

RICHARD BLAKEMORE

PEGASUS BOOKS

NEW YORK LONDON

For My Students

ENEMIES OF ALL

Pegasus Books, Ltd.
148 West 37th Street, 13th Floor
New York, NY 10018

ISBN: 978-1-63936-633-0

10 9 8 7 6 5 4 3 2

Printed in the United States of America
Distributed by Simon & Schuster
www.pegasusbooks.com

CONTENTS

Part III: Black Flag 205

FOREWORD

In January 2018, maritime archaeologists working in North Carolina announced an amazing discovery. They were excavating the shipwreck of the *Queen Anne's Revenge*, captained by Edward Teach – more famously known in his own day and ever since as Blackbeard, perhaps the most famous pirate of all.

Two years earlier, they had recovered several scraps of paper, seemingly among the least prepossessing of 400,000 items brought up from the seabed over several decades. Yet because one bore the unusual toponym 'Hilo', referring to Ilo in Peru, after some cross-checking, these researchers were able to identify the book, and the page, from which these papers came.

That book was Edward Cooke's *A Voyage to the South Sea*, published in 1712, six years before the *Queen Anne's Revenge* ran aground. Evidently the pirates' reading materials (whether acquired through theft or more respectable means) were up to date, and also topical. *A Voyage to the South Sea* narrated Cooke's travels with Woodes Rogers aboard the *Duke* and the *Dutchess* in 1708–11. During that long cruise, Rogers and Cooke plundered Spanish shipping in the Pacific Ocean. They also rescued Alexander Selkirk, the castaway who probably inspired Daniel Defoe's *Robinson Crusoe*, which first appeared in print the year after Teach's death.

There are practical reasons why Cooke's tome, over 400 pages long, might be found aboard the *Queen Anne's Revenge*. Like many contributions to the burgeoning maritime literature of the day, Cooke's work included detailed navigational information, albeit focused on the Pacific coast of South America and the Indian Ocean, both some way from Teach's usual cruising grounds.

The circumstances of the discovery point towards a more prosaic explanation: these scraps were found in a cannon, covered in gunpowder, so they were probably used as wadding. Maybe the pirates put their books to this messy end once they had finished with them. Maybe Teach's crew never actually read these books at all.

And yet. A book by a sailor and plunderer, about sailing and plundering, aboard a ship of sailors and plunderers; a book about travelling, itself travelling and then sinking among the islands and inlets of the Carolina coast ... it is far too intriguing a prospect to dismiss entirely.

My own favourite interpretation is that pirates simply enjoyed reading about pirates.

A week or two after this announcement, I began teaching an undergraduate course on the history of piracy. That (for me, extremely well-timed) archaeological announcement instantly became, and remains, the introductory vignette for my first lecture. It so perfectly encapsulates a key theme of that course and also of this book: that the history of piracy is not just a matter of what pirates did. It is as much, if not more, a question of the stories told about piracy, and the stories that pirates themselves told.

You know what a pirate is. You know how they dress, how they speak. If you think of the word 'pirate', I bet I can guess which images and associations leap to your mind, reinforced by depictions you can find pretty much anywhere in modern culture – especially if, like me, you have young children (though I admit my son's interest in pirates and collection of related toys may be neither coincidental nor representative).

We have a remarkably clear picture of pirates, and it is dominated by figures like Teach. It is only Teach's reputation as Blackbeard that made that archaeological discovery a headline at all. A few years after Teach's death he was described as a man of 'uncommon Boldness, and personal Courage', known for his 'Frolicks of Wickedness'. His 'Cognomen of *Black-beard*' derived from the 'large Quantity of Hair, which like a frightful Meteor, covered his whole Face, and frightened *America* more than any Comet'. Into this beard and hair he twisted ribbons, and during battle 'he wore a Fur-Cap, and stuck a lighted Match on each Side, under it ... his Eyes naturally looking Fierce and Wild, made him altogether such a Figure, that Imagination cannot form an Idea of a Fury, from Hell, to look more frightful.' You cannot get much more piratical than that.

Portraits of Edward Teach,
or Blackbeard, from various
English and Dutch editions
of the *General History*.
(Courtesy of the John Carter
Brown Library)

This vivid description comes from another eighteenth-century book, published in several editions and volumes under various titles but usually known as *The General History of the Pyrates*. More than any other, this text, first appearing six years after Teach's death, has defined the idea of pirates across three centuries. Translated into many languages and often reprinted, its characterful pen portraits and striking illustrations have shaped a now self-replicating genre of novels, films, computer games, TV shows, toys, costumes, and all manner of other things.

That image of piracy is very specific in historical terms. Maritime plundering has happened in most regions of the world, through most ages of human society, but only in one period, roughly the late seventeenth and early eighteenth centuries, did pirates look and act anything like we now imagine them.

I find that fascinating. Why has that one relatively short moment come to stand for all sea raiding across time and space? Partly it is because there was indeed a lot of marauding going on then, and that marauding had a huge impact on world history. Even more importantly, I would argue, it is because of contemporary debates about and popular representations of piracy. It is the combination of what pirates did and the stories told about them that created this image, and it is this combination that I will explore in this book.

The *General History* included a summary of contemporary laws concerning piracy, which is, in its most basic definition, a crime. This legal 'Abstract' opened with the phrase: '*A Pyrate is* Hostis humanis generis, *a common Enemy*'. Here, and in its sensationalisation of pirates from the 1690s and early 1700s, the *General History* tapped into one of the most persistent stories about pirates: the idea that they are 'enemies of all'.

This concept is generally credited to the Roman lawyer Cicero, who observed in his *De Officiis* that, while one must keep an oath with a lawful enemy, according to the rules of war, the same is not true for pirates, who he termed '*communis hostis omnium*', the common enemy of all. Alberico Gentili expounded the same concept more fully in the late sixteenth century. An Italian Protestant, Gentili became Regius Professor of civil law at Oxford and an advocate in the English High Court of Admiralty, regularly acting in high-profile lawsuits with implications both for European diplomacy and the nascent development of international law. Gentili published *De Jure Belli* (*On the Laws of War*) in three volumes across 1588 and 1589, years when the Spanish Armada threatened England and a counter-strike sailed against Spain. Among other things, Gentili argued that all nations shared a war against pirates, calling them '*communes hostes omnium*' who violated 'the common law of nations and the fellowship of human society'.

This idea became extremely prominent, recycled in treatises down the ages. It is more than an abstract theorem: it appeared in legislation and trials concerning piracy, and it has been adopted beyond its original context. During the French Revolution, Jacobins justified the Terror by decrying counter-revolutionaries with the same label. Israeli attorney general Gideon Hausner used the phrase '*hostis humani generis*' when prosecuting Nazi war criminal Adolf Eichmann, as did philosopher Hannah

Arendt in her writings about that trial. The concept continues to influence legal thinking today.

It fits neatly with the dramatic, outlandish image of Teach and others presented in the *General History*, as 'inhumane Wretches' occupying a unique 'Common-wealth', with their own distinctive laws and customs. However, this concept of 'enemies of all', which implies a perpetual and universal status for all pirates, begins to break down almost immediately when we examine the evidence a little more closely – and not just the evidence of piracy, but even for the concept itself.

Cicero, for example, aimed for evocative effect in *De Officiis*, and his primary concern in that passage was not piracy but perjury. Similarly, when prosecuting Gaius Verres, governor of Sicily, Cicero accused him of protecting pirates, not only 'cruel and deadly' enemies of Rome but 'a common enemy of all nations and peoples', using suitably compelling language to sway the court.

However, Cicero further claimed that Verres himself acted as pirates did, explaining, 'Though they are the general enemies of all mankind, there are some people of whom they make friends, not only sparing them but enriching them with stolen wealth.' Cicero's 'enemies of all' are not enemies of quite everyone.

Nor were pirates the only 'enemies of all' he mentioned: Cicero also said 'we have no ties of fellowship with a tyrant, but rather the bitterest feud … those fierce and savage monsters in human form should be cut off from what may be called the common body of humanity' (and this lineage of tyranny, as much as piracy, appealed to the Jacobins). In none of these instances did Cicero establish a concrete legal principle: his words should be understood as a rhetorical use *of* piracy, more than a rationale *for* it.

The slightly different phrase that appeared in many legal texts and found its way into the *General History*, *hostis humanis generis*, meaning 'enemies of all mankind' (or of 'mankind itself'), also has a curious history. Some scholars attribute it to the fourteenth-century writer Bartolus de Sassoferrato, but in fact it appears in a marginal note to one of his works printed in the 1490s, probably added by a later editor. While this note does mention pirates, it actually attaches the label 'enemies of all mankind' to hypocrites, though that did not stop later writers from adopting it for pirates instead.

It strikes me as perfectly apt that the development of what is supposedly one of the clearest, and certainly one of the most enduring, ideas about piracy was so bedevilled by these inconsistencies from its very beginning.

The legal status of piracy as a crime has been reasonably stable from the medieval period onwards, at least in Europe, and was considerably reinforced through the sixteenth, seventeenth and eighteenth centuries, not least due to this idea of 'enemies of all'. However, the application of that legal status in reality has always been something of a challenge.

Consider, if you will, the terminology around piracy and plunder. I am, as my students (and my family) can tell you, rather obsessed with terminology, but I hope it goes beyond mere pedantry. These words, the relationships between them, and their changing meanings can illuminate trends of thought concerning maritime raiding.

'Pirate' comes from Greek *peirata* and Latin *pirata*, with a clutch of fairly close cognates: *pirate* in English and French, *pirata* in Italian and Spanish, *Pirat* in German, *piraat* in Dutch. Originally it was probably not a legal term, as Roman lawyers often preferred *praedones* or *ladrones*, meaning 'thieves' or 'plunderers'. *Pirata* applied more generally to maritime raiders, though still in a derogatory sense, as with Cicero. That broad and somewhat more colloquial use has survived, even while 'pirate' has also since acquired its more specific meaning of an illegal plunderer at sea.

Yet pirates are not the only kind of maritime plunderers. Indeed, for much of history most plunderers vociferously claimed that their actions were entirely legal, hence the plethora of alternative terms available. Many of these have a more complex multilingual genealogy, which is no coincidence given how important these designations have been in international law and politics.

For example, 'corsair' in English is often, though not always, associated with Mediterranean raiding, and usually, though again not always, a legally permissible version. It derives from *corso*, meaning to chase: a label for the extended and messy conflict between Islamic and Christian raiders – if only in principle, since they often plundered coreligionists too. The terms *piratae* and *cursarii* were sometimes used interchangeably in medieval documents.

In Spanish and French, however, *corsario* and *corsaire* have drifted away from their geographical and religious roots and can mean any maritime plunderer, legal or otherwise. Spanish documents called Francis Drake – whose actions they definitely considered illegal – a *corsario* more often than a *pirata*, but the term was (and is) not always used in this way. In French, *guerre de course* became a technical term for officially sanctioned raiding by private ships, in contrast to the *guerre d'escadre* or 'war by squadrons'.

Kaper is similarly capacious in Dutch, though often with a pejorative slant; so too *vrijbuiter*, meaning 'free-plunderer', giving us 'freebooter' in

English and *flibustier* in French. *Commissievaarder* means someone sailing with a legal commission. The most well-known English cognate of *commissievaarder* is 'privateer', often used anachronistically because, as we shall see, it did not appear until the mid-seventeenth century, and its meaning has changed since then.

The list goes on. Dutch *zeerover*, and *Seeräuber* in German, mean 'sea-robber', not quite the same as the related English 'sea rover'. French documents often call maritime raiders *forbans*, which can mean 'rogue' in a wider sense. One of my personal favourites in English is 'pickaroon', from Spanish *picaro*, another word for a rogue (see also *'picaresque'*).

Of course, those are all examples from European languages. Ottoman Turkish adapted *qursan* from *corso*. In Chinese, *haikou* and *haidao* are often used in literary texts, meaning sea robbers or robbery, while imperial laws refer simply to *dao* (theft) or *daozei* (theft with violence). *Wokuo* is another derogatory term, applying to Japanese smugglers and raiders, though many people labelled *wokuo* were actually Chinese. There is no specific Arabic term for 'pirate', but words like *salaba*, to plunder or loot, were used, or a combination like *liss al-bahr* (sea robber), and similarly *duzd darya'i* in Persian. Comparable combinations of *samudrii* (maritime) with *chaurya* (theft) or *daakaa* (attack) appear in Marathi and Hindi. Many of these terms are translated into English as 'pirate', but this is misleading, because the phrases in these other languages do not always carry the specific connotations that 'pirate' does.

The linguistic variety is bewildering, but this very complexity conveys a crucial point. Not all plundering by sea was piracy, in the strict sense. The status and perception of maritime raiding varied according to circumstance.

For that reason we must think very carefully before we use the word 'pirate', or accept it uncritically when we find it in historical sources, though I admit that it is very hard to find a suitable alternative, at least in English, that is quite as flexible as *kaper* or *corsario*. To call someone a pirate – especially as that term became so strongly associated with the idea of 'enemies of all' – is to make a legal and political judgement about them.

It is the judgement, as much as the act of maritime violence itself, that makes someone a pirate. We are back to that combination of actions and stories. The ways in which people made and challenged these judgements have not only created the image of piracy that we have today, but have also, as historians have come to realise over the last few decades, profoundly shaped world history.

In this book I am concerned with what aficionados of piratical history often call the 'golden age', although, like so many other labels pertaining to this subject, it was never used by pirates themselves and its meaning varies. When first coined in the 1890s, it referred to the later decades of the seventeenth century, but some historians have stretched it to cover the period roughly from 1650 to 1730, and others have shrunk and shifted it to the 1710s and 1720s – the decades that featured Teach and his chums, and the *General History*.

When you think of pirates, it is almost always *these* pirates that you are thinking about. During this not-quite-a-century, three overlapping generations of plunderers took to the seas, and while that was nothing new, their voyages, and the discussions they provoked, contributed to the world-changing rise of European empires and created the image of piracy that remains with us.

I will explore the international and global dimensions of these plunderers, but in some places I focus on the British Empire. All empires both supported plundering and condemned piracy, but the conversations around piracy seem to have been particularly fervent within the British Empire in this period. Though I do not wish to make any claims for national exceptionalism, changes within that empire have been particularly impactful for how we imagine and understand piracy. Perhaps that explains some of the multilingual diversity I mentioned.

Each part of the book looks at one of these three generations. In the first I discuss the buccaneers who rampaged across the Caribbean from roughly 1650 to 1680. As the Spanish Empire extracted vast amounts of wealth from the Americas and northern European challengers established competing colonies, plunder became a mainstay for colonial economies. Imperial control remained relatively weak and local governors acted with considerable autonomy, often supporting buccaneering.

These raiders, led by Henry Morgan, François l'Olonnais, and others, therefore operated at the very edge of, if not beyond, contemporary laws of war and plunder, and in doing so drove forwards those very same legal conventions. They were not 'enemies of all', but they provoked further discussion around piracy. Once the profits from plunder were invested in sugar and slavery, the buccaneers' appeal began to wane, at least in some colonies. Jamaica, at first a buccaneering hotspot, had officially turned away from them by the 1680s.

In that decade a new generation of these buccaneers, and some of the old, began to expand into the Pacific and Indian Oceans. Several then published accounts of their voyages, which helped to shape ongoing conversations about plundering, as well as providing grateful historians with much of our evidence. These plunderers still usually sailed with lawful commissions during global wars, and found support in French, English and other colonies. They cannot easily be categorised as 'enemies of all' either, but their actions caused increasing trouble for imperial rulers.

This issue came to a head in the Indian Ocean, when marauders disrupted lucrative trade with the powerful Mughal Empire, prompting more determined efforts to suppress these raiders and to wean colonial communities off their plundering habits. These efforts, culminating in several high-profile piracy trials such as those of Henry Every and William Kidd around the turn of the eighteenth century, struggled to convince everyone, but did result in a new and more consistent legal framework for dealing with piracy on a worldwide scale.

That framework came to fruition only with the final generation of pirates discussed here, after the Treaty of Utrecht in 1713 ended another global war. Changing economic and political circumstances altered colonial attitudes in ways that government fiat could not, and the increased military resources as a result of war were another important factor. A burst of plundering centred on the Bahamas, which seems to have begun in a similar fashion to previous episodes, quickly spiralled outwards into probably the most definitive moment in the history of piracy.

Those pirates came closest to being 'enemies of all', raiding indiscriminately while imperial authorities pursued, captured, prosecuted and hanged them wherever they could. Some, like Teach, Charles Vane, Calico Jack, Anne Bonny, and Mary Read, were extravagant and rebellious figures. Yet even at this time the relationship between pirates and imperial authority was more complex than it at first appears, and we must also pay careful attention to how the *General History* has shaped our understanding of this period and its legacies.

Are you sitting comfortably? Yes? Then anchors aweigh ...

A Note on Conventions

This book covers several centuries, continents and oceans, across which many different languages and calendars were in use, most of them changing over the course of this period. For the sake of simplicity, unless otherwise stated I have given dates in the Julian calendar used in Britain and its colonies until 1752. Most of Europe changed to the Gregorian calendar from 1582 onwards, ten days ahead of the Julian calendar. Many other calendars were in use around the world, though not usually by the plunderers under discussion here.

Wherever possible I have given an individual's name in their own language. For locations I have used the modern Anglicised name, except where it is customary to use the original name in English. Where this becomes a matter of personal taste, I have followed my own.

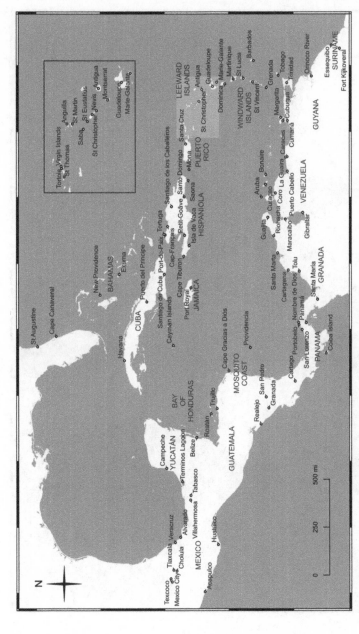

European colonies in the Caribbean.

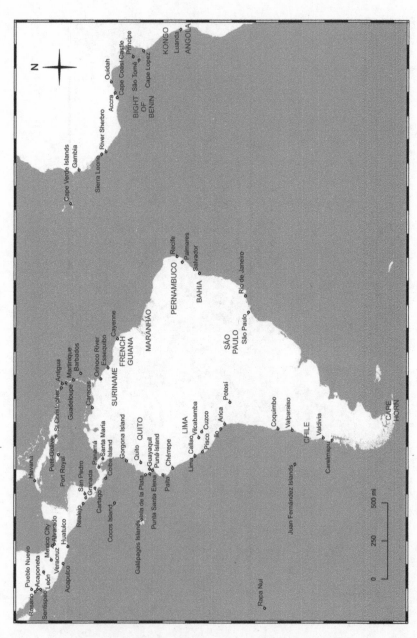

The South Atlantic.

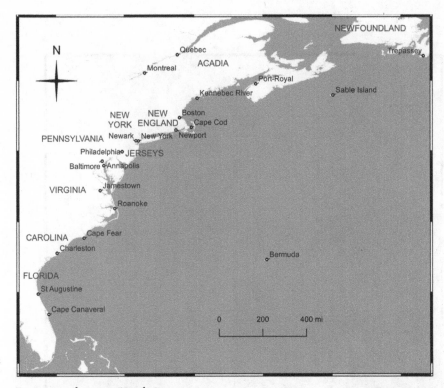

European colonies in North America.

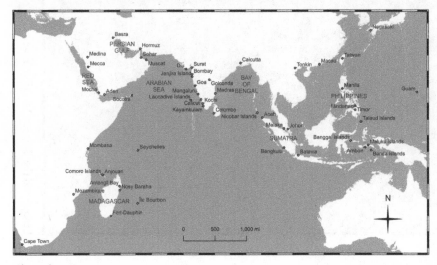

The Indian Ocean.

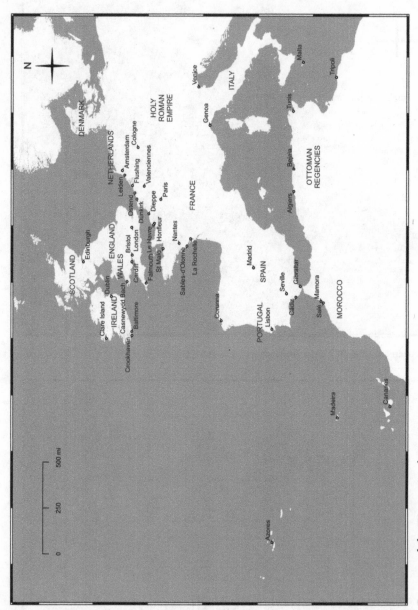

Europe and the Western Mediterranean.

I
BUCCANEERS

PORT ROYAL, JAMAICA
TUESDAY, 7 JUNE 1692

The earthquake struck just before noon with a sound like thunder and a sky suddenly as dull and red as a glowing oven. It came without warning, on a clear day after weeks of hot, calm weather, in three shocks of increasing intensity and devastation.

Port Royal stood at the tip of a spit protecting the long bay that served as a natural harbour. One witness wrote that this sandy ground 'heav'd and swell'd like the rolling sea'. Fissures engulfed terrified inhabitants as 'whole streets were swallowed up by the opening earth'. Surging waves capsized ships and crashed over the fortifications, submerging the wharf, where the town's best brick houses stood, and another two streets behind. Only the tallest buildings remained above water. A captured French ship was swept from the harbour to the marketplace. The town's burial ground was torn apart; disinterred corpses floated along the shore beside new victims.

Emmanuel Heath, rector of St Paul's, had read prayers in church before meeting John White, president of the Council of Jamaica, for a glass of wormwood wine before lunch. White kept 'very composed, being a very grave man'. He met the first shock with considerable *sangfroid*, smoking his pipe and commenting 'it's an earth-quake; be not afraid, it will soon be over'.

White was, in a way, correct. Heath noted that the quake began at half past eleven, and 'in the space of three minutes' the town 'was shaken and shattered to pieces'. An archaeological excavation in 1959 found a pocket-watch, made six years before the earthquake by French watchmaker Paul Blondel, its hands stopped at 11:43.

Port Royal was only 37 years old. The town appeared in the space of a single generation. Yet it was the largest settlement in England's Caribbean possessions, twice the size of Bridgetown in Barbados, and in the English American colonies only Boston was bigger. Heath called Port Royal 'the fairest town of all the English plantations, the best emporium and mart of this part of the world, exceeding in its riches, plentiful of all good things'. Another resident proclaimed it 'the Storehouse or Treasury of the *West-Indies*', adding that there was more ready cash per person here than there was in London. Over 100 ships visited each year, and the town had its own fleet of small, locally built sloops perfect for trading, smuggling and catching tortoises – or other, more lucrative, prey.

The speed and scale of destruction was therefore astonishing. Heath called it 'that fatal day, the most terrible that ever I saw in my life', while another witness wrote of 'such crying, such shrieking and mourning, [as] I never heard ... this town is become a heap of ruins'. Three-quarters of Port Royal was destroyed almost immediately. The earthquake hurled water from deep wells, caused a 2m tsunami and smaller shocks and landslides, and wrecked churches, dwellings and sugar works across the island. Tremors, thunderstorms and foul weather continued for several months.

The death toll, including from injuries or disease in subsequent days, was estimated at 4,000, heavily concentrated in Port Royal, whose population just before the calamity was about 6,500. The minister of another Jamaican parish assessed the damage to Port Royal at £400,000, an enormous sum worth over £50 million today.

This natural disaster was compounded by other troubles. Shortly afterwards a French force attacked the north coast; this all occurred in the middle of the Nine Years' War. They were seen off, but another peril lurked closer to home. Heath wrote that on the night following the earthquake miscreants broke open warehouses and deserted homes 'to rob and rifle their neighbours', though the earth still trembled and some looters died under collapsing buildings. Another report described how English and Spanish mariners aboard those ships still afloat purloined goods instead of rescuing people, some contenting themselves with flotsam, others pillaging houses, and 'the following night those villains were more savage ... our enemies could not have treated us worse than the seamen'.

Such behaviour was hardly a surprise, considering Port Royal's reputation. Heath thought the earthquake a 'terrible judgement of God' upon 'a most ungodly debauched people ... so desperately wicked, it makes me afraid to stay in the place'. In England, where a smaller and less destructive earthquake occurred a few months later, the sins of the town were condemned in numerous tracts lambasting the failings of both colony and country.

For some, it showed a divine condemnation of the reigning king and queen, William and Mary, who a few years before had usurped Mary's Catholic father, James VII of Scotland and II of England (at this time separate kingdoms sharing a single monarch). For others it carried a message regarding England's growing empire, and Jamaica's place therein. One Nonconformist preacher wrote of it as 'so remarkable a providence upon the English plantation in Jamaica', which he called 'a part of England itself ... though beyond the sea'. He noted that 'it fell so particularly upon that town ... that bore the ensigns of sovereignty and government ... the key of the island ... the seat of the King's House'.

Similar attitudes could be found in other colonies, too. Cotton Mather, a minister in Massachusetts, wrote to his uncle that he had heard of the downfall of 'the rich town of Port Royal', comparing it to the ancient Phoenician trading city of Tyre, 'but a very Sodom for wickedness … Behold, an accident speaking to all our English America'. In this letter, Mather also mentioned the notorious Salem witchcraft trials of that year; he was a correspondent and advisor to the judges who prosecuted 150 people, and condemned twenty of them to death. For Mather and these other writers, England's Atlantic empire stood poised between a pious and profitable future and the literally damning behaviour of colonial reprobates.

Casual and copious alcohol and sex featured heavily in contemporary descriptions of Port Royal (witchcraft not so much). One anonymous writer called it 'a sink of filthiness', while Heath complained that following the catastrophe 'those audacious whores that remain upon the place, are as impudent and drunk as ever'. Another observer commented that the earthquake had not dissuaded the surviving residents from 'the same whoring and drinking, the same cursing and swearing'.

Or the same plundering – for these were not just any sinners. They were, as Heath put it, 'a company of lewd rogues whom they call privateers'. Sea raiding was an old practice, but here Heath used a relatively new word, which at the time had begun to replace the previously common and rather cumbrous 'private men of war'. In 1661, six years into Port Royal's existence, Edmund Hickeringill, in a book called *Jamaica Viewed*, wrote that the town was first built 'for the accommodation of Sea-men, especially the *Privateers*, who are their best Customers'.

These '*Privateers of Jamaica*', he went on, were 'often fingering the Plate, and other precious commodities' that they had seized from Spanish ships and towns. Later in the same decade Samuel Pepys, the famous diarist and naval administrator, recorded that 'we have done the Spaniard abundance of mischief in the West Indys, by our privateers at Jamaica'. Hickeringill also mentioned 'buccaneers', likewise a brand-new word, and *flibustier* also arrived in French around this time (though the Dutch *vrijbuiter* had been around for longer).

The appearance and the changing meanings of these neologisms show how significant and remarkable these sea rovers were. They were essential to the rapid growth of places like Port Royal into a famous 'store-house or treasury', before being blamed for its equally notorious ruination. Despite the disapproval of respectable reverends like Heath or Mather, the colonial history of the Americas is inconceivable without this 'company of lewd rogues'.

I

BEYOND THE LINE

In 1618 Henry Mainwaring presented a manuscript to James VI and I, the Stuart monarch who first ruled both Scotland and England, with the title 'On the Beginnings, Practices, and Suppression of Pirates'. Mainwaring knew whereof he spoke, for he had gone a-pirating. This treatise helped his rehabilitation: he called himself 'your own Creature', who was 'newly recreated and restored by your gracious Pardon'.

It helped that Mainwaring could claim a good family and education – at Brasenose College, Oxford – and 'fell not purposely but by mischance into those courses', never plundering English ships, or so he said. He later served as lieutenant of Dover Castle and deputy warden of the Cinque Ports, travelled on a diplomatic mission to Venice and ended up as Sir Henry, a vice-admiral in the navy and a gentleman of the royal bedchamber.

Mainwaring wrote that 'English Pirates do first arm and horse them-selves within your Highness' Dominions', since a group of ten or twelve men could easily steal a small ship. With that, and some new recruits, they would make for Brittany or thereabouts and seize a larger ship, 'and so little by little reinforce themselves'.

There are several popular piratical computer games that resemble the process Mainwaring described, the player starting out with a small vessel and 'reinforcing themselves' as they go along. Modern scholars too have been drawn to the idea of escalating 'pirate cycles', a term coined in the 1930s, to explain why piracy appears, flourishes, and declines.

One such model suggests three types of plundering: *parasitic*, preying on well-established trade routes; *episodic*, a response to specific economic or political disruptions; and *intrinsic*, embedded in the social and economic fabric of a community. Of course, these three modes are not distinct, and any one historical example might fit two or all three of these definitions.

The surge of piracy around 1610, in which Mainwaring participated, is a case in point: targeting lucrative Mediterranean trade routes, occurring at the end of a major war, sustaining and sustained by coastal communities in Ireland and North Africa.

Others emphasise the importance of market forces, particularly the balance of demand and supply. Merchants unable to acquire desired goods through legal routes, or at the right price, sometimes turned to plundering. Raiders as often redirected commodities as destroyed or consumed them, although their impact on the original producers and shippers was undoubtedly destructive (economically and literally).

Or plunderers could themselves supply protection. The theory of 'protection costs' suggests that one role of empires was the coordination and sale of protection to traders, through commercial monopolies and military resources. Those who ensured lower protection costs enjoyed a competitive economic advantage, which could be more substantial than that conferred by other factors like technology. Where protection was not organised by state authorities then merchants, or other groups, might engage private providers such as plunderers – sometimes for protection from other plunderers.

A third interpretation considers labour supply the most significant cause. Without sailors there can be no piracy. When the maritime labour market could not absorb a surplus, this might spill over into plundering, especially at the end of a conflict during which seafarers had been employed in warfare. The 'pirate cycle' ends when this labour surplus dissipates through death, retirement, or transfer into other sectors.

Mainwaring would have recognised this last analysis, though perhaps not its theoretical language. He wrote that 'the common sort of seamen are so generally necessitous and discontented' that they turned to piracy. His contemporary John Smith, a soldier, sailor, and sometime governor of Virginia, agreed. When James signed a treaty with Spain, ending decades of fighting, 'those that were poore and had nothing but from hand to mouth, turned Pirats ... some, that had lived bravely [during the war], would not abase themselves to poverty'.

However you explain it – and I favour the labour supply theory myself – sea raiding requires certain preconditions. There must be ships and cargoes, or other prizes, to plunder. Sailors must have both the incentive and the resources, including their own ships and, even more importantly, the means to repair, resupply, and replace those ships, which are intensely perishable while operating in a hostile environment. People must be willing to buy the plunder. Often, though not always, political connections provide some shelter. All major episodes of sea raiding combine some of these factors. We find them arising in the Caribbean during the sixteenth and seventeenth centuries.

Spanish voyagers first invaded the Caribbean and the Americas in the 1490s, beginning with Cristoforo Colombo (in his native Italian; you probably know him as Columbus). After Portuguese voyagers reached the Cape of Good Hope in 1498, a series of treaties, negotiated by the Spanish-born pope, divided the world between these two monarchs. The Spanish Crown claimed possession of all lands beyond a meridian 370 miles west of the Cape Verde Islands, roughly where São Paulo lies today; afterwards Portuguese ships stumbled into, and invaded, eastern Brazil. A slightly later pact designated the Indian Ocean as Portuguese territory, and the Pacific as Spanish.

Following a succession crisis in 1580, Felipe II of Spain seized the Portuguese throne. From then until 1640 the two kingdoms, in principle still separate, belonged to a single Spanish Habsburg ruler, forming one worldwide empire. Milanese Jesuit Giovanni Botero, in his *Relationi Universali* of 1592, celebrated what he called '*l'imperio del' Oceano*'.

Such claims tried to place the world under Iberian sovereignty, and to Europeanise it. So too did documents like the *Requerimiento*, introduced in 1513 and read out in Latin or Spanish at the start of each conquest, proclaiming possession of a region and its inhabitants and rendering any resistance, in Spanish eyes, rebellion. The Antilles in the Caribbean were named after Antillia, an island from medieval European myth, while Venezuela, 'little Venice', comes from a 1499 voyage that spotted villages on stilts. Amerigo Vespucci, a Florentine sailor in Portuguese service, published his letters describing this *Mundus Novus* or 'new world' in 1503; these raced through sixty editions, in multiple languages, by 1520. From 1507 these included maps that called the continent 'America', in Vespucci's honour.

These ideas wildly exaggerated the extent of Spanish 'conquest'. Spanish colonists remained relatively few, especially in the first decades, and their early campaigns exploited conflicts that already existed. Hernán Cortés allied with enemies of the Aztecs, including Ixtilxochitl, ruler of Texcoco, formerly part of the Mexica triple alliance. Thousands of Totonac, Tlaxcalteca, and Cholulteca soldiers marched on Tenochtitlán in 1521, though Cholula only joined Cortés after a massacre there by Spanish soldiers.

In Peru, too, Francisco Pizarro and a few hundred *conquistadores* joined a civil war raging between the half-brothers Atawallpa and Waskar Inka. Pizarro captured Atawallpa and killed him, before backing Waskar's younger brother Manqu Inka Yupanki. Manqu then turned against Pizarro, but was forced to retreat by Diego de Almagro in 1537. The next year Almagro allied with Manqu's half-brother in a rebellion against Pizarro, but was captured and executed in 1538. Like in Mexico, Indigenous soldiers did most of the actual fighting.

Spanish forces had fairly quickly seized control of the Greater Antilles, the larger islands lying along the north side of the Caribbean Sea belonging to Taíno communities, an Arawak-speaking group. They made much less headway in the Lesser Antilles, the chain of small islands marking the eastern edge of the sea. The northern cluster, later named the Leeward Islands, was occupied by Tainó, and the southern, later the Windward Islands, by separate Arawak speakers, known as 'island Caribs' or Kalinago.

Elsewhere, too, Spanish territorial control fell far short of their grand claims. The invasion of the Yucatán peninsula, again largely reliant on Nahua soldiers, dragged on for a century and a half, as some Mayan cities allied with the *conquistadores* while others fought back. Further south, Manqu Inka held on around Vilcabamba until his death in 1544, and the region resisted conquest until the 1570s. Indigenous groups such as the Mapuche in what is now Chile, the Chocó south of Bolivia, and the Charrúa in Uruguay, or the Guale, Apalachee, and Apalachicola in what is now the southern USA, defeated Spanish expansion well into the seventeenth century, and in some cases the nineteenth. In typically high-handed (and inaccurate) fashion, Spanish authorities deemed the areas beyond their control *despoblado*, 'uninhabited'. Portuguese settlers in Brazil also hugged the coast and only slowly began to expand inland.

Not even conquered regions remained quiet. Major rebellions erupted in the Andes in the 1560s, and northern Mexico throughout the seventeenth century. Many of the enslaved African people shipped across the Atlantic in ever larger numbers escaped and formed independent settlements, called *quilombos* (from *kilombo*, an Angolan word) in Brazil and *palenques* in the Spanish Empire. Their inhabitants were known as *cimarrónes* or maroons. One of the largest, Palmares in north-eastern Brazil, began in 1605 and grew to a population of perhaps 20,000 in a dozen villages spread over 90 miles by the time it was destroyed, in 1694, by a combined Portuguese and Indigenous army from São Paulo.

Over these centuries, the Caribbean and neighbouring regions in the Americas became a theatre of continuous conflict involving the Spanish

Empire, their enemies and allies among the Indigenous and *cimarrón* groups of the region, and interlopers and challengers from northern Europe. This strife created opportunities for maritime plundering.

The Spanish Empire was built on plunder. Cortés took 160,000 *pesos* even before deposing Moctezuma in Tenochtitlán; Pizarro looted 2 million *pesos* in Cuzco. Tribute demands in Hispaniola were so harsh they led to mass Taíno suicides. One *cacique* or Taíno leader called Hatuey reportedly observed that the newcomers 'worship some covetous and unsatisfied Deity, and to content the greedy worship of that Celestial Power, they require many things from us, using all their endeavour to murder and enslave us'.

Caribbean gold fields were largely exhausted by the 1530s, but mining continued in Mexico. Both were then eclipsed by the discovery of the world's biggest silver deposit, at Potosí in modern-day Bolivia. This city, founded in 1545, was at one time the second largest in the Americas, with a population of 160,000 in the early seventeenth century – a little more populous than Seville, a third of the size of Paris or London.

Here was the economic basis of Spanish global power, and the empire was remarkably successful at extracting wealth in natural materials. The *Carrera de Indias*, the fleet of treasure galleons and other ships sailing regularly to the Caribbean, consisted of only 35 vessels in 1506 but over 200 by mid-century. All commodities from the Americas were supposed to be imported through the *Casa de Contratación* in Seville, keeping this trade under royal control. The volume of that trade increased by 800 per cent across those first fifty years, including pearls, hides, and dyestuffs like cochineal and indigo, though gold and silver were most important to the Crown. The Spanish *peso de ocho*, a silver coin worth eight *reales*, became a global currency. In English *pesos* were known as Spanish dollars, or, more famously, 'pieces of eight'.

To rule the new territories and coordinate this extraction, the Habsburg emperors established a hierarchy under two viceroyalties: New Spain, comprising Mexico, the Caribbean, and Venezuela, with pretensions to North America as well; and Peru, which claimed jurisdiction over most of South America. Below the viceroys stood regional *audiencias* or courts, local officials called *corregidores* and, for major towns, mayors (*alcaldes mayores*) and councils (*cabildos*). The Church played a crucial role in this structure, too. The Spanish Crown had direct control over appointments to colonial bishoprics, while religious orders like the Dominicans, Franciscans, and Jesuits travelled through the Americas, expanding the Spanish presence, but acting semi-independently and in some ways challenging imperial authorities.

Though the Spanish 'conquest' was more complicated than contemporary or later myths suggest, over the sixteenth century this plundering empire did become the dominant regional power, especially in the Caribbean, and transformed societies in the Americas. One of its most devastating impacts was to bring diseases like smallpox, measles, typhus, influenza, plague, malaria, and yellow fever, which spread rapidly and fatally among people with no previous exposure to them. Estimates vary, but the Indigenous population of the Americas fell from roughly 60 million to 6 million within the first century and a half of this biological contact, as well as through imperial violence.

The social and cultural consequences were enormous. Epidemics coincided with pivotal moments in the collapse of the Aztec and Inka empires, and in later conflicts, and communities who had no direct contact with Europeans were affected. The complex Mound Building societies of the Mississippi region disappeared, for example, evolving into new communities including the Cherokee, Creek, Catawbas, and Chickasaw.

The Caribbean was hit particularly hard. There were probably some 300,000 Taíno people in Hispaniola in 1492, and only 500 in 1548. Yet that population did not disappear. Communities of Taíno, Kalinago, and Kalina-speaking 'mainland Caribs' all persisted in the Caribbean. DNA analysis suggests that their descendants remain there today, though this is a subject of some debate. Across the Americas as a whole, of 1,284 recorded Indigenous languages, 1,090 are still spoken: a testament to cultural resilience.

In principle the '*indios*', as the Spanish authorities called Indigenous people under their rule, remained separate, a '*república de indios*' subject to the Crown. At least initially, some Indigenous elites held onto their position as landowners paying tribute to the new overlords. However, the *conquistadores*, through tenurial holdings called *encomiendas*, grabbed specific regions and communities, with brutal results.

Regulatory efforts such as the Laws of Burgos of 1512 and the New Laws of 1542 sought to control the worst excesses of the *encomienda* system and eventually remove it altogether, but were resisted by the powerful *encomenderos*. Meanwhile, large numbers of enslaved or coerced workers toiled on estates and in the mines, initially from local Indigenous communities as a tribute called *repartimiento* (or *mita* in Peru, a name derived from

Inka labour levies), and later from Africa, subjected to constant brutality
and danger. Villages held funerals for these conscripted labourers before
they left for Potosí.

The theoretical separation of the 'república de indios' proved impossible.
By 1600 there were only about half a million Iberians in the Americas,
and these colonists, who were overwhelmingly male, married or had less
formal sexual encounters with American women. In 1504 the Crown even
ordered forced Spanish–Taíno marriages in Hispaniola.

These encounters ranged across all social levels. Cortés depended on
Dona Marina, whose original name is variously recorded as Malinali,
Malinche, or Malintzin, a Nahuatl-speaking prisoner given to him as a
tribute by Tabasco, a Mayan state in the Yucatán. She proved a pivotal
negotiator and interpreter, and she and Cortés had several children before
she married another conquistador. Women from Moctezuma's family, and
from the Inka elite, married Spanish leaders. Such relationships, often
forced or abusive, also involved (usually, but not always, enslaved) African
women and some Indigenous and African couples.

Ideas about ethnicity and biology had, at that time, not yet evolved
into later theories of 'race'. Language, culture, and community were more
important signifiers, even among Europeans who identified themselves
with Europe, or rather with Christendom. There is little evidence that
Indigenous American and African peoples placed themselves within 'racial'
or continental categories, outside of their contact with European empires.

Spanish colonists, however, brought with them the concept of limpieza
de sangre, 'purity of blood', derived from the centuries-long reconquista war
in which the last Islamic emirate in Iberia had only recently been defeated.
The Crown forbade Muslims and Jews, and even the children of moriscos
and conversos, converts to Christianity, from travelling to the Americas,
though some still did. The Inquisición established tribunals at Lima and
Mexico City, partially due to suspicions about these 'New Christians'.

The Spanish authorities therefore imposed hierarchical casta or 'lineage' laws that, at least in theory, determined social status and legal rights
by the amount of Español in an individual's bloodline. Indigenous and
African peoples were positioned at the bottom of this pyramid, though
enslaved people could and did purchase their freedom, or were manumit-
ted, creating communities of free people of colour in Spanish towns.
They served in colonial militias and sometimes became overseers or slaveholders themselves.

Spanish documents call people of African and European parentage
mulato, those of Indigenous and European parentage mestizo, and those

of African and Indigenous parentage *zambo*. Similar terms in Portuguese included *pardo* (African–European), *mestiço*, *mameluco* or *caboclo* (Indigenous–European) and *cafuso* (African–Indigenous); also *cabra* for all three. These pejorative terms represent efforts to classify and regulate, through prejudices about skin colour and genealogy, an increasingly diverse society. When they appear in contemporary sources we can never be sure they tell us what a person thought about their own ethnicity or identity, but these are often the only clues we have about them.

The Spanish Empire's plundering soon drew the attention of other plunderers from northern Europe. Opportunists waited near the Azores or the Spanish coast for returning fleets, but others made for Africa, Brazil, and the Caribbean. A few scouted northwards but several began to attack Spanish shipping from makeshift bases in the Bahamas. Not all of them struck it rich. A French raiding party making for the pearl fisheries at Cubugua in Venezuela was defeated by two vessels manned with Indigenous archers in Spanish service, shooting poisoned arrows, after which French mariners avoided the island.

France and Spain, old enemies, fought one another in every decade during the first half of the sixteenth century, and again in the 1580s and 1590s. French plunderers reportedly captured more than 300 Portuguese ships sailing to Africa in the first three decades of the century, and twenty-two French raids occurred in the Caribbean between 1535 and 1547, including against Nombre de Diós, Santo Domingo, Havana, and an attack on Cartagena that seized 150,000 *ducats*. Even after peace in 1544, the *audiencia* of Santo Domingo complained that French ships carried on cruising, and in any case the peace was short-lived.

One of the most prominent of these raiders was François le Clerc, called *Pata de Palo* in Spanish and *Jambe de Bois* by his compatriots due to his wooden leg, probably the first known example of this popular pirate image. During the 1550s Le Clerc and others raided Madeira, Mona, Saona, Puerto Rico, Puerto Cabello, Hispaniola, and Havana. In 1554 he sacked Santiago de Cuba, seizing treasure worth 80,000 *pesos* and damaging the town so much that it never recovered its status as the island's capital. Another captain, Jean d'Argo or Ango of Dieppe, seized nine Spanish galleons, and still others raided Portuguese shipping near Brazil.

In 1559 the Treaty of Cateau-Cambresis brought a longer peace between Spain and France, but the terms of the treaty did not extend to the Americas, meaning that acts of hostility there would not provoke war in Europe. Probably unintentional, and initially applying only to French ships, this principle of 'no peace beyond the line' soon spread.

Many early voyages, however, sought to trade rather than raid. Most French trips to Brazil in the first decades aimed to purchase brazilwood, also used in dyes. In the 1560s, John Hawkins and his young accomplice Francis Drake endeavoured to break into the Portuguese slave trade to Spanish colonies. With a partner in the Canaries and contacts in Hispaniola, they recruited a Spanish pilot, and sometimes teamed up with French smugglers too. Through a mixture of negotiation or alliance with African rulers and outright violence, they captured several hundred people in West Africa and transported them to the Caribbean.

Some Spanish colonists willingly did business with these smugglers, especially when heavily armed ships took hostages or threatened bombardment if rebuffed. Low prices appealed, too, because goods shipped from Spain were taxed on departure, on arrival in the Caribbean and on transshipment between colonies – many had already been imported to Spain and taxed then too. The same item cost several times more at Potosí than at Panamá, and considerably more in Panamá than in Europe. Contraband traders brought out manufactured goods and enslaved people, sometimes captured from Portuguese ships, and traded for tobacco, hides, cochineal, indigo, and logwood, another dye ingredient.

During his first voyage Hawkins sent his cargoes to Iberia, intending to clear them through some local agents, but his ships were seized in Lisbon and Seville. Hawkins' trading, like the other smugglers', contravened the Spanish government's decree that any unauthorised ship in those waters, no matter their intentions, was illegal. Spanish subjects who crossed the Atlantic without official permission could be fined, banished, whipped, or condemned to years chained to an oar in the king's galleys; increasingly those harbouring smugglers were punished too. Foreigners captured in the Caribbean by the *guardacostas* faced prison, execution, or forced labour in the mines or on royal building projects.

In 1549, alarmed by the growing presence of foreign interlopers, Carlos V granted Pedro Menéndez de Avilés a commission against '*corsarios y robadores*', with which he raided French settlements in Florida, while others received similar commissions as '*contra-corsarios*'. Nor did a Spanish licence to trade always bring security, as Captain Borgoing, of Le Havre, found at Margarita Island off Venezuela in 1568. The colonists invited Borgoing and his men ashore, then ambushed them and displayed their corpses along the shoreline.

Hostilities escalated during the later sixteenth century, as religious conflict added to the mix. Under Henry VIII, England allied with Spain against France, until Henry's break with Rome, and again for Mary I's reign in 1553–58, through her marriage to Felipe II. When Elizabeth I succeeded to the throne in 1559, England became an officially Protestant kingdom once more, drifting into enmity with the Spanish Crown. In the later 1560s a Protestant rebellion, supported covertly by England, broke out in the Burgundian Netherlands, until then part of the Habsburg patrimony. Several of the northern provinces signed a mutual treaty in 1579 and declared their independence from Spain in 1581.

These Protestants cared little for papal paperwork or Spanish and Portuguese pretensions to global *imperium*. Indeed, for the fledgling Dutch Republic, war with Spain was a struggle for its very existence. From 1569 onwards some of the *watergeuzen*, the militant 'Sea Beggars', marauded in the Caribbean, though Dutch merchants went smuggling too, sometimes with the cover of legal agents in Seville.

Captured Dutch and English intruders, now likely to be *corsarios luteranos*, came to the attention of the *Inquisición*. So too did French Protestants, called Huguenots; in one early attack a Huguenot captain and his men hacked a statue of the Virgin Mary to pieces. Huguenot strongholds like Rouen, Dieppe, Caen, Saint-Malo, and La Rochelle sent ships across the Atlantic, although France's own wars of religion in the later sixteenth century prevented major Caribbean campaigns.

In 1568 Hawkins and Drake made their third trip, the fourth Hawkins had financed. They traded at Riohacha after first firing on the town, avoided the heavily defended Cartagena, and then ran into a Spanish fleet in the harbour of Veracruz. Only two English ships escaped from the ensuing battle, leaving behind a vessel leased from the queen herself and many English prisoners. Drake, eager for revenge, led numerous later voyages, including attacks on the isthmus of Panamá in 1572–73, enabled by an alliance with local *cimarrónes*, and on Santo Domingo and Cartagena in 1585–86. He died during his final voyage to the Caribbean in 1596.

When England officially allied with the Dutch Republic in 1585 it brought a marked change of pace to English raiding in the Caribbean. Between 1568 and 1585, there were only fourteen raiding trips, and Elizabeth tried to maintain some semblance of plausible deniability about her involvement. From 1585 until the end of her reign in 1603, the number of expeditions increased fivefold. The famous Armada of 1588, itself in part a response to these raiders, provoked more voyages and provided extra justification.

Drake's expeditions were often large operations, and some took considerable amounts of plunder. In 1577–80 Drake circumnavigated the globe and brought back £800,000 worth of Spanish treasure: a 4,700 per cent profit for the investors, of which £16,000 went to the queen. Most late-sixteenth-century plundering expeditions were much smaller affairs, and several returned home empty-handed. Nevertheless, the overall effect was significant. Between 1585 and 1591, when at least 235 English warships cruised the Atlantic, they brought back around £400,000 in total, equivalent to over one-tenth of English imports, or a little more than the Crown's annual revenue. This influx of silver may have helped the queen to maintain the value of sterling and avoid debasing the coinage.

Nor did smuggling cease. Preserving the catch from North Sea fishing fleets, vital to the Dutch economy and diet, required large quantities of salt, which they could no longer get from Portugal. Dutch *schippers* sailed further west: between 1599 and 1605, around 100 Dutch ships, as well as some English and French ones, visited Venezuela's saltpans each year. Luis Fajardo led a large Spanish expedition in 1605 that captured some sixteen ships as prizes, executing most of his prisoners as pirates, on the authority of a royal *cédula*, or proclamation, issued that year.

Fajardo was back the next year, and seems to have driven away the salt smugglers, but soon Dutch ships were trading for tobacco instead, at Cumaná, Trinidad, and the Orinoco River. The Spanish government outlawed tobacco production in those regions and forcibly relocated Spanish settlers away from the exposed west of Hispaniola, but could not halt the illicit commerce.

Both raiders and smugglers compelled the Spanish Empire to fortify its major harbours and defend its shipping routes. In 1522 Seville's merchants appealed for naval protection, and the *Casa de Contratación* introduced *averías*, taxes on colonial trade, to pay for it. From 1525 ships were required to sail in convoys, by 1552 merchant ships had to go armed, and in the 1560s the *Consejo de las Indias*, the imperial council in Madrid, decreed that all treasure should be carried aboard fast and heavily armed *gallizabras*. During the 1580s the first permanent naval patrols arrived in the Caribbean and were then consolidated into a new *Armada de Barlovento* to defend the region.

After 1561 all ships were ordered to cross the Atlantic with the official *Carrera*, which left Spain in January and August. In the Caribbean they divided, those known as the *flota* heading for Veracruz to collect the treasure from Mexico, and those called the *galeones* sailing to Cartagena, accompanied by the *Armada de la Guardia*. Bullion brought to Panamá from Peru up the Pacific coast was carried across the isthmus (originally to Nombre de Diós, later to Portobelo), loaded onto local vessels alongside cochineal and indigo, hides and cocoa, pearls and emeralds, and sent to Cartagena for the *galeones*. Both fleets then converged on Havana and returned to Seville, protected in the Atlantic by the *Armada del Mar Océano*.

Marauders were not the only perils. The storm-wracked Caribbean provided harsh sailing conditions, and even in calm seasons teredo worms munched into wooden hulls. Tempests and hurricanes wrecked or scattered a number of ships throughout the 1550s and 1560s. In 1590 fifteen of the *flota* sank during a storm while anchored at Veracruz, and in 1601 fourteen more while approaching the port; in 1591 sixteen ships were driven ashore at Terceira in the Azores.

Atlantic shipping was a costly and deadly business, and the attacks of the later 1500s took their toll. The *Armada de la Guardia* cost 1.4 million *pesos* per trip, and, with its vast military commitments in Europe as well, the Spanish government relied heavily on loans from German, Flemish, and Italian bankers. Interest rates rose continually, since the Spanish Crown defaulted on its debts six times between 1557 and 1637. The *averías* jumped from 2 per cent in 1585 to 8 per cent by 1591, as military architects arrived in the Caribbean to build new defences. The taxes would soar to 23 per cent and even 40 per cent at times in the early seventeenth century.

That made smugglers' prices more attractive, of course, and the transatlantic sea rovers of this era inspired popular legends that influenced later ideas about piracy, as we shall see. Yet they did not immediately topple the Spanish Empire, or greatly inhibit its successful plundering of American silver. The *Carrera*'s cargoes increased tenfold by 1580 and peaked at 45,000 tons in 1608. Their total value exceeded several million *pesos* in most years of the later sixteenth and early seventeenth centuries. Hundreds of tons of silver in the 1540s became thousands by the 1590s: between 1500 and 1650 a total of 16,000 tons of silver flowed through the *Casa de Contratación*. That is only the official amount. Over its first century of Atlantic empire, Spain's supply trebled the gold and silver circulating in Europe. An estimated 85 per cent of the world's silver, and 70 per cent of its gold, originated in the Americas between 1500 and 1800.

Just as the *Carrera*'s shipments hit their highest point during the early seventeenth century, though, the activities of the northern European empires entered a new phase that would, eventually, tip the scales against Spanish pretensions to hegemony in the Americas: rival colonisation.

2

BRETHREN OF THE COAST

Northern European venturers attempted colonies of their own during the sixteenth century, but met with little early success. Like Columbus, some of the earliest voyages involved Italian sailors with English or French sponsorship, such as Giovanni and Sebastiano Caboto, or Giovanni de Verrazzano, and mainly concentrated on North America, where Jacques Cartier also made three voyages during the 1530s and 1540s. Fishermen cruised these waters in increasing numbers, with 150 French, Spanish (probably Basque), English, and Portuguese ships reported off the Grand Banks of Newfoundland in 1578.

Some of these transatlantic voyages passed through the Caribbean. The circular, clockwise winds and currents of the North Atlantic gyre made it quicker to sail from Europe to the Azores or Canaries then catch the 'trade winds' west to the Caribbean, before striking north and eventually east. The anticlockwise gyre of the South Atlantic imposed similar constraints – which is why Portuguese ships returning from Africa found themselves on the coast of Brazil.

Irregular trading posts sprang up around the Caribbean, often swiftly abandoned. French, mostly Huguenot, settlements existed in Florida during the 1560s, but Spanish forces had destroyed them all by 1565. France Antarctique, established in 1555 in Guanabara Bay, was similarly demolished by three Portuguese expeditions between 1560 and 1567, and replaced by Rio de Janeiro.

Indigenous allies played a key role once again, especially in Brazil, where Potiguar groups joined French raids in the north-east, as did Tupinambá further south, including those already fighting the Iberian empires. Other Indigenous communities sided with the Portuguese authorities: when the governor of Pernambuco expanded his territory in 1569, it was with the help of 20,000 Indigenous soldiers.

Further north, Walter Ralegh received a royal charter for an area he named Virginia in the queen's honour, but his efforts at Roanoke, in what is now North Carolina, lasted barely a few years. A ship arriving there in 1590 found the place deserted, and the mystery of what happened to those colonists has never been solved. In the decades either side of 1600 further efforts on the St Lawrence River, Sable Island, the Bay of Fundy, Cape Cod, and the Amazon by French settlers, the Kennebec River by English ones, and in Guaiana and Cayenne – and elsewhere – by Dutch, English, and French groups all failed.

It was only in the 1620s and 1630s that such colonies achieved a permanent footing, and that was not immediately guaranteed. Dutch communities in Nieuw Nederland and French ones at Québec and elsewhere on the St Lawrence River remained small. They mainly purchased furs from Mi'kmaq, Wendat (whom the French called Huron), Algonquin, and Iroquois trappers.

Wild ambitions of discovering a new Potosí were disappointed in new settlements in Virginia, New England, and Maryland, officially English but with colonists from the other Stuart realms as well. The Chesapeake colonies eventually turned a profit through tobacco, with Virginian exports increasing from 20,000lb in 1617 to 350,000lb in 1621. Still, they took some time to build up a secure base. The Virginia Company, granted a charter in 1606 by James VI and I, had acquired such high debt by 1624 that it was taken under royal management. Bermuda, meanwhile, was settled by accident in 1609 when a ship bound for Jamestown wrecked there, possibly inspiring Shakespeare's *The Tempest*.

Some coastal Caribbean trading posts persisted, such as Fort Kijkoveral on the Essequibo River, established in 1616, which grew into Nova Zeelandia. However, the northern European empires concentrated on the Lesser Antilles. Spanish attention was fixed elsewhere, and with the prevailing easterlies it was much easier for ships to sail downwind towards the Spanish colonies than it was for Spanish ships to reach the smaller islands. These conditions made Spanish counterattacks more difficult, though it did not stop them entirely.

Colonists from Britain and Ireland settled on Barbados, Nevis, Antigua, and Montserrat, and French *colons* claimed Guadeloupe, Martinique, St Lucia, and Grenada. St Christopher was shared between English and French planters, and St Martin or Maarten between French and Dutch ones.

The Dutch *West Indische Compagnie*'s other territories included Saba and St Eustatius (known locally as Statia), plus Curaçao, Bonaire, and Aruba off Venezuela. Spanish expeditions in 1637 and 1641 drove French settlers off Santa Cruz, near Puerto Rico, and also struck at St Christopher in 1629–30 and St Martin in 1633, but could not dislodge those new arrivals.

Many of these colonies continued with the old trades of plundering and smuggling, especially in the Lesser Antilles, whose tobacco growers could not compete with the northern mainland, while efforts with cotton failed to provide a sustainable staple crop. For some, plunder was their explicit *raison d'être*. In 1629 English colonists settled on Providence Island (now Providencia), in the far west of the Caribbean, precisely because it was well placed to strike at Spanish shipping. Its position also made it vulnerable to retaliation, though, and Spanish soldiers recaptured the island in 1642.

A resurgence of international warfare explains the timing and economic viability of these colonial efforts. The Dutch provinces had agreed a truce with Spain in 1609, but this paused, rather than ended, their enmity, and it expired in 1621 with Spain still refusing to recognise the seven provinces as anything but rebels. On his accession to the English throne in 1604, James VI and I made peace with Spain and unsuccessfully tried to marry his son to the Spanish *infanta*, but soon after Charles I acceded to the throne in 1625 he declared war on Spain, partially because of his frustrated romantic ambitions.

France and England also fought in the later 1620s, when England supported Huguenot rebellions, but the common foe remained Spain. Cardinal Richelieu, rising to power at this time, covertly supported Spain's enemies until war broke out again in 1635. A Portuguese revolt erupted in 1640, adding more combatants to the fray.

The *West Indische Compagnie* mounted the greatest challenge to Spanish hegemony. Founded in 1621, at the renewal of war, the *Compagnie* purchased or commissioned more than 200 ships of its own during its first two decades, and dispatched around 800 for war or trade. They captured or destroyed more than 800 Spanish ships while attacking many towns in the Americas, sailing under captains like Cornelis Jol, known (like François le Clerc) as *Houtebeen* or 'wooden leg', and Diego de los Reyes, alias Diego el Mulato, who escaped slavery in Havana and joined a Dutch ship, later rising to command. Some were captured or killed by Spanish forces, but others seized valuable prizes, and they played havoc with Spanish shipping. In 1644 the bishop of Puerto Rico wrote to Madrid that local fishermen were so fearful of Dutch ships that they would not set sail.

One voyage ranks among the most lucrative plundering trips ever. In 1628 Piet Hein commanded thirty-two ships and some 3,500 men, just one of four Dutch fleets sent to the Caribbean that year, and encountered a small *flota* off the coast of Cuba. Hein chased several ships aground, seized all the cargo and half the ships, and burnt the rest. He had met one half of the treasure fleet, while the other half hid in port, but even that plunder was estimated at between 4 and 8 million *pesos*, worth well over £100 million today. Shareholders received dividends of 75 per cent, while unpaid sailors rioted in the streets of Amsterdam. Spain lost a year's income and its interest rates on future loans soared.

The *Compagnie* attacked Bahia in 1624 (Hein sailed in this fleet too), and though Fadrique de Toledo retook it the next year, a large Dutch force then seized Penambuco, further north, in 1629–30, while another destroyed De Toledo's fleet in 1625, robbing Spain of expensive ships and skilled sailors, both of which took years to replace. Here, again, Potiguar and other Tupi-speaking combatants joined the Dutch armies; a few travelled to the Netherlands. This long conflict ended with Portuguese victory and the expulsion of the *Compagnie* in 1654, but the temporary

'A figure of how General Pieter Pietersen Heyn conquered the Silver Fleet Anno 1628', from 1651–52. (Rijksmuseum, Amsterdam)

Dutch presence in Brazil had momentous consequences because it transmitted sugar cultivation to the Caribbean.

Dutch raiders posed the biggest problem for Spanish governors, but they were not the only ones. Far fewer in number, especially when their kingdoms were nominally at peace, English and French plundering trips nevertheless continued. English colonists in the north attacked French Acadia several times, and the earl of Warwick, a Protestant zealot, supported various ventures, including the Providence Island Company and other plundering voyages. A minister in Bermuda described 'Spaniards' as 'lyms [limbs] of Antechrist', and thought that robbing them should be 'greatly comended'.

The Spanish authorities had always feared this would be the case. Pedro de Zuñiga, ambassador in London, warned in 1607 that English colonisation could have no other purpose but to attract unemployed plunderers, who would ruin Spanish trade and interrupt the flow of silver. It was, he thought, 'the most useful way they have found to play the pirate'.

De Zuñiga's warnings showed perceptive foresight, but may have seemed premature, coming at the height of the *Carrera*'s traffic. If the *Compagnie*'s raiding revealed the vulnerability of the Spanish Empire, these new competitors developed slowly. Moreover, while the Spanish Empire possessed a single hierarchy, and the various captaincies of Portuguese Brazil were reconstituted into two *Estados* (Maranhão in the north and Brazil in the south) in 1620 with a central overseas council from 1642, the northern European empires were much less coordinated and received limited support from their rulers.

The *West Indische Compagnie* combined several previous companies under a single charter and structure, topped by a central committee called the *Heren XIX*, but these nineteen gentlemen represented five distinct *kamers* in different Dutch provinces, all with their own interests. Amsterdam oversaw Curaçao and Nieuw Nederland, Zeeland controlled Nova Zeelandia (and most raiders hailed from Zeeland), and Groningen managed trade at the Gambia River. Only the invasion of Brazil was a united endeavour. Some of the colonies were sold to individual *patroons*, although later brought back under *Compagnie* control. A disgruntled Dutch merchant also helped the Swedish Crown set up Nya Sverige in the Delaware Valley in 1638, until it was captured by soldiers from Nieuw Amsterdam in 1655.

The English and French empires were even more of a hodgepodge. Different French syndicates competed in North America, despite a monopoly granted by Henri IV to the Huguenot Pierre du Gau, backed by merchants from La Rochelle, as *lieutenant-général* of Acadia and Canada. Cardinal Richelieu, who tried to centralise royal power within France, installed a *gouverneur général* of the French Antilles in 1628, and founded the *Compagnie des Cents-Associés* in 1627, with a fifteen-year monopoly between Florida and Canada, and the *Compagnie des Îles d'Amérique* in 1635, for the Caribbean. Neither *Compagnie* lasted, though, and Richelieu's successor Cardinal Mazarin sold off the rights for islands or fur-trading concessions.

Similarly, some English colonies had Crown-appointed governors, including Virginia after 1624, but others, such as Massachusetts Bay and Providence Island, were organised by an independent company or, as in the case of Maryland and most of the Lesser Antilles, by individual or collective proprietors, meaning they were often known as 'private' colonies. An associate of Warwick proposed an English West India Company in 1621 to launch a combined naval and private fleet that would capture Santo Domingo, Portobelo, and Panamá, but this overambitious scheme never went anywhere.

Besides the fierce rivalries between empires, and between colonies within each empire, there was inter-imperial trade and cooperation as well. All these colonies depended on Dutch shipping: the largest commercial fleet in Europe. Amsterdam alone boasted 600 fishing vessels and 1,750 merchant ships, with thousands of German and Scandinavian immigrants among their crews. Many Dutch merchants resided in English and French ports. When the *Compagnie* retreated from Brazil, Dutch sugar planters found new homes in Barbados, Guadeloupe, and Martinique. By 1669 even the leader of the French Jesuit missionaries on St Christopher owed money to Dutch merchants.

Such inconsistencies are not surprising, since even Spanish colonial efforts, while based on ideology derived from Roman concepts and endorsed by royal delusions of grandeur, did not spring from any coherent or predetermined plan. Indeed, the fragmented nature of these empires reflected the fragmented structure of politics in Europe, characterised by strident local identities and institutions – for example in both the Dutch and French provinces, or indeed the Spanish realms that had been dynastically united shortly before Columbus sailed.

The first use of the term 'British Empire', by courtier, alchemist, and supposed magician John Dee, included extensive claims to the North

Atlantic and even Scandinavia, but Dee was particularly interested in English territorial ambitions within Britain and Ireland. Elizabeth never realised those ambitions, and when her Stuart successors combined the Scottish and English Crowns (together with the latter's claims to Wales and Ireland), the elite of both kingdoms rejected James' proposals for a legal and political union.

The middle of the seventeenth century brought more aggressive state intervention, both in Europe and across the Atlantic. For Britain this resulted from two decades of civil war, during which England's interregnum government, established after the execution of Charles I in 1649, invaded both Scotland and Ireland. Merchants involved in colonial trade took roles in this government and its naval administration, including Warwick, who served as admiral of the Parliamentarian fleet.

A newly formed committee for trade and plantations introduced laws in 1647 concerning colonial trade, which expanded in 1651 into the first Navigation Act. Directly and deliberately challenging Dutch commercial dominance, and contributing towards the First Anglo-Dutch War, this legislation prohibited English colonies from trading with other empires and demanded that all colonial commodities go through England and be taxed there, carried on English ships, sailed by majority-English crews. After his restoration to the British thrones in 1660, Charles II continued these measures.

Similar efforts occurred in France a little later – perhaps also influenced by the internecine mid-century strife of the Fronde, though no Bourbons were beheaded then. In 1658 Mazarin introduced a tariff system, resembling the Navigation Acts in its aim to boost French shipping and cut out Dutch merchants. During the 1660s and 1670s Jean Colbert, chief minister to Louis XIV, continued this approach with further tariffs on Dutch goods and a new *Compagnie des Indes Occidentales*, which monopolised and taxed colonial trade, and a counterpart *Compagnie des Indes Orientales*.

These efforts at centralisation were very stop–start. In 1672 Louis withdrew financial support for the *Compagnie des Indes Occidentales* as he concentrated on an invasion of the Netherlands. The *Compagnie* was dissolved in 1674, and a replacement lasted only a year, after which Louis granted colonial tax-collecting rights, the *Ferme d'Occident*, to a private merchant in return for 350,000 *livres* per year and an undertaking to supply the French colonies with enslaved African labour. These governments' interest in, and commitment to, colonies was not guaranteed.

The newer colonies were quite different from the Spanish Empire in social composition. Many of them were sparsely populated: a few hundred French *colons* in North America by the 1640s; several thousand in the Caribbean, later joined by around 1,000 Dutch settlers from Brazil. There were a few hundred thousand across the English islands, including Scottish and Irish migrants, and about 23,000 in Massachusetts Bay.

None of these new colonies ruled over large Indigenous populations in the Spanish fashion, though everywhere they depended on Indigenous assistance, most obviously in the northern fur-trading outposts. These witnessed the closest cross-cultural interactions, including marriages, where some Dutch and French traders adapted to Indigenous cultures, while French Jesuits travelled widely in the region.

If some northern Europeans acquired land by negotiation, others seized it by violence, and even when cooperation and trade occurred, conflict was never far away. The first Virginians traded with the Powhatan confederacy, but escalating clashes led to an attack on the colony in 1622, which contributed to the collapse of the Virginia Company. The self-styled pilgrims in New England depended on the help of their Wampanoag neighbours, and with them and Mohegan allies they defeated their Narragansett rivals and entirely wiped out the Pequot confederacy (formerly allied with Dutch settlers) during the 1630s and 1640s.

Indigenous communities in the Lesser Antilles were scarcer after over a century of European diseases and marauding, but still occupied some islands, and Taíno or Kalinago raids destroyed some colonial efforts, such as English attempts at St Lucia in 1605 and Grenada in 1609. Colonists on St Christopher initially made an agreement with one 'King Tegreeman', but there was soon fighting, during which 'Tegreeman' himself was killed. Subsequent raiding continued, there and elsewhere. It was not until 1660 that fifteen Carib *caciques* and various Antillean governors concluded a formal treaty.

Indigenous groups who helped colonists frequently suffered for their generosity. In 1627, early in the settlement of Barbados, Henry Powell visited the Essequibo River and, after trading with Dutch colonists and Kalina communities, recruited (apparently peaceably) some thirty-two Kalina men, women, and children to come to Barbados. Their knowledge of Caribbean flora and fauna proved invaluable, but within twenty years only five remained, and these five had been enslaved – though Powell, when he found out, protested that they should be freed. Enslaved people remained a minority on these islands during the first decades of colonisation, but slavery, whether of Indigenous people or through the transatlantic slave trade, was present from the beginning.

A few wealthy European planters settled in some colonies, but poor labourers formed the majority, mostly young and male, with relatively few European women arriving in the Americas in these years. Many were indentured servants, or *engagés* in French, contracted to work for a set term, usually five or seven years (three for *engagés*), to pay off the cost of their sea travel. Some were criminals or prisoners, forcibly transported.

Montserrat, and other English settlements too, had a large proportion of Catholic workers from Ireland, and during the British civil wars the interregnum regimes shipped over political dissidents and defeated soldiers. Josiah Child, governor of the East India Company and a prominent political economist, wrote sneeringly in 1693 that Virginia and Barbados '*were first peopled by a sort of loose vagrant people*, vicious and destitute'. Jean-Baptiste du Tertre, a missionary who travelled to the French colonies in the middle of the century, described them as 'gathered from all sorts of people: from all the nations of the earth, of all estates, [and] all ages'. He added that some colonies included 'a great number of renegades, apostates of faith and religion, and a number of criminals'.

They usually lived in rough wooden huts, though the wealthier planters built themselves better houses over time. Some colonists borrowed local construction techniques, and in the Caribbean adopted the 'hamacco' for sleeping, just as sailors had begun to do. They initially sought to replicate European foods, planting wheat and only slowly adapting to American crops like cassava, maize, and yams. Some hunted, and propagandists eager to advertise the colonies to those back home extolled the variety of fruits, plants, and wildlife and the merits of coastal waters teeming with fish and turtles.

The reality was less glamorous, with times of starvation in both the Caribbean and on the northern mainland, including in Virginia in 1609–10 (when 85 per cent of settlers died) and Barbados in 1630–31, partially because the planters concentrated on growing tobacco rather than food. Richard Ligon, who visited Barbados in the 1640s, noted that servants and enslaved people regularly ate 'lob-lollie', an unappetising maize gruel, and only tasted meat whenever their working oxen died.

Alcohol, however, was widely available, imported from Europe or made locally. Popular drinks included 'mobbie', a liquor fermented from sweet potatoes, and 'perino', made of cassava root, both from Taíno or Kalinago recipes. Once sugar production began several alcoholic side-products appeared, known variously as garapa, aqua ardente, 'kill-devil', and rumbullion.

The bad treatment of servants became so notorious that 'spirits' or kidnappers operated in European ports, conning or capturing new labourers for the colonies. Ligon wrote of their 'tedious hard labour, slight feeding, and ill lodging' and 'very wearisome and miserable lives'. They toiled all day in debilitating heat, tormented by mosquitos and other pests, especially when clearing the tropical jungle. Many succumbed to dysentery or tropical diseases, which might strike on ship well before they reached their new homes, and plague hit some colonies. A third, perhaps more, died in servitude.

Indentured service was certainly not slavery, with important differences in legal and social status, but there was little protection for servants against the beatings and sometimes torture inflicted by brutal masters or overseers. Any found guilty of theft or absconding might see their indenture extended for several more years. Female servants who got pregnant, and the father if he too was indentured, received a similar punishment. Those fortunate enough to survive their contracted time faced poor prospects afterwards: the struggle for a new small freeholder became harder as unclaimed land on each island shrank.

These hardships among indentured servants, together with the varied origins, faiths, and circumstances of the colonists, made for unstable and combustible communities. When a Spanish squadron attacked St Christopher in 1629, servants swam out to the ships to inform them about the island and its defences. In 1634 a conspiracy among rebellious servants was discovered in Barbados, and another in 1649, the latter only only the day before it was set to ignite. Others drifted from one colony to another as free workers or fugitive servants.

Some ran away to join the buccaneers.

The word 'buccaneer' comes from the French *boucan*, a corruption of *buccan* or *mukén*, either from Arawak or Tupi, meaning a frame for smoking meat ('barbecue' similarly comes from Arawak). Edmund Hickeringill, in *Jamaica Viewed*, wrote of 'a few *Buckaneers* or Hunting *French-men*, that follow the game'. The first buccaneers were not pirates, or maritime raiders of any sort, but hunters.

They followed a rough, roaming life on small islands and along the fringes of Caribbean colonies, stalking wild cattle and hogs – thriving invasive species introduced by Spanish settlers. Hickeringill commented that the *boucaniers* 'live by killing the wild beeves for their hides' and

Scenes of *boucanier* life from *Histoire des avantiers flibustiers*, a later French translation of Exquemelin's *Zee-roovers*. (Courtesy of the John Carter Brown Library)

that each man had a dog and a gun, both 'more industriously tended then [*sic*] themselves'.

They smoked or grilled the meat and dried the hides, bartering these with colonial settlements, passing ships, or Indigenous groups for tobacco, alcohol, and ammunition. Some *boucaniers* set up camps around Campeche and Belize in the Yucatán to cut logwood, despite *guardacostas*' attempts to drive them away. Many gathered in western Hispaniola.

In 1647 the governor of Santo Domingo established two militia companies to patrol the coasts, composed mostly of African or '*mulato*' soldiers and officers, and in 1653 those patrols brought in English, French, Irish, and Dutch prisoners. These *boucaniers* were an international bunch. There were likely *cimarrónes* among their number, since Hickingerill referred to '*French Buckaneers*, or Hunting *Marownaes*', and perhaps some Taíno or Kalinago individuals too. One contemporary called them an 'ungoverned rabble'. In a 1687 translation of *Don Quixote*, a scurrilous innkeeper was called 'an *Andaluzian* Bully, a Jamaican *Buckaneer*, as true a Thief as ever sung *Psalm* at *Tyburn*' – this last a reference to London's site for criminal execution. They evidently had a pretty poor reputation.

This 'rabble' may have developed their own social rules and communal identity, though the evidence is questionable. Le Pers and Labat, two more missionaries who visited the Caribbean during the 1690s and early 1700s (both, like Du Tertre, called Jean-Baptiste), noted that *boucaniers* formed 'small societies'. According to these accounts, they practised '*matelotage*', a distinctive form of partnership sharing possessions and resources, each *matelot*, from the French word for mariner, inheriting from his partner in the event of their death. Le Pers also wrote that these *avanturiers*, as he called them, named their whole community the *frères* or *gens de la côte*.

This idea of 'brethren of the coast' is another oft-told tale about pirates. It appeared in the work of influential writers like Voltaire and Abbé Raynal in the 1760s and 1770s, both most likely taking the idea from Le Pers, and in numerous translations thereafter. By the nineteenth century this fraternal appellation had become, and remains, a feature of historical writing on the Caribbean and on piracy.

Yet it was probably never used by the men themselves, and it exaggerates the unity among these communities. Alexandre Exquemelin, himself a buccaneer during the 1660s, wrote of them calling one another '*broeders*' (brothers), but never spoke of 'brethren of the coast'. The terms *frères* or *gens de la côte* are absent from an unpublished description of the French Caribbean dated around 1660 that survives in the Archives Nationales d'Outre-Mer, and from the earlier writings of Du Tertre.

Le Pers only knew the very end of the buccaneering era, so I suspect this concept of a united fraternity was at the very least a late development, and more likely another fictitious ingredient in our piratical imagination. In fact, when Du Tertre visited in the middle of the seventeenth century, developments in two locations had only just begun to transform these scattered, roaming *boucaniers* into the buccaneers of later fame. Those two places, also now legendary in piratical lore, were Tortuga and Port Royal.

The small island of Tortuga lies just a few miles off the north-western corner of Hispaniola. It was named by Columbus in 1492, supposedly because its shape reminded him of a turtle's shell. The northern shore is formidably rocky, the southern side more accessible, with a natural harbour sheltered by reefs. That geography, together with the island's location midway along the Greater Antilles and near to the shipping routes from Cuba, rendered it particularly suitable as a raiding base.

From the 1620s onwards *avanturiers* gathered here. Among them Jean-Baptiste le Pers noted both *boucaniers*, the hunters, and *flibustiers*. It is likely that some of these *avanturiers* were both, alternately hunting on land and roving at sea. For example, at some point in the middle decades of the century, though the exact date is unrecorded, Pierre le Grand and twenty-eight others were fortunate or crafty enough to take a Spanish silver galleon by surprise, promptly sailing back to France with it.

These *avanturiers* were much less numerous and well organised than the Dutch fleets operating out of Curaçao and elsewhere, or the English raiders of Providencia. The Providence Island Company sent a governor to claim Tortuga in 1634, but he died within a year. Nevertheless, the *avanturiers* were a nuisance, and every so often soldiers from Santo Domingo drove them off the island. They always returned shortly afterwards, along with a few resident *colons* and enslaved people.

By 1640 one Jean le Vasseur was in Tortuga. A Huguenot and a military engineer, he held no official command from the French Crown, but secured control of the island by building a substantial fortress overlooking the harbour, Fort de Rocher, nicknamed 'the dovecote'. He named one of his castle's dungeons 'purgatory', possibly out of hostility towards Catholicism. When another Spanish force attacked in 1643, Le Vasseur's cannon defeated them.

The fort strengthened Tortuga's appeal as an occasional base for the footloose *avanturiers*, offering commerce and carousing. Hickeringill described how the *boucaniers* might have grown rich from hunting and trade, had 'not their lavish riotings ... exceed[ed] the hardship of their incomes' whenever they visited Tortuga. Spanish estimates placed its population at around this time at 700 Frenchmen, 200 enslaved African people, and 250 enslaved Maya, probably captured by logwood cutters.

Well ensconced and avaricious, Le Vasseur taxed all this marketing and revelling, and monopolised the commerce in brazilwood from the island. In 1646 Le Vasseur's niece set sail to join him, suggesting a certain confidence in his position, and at one point he resisted an attempt by Phillippe de Longvilliers de Poincy, *gouverneur* of French St Christopher, to evict him in favour of de Poincy's own nephew. When two of Le Vasseur's henchmen murdered him during a quarrel in 1653, De Poincy swiftly sent in a new governor, who was driven from the island by yet another Spanish expedition in January the following year.

If that expedition removed one threat to the Spanish Empire, another very swiftly appeared. Early in 1655 a naval fleet of twenty vessels and 2,500 men arrived at Barbados, the first time English military forces had come to the Caribbean, rather than privately organised ventures. This 'Western Design', as it is known to historians, was motivated by Lord Protector Oliver Cromwell's hostility towards Catholic Spain, backed by the ambitions of the colonial merchants in government.

The expedition ignored Spanish friendliness towards the Commonwealth: Spain was one of the first countries to recognise the regime after it executed Charles I, and in 1650 Spanish ports welcomed Parliamentarian ships and banned Royalist ones. That friendliness did not extend to the Caribbean, though. John Milton, poet and polemicist for Cromwell, penned a justification that lamented the Spanish authorities' continued punishment of innocent sailors and merchants merely for sailing to the Americas.

Another key instigator of the Western Design was Thomas Gage, an Englishman born into a genteel Catholic family who travelled through the Spanish Americas as a Dominican priest, before converting to Protestantism and publishing a narrative of his journeyings. Gage reckoned that Cuba and Hispaniola would be easy to capture, and he went along as chaplain. After recruiting several thousand more troops in Barbados and other English islands, they launched two attacks near Santo Domingo, meeting defeat both times. Despite their experience as civil war veterans, the two commanders, Admiral William Penn and General Robert Venables, were ill prepared for campaigning in tropical conditions and spent much of their time arguing while their men succumbed to disease and starvation.

They turned their attention to Jamaica. With more mountainous terrain and little in the way of precious metals, this island was of much less interest to Spanish rulers than its neighbours. It had only a few thousand denizens, including Spanish colonists, enslaved Taíno and African people, *cimarrónes* who had escaped into the highland interior and visiting *boucaniers*. A previous English expedition in 1642, commanded by William Jackson (another of Warwick's associates), briefly captured the capital Santiago de la Vega after raiding along the South American mainland, ransoming it for 7,000 *pesos* plus 200 cattle and 10,000lb of manioc bread.

The town was no better defended, and probably no wealthier, when Penn and Venables attacked in May 1655. The island fell swiftly, but, apart from the speed of the victory, it was an inauspicious beginning. Leaving a small and poorly supplied army there, Penn and Venables hurried back to England, where Cromwell threw them in the Tower of London. The terms of surrender on Jamaica required the Spanish colonists to depart immediately, but several retreated to the mountains and harried the English settlers, while counterattacks came from Cuba in 1657 and 1660. However, Colonel Edward D'Oyley, another civil war soldier who took command from October 1655, managed to hold out.

On their first arrival, the English forces landed at the capacious natural harbour just a few miles to the south-east of Santiago de la Vega, which they called Cagway Bay, from the Spanish and possibly Taíno name Caguaya. While Spanish colonists had only used the outer peninsula to repair ships, the English soldiers and sailors began to fortify it as early as September 1655. They raised a round stone tower and several gun platforms, and soon these defences expanded and a town grew up around them.

Within a couple of years there was a church that also served as a market hall and at least three rows of dwellings beside the wharfs along the inner shore. The population of the island in 1658 was probably around 4,500 Europeans and 1,500 enslaved African people, many of them in the town, which was already growing larger than most colonial settlements. By 1660 there were about 200 houses, and double that within another four years.

Presumably the town acquired the name Port Royal around this time, after Charles II's restoration, just as the original Fort Cromwell was obsequiously rechristened Fort Charles. Port Royal offered similar benefits to the adventurers, hunters, smugglers, and freebooters as Tortuga had done: a secure and safe harbour within a handy distance of their cruising grounds, buyers for their wares, material necessities, and a variety of insalubrious diversions.

One consequence of this invasion was the revival of Tortuga. In 1656 D'Oyley commissioned Elias Watts, a newly arrived merchant, to re-occupy the island, which the Spanish soldiers had abandoned to defend Santo Domingo. Three years later Jérémie Deschamps, *seigneur* du Rasset, possibly a former resident of Tortuga under Le Vasseur, persuaded the Council of State in England to give him a new commission as governor, having prudently secured another as *gouverneur* from Louis XIV. He displaced Watts and subsequently quarrelled with D'Oyley, who feared that Deschamps' free hand with *flibustiers* would land them both in trouble.

Deschamps responded by declaring himself, and Tortuga, for the French Crown, and English attempts on the island in 1660 and 1662 failed. Deschamps later returned to France and spent some time imprisoned in the Bastille; he may have been scheming with the English government to seize the island for them again. Nevertheless, Tortuga remained in French hands, with further fortifications added in the 1660s, just as in Port Royal, and would later expand onto the mainland of Hispaniola as the colony of Saint-Domingue.

Throughout the late sixteenth and early seventeenth centuries, hunters, freebooters, logwood cutters, and smugglers had drifted around the colonies of the Caribbean. Raiders had troubled Spanish settlements; some had made a fortune. However, these were mostly itinerant, intermittent, and often small-scale activities. Larger expeditions, like those commanded by Drake or sent by the *West Indische Compagnie*, often launched from Europe and returned there, rather than from Caribbean bases, though Curaçao and Brazil provided havens for *Compagnie* ships. These expeditions had, more often than not, occurred as part of recognised wars, or within legal frameworks of plunder.

The continuous occupation of Port Royal and Tortuga from the later 1650s brought a new phase of maritime plundering to the Caribbean, providing centres for English, Dutch, and French raiders at the same time as the *West Indische Compagnie* largely ceased its warfare against Spain. The Peace of Westphalia in 1648 brought official Spanish recognition of the Netherlands, including their Caribbean possessions, and from then on Dutch merchants concentrated on commerce and smuggling, especially the slave trade.

Cromwell's death in 1659 was marked by thanksgiving services in Mexico City, while the Treaty of the Pyrenees the same year, followed by Charles II's restoration in 1660, meant a formal end to Spain's wars with France and Britain. Yet, unlike the *West Indische Compagnie*, the *avanturiers* or freebooters did not respond to these events by adopting less hostile courses. On the contrary, buccaneers gathered in Tortuga and Port Royal, pursuing a sustained campaign against the Spanish Empire and launching raids that stunned the world in their daring and brutality. These buccaneers occupied more ambiguous political positions that, as we shall see, stimulated new debates about the status of piracy and sea raiding.

One of their most famous leaders, whose campaigns did more to provoke these debates than any other, has come to stand as a symbol of the buccaneering era. His name was Henry Morgan.

3

ALL THE ROGUES
IN THESE SEAS

When Henry Morgan arrived in Jamaica, nobody, probably not even Morgan himself, could have known how closely intertwined his fate and that of the colony would become. During Port Royal's heyday, Morgan was its most famous resident; to his fellows a revered leader who won military victories and material wealth; to Spanish colonists a fearsome pirate who preyed on the defenceless.

The most well-known image of Morgan today appears on bottles of Captain Morgan rum, flashily dressed and heroically posed; his 'dashing spirit' is also punningly mentioned. Nor is Morgan the only Welsh sea rover honoured in this way. In 2017 a new seaweed-flavoured brand of rum appeared, named Barti in honour of 'Black Bart' Roberts, whom we will meet in another chapter. Any deeper meaning to this connection between Welsh culture, piracy, and alcohol, I will leave you to contemplate.

Barti is distilled in Pembrokeshire, close to where Roberts was born; the Captain Morgan brand has nothing to do with its namesake. It was created in 1944 by a Canadian distilling company, although the rum was initially produced in Jamaica, and later in Puerto Rico, so there is a Caribbean connection. Nevertheless, the advertising invokes popular ideas about buccaneers that define how we still interpret that period of plundering.

Two contemporary images of Morgan survive, and neither is quite as romantic. A portrait held at Tredegar House, home to his wealthy cousins, shows a young man dressed and bewigged in a well-heeled if plain manner, with a confident and direct stare. It must have been made before he departed for the Caribbean.

The other appeared in variations across the different editions and translations of Alexandre Exquemelin's *De Americaensche Zee-roovers*, first published in 1678. Depicting Morgan at the height of his buccaneering career, it has a certain resemblance to the earlier portrait, but by this time Morgan is solidly built, opulently dressed, slightly smirking as his hand firmly grips the baton that was a contemporary symbol of military command. Behind him a fleet burns in battle. His eyes no longer meet your gaze, focusing off to the side – is he evasive, or determined?

Morgan was probably born in 1635 near Cardiff, to a poorer branch of the Tredegar clan. A local pub and community hub, Llanrumney Hall, lays claim to being his childhood home. We do not know how or when he reached the Caribbean. Two buccaneers-turned-authors gave different accounts: Exquemelin wrote that Morgan, under whom he served, had first gone to Barbados as an indentured servant, while Bartholomew Sharp had him sail as a soldier with the Western Design.

Of the two, I find the former a more intriguing tale (if only because Morgan himself denied it so hotly) but the latter a more likely one. By 1662 Morgan was an officer of the Port Royal militia and a captain in a raiding expedition, suggesting prior experience in combat. Morgan's only surviving comment on his childhood was that he 'left the schools too young to be a great proficient in either [admiralty] or other laws, and

Portraits of Henry Morgan from the Dutch and Spanish editions of Exquemelin's *Zee-roovers* (both misnaming him 'John Morgan'). (Courtesy of the John Carter Brown Library)

have been much more used to the pike than the book'. He disingenuously downplays his knowledge here, probably to excuse alleged mistakes during his long tenure as Jamaica's admiralty judge, but it suggests he started his military career early.

A soldiering life fits his family background, too. One of his great-uncles commanded the English garrison at Bergen-op-Zoom in the Netherlands during Elizabeth's reign. Two of his uncles, Thomas and Edward Morgan, fought in Europe during the Thirty Years' War and then, on opposing sides, during the British civil wars.

Thomas served with the Parliamentarian commander George Monck, who played a crucial role in the restoration of Charles II, and it was probably through this connection that Thomas became governor of Jersey in 1665 and died there in 1679. Edward, meanwhile, was captain-general of Royalist forces in South Wales, perhaps schooling his young nephew. The region saw fierce fighting, and Edward fled into exile in 1651, for which loyalty the king would later reward him.

Another possibility is that Morgan went to sea as a young man. Parliament's Irish Sea squadron operated out of Milford Haven, while Royalist raiders were for a time based in Bristol, both within striking distance of Llanrhymni. Large naval squadrons and many 'private men of war' cruised during the First Anglo-Dutch War of 1652–54. I am speculating here, though.

If Morgan reached the Caribbean in 1655, then at Santo Domingo he got a signal lesson in how *not* to conduct a campaign. Alternatively, he may have arrived in the following few years. All new settlers were exempted from excise taxes or customs duties for seven years, which might have been an attractive prospect.

If he was not a soldier to begin with, he soon joined up. In 1661, Governor D'Oyley detained two ships he had commissioned, which had attacked a Dutch vessel instead of their approved Spanish targets. D'Oyley threatened prosecution for any who should 'comfort or abett the said Theeves and piratts'. One of the twenty-five accused was 'henry Morgan, souldier', though it is not certainly the same man. In any case, the culprits escaped punishment.

Perhaps that is not surprising. Despite the treaties of the past two years, the Caribbean was still a warzone.

By the 1650s, Spanish imperial power was crumbling under the strain of a century and a half of warfare. The populations of other European countries increased across the seventeenth and eighteenth centuries, doubling or more in Britain, the Netherlands, and Portugal; the population of Spain rose by less than a third in the 1600s and stagnated in the 1700s, reflecting economic disparities.

During the first half of the seventeenth century, the gross tonnage of Spanish trade to the Americas fell by over half, and even the policies of reformist politician Gaspar de Guzmán, *conde-duque* de Olivares, could not reverse the trend. In 1656–57, Admiral Robert Blake blockaded the Spanish coast and destroyed the *flota* at the Canaries, capturing 2 million *pesos*. The other 10.5 million, hurriedly ferried ashore, now lay stranded, interrupting Spain's payments to its armies and creditors.

When Felipe IV died in 1665, his 3-year-old son Carlos II succeeded to the throne, the last Habsburg king of Spain. During Carlos' youth his mother, Mariana of Austria, governed as queen regent, facing factional rivalries within Spain besides the structural and economic issues that plagued the empire. By 1670, less than half of the millions of *pesos* imported to Spain remained there, because so much wealth went to paying off the Crown's debts.

Though the bureaucratic and indecisive nature of this empire has been exaggerated, playing up contemporary ethno-national stereotypes, the Spanish Crown did lay restrictions on its servants. A *cédula* of 1633 ordered that no governor take money from the royal coffers for defence unless 'it is truly and probably held as certain and evident that there are enemies on the coast', and a *junta* of royal treasury officials must sign it off, allowing 'only exactly what is necessary'. Of course, by then it would often be too late.

Spanish records reveal the decline in colonial defences. Portobelo had three castles but only a small royal guard and a militia that, in 1667, mustered 129 men (divided into four companies along *casta* lines). Panamá was unfortified and had a few hundred regular troops plus the militia, although Spanish forces destroyed many of the *cimarrón* communities and established *doctrinas*, villages of Indigenous converts, who were allies rather than enemies. Cartagena maintained some 400 regular troops across three castles with 50 cannon between them, but here as elsewhere the soldiers went unpaid for months or years, and many deserted.

Governors tended to protect their own domain and hesitated to send scarce resources to assist others. Most smaller towns had no defences at all.

Their favoured tactic was to hide their possessions and themselves in the surrounding countryside until any peril had passed.

The valuable cargoes continued: at Portobelo in 1669 the ships loaded 5 million *pesos* of merchandise and 17.5 million of silver coin and bullion. However, the *Carrera* no longer sailed every year, and though the *Armada de Barlovento* nominally defended the Caribbean, ships were recalled to Europe, or wrecked, and sometimes none of them were present at all. A new squadron set up in Puerto Rico in 1641 did not last long. Only in 1665 was the *Armada de Barlovento* reinstituted, and even then it did not reach the Caribbean for two years, although Spanish ports often set out *guardacostas*.

Many Spanish settlements were still wealthy, though. Silver and gold flowed more intermittently, but it flowed. Churches and cathedrals in Panamá, Cartagena, Havana, and elsewhere were stocked with rich ornaments, while merchants dealt profitably in local products. Most of the major towns also had large numbers of enslaved people. Of Panamá's 6,000 inhabitants in 1607, around 1,000 were European and the rest Indigenous, African, or of mixed parentage, though not all of that majority were enslaved. The population probably increased a little over the century, and planters in the colonies of northern European empires saw this enslaved labour as another form of wealth they wished to steal.

Riches and defensive weakness on the Spanish side were matched, among their enemies, by a siege mentality of their own, as Jamaica and Tortuga seemed precarious throughout these decades. Communicating with Europe took several months, and colonial governors dealt with matters on the spot as they saw fit. Rulers in Europe sent vague instructions that may have implicitly recognised this fact, but were also reluctant to commit much in the way of resources to defending colonies that had, as yet, shown little promise.

The recent treaties had not formally acknowledged any English or French colonies. The inhabitants of Tortuga and Jamaica could not know that no future Spanish attack would wrest the islands from them, and it was not for want of trying. Nestled among the Greater Antilles, they were both more strategically valuable and more vulnerable than their fellows further eastward.

Nor had those treaties permitted foreign ships to call at Spanish ports. Smuggling to the Spanish colonies was rife, but risky. Capture by the *guardacostas*, whom Dutch, English, and French sailors accused of piracy, remained a common occurrence, with execution or imprisonment and hard labour a frequent outcome. Even the small number of ships issued with licences were sometimes seized.

Before those treaties, the last years of war in the later 1650s laid the foundations of later buccaneering. The ships left over from the Western Design, hanging around in Jamaica in 1655–57, raided Spanish settlements in the Guajira Peninsula and Riohacha, and cruised in the Florida Strait, forcing the *flota* to overwinter in Mexico. Recruits from the *avanturiers*, *vrijbuiters*, and rovers already present in the Caribbean bolstered their numbers, and over time they drew more volunteers.

When D'Oyley wrote to Tortuga in 1657 encouraging residents to relocate to Jamaica, he was probably most interested in *boucaniers* who could help to feed the colony, but he did employ private warships. So too did Elias Watts during his brief tenure in Tortuga, granting a commission to around 400 men, who borrowed a frigate that had just arrived from Nantes and descended on Santiago de los Caballeros in Hispaniola, pillaging the town and denuding its churches. When they returned to Tortuga each man received 300 *pesos* for his share, equivalent to several years' wages for a sailor on a merchant or navy ship.

Newly arrived naval officer Christopher Myngs defeated an attempt to retake Jamaica in 1658, before leading several combined expeditions of naval and private ships. He looted Cumaná, Puerto Cabello, and Coro along the coast of Venezuela in 1658, then (despite the end of war) Santiago de Cuba in 1661–62, and Campeche in 1663. At Coro, Myngs seized twenty-two chests of silver, valued at a princely £300,000 when he returned to Port Royal.

That success led to squabbles with D'Oyley, who had instituted a rough and ready version of the legal procedure for prizes (ships captured from the enemy). Myngs did not observe even these rules, so D'Oyley sent him to England to stand trial for some irregularities, but then had to sail home himself when Myngs started a retaliatory lawsuit.

While Myngs returned in 1661, D'Oyley did not. Charles II sent out his own governor, Lord Windsor, who set up a more official admiralty court and cancelled all of D'Oyley's commissions – then swiftly handed out his own, issuing at least sixteen by 1663. He had a stake in this: his annual salary depended on the proceeds of the prize court.

Port Royal's maritime potency and plundering profits quickly grew. The Santiago raid involved eleven ships and 1,300 men, plus Thomas Whetstone, whom they met at sea. Oliver Cromwell's nephew but a former Royalist, Whetstone now commanded a private ship with many Indigenous crewmembers. By 1660, a Spanish visitor reported more than twenty warships based in Port Royal; another source mentioned thirty vessels crewed by some 3,000 men. Myngs' final Caribbean campaign in

1663 comprised 740 men and more than a dozen ships from Port Royal, plus 250 men in four ships from Tortuga, and three Dutch ships with 100 men.

The buccaneers became even more important after Myngs and his naval frigates departed that year, recalled by a government in London looking to cut costs. They now had an informal leadership, fostered during Myngs' raids. In 1658, Myngs sold three prizes to Robert Searle, Lawrence Prince (a *vrijbuiter* from Amsterdam), and John Morris, all of whom became prominent captains. The 1663 expedition involved Morris, Searle, and two future commanders of note: Edward Mansfield, probably an experienced captain already, and Henry Morgan, for whom it was his first voyage at that rank, or at least the first on record.

Only a few months after that voyage, Morgan set sail with Morris and a few others, including the Dutchman David Marteen. Morgan was probably not commander at the start, as the others were more experienced (Marteen was later described as 'the best man in Tortuga'). Morgan may have taken charge at some point. Their first target was Villahermosa in Campeche, 50 miles inland. As previous voyages had, Morgan and his companions depended on Indigenous guides. They seized the town and 300 prisoners, but while they were ashore, some passing Spanish vessels happened upon, and captured, their five ships, then ambushed the buccaneers when they returned.

They defeated this ambush but could not regain their ships. Seemingly undaunted, they seized two Spanish barques and four large canoes and travelled 500 miles, against strong currents, round Yucatán to Honduras and the island of Roatán. They sacked Trujillo, then sailed a further 450 miles south (bringing their total at this point to 2,600 miles), where they struck upriver and attacked Granada, a town at the northern tip of Lake Nicaragua and, lying 150 miles from the Caribbean Sea, largely undefended. Granada was bigger than Portsmouth, with seven churches and a cathedral, and the buccaneers spent sixteen hours plundering the place. Once again they joined with local Indigenous groups, around 1,000 of these allies participating in the attack, who afterwards 'secured themselves in the mountains', except for a few who joined Marteen's ship.

As they sailed away for Port Royal, Morgan and his fellows no doubt congratulated one another. When they returned, almost two years after they set sail, they found there was a new governor in town.

Thomas Modyford arrived in Jamaica on 11 June 1664. He had been a planter in Barbados, which recommended him for the role of governor. His mission was to turn the colonists away from plundering and towards sugar cultivation.

It was a tricky task. Before Modyford's arrival Thomas Lynch, a Jamaican merchant acting as interim governor, wrote to England that some 1,500 buccaneers in twelve ships sailed from Port Royal. It would be 'a remote and hazardous expedient' to revoke their commissions without the naval strength to back it up, since the buccaneers would most likely up anchors for Tortuga, and might turn their attention on Jamaican ships. 'What compliance can be expected,' Lynch asked, 'from men so desperate and numerous, that have no other element but the sea, nor trade but privateering?'

I will pause here to indulge in some more lexicographical pondering. As I noted earlier, 'privateer' in modern English usually means a sea raider with a legal commission, distinct from pirates, although scholars are quick to point out that such paperwork does not guarantee law-abiding behaviour.

In the first appearances of the word during the 1650s and 1660s it did not, I think, carry this direct connotation of legality and authorisation. Rather, like its forerunner 'private men of war', it points to the ownership of the vessel. The 'privateers' of the later seventeenth century might carry a commission, sometimes more than one, but not all of them did, and the absence of such documentation would not prevent them from being called a privateer – nor render them, automatically, a pirate.

In a curious hint towards this ambiguity, Thomas Blount's *Nomo-lexikon* of 1670, a dictionary of legal terms, offered 'Sea rover ... See Privateir', though it gave no separate entry for the latter. A rival text, John Cowell and Thomas Manley's *Nomothetes*, appeared two years later and queried whether privateer was 'not the same with Pyrate', to which Blount conceded in another book, while accusing Cowell and Manley of plagiarism, that in *Nomo-lexikon* 'Privateir' had been a misprint for 'pirate'. This obscure spat among glossographers intriguingly reflects the uncertain and unsettled definitions of the time. Only gradually did clear linguistic and legal distinctions emerge.

I have generally preferred 'buccaneers' here, even though people did not use that label in the 1660s and 1670s, except, like Edmund Hickeringill, to mean the hunting *boucaniers*. It too changed its meaning over time, but in English it came to stand for Caribbean sea raiders by the 1680s; by 1684 one such plunderer wrote of 'our Profession, that is to say, a true Bucanier'. More importantly, it avoids confusion with the modern implications of 'privateer'. These changing meanings are themselves a crucial part of our story.

Whatever we call them, Port Royal was soon notorious for its raiders. Lynch wrote that 'the Spaniards call all the rogues in these seas, of what nation soever, English'. As his fears about Tortuga show, this was an inaccurate epithet. Bertrand d'Ogeron, the new governor for the *Compagnie des Indes Occidentales*, wrote in 1665 that the *boucaniers* still roamed Hispaniola, with around 800 of them spread in small groups. He reported that they 'live like savages ... and they commit a thousand robberies', including against Dutch and English ships; here again we see that *avanturiers* could be both *boucaniers* and *flibustiers*.

Ogeron noted that they had 'a leader of their own', recognising no other authority, suggesting that the *avanturiers*, like the buccaneers in Jamaica, had become more coordinated. He nevertheless sought to use these 'savages' for his own purposes, establishing a base at Petit-Goâve, on the south-west coast of Hispaniola, and offering commissions both on his own French authority and on behalf of the ongoing Portuguese rebellion.

At first Modyford took a different line. Within a month of arriving, he prohibited further violence against Spanish ships and ordered British sailors not to take foreign commissions. Just as Robert Searle sailed into Port Royal in September 1664 with two prizes from Cuba, Modyford received renewed orders from London to cease hostilities and make necessary restitution. Modyford and the Council of Jamaica resolved to return the prizes to Cuba, rescind Searle's commission, and declare that anyone who carried on raiding would be 'looked upon as pirates and rebels'.

When another formerly commissioned buccaneer, Captain Munro, began to attack English ships, he was captured and publicly executed for piracy, but it no doubt intensified anxieties about what disappointed plunderers might do. Modyford shared Lynch's worries that buccaneers could relocate to Tortuga. He informed London that he must proceed 'by degrees and moderation'.

Modyford refrained from issuing new commissions, but his brother-in-law, one Mr Kendall, proposed to the Privy Council in England that prizes brought in under existing commissions should be permitted. Otherwise, he warned, the colony would lose over 1,000 'stout men', whom he also described as 'desperate people' after a decade or more spent at sea. When in February 1665 Modyford condemned fourteen men for piracy, he promptly pardoned all but three of them.

Jamaica needed those stout and desperate men: the Second Anglo-Dutch War was brewing. In January 1665, before war was formally declared, Michiel de Ruyter attacked English trading posts in West Africa, crossed the Atlantic, menaced Barbados, and raided Virginia and New England. Modyford's new lieutenant-governor was Henry Morgan's uncle Edward, appointed because of his demonstrated devotion to the Stuarts, his family connection with Monck, now the duke of Albemarle and a royal advisor, and perhaps also his experience of Dutch warfare.

Modyford duly issued commissions against Dutch shipping, and he and Morgan planned an attack on Curaçao. Morgan assembled 9 ships and 500 soldiers, whom Modyford called 'reformed privateers ... [and] resolute fellows', including Searle. They were hired 'at the old rate of no purchase, no pay', so Modyford reassured London that the expedition 'will cost the King nothing considerable'.

It did not gain the king much, either, nor the buccaneers. Setting off in several groups between late March and mid-April 1665, they made a hard voyage, almost 1,000 miles to windward, and were refused permission to resupply in Hispaniola on the way. Efforts to establish peaceful trade with Spanish ports were not going well: 'We and they have used too many mutual barbarisms to have a sudden correspondence,' Lynch wrote ruefully to London. The expedition captured St Eustatius, and 900 enslaved people, but Edward Morgan died, not in battle but 'being ancient and corpulent, by hard marching and extraordinary heat'.

His second-in-command and successor Colonel Cary persuaded the 'reformed privateers' to assault Saba nearby – many Sabans today are proud of their piratical heritage and hold that moment as its beginning – but the men refused to continue to Curaçao. The following year Searle captured Tobago, but overall the buccaneers had little impact in this war.

Late in August 1665, David Marteen was the first of Henry Morgan's companions to sail into Port Royal, bringing rather poorly timed news of their rampage along the Spanish mainland. Marteen soon slipped away to Tortuga, fearing that Dutchmen were now *personae non gratae* in Jamaica. When the others arrived, they maintained that under Lord Windsor's commissions they had acted lawfully, and that in their wanderings they had never received the orders cancelling hostilities against Spain.

Modyford continued his permissive policy on previous commissions, and the plunder from this voyage made Henry Morgan a wealthy man. He married his cousin, Mary Elizabeth Morgan, purchased his first plantation, and resumed his role as a captain in the Port Royal militia. I wonder if

he considered settling down – but if he did, circumstances soon changed
his mind.

News reached Port Royal late in 1665 of a 'parcel of privateers' who
had Portuguese commissions (probably from Ogeron), 'cared for dealing with no enemy but the Spaniards', and planned to attack Cuba. They
were led by Edward Mansfield, who may have been Dutch or German;
Modyford called him 'the old fellow', so he probably had a long career
at sea. Modyford sent out two ships to find them, and by March 1666 he
reported them 'professing much zeal in his Majesty's service, and a firm
intention to attack Curacao'.

His judgement proved optimistic. Mansfield raided the Cuban coast
anyway, to gather supplies, then in January 1666 sailed south-east.
Discouraged by the difficulties of beating hundreds of miles to windward, several ships abandoned the fleet, and Mansfield later claimed that
his disobedient sailors had forced him to literally change tack. Inspired
by information from a Spanish prisoner, they made for the never-before-
plundered inland town of Cartago, about 1,000 miles west of Curaçao.
However, the landing party bickered while Indigenous scouts warned the
garrison, forcing a retreat.

Mansfield did not return to Port Royal straight away. Learning once
again from prisoners, one Spanish and one 'mestizo', that the garrison on
Providencia had dwindled in recent decades, he selected this new target,
ideally suited as a base, lying within a few hundred miles of most of the
Spanish mainland. Guided by his prisoners, Mansfield snuck through the
encircling reefs and overran the few defenders. Spanish records suggest
that he seized around 70,000 pesos, although he never admitted it.

If he had misgivings about how Modyford would respond to the news
that he had captured a Spanish island instead of Curaçao, Mansfield was
fortunate. Modyford, in frustration, had written to London some months
earlier that he would continue to 'restrain [the buccaneers] from further
acts against the Spaniards', but significantly added 'unless provoked by
new insolencies'. 'It must be force alone,' he warned, 'that can cut in
sunder that unneighbourly maxim of their government to deny all access
to strangers.'

After consulting with the Council of Jamaica about the guardacostas'
depredations and the decline of Port Royal's defences, Modyford declared
on 4 March 1666 that he would once again issue commissions against

Spanish shipping. Conveniently, Albemarle had authorised him to commission ships 'as he found it for the advantage of his Majesty's service and
the good of this island' – a perhaps deliberately broad remit. Very soon
Modyford crowed that Tortuga men were coming over to him, including
David Marteen with two frigates.

When Mansfield arrived in June 1666, Modyford endorsed his *fait accom-
pli* – indeed Modyford had heard about Mansfield's plans, and reported
them to London, before Mansfield even reached Providencia. Restoring
a former English possession had a better look than burning a Spanish
town. Modyford sent a garrison to reinforce the island, commanded by
Major Samuel Smith and ferried over by Thomas Whetstone. However, at
Providencia these reinforcements did not meet the fate they were expecting.

Mansfield allowed the Spanish commander of Providencia to sail for
the mainland with his men, and he promptly complained to Juan Perez
de Guzmán, president of the *audiencia* of Panamá, who dispatched José
Sanchez Ximenez, *sargento-mayor* of Portobelo, with a force of 125 men,
including twelve '*indios*'. They embarked on an English ship in Portobelo,
which had been impounded even though it was employed by the Genoese
merchants who then held the *asiento*, the official contract for the slave trade
with Spanish colonies.

This relief force called at Cartagena, where the governor called a *junta*
and reluctantly provided an additional sixty Spanish and sixty '*mulato*' soldiers, probably because of threats from Perez to report any backsliding to
Madrid. At Providencia it was the English soldiers' turn to be heavily out-
numbered, and though they apparently used organ pipes from the church
as makeshift artillery, Sanchez swiftly took the island. Unlike Mansfield,
he did not release his prisoners, sending them to Portobelo and Panamá,
where some were imprisoned for several years.

In July 1667, the Second Anglo-Dutch War ended with the Treaty of
Breda, and Spain and Britain agreed a new alliance in September. It took
months for word of these treaties to reach the Caribbean, long after news
from Providencia arrived in Jamaica and seemed to confirm Modyford's
fears of Spanish aggression. Mansfield himself had left for Tortuga, only
to be captured and reportedly executed in Havana. Modyford needed a
new commander.

He chose Henry Morgan, whom he instructed to capture prisoners and
gather intelligence. It seems unlikely that Morgan ever intended to confine
himself to these objectives. His commission, authorising him only to capture Spanish ships, paradoxically encouraged him to raid ashore, because
the buccaneers could keep that plunder to themselves.

A copy of the articles agreed by Morgan and his fellows for this voyage, in January 1668, was captured and survives in the Archivo General de Indias in Seville. These articles mandate that anything taken ashore 'shall be divided man for man as free plunder', whereas a quarter of anything captured at sea would go to the shipowners, after deducting the shares due to the king and lord admiral. Even Modyford later acknowledged that for 'plunder from shoare they pay nothing because not comissionated to it'.

First Morgan needed to interrogate some prisoners. Allying with *avanturiers* from Tortuga and Hispaniola, Morgan seized Puerto del Principe in Cuba. Some of the residents admitted, possibly under torture or the threat of it, that they had been pressed into service for an attack on Jamaica, and that major forces were expected from Veracruz, Campeche, Portobelo, and Cartagena. The state of the garrisons in those towns renders this statement highly dubious, but Morgan may have believed it, and in any case, he could now justify an attack on any major Spanish port.

He also demanded a ransom for the town, but when it became clear that the townspeople were playing for time in the hope of rescue, he settled for 1,000 cattle and whatever plunder his men had already gathered. At a council of war held at Cape Gracias a Diós, on the north-east coast of what is now Nicaragua, Morgan proposed Portobelo as the target, probably hoping that the town would be full of silver and other riches awaiting the *galeones*. His French allies considered it too dangerous and sailed off.

Left with only 500 men, Morgan reassured them that Portobelo would fall easily. He had learnt from an 'Indian' informant about the poor state of the defences. Approaching the city, they captured a boat with a '*zambo*' sailor aboard who offered to land them safely near the town. Once again, Indigenous knowledge was crucial to the buccaneers' success. They also encountered a canoe carrying some escaped English prisoners, starving and ragged.

Morgan attacked on 26 June 1668, avoiding the heavily fortified harbour and landing west of the city. The buccaneers easily swept past the outer defences and the western castle of Santiago, which was both scantily manned and poorly situated below an overlooking hill from which buccaneer sharpshooters pinned down the garrison, while their fellows passed by.

Although warned by a scout canoe and the sound of gunfire, the citizens of Portobelo were unprepared. As the drum beat for the militia to gather, many townsfolk instead tried to hide their riches, or fled, or simply ignored the summons. The buccaneers rushed through the streets to the incomplete castle of San Geronimo in the harbour, led by the escaped prisoners who had been labouring on it; the terrified castellan swiftly surrendered. Here they found eleven more prisoners, captured at Providencia, who told them that a 'great man' had recently been transferred from there to Peru. The implication was that this might be Prince Maurice, Charles II's cousin, whose ship had disappeared in a hurricane some years before.

It took about half an hour from the buccaneers first reaching Santiago to capturing San Geronimo. The sun was only just rising. The buccaneers looted through the streets, seizing the royal treasury, where they freed still more English prisoners. Others went to the hospital and convent. They detained the city's survivors, those who had not escaped, in the biggest church.

To finish off Santiago, Morgan adopted a ruthless ploy that has become part of his legend. He forced the mayor and some friars, nuns, and old men to walk ahead of his soldiers. Alexandre Exquemelin described this episode with savage relish in his *Zee-roovers*, and though Morgan later denied it, the official Spanish reports back up Exquemelin on this occasion. Despite the terrified entreaties of their unfortunate compatriots, the garrison kept firing, but they could not hold off the renewed assault. It did not take long for the buccaneers to capture a third castle, San Felipe, across the bay; the castellan lost his nerve, surrendered, and immediately committed suicide.

It was a swift victory, but not a surprising one. Morgan conveniently exaggerated the strength of Spanish defences in his reports, and, though it is possible that Spanish commanders also underestimated, for the sake of their reputations, the defenders were probably not ready to resist an attack. Morgan also, laconically and rather misleadingly, stated that he had been 'enforced to assault the castle' when 'we could not refresh ourselves in quiet'.

Not that the buccaneers refreshed themselves 'in quiet'. Exquemelin described them 'merrily lording with wine and women' and suggested that fifty sober men might have recaptured the city that night. Both Spanish and English witnesses recounted gruesome tortures to make prisoners reveal their wealth, targeting women in particular. Morgan denied it all and claimed that his female prisoners preferred to remain with him rather than take their chances among the 'rude Panama soldiers', but I doubt this is true, and even if it is, Morgan probably extended his protection only to women of high status.

In Panamá, the interim governor Agustin de Bracamonte acted swiftly when he heard the news (Juan Perez de Guzmán had been arrested on

Depictions of buccaneer raids and incidents from Exquemelin's *Zee-roovers*. Note the encounter with a crocodile, top right. (Courtesy of the John Carter Brown Library)

charges of embezzlement the year before by the *conde* de Lemos, viceroy of Peru, and imprisoned in Lima). De Bracamonte summoned around 700 men and set out across the isthmus, but he was slowed by delays in collecting food and weapons, and when he learned of the fall of San Felipe his momentum disappeared.

Rather than attack the city, the Spanish commanders instead marched to Matapalo, a poor choice for a camp, where torrential rains and mosquitos laid their soldiers low. When two Spanish mariners snuck out of Portobelo with the alarming, and entirely untrue, news that this was just a distraction while a French force struck at Panamá, a hastily convened *junta* chose to retreat across the isthmus.

Morgan wrote to De Bracamonte demanding 350,000 *pesos*, or he would burn the city. The governor replied curtly that he would not negotiate. Morgan sent another letter, this time with an insolent flourish that became his signature style. He awaited the Spanish army, Morgan said, and if they did not come to him, he would visit them in Panamá. He signed off with a grandiloquent brag: 'Portobello city of the king of England.'

He had no intention of holding the city, of course, and accepted a lower ransom of 100,000 *pesos*, though refusing the governor's ingenious proposals that the ransom be paid half up front and half by bills of exchange, or delivered after the buccaneers had left. Morgan was only interested in cash down.

The wealthy merchants of Portobelo collected 56,000 *pesos* in silver bars and plate, 40,000 in silver coin, and 4,000 in gold. The total plunder probably came to something like 250,000 *pesos*, and each of the surviving buccaneers received around eight or ten years' wages for a merchant sailor. Many prisoners, especially those of African or mixed parentage (regardless of whether they were legally free or enslaved in Portobelo), were also carried back to slavery in Jamaica.

Portobelo, like the expeditions over the preceding decade, laid bare the challenge of defending an under-resourced and overstretched Spanish Empire. De Bracamonte had sent out hurried appeals to Cartagena and Lima, and both dispatched relief expeditions, but these set out, within six days of each other, several weeks after Morgan and his fellows left the city. The viceroy of New Spain did not hear about Portobelo for months. The newly recomposed *Armada de Barlovento*, in Havana, never even set sail.

4

HAZARD OF BATTLE

At some time in 1668, probably while Morgan was away at sea, an infamous *flibustier* arrived in Port Royal with a captured Spanish brigantine: François l'Olonnais, the most prominent captain then sailing out of Tortuga. Morgan's voyages were just part of a wider pattern of marauding in the later 1660s, although they were among the largest and had the greatest impact.

L'Olonnais sold his prize to a *vrijbuiter* based in Jamaica, Roche (or Roc) Brasiliano, so named because he had formerly served the *Compagnie* in Bahia, though he may have been born in the Netherlands. After the Dutch retreat in 1654, Brasiliano relocated to the Caribbean, possibly by way of a mutiny, and brought in at least one valuable prize to Port Royal. He had been captured by Spanish forces and escaped at some time before he purchased this new ship from L'Olonnais.

Brasiliano and his first mate, another Dutchman called Jelles de Lecat (or Lescat), cruised near Cartagena and Portobelo, soon capturing a prize, which De Lecat took as his own ship. In 1669 the pair, together with an English buccaneer called Joseph Bradley, went on another voyage, in which Bradley and Brasiliano blockaded Campeche while De Lecat loaded logwood.

De Lecat later sailed with Jan Erasmus Reyning, who may in fact have been dispatched to capture him before joining forces instead. Reyning was born in Flushing, Zeeland, in 1640, the son of a Danish mariner and a local woman. He went to sea with his father, was captured during the Second Anglo-Dutch War, and then travelled to the French plantations in Hispaniola as an *engagé* before joining the *avanturiers*.

Brasiliano and L'Olonnais got their own sections in Exquemelin's *Zee-roovers*, and like Morgan both were depicted in portraits. They too stand before scenes of battle and destruction, and they make rather more fearsome prospects than Morgan. Unlike his baton of office, they brandish cutlasses, and L'Olonnais wears an expression of insolent contempt. Exquemelin's account of their voyages also included lurid details of brutality towards Spanish prisoners; L'Olonnais is supposed to have ripped out and eaten one man's still-beating heart.

L'Olonnais, like De Lecat and Exquemelin himself, arrived in the Caribbean as an *engagé*, coming originally from Sables-d'Olonne, hence his name. He may have been in Tortuga when Deschamps took over in 1659, and at some time around then became a *flibustier*. Exquemelin wrote that L'Olonnais was shipwrecked in Campeche early in his career, where Spanish soldiers slaughtered his crew, while he survived by hiding among the bodies, covered in blood. He snuck into a town and with a group of enslaved people escaped on a canoe, eventually returning to Tortuga. This episode apparently began his implacable hatred towards the Spanish Empire.

L'Olonnais allied with another *flibustier* leader, Michel de Maristeguy, more famously Michel le Basque, again a nod to his origins. He had already tasted success after starting out as a *boucanier* around 1657. Ogeron appointed Le Basque a district official in Hispaniola, but he returned to sea and captured one of the *galeones*. In 1666 Le Basque and L'Olonnais, with eight ships and 650 men, set sail for Maracaibo, lying on Lake Maracaibo in Venezuela. Seizing some prizes and then skilfully navigating through

Portraits of François l'Olonnais and Roche Brasiliano, from Exquemelin's *Zee-roovers*. (Courtesy of the John Carter Brown Library)

the treacherous Gulf of Venezuela to the narrow entrance of the lake, they fell on the town without warning and captured some 4,000 inhabitants.

From there he attacked Gibraltar, at the other end of the lake, where he seized more plunder but his men fell sick. After six weeks he burnt Gibraltar, returned to Maracaibo and pillaged it a second time. The total amount from the raid was some 260,000 *pesos*, plus many valuable objects, on par with Morgan's Portobelo voyage two years later.

L'Olonnais next set out for the Mosquito Coast with 700 men in 1667, but this expedition did not go so well. The ships met a tempest in the Gulf of Honduras and, avoiding larger targets, pillaged the small towns of the coast, mostly Miskito villages or turtle fishermen. L'Olonnais captured one ship and chose to strike inland, forcing some prisoners to guide him to San Pedro, near Lake Nicaragua, despite difficult terrain and counter-attacks by Spanish soldiers. After a stiff defence he captured the town, but most of its denizens had fled.

A depiction of L'Olonnais torturing his prisoners, from Exquemelin's *Zee-roovers*. (Courtesy of the John Carter Brown Library)

Following a few other raids in the area, fierce skirmishes with Miskito parties eventually drove L'Olonnais back to the coast. At some point he must have sold his prize in Port Royal, before he returned to cruise near Cartagena. He was then captured by some 'Indios Bravos' of the Darién region, who, according to Exquemelin, butchered L'Olonnais in a fashion gruesomely similar to his own violent excesses.

L'Olonnais and Morgan, and Myngs before them, were distinctive in gathering large forces and seizing major towns. Many of the buccaneers – like Brasiliano, De Lecat, Reyning, and Bradley – sailed in much smaller groups on cruises against Spanish shipping, though they also accompanied L'Olonnais and Morgan (the French ships that left Morgan before Portobelo may have gone to L'Olonnais). L'Olonnais' grisly end shows that death was as probable a fate for any buccaneer as wealth and fortune, even for their leaders – but not for Morgan. By the time of the famous *flibustier*'s demise, Morgan was already embarked on another plundering venture.

From Portobelo, Morgan brought back his plunder and the reports of an invasion aimed at Jamaica. Deeming these credible, and without any countermanding orders from England (or much in the way of orders at all), Modyford and Morgan decided to press on with defence through pre-emptive attack. Modyford had also received news that his own son Jack, whose ship had disappeared some years previously, had been captured by Spanish forces and was either dead or imprisoned.

In October 1668, Morgan began once more to round up recruits, announcing a rendezvous at the Isla de Vaca off the south coast of Hispaniola. Soon after Morgan departed, the *Oxford* arrived, the first naval ship to reach Jamaica for several years, and with thirty-four guns one of the most powerful vessels in the Caribbean. On arrival in Port Royal the captain quarrelled with and murdered the ship's master, then ran away, so Modyford placed Edward Collier, an experienced buccaneer, in command.

Collier soon captured *Le Cerf Volant*, a ship from La Rochelle whose captain was accused of seizing a Virginian vessel. The Jamaican admiralty court condemned the captain for piracy, reprieving him but taking his ship, now renamed the *Satisfaction*. Both the *Oxford* and the *Satisfaction* sailed to join Morgan, and with them went Richard Browne, a surgeon with his own political contacts in London. Browne's letters home provide an alternative and not quite so laudatory perspective on Morgan's voyages, although whatever Browne's criticisms he still participated.

Collier and Browne found that Morgan had already gathered 12 ships and almost 1,000 men. Morgan took the *Oxford* as his flagship and, on 2 January 1669, called a council of war aboard. The captains decided on Cartagena, one of the biggest Spanish cities, suspected of gathering invasion forces. After the council came the revels that, according to Exquemelin, included 'shooting of healths', a combination of drinking toasts and gun salutes.

This 'good cheer' proved deadly when a stray spark hit the powder magazine and the *Oxford* exploded. Only six men and four boys survived: those feasting on one side of the table in the great cabin all lived, including Morgan and Browne, and those on the other side all perished. The king's ship had lasted barely a few months in the Caribbean. Rumours claimed it was a deliberate French revenge for *Le Cerf Volant*, while the denizens of Cartagena were sure that their saintly patron was seen returning the next morning to her namesake monastery, Nuestra Señora de Popa, after visiting a terrible judgement on the *corsarios luteranos*.

Whether vengeful, providential, or accidental, losing the *Oxford* forced a change of plan. Cartagena was out of the question, and Collier took the *Satisfaction* for an independent cruise to Campeche. Morgan transferred to the *Lilly*, a ship half the strength of the *Oxford*, and waited an extra month to gather more reinforcements. He resolved to sail to Trinidad and from there raid along the Venezuelan coast, as Myngs had done in 1658.

Like others before them, though, this fleet struggled in the tough sailing conditions of the long windward voyage. Three ships and 300 men gave up, leaving Morgan with 8 ships and about 500 buccaneers. Among them was at least one *flibustier* who had sailed with L'Olonnais, and who suggested they set course for Maracaibo. The defences had been weak in 1666, he recalled, and during the intervening years the city had probably restored its wealth.

After stopping briefly at Aruba to resupply, this *flibustier* guided the fleet through the Gulf of Venezuela towards the Barra de Maracaibo, three islands blocking the narrow entrance to the lake. Here they discovered a newly built castle, the Fuerte de la Barra. Well supplied and armed with eleven cannon, its garrison of only nine men bombarded the buccaneers for a day before sneaking away at night. In a dawn assault Morgan found the island deserted, but, according to Exquemelin, stumbled across and extinguished a burning match left behind in the powder store, only a few inches from disaster. The luck that saved him on the *Oxford* seemed to be holding.

The buccaneers threw the guns from the castle walls, rather than garrison it themselves, and pressed on for Maracaibo. They found the town deserted too: its 400 or so families had fled, taking as much as they could carry. The buccaneers spent about a week there, sending out parties by day to round up cattle and prisoners, who they held in the church and subjected to the same brutal treatment as their victims at Portobelo.

Morgan then decided, as he later wrote, 'to sayle farther to discover the Lake for the service of our King and country'. Most of the lakeshore was deserted, so he followed further in L'Olonnais' footsteps towards Gibraltar. Driven back at first by the batteries of this town, the buccaneers landed the following day and found it empty as well.

Out went the raiding parties, gathering in around 250 prisoners, plus five local craft and a Cuban ship. These vessels, so Exquemelin said, hid in a nearby river with the governor of Gibraltar, until betrayed by an enslaved person among Morgan's prisoners, though the governor escaped with much of the merchandise. Exquemelin again filled his pages on this episode with graphic descriptions of torture, though none of the official Spanish accounts mention it.

Morgan and his companions returned to Maracaibo early in April 1669 carrying *pesos*, silks, jewels, and captives. They found that leaving Lake Maracaibo would prove more difficult than getting in. They were trapped.

As Morgan prepared at the Isla de Vaca and then sailed for Venezuela, reports reached Alonso de Campos, commander of the *Armada de Barlovento*, travelling by way of an escaped prisoner from Jamaica, a Spanish herdsman, a Dutch *schipper*, and other wanderers. De Campos set sail with his three ships, which together wielded more firepower than the whole of Morgan's fleet.

Heading for Trinidad, the *Armada* met a Dutch ship from Curaçao with up-to-date information and soon reached the Barra, blocking the channel and repairing the Fuerte's armaments. De Campos sent to Coro for local pilots and to Caracas for reinforcements. Here was an unparalleled opportunity: a large force of buccaneers and one of their most successful leaders, bottled up.

De Campos wrote to Morgan, offering mercy if he surrendered, with all his men, their plunder and their enslaved captives; otherwise he meant to 'put you all to the sword [...] for the injustices you have done to the Spanish nation in America'. Morgan replied that he would free Maracaibo and leave behind the enslaved prisoners, if he and his men could sail off with their plunder. Both commanders refused these offers.

Morgan consulted with his men, who preferred to fight rather than yield their spoils. 'I shall save you the labour with your nimble Frigotts to come here,' he wrote to De Campos with his characteristic brazenness on 7 April 1669, 'being resollved to visite you with all expedition, and there wee will putt to hazard of Battle in whose power it shall be to use Clemency.'

The buccaneers deployed two deceptions, in what strikes me as their most dramatic and desperate escapade. De Campos' spies watched the buccaneers convert their Cuban prize, adding extra guns, and learned also that they were preparing a fireship. The new flagship, bravely decked out with the commander's colours, led Morgan's fleet towards the Barra. To the astonishment of the Spanish sailors, it aimed directly for the *Armada*'s largest and most powerful ship. De Campos must have assumed that Morgan was overconfident and overmatched.

Until, that is, the ships crashed together, smoke billowed from the Cuban vessel and the twelve buccaneers on deck leapt overboard. The flagship *was* the fireship, sporting logs for guns and wooden mannequins in sailors' caps. While De Campos and his men abandoned ship, Morgan's fleet attacked the other two vessels of the *Armada*. Both ran aground, one of them protected by the Fuerte's guns, the other seized by the buccaneers. In a single battle, Morgan had destroyed the *Armada*, as well as recovering around 20,000 *pesos* from the wrecks.

De Campos still held the Fuerte. Morgan offered to free his hostages in return for passage, but De Campos had no sympathy for those who should, he declared, have fought harder in the first place. The buccaneers knew that time was not on their side; Spanish reinforcements might be on their way. They had to move soon. From the walls of the Fuerte, the soldiers watched as boats ferried Morgan's men ashore, to the cover of some mangrove swamps. De Campos accordingly repositioned several cannon to the landward side of the fort.

That night De Campos allowed most of his men to rest, anticipating a dawn attack. Meanwhile, Morgan's fleet sailed past the islands. The buccaneers in the boats had been the second deception, lying down for each return trip, or so Exquemelin's story goes. When Spanish lookouts raised the alarm, many of their cannon were facing the wrong way. The buccaneers passed with little damage, pausing only to unload their hostages and fire a final mocking salute.

De Campos returned to Spain in disgrace. Morgan reached Port Royal on 17 May 1669 to a hero's welcome. The plunder from this voyage has been estimated at 250,000 *pesos*, similar to Portobelo (and not counting the value of merchandise and enslaved prisoners), though both Thomas Modyford and his brother James thought that the takings, for individual sailors and as a whole, were lower than the previous voyage. Morgan had cemented his reputation as the most daring buccaneer commander in the Caribbean.

Port Royal's celebrations after Maracaibo did not last very long. Lord Arlington, a royal minister less militant towards Spain than others, ordered Modyford to cease plundering. About a month after Morgan's return, Modyford duly called in all commissions. He had the same concerns as before regarding Tortuga, but there were no commissions on offer there either, due to peace between France and Spain.

A small number of 'knaves', as Modyford called them, continued roving, landing their plunder clandestinely in Jamaica, but others turned to smuggling or logwood cutting. Robert Searle arrived in Jamaica but kept away from Port Royal for fear of a cool reception, since he had recently sacked St Augustine in Florida, after a Spanish attack on New Providence in the Bahamas. When he did venture into town he was arrested and kept in prison, awaiting judgement from London.

This tremulous peace was, yet again, of short duration. A few months before Modyford's proclamation, stung by news of Portobelo, Mariana and the *Consejo de las Indias* sent an order to the Caribbean to 'cause war to be published against that nation, and to execute all the hostilities which are permitted in war'. Those orders arrived in the autumn and winter of 1669, but suitable vessels were in limited supply following the destruction of the *Armada de Barlovento*. There was no sudden rush of volunteers. Nevertheless, Jamaica was winding down its military resources at the same time that the Spanish Empire prepared to retaliate.

The most active and flamboyant figure to take up the call was Manoel Rivero Pardal, a Portuguese captain in Spanish service, who received a commission in January 1670 and set sail soon after. Rivero cruised first to the Caymans, seizing small vessels that he took to Cuba. There he surprised and captured the *Mary & Jane*, commanded by Bernard Claesen Speirdijk, a well-known *vrijbuiter* often called Captain Barnard or Bart.

Speirdijk had just carried Modyford's letters of peace to the governor of Cuba, as well as some prisoners released from Jamaica, and then engaged in some trading. Rivero approached flying English colours and then attacked, loudly declaring himself 'a punishment for heretics'. After a fierce fight lasting seven hours, in which Speirdijk was slain, Rivero sent nine prisoners to Jamaica with the threat that he sought revenge for Portobelo and was only just getting started. The rest, with the prize, he carried to Cartagena.

This new attack caused consternation in Jamaica, especially as other attacks followed. Some ships, including those manned by former buccaneers, turned the tables and brought their attackers as prizes into Port Royal; others were not so lucky. James Modyford, the governor's brother, wrote to Thomas Lynch that he intended to sell his Jamaican plantation as soon as he could, because 'the Spaniards begin to take the right course to ruin us'.

The old rumours of invasion circulated, but now there seemed to be more solid proof, as Willem Beck, the governor of Curaçao, sent Thomas Modyford a Spanish commission that had come into his hands, together with a copy of the queen's orders. A captured English Catholic convert reported that proclamations of war had been made at Cartagena.

It did not matter that on the very same day Mariana signed these orders in Spain, Morgan had been plotting his breakout from Maracaibo after plundering two Spanish towns. Indeed, buccaneers less patient than Modyford were said to be gathering in the Caymans, contemplating revenge for Speirdijk. Modyford wrote to his superiors in London that he would try to 'divert them or moderate their councils'.

Rivero reappeared on the northern coast of Jamaica late in May 1670, together with a former *flibustier* ship that he had captured, *La Gallardina*. For a couple of months he plundered coastal shipping and burned isolated settlements. After one raid he left a written challenge broadcasting his achievements thus far, and ending, 'I come to seek General Morgan [...] I crave that he would come out upon the coast and seek me, that he might see the valour of the Spaniards.'

It was too much for Modyford and the Council of Jamaica, who met on 29 June 1670 and considered the dire consequences if these provocations went unanswered. Modyford's instructions as governor included the power to take extraordinary action when circumstances demanded, and the councillors felt that this was such a moment. They advised him to commission Morgan once again to seize Spanish vessels, attack any invasion forces mustering, and pursue 'all manner of Exploits which may tend to the preservation and quiet of this Island'.

Modyford agreed, writing to Arlington that the Spanish colonies had 'plunged themselves into this war'. He had no choice, he argued, but was optimistic that 'a little more suffering will inform them of their condition and force them to capitulations more suitable to the sociableness of man's nature'.

Juan Perez de Guzmán returned from Lima to Panamá, cleared of all charges, at the start of 1669, when Morgan was gathering forces for the Maracaibo voyage. Concerned about the attack on Portobelo during his absence, Perez concentrated his efforts, constrained though he was by limited funds, on bolstering his *audiencia*'s defences, especially San Lorenzo Castle at the mouth of the River Chagres.

In June 1670 Perez heard that 1,500 buccaneers were preparing in Jamaica to strike at Panamá. Though this rumour arrived before Modyford and the Council had even met, it was a prescient one. Nor was it the only prescience around. A Franciscan friar preached in Panamá's cathedral of a vision vouchsafed to one of his fellows in which a man from Jamaica destroyed their city. The visionary even commissioned a painting for their convent depicting this terrifying premonition.

Morgan actually received his commission on 1 August, but he did not hang around. Within eight days he issued ten commissions, took the newly returned *Satisfaction* as his flagship, and sailed on 14 August for Isla de Vaca. By November he had some 2,000 men there, Dutch, English, and French: one of the largest buccaneer gatherings ever. In 1671 the *gouverneur* estimated that there were 1,000 *flibustiers* and 100 *boucaniers* in Tortuga, while Jamaican governors consistently numbered the buccaneers of Port Royal at roughly 1,500. If these numbers are accurate, something like four out of every five buccaneers then present in the Caribbean now joined Morgan, who wrote to Jamaica asking for more ships to transport them all.

With him was a roll-call of buccaneering captains: Searle, newly released from prison for the expedition, Richard Norman, Bradley with his comrades Brasiliano and De Lecat, Reyning, and Francis Witherborn. Richard Browne was surgeon general. Lawrence Prince sailed in with two other ships after a cruise that attacked Granada on Lake Nicaragua, just as Morgan had done six years before. On their arrival in Jamaica Modyford reproved them for acting without a commission, then swiftly sent them to join Morgan.

An especially welcome sight was John Morris, because he brought with him Rivero's ship. Morris had met Rivero off Cuba and struck first;

Rivero died in the assault. Aboard, Morris found both Rivero's commission and an epic poem, composed by the *capitán* during his time at sea, celebrating his own career. He sent these to Modyford, renamed the prize the *Lamb* (possibly an ironic comment on its blustering former commander?), and brought it with him to the rendezvous.

With Morris was Juan de Lao, an Indigenous cook, now forcibly employed in the same job among the buccaneers. De Lao later escaped and reported to the Spanish authorities, giving another view on the voyage. One of De Lao's more intriguing, but probably fanciful, assertions was that an old English witch accompanied Morgan, 'brought along to prophesy for them and through her diabolical arts to advise them what they should do'.

Morgan dispatched Collier to capture provisions and prisoners, targeting Riohacha on 6 September 1670. There he seized Rivero's former consort *La Gallardina*, thirty-eight prisoners and foodstuffs, as well as executing two of the garrison after the castle refused to surrender. He apparently missed 200,000 *pesos* hidden in the fort.

Back at Isla de Vaca by late October, Collier and Morgan interrogated the prisoners. Marco de Luba, the Canarian former master of *La Gallardina*, admitted, possibly under torture, that military preparations were under way at Cartagena and a fleet from Spain soon expected in Panamá, to invade Jamaica. He was half right: forces were gathering, but for defensive purposes, in response to Collier's attack and Morgan's growing fleet. Some Spanish officials speculated that Charles II's brother, the duke of York, might himself lead this campaign, though he never visited the Caribbean.

Morgan gave *La Gallardina* to the *flibustiers* with him and, moving the fleet to Cape Tiburon, called a council of war. They considered several options and resolved to attack Panamá, a lynchpin of the silver route from Peru to Spain. Did Morgan also remember his swaggering promise, issued in that letter from Portobelo some years before, to visit this city?

They sailed on 8 December 1670; Morgan notified Modyford, but was carefully vague about their destination, either to preserve Modyford's exculpatory ignorance or to prevent any late countermanding orders. En route the buccaneers retook Providencia, where the commander agreed to surrender after a pretend battle to preserve his honour; at least, that is Exquemelin's tale. De Lao, aboard one of the ships, remembered that he heard much firing, even though there were no casualties recorded on either side.

Here, they recruited some guides from among the 'rascals and evildoers' who, according to Exquemelin, had been banished to the garrison there as punishment. One Indigenous volunteer called Antonillo knew the River Chagres well, which would be crucial, because this was the route they had chosen across the isthmus.

First, though, they had to deal with San Lorenzo Castle, occupying a strong clifftop position, with bastions and gun platforms facing both landward and seaward. Its garrison numbered 400, including many African and Indigenous soldiers, and Perez may have concentrated his best forces here in the hope of halting the invasion before it began.

Morgan sent Joseph Bradley with 470 men to take the castle, following a few days later. Bradley landed 4 miles from the castle and circumvented an ambush, but the buccaneers then had no choice except an all-out charge across a killing ground cleared before the castle. After two assaults, a Spanish witness wrote, 'one could not see the *campana* [the open ground] for the dead bodies'.

The third charge reached the walls, made of timber packed with earth and roofed with palm-thatch, and soon they were on fire; according to one account this happened after an enterprising buccaneer seized an arrow shot by one of the Indigenous defenders, set it alight and fired it back from his musket. A grenade struck the castle's magazine. Half the garrison fled, the other half refused quarter and were cut down as the buccaneers broke through. The buccaneers lost more than a quarter of their men, including Bradley, in probably the bloodiest battle of any of their campaigns. It must have made a grim scene the next morning.

Richard Norman took charge and had almost finished the repairs when, five days later, the rest of the fleet sailed in – the *Satisfaction* and four other ships straight onto a reef, though most of the crews escaped. Morgan did not take very good care of his ships, perhaps because he was confident of always seizing another one. Ten men drowned and so too, De Lao later claimed, did the old witch.

Morgan spent a week at San Lorenzo and left Norman with 400 men there, plus some on the ships who went marauding along the coast. The remaining force, of over 1,400, set off up the Chagres in seven of the smallest ships and thirty-six boats and canoes.

It was a gruelling march. Navigating the Chagres' twists and tributaries took three times longer than the direct distance. When they left the ships behind they took only ammunition, struggling for three days without food, plagued by insects and obstructed by the jungle. According to Exquemelin, the desperate buccaneers ate grass, raw maize, and empty leather bags.

They met no resistance, apart from one small ambush. There were four stockades along the Chagres, but the buccaneers found each one abandoned, as the 400 men assigned to them had already retreated. Some 300 others, together with one Black and two '*mestizo*' volunteers from Panamá gaol who knew the terrain, set off to recapture San Lorenzo but also, seeing the number of the buccaneers, fled into the mountains.

It might have been a shrewd tactic. Each empty stockade dashed the buccaneers' hopes of fresh food. At Venta de Cruces, where the Chagres met the mule trail across the isthmus, the ravenous buccaneers found sixteen jars of Peruvian wine, predictably resulting in drunkenness followed by sickness. Morgan astutely declared the wine to be poisoned and disposed of it.

Hungover and demoralised though they were, the buccaneers could only push on through high woodlands and deep ravines. Now they were harried by 400 Indigenous archers and 300 musketeers under Joseph de Prado, a Black *capitán* who had led the evaded ambush at San Lorenzo. They held out until their *capitán* was slain, but could not stop the buccaneers from pushing through to the savanna between the mountains and the city, where they met herds of cattle and horses, on which they fell with savage delight.

Perez, sick and bed-bound when the news of San Lorenzo arrived, had mustered most of his men at Guyabal, a plateau from which he could watch all routes over the isthmus. A *junta* there proved indecisive, but then the Spanish commanders found the decision made for them, when they awoke to find two thirds of the army had already retreated during the night. Perez could only return to Panamá where, on Sunday, 15 January 1671, he heard Mass in the cathedral and then exhorted all citizens to fight, swearing a vow to the statue of the Virgin Mary that he would protect her with his life.

He positioned his army, 1,200 infantry and 400 cavalry, across the road to the city, beside a hill that he thought would protect his right flank, and with two herds of oxen and bulls ready to stampede in the wake of a cavalry charge. Two days later, the buccaneers made camp within sight of Perez's army.

The next day, 18 January 1671, was hot and clear. Morgan's army began their advance at seven in the morning. Perez's decision not to occupy the hill proved flawed. Buccaneers and *flibustiers* in the vanguard drove off a cavalry charge by fierce fire and then secured the high ground; as those horsemen fled to Panamá, Spanish soldiers began charging without orders, so Perez led a general attack that ended in disaster. Even the oxen and bulls, when released, were turned back into the Spanish ranks, which by then were in full retreat. Perez intended to honour his vow to die in battle, but his priest persuaded him otherwise. By late morning the buccaneers had broken through.

Perez's captain of artillery had orders to destroy the city armoury if necessary. He did so as fleeing soldiers streamed through the city; the explosion could be heard 6 miles away. Somehow word got around the defenders to burn everything, even as buccaneers broke into anything still standing. Apart from a few stone buildings, everything was flammable: fine houses of mahogany and cedar, poorer districts of cane and straw. By midnight, Morgan wrote, 'Thus was consumed that famous and ancient City of Panama, which is the greatest mart for silver and gold in the whole world.'

Among the ashes, the buccaneers went through their usual business after victory. Whatever treasures had not been carried away were ferreted out of the ruins. Churches and religious houses were looted, Perez's library torn up. Morgan claimed that he rounded up 3,000 prisoners, sending hunting parties out as far as 20 miles.

Perez reported shocking tortures practised on these unfortunates, while Browne wrote 'what was [done] in fight and heat of blood in pursuit of a flying enemy, I presume is pardonable', describing Morgan – for whom he had no particular affection – as 'noble enough to the vanquished enemy'. He added, 'As to their women, I know nor ever heard of anything offered beyond their wills,' though this may be special pleading, and implies a rather dismissive and misogynistic judgement.

Most of the clerics and wealthier citizens had escaped by sea, with much local shipping either burnt or fled, but Searle seized a barque and raided the islands in the Bay of Panamá. He captured one ship, sailing in unawares, with 20,000 *pesos* aboard, though apparently missed an even wealthier prize when the seamen got drunk on one island.

Perez, meanwhile, retreated 70 miles south-west and spent weeks unsuccessfully trying to gather up his scattered army. He wrote to Cartagena and Lima for help, though taking a little longer to report to Madrid; Juan de Lao, who had escaped, also reported his experiences in Cartagena. The governor there concentrated on his own defences, but De Lemos sent a substantial force north from Peru.

As at Portobelo, they arrived far too late. Morgan left Panamá at the end of February, burning the ships to prevent 100 or so men who wished to continue raiding the Pacific coast. They crossed the isthmus with about 170 mules carrying plate and coin, and 600 prisoners whom Morgan intended to ransom. He also tried to ransom San Lorenzo, but the denizens of Portobelo, bitterly remembering their own payments three years earlier, refused.

Before they went their separate ways, the buccaneers shared out all the plunder, according to Exquemelin first searching everyone, Morgan included. Morgan later wrote that the total plunder amounted to £30,000, half of what had been taken at Portobelo, though he was probably undervaluing it and other estimates ran as high as 400,000 *pesos*.

That sum was split among a much larger number of men, and some contemporaries reckoned the figure per head at £10 or £16, while Exquemelin suggested 200 *pesos* (about £40) – much less than the buccaneers had expected. Inevitably there were suspicions that Morgan had snuck away with a much larger share, exacerbated when he unexpectedly sailed off – possibly he feared unrest, or simply wanted to get to Jamaica first with his version of the story, which he did, in April 1671.

Between 1655 and 1671, buccaneers and *flibustiers* attacked eighteen Spanish cities, four towns, and thirty-five villages around the Caribbean, including Maracaibo and Gibraltar twice, Santa Marta and Campeche three times, Riohacha five times, and Tolu, near Cartagena, an astonishing eight times. Panamá was the most devastating campaign: almost a quarter of the population of the *audiencia* perished, in battle or in the epidemic that ravaged the region afterwards.

Yet recovery was remarkably swift. A new Panamá City, on a site both more defensible and more accessible for ships, quickly flourished. In August 1672 a treasure fleet from Peru brought 20 million *pesos* through the city – far more than the buccaneers had plundered. Within a few years there were 100 houses and a new cathedral.

While Modyford had probably not anticipated the extent of Morgan's expedition, it achieved its publicly stated aim. The Council of Jamaica concurred, thanking Morgan for his actions. James Modyford wrote that the colonists could feel 'prettie well revenged' for Rivero's previous attacks.

However, the campaign left Modyford and Morgan in a predicament. Even before Morgan sailed, they knew that a treaty between England and Spain was in the offing, and word of its official signing now started to arrive. The governor of Cartagena, when he first heard of Panamá, wrote to Morgan accusing him of already knowing about the treaty. Modyford sent word to Spanish governors offering 'civility and friendship' (and perhaps hoping that the 'little more suffering', as he put it, would make them amenable).

His governorship was already on borrowed time. In January 1671, as Morgan sailed towards San Lorenzo, Thomas Lynch received a royal commission to replace Modyford, with secret orders to arrest him, due to the ever more clamorous protests of the Spanish ambassador. Lynch arrived in Jamaica in July and, though Modyford greeted him warmly and offered assistance, on 15 August Lynch carried out those orders. Shortly afterwards, Modyford sailed for England.

At the end of the year, Lynch received further instructions: arrest Morgan. Modyford's arrival in London under guard had not satisfied the Spanish ambassador – though the Council of Jamaica, even after Modyford's arrest, passed a resolution confirming the validity of Morgan's commission.

Lynch delayed, partly because Morgan was ill and partly for fear it would spook the buccaneers, to whom he offered pardons. Eventually, in April 1672, Lynch carried out the order. Morgan arrived in London three months later, still very sickly, to await the pleasure of the king.

5

JAMAICA DISCIPLINE

In 1669, a dispatch from New Spain to Madrid included a report from a man who spent five years imprisoned in Jamaica. He described the buccaneers as 'men of the sea, commoners of little social pretension'. In many ways, the life of buccaneers resembled that of other 'men of the sea'. Many buccaneers had been merchant or naval sailors first, and returned sometimes to other maritime trades.

Yet they may have been unlike other mariners in certain ways. One aspect that particularly intrigues historians is the suggestion that, as an account from Jamaica early in Charles II's reign put it, these 'rovers' followed 'no rules but some of their owne by tradition'. The idea of 'brethren of the coast', of a communal, egalitarian, and even democratic culture, has become firmly attached to the popular image of buccaneers and pirates more generally.

This culture is often described as the 'Jamaica discipline', a term that first appeared in 1726 in George Shelvocke's *Voyage round the World*, narrating his own Pacific voyage in 1719–20. When some of his shipwrecked crew mutinied and deposed him, he wrote, they 'form'd a new regulation, and new Articles ... [and] regulated themselves according to the *Jamaica* discipline'.

Shelvocke here sought to discredit his mutinous men by association with the disreputable world of Jamaican rovers, and I read the phrase in a scathing or sarcastic tone. Like 'brethren of the coast', this popular image is misleading, and probably a later pejorative invention. There is no evidence that the concept (or the phrase) of a coherent 'discipline' existed during the later seventeenth century among the buccaneers. It is another story we tell about pirates.

Nevertheless, there may well have been elements of distinctive social practice and communal identity among the buccaneers. Whereas the precursor 'private man of war' always referred to a ship, during the 1650s and 1660s a 'privateer' could be a ship (especially in legislation) but was also used, by Modyford, Lynch, and others, to mean the men themselves. This seems to me an intriguing and significant linguistic development, which does indeed suggest that here was a recognised social grouping. A sailor might become a 'privateer' by stepping aboard a 'privateer' ship, alternating with other employments; but some, at least, remained identifiably 'privateers' betweentimes.

They may have recognised one another as fellow buccaneers, too. The correspondent from New Spain described them as 'very happy, well paid, and they live in amity with one another', their plunder and prizes 'shared with much brotherhood and friendship'. Alexandre Exquemelin similarly wrote that 'they are faithful and helpful to each other' and 'do justice among one another', adding that if anyone had nothing, others would support him until he was back on his feet.

Exquemelin explained that at the start of any voyage the participants 'with a common voice' made an 'accord' concerning objectives and conditions, set down in 'articles'. Morgan certainly called councils, though it seems likely that only captains and officers participated. Such articles, agreed separately for each voyage, followed a similar pattern, setting out the shares due to each rank; punishments for negligence or drunkenness; and rewards for those who tore down the Spanish flag or ran up the English or French one, who brought in a prisoner with valuable intelligence, or who threw grenades into a Spanish fort.

They also mandated compensation for injuries, although this custom was found on medieval voyages too. On the Panamá expedition, the sums were 600 *pesos* for a right arm lost, 500 for a left, and 100 for a finger or an eye – much more generous payments than those offered to wounded merchant or naval sailors. Exquemelin wrote that they swore an oath on the Bible not to cheat one another, and anyone swearing this oath falsely was 'banished and may never again come into their company'.

Of course, Exquemelin probably exaggerated this solidarity. The Panamá raid provoked sour recriminations over the division of spoils, and Richard Browne wrote that on returning to Port Royal the voyage's commanders dared not face the 'widows, orphans, and injured inhabitants' who had loaned them money.

Nor were voyages devoid of other tensions. Early in Morgan's Portobelo voyage, Exquemelin wrote, a buccaneer and *flibustier* fell out over the prized bone marrow of one of the butchered oxen, and in the ensuing duel the Englishman shot the Frenchman in the back. Morgan, to prevent further fighting, arrested the assailant and took him back to Jamaica in chains for trial. If the buccaneers did possess a shared set of rules and a sense of brotherhood, it did not make them impervious to internal conflict.

Indeed, like the *boucaniers* who came before them, these marauders were a motley crowd. The men with Morgan at Portobelo were mostly English, but there were also forty Dutchmen, some *flibustiers*, and Italian, Portuguese, '*mulato*', and African buccaneers aboard, plus at least one Spanish sailor. Two intriguing names among those recorded on the voyage are Ipseiodawas and John Mapoo, names that suggest an Indigenous or, in Mapoo's case, perhaps African heritage. If Morgan's voyages gathered an unusually wide range of participants, any buccaneering ship might combine men from different backgrounds. The same was true of most seventeenth-century ships, but it was especially common in the international melting pot of the Caribbean.

Buccaneer ships were, for the most part, small and fast. The largest frigates, such as the *Satisfaction* and *Oxford*, or the ships of the *Armada de Barlovento*, had only one gundeck and carried twenty or thirty cannon. Few were more than 100 feet long or 30 feet wide. These vessels were small fry compared to the massive battleships that fought major sea battles in the Anglo-Dutch wars during these decades.

Frigates first developed during the late sixteenth and early seventeenth centuries in the Spanish Netherlands, especially Dunkirk, from where plunderers in their swift new vessels sailed out against Dutch and English commerce. 'Dunkirkers' captured hundreds of Dutch and English ships in the 1620s, and 'Ostenders' and 'Flushingers' were two other toponymic synonyms for these sea raiders, especially after a combined Anglo-French force (including George Monck and Thomas Morgan) captured Dunkirk in 1658.

Even frigates were relatively rare in the Caribbean, and most buccaneers sailed in some variation of the Bermuda or Jamaica sloop, another new type of vessel, developed specifically for these waters. They may have come to Bermuda by way of Jacob Jacobsen, 'an excellent Dutch Carpinter' shipwrecked on the island, who, according to John Smith, was soon employed to make boats. These boats grew in size to become ocean-going ships of up to 70 feet long, though Jamaican sloops were usually smaller than their Bermudan counterparts.

Even if he did not introduce them, these ships took their shape and rig from the *jachts* of Jacobsen's homeland. Most European ships of the seventeenth century used square sails except on their rearmost mizzen

A Dutch frigate, drawn by Wenceslaus Hollar in 1647; larger buccaneer vessels would have been of a similar size. Note the lateen rig on the mizzen mast; the other masts are square-rigged. (Rijksmuseum, Amsterdam)

mast, which often had a lateen sail, triangular and rigged fore-and-aft, to help steer and steady the ship. *Jachts* and sloops adapted the lateen for their mainsail, helping them to travel upwind, and the design morphed into what would now be called gaff-rigged: a four-cornered, sometimes trapezoidal shape. The style was so well established by 1680 that one Samuel Fortrey wrote to Samuel Pepys about it, suggesting improvements. Its evolution reflects the international interactions in shipbuilding and maritime technology of this time, and the 'Bermuda rig', now usually with a triangular rather than a gaff mainsail, is standard today for dinghies and yachts across the world.

Buccaneers also used canoes regularly; the word comes from *canoa*, a Caribbean term. These were quite different to modern canoes. Made from hollowed-out tree trunks – a technique employed all along the American seaboard – the largest carried 150 people, using sails as well as oars. Smaller dugout vessels, commonly used for fishing, were known as 'pirogues', from the Kalinago *piraua*; like 'canoe' a word that was later exported to other contexts.

Large crews of 100 or more crammed into these vessels: even frigates were less than half the length of a football pitch. The crew were most likely divided into two watches; John Smith, earlier in the century, wrote of a 'larboard' and a 'starboard' watch ('larboard' was not officially replaced by 'port' in the British and US navies until the 1840s). These watches alternated on duty, except when emergencies or combat demanded all hands on deck.

Buccaneers at sea could therefore expect little privacy, but would experience a repetitive routine leavened by extreme danger, challenging physical conditions, and rudimentary material comforts, especially on the smallest vessels, with only one deck open to the sea and sky. Meals would have involved tough preserved food, salted beef, and hard-baked biscuit, as well as stagnant water or beer, though sailors had begun to eat rice and indulged in spirits like brandy or rum as well. Buccaneers also fished when they could (turtle was a favourite), or raided ashore to secure an occasional supply of fresh victuals, including fresh meat for their *boucans*.

For men of their social status, the hardship of life at sea was probably not much worse than circumstances ashore, and we can focus too easily on the grim conditions at the expense of other dimensions, such as the importance of community and camaraderie. Buccaneers may have grouped into messes for meals, as was common in other ships, forming a familiar and supportive small group within the larger crew. Smith described 'consorts', a partnership in which two sailors on different watches shared a bed or hammock, though not at the same time, perhaps the origin of *matelotage* among the *boucaniers*.

There was also plenty of idle time, though a lot of energy and skill went into repairing and maintaining the fragile fabric of a ship. Some seventeenth-century sailors taught themselves reading, mathematics, and navigation at sea, while several buccaneers kept journals. Literate men may have read aloud to their illiterate shipmates, a common practice in this era. Craft practices like drawing, carving scrimshaw, and needlework may have occupied buccaneers just as they did sailors on later voyages. All were well within the skillset of experienced 'men of the sea'. Gambling was a common pastime too.

Religion may have provided another element of daily routine. Larger naval ships employed chaplains, and on merchant vessels the master might read a lesson on Sundays, or the crew gather to sing a psalm at the changing of the watch. Perhaps not all buccaneers were devout, but Morgan was certainly involved in the local church in Port Royal, and some were motivated by their faith. Protestant buccaneers targeted Spanish clerics and churches, while Catholic *flibustiers* showed them respect. Jean-Baptiste Labat recorded an incident where he was invited to say Mass for *flibustiers* and, when one of the crew misbehaved, the *capitaine* abruptly shot the miscreant.

Nor were psalms the only music aboard. One sailor of the 1650s and 1660s, who spent his time in merchant ships and naval frigates in the Mediterranean and eastern Atlantic, recalled men singing both psalms and obscene songs during the voyage, though he is coyly reticent about the latter.

Buccaneers and other plunderers are often associated with sea shanties – in the online game *Sea of Thieves*, players can gather for a nautical jam session. The shanties we know today were mostly collected in the nineteenth century, but some may have older origins. I think it likely that rhythmic work songs of some kind featured in seventeenth-century sailing. There were plenty of printed ballads about sailors, sea life, and plundering circulating at this time, which could be pasted up on tavern walls and perhaps carried to sea.

Ships used drums and trumpets for signalling, which may have provided entertainment too, besides other musical instruments; Francis Drake took several musicians along on his circumnavigation. Modern representations often depict pirates playing the accordion or some variant of it (also featured in *Sea of Thieves*), but those instruments did not exist until the 1820s. Much more likely, if they played anything at all, would be contemporary European instruments such as lutes or early guitars, viols, recorders, flutes, hurdy-gurdies, and bagpipes, among many others.

Another intriguing possibility is some form of banjo, a peculiarly Atlantic instrument, played among enslaved people in the Caribbean, later migrating with them to North America. Similar instruments, descended from a common musical tradition, are played in West Africa today, sometimes with techniques that resemble those found in America.

Travellers commented on these instruments, including Labat and Hans Sloane, a doctor who visited Jamaica in the 1680s and whose collection of flora, fauna, and other objects formed the beginnings of the British Museum. Sadly, the 'Jamaican strum strums' he acquired have not survived, but his *Voyage to the Islands* printed the first ever musical notation of Caribbean enslaved peoples' songs, written down for him by one Mr Baptiste, possibly a free person of colour from the French colonies.

I have no proof of this putative connection, beyond the fact that buccaneers and banjos existed in the Caribbean at the same time, but it is possible that the *cimarrónes* among their number brought musical traditions with them, or that buccaneers encountered this music ashore. Those traditions developed into jazz, blues, rock, calypso, reggae, gospel, and a host of other styles that profoundly shaped modern popular culture.

The fact that this particular idea occurred to me shortly after acquiring an antique banjo of my own is, of course, pure coincidence.

If buccaneers developed their own culture and community – through friendships and shared pastimes as well as articles and oaths – they also shaped the social life of Port Royal and Tortuga. The latter expanded from some 900 people in 1661 to about 6,500 by 1681, of whom around a third were people of colour, making the two settlements similar in size. For both towns this growth was driven by contraband trade and plunder from the Spanish colonies, and by the presence of the smugglers and plunderers.

Town leaders understood this fact. When in March 1666 Thomas Modyford and the Council of Jamaica justified commissions against Spanish shipping, their reasons were principally economic: cheap prize goods would attract merchants; small planters could sell provisions; new settlers from the Lesser Antilles might be tempted across. Only belatedly did the councillors remember the defensive advantages and, as a final point, that they might force a 'free trade' with Spanish colonies.

Modyford wrote after this decision 'what an universal change there was on the faces of men and things'. Debts were paid, ships prepared. When Morgan returned from Portobelo, James Modyford, then chief judge of the admiralty court, noted the 'plunder and jewells, gold and silver' available in the town, and John Styles, another planter, commented that 'trade now consists principally in plate money, jewels, and other things brought in by the privateers'. Without buccaneering, these towns stagnated. On one occasion when commissions were cancelled, a Jamaican settler wrote to a friend in London asking for cash, since 'ready money will be hard to come by'.

Merchants flocked to Port Royal and Tortuga for cheap bargains. James Modyford thought that he could have doubled or trebled his investment if he had had any spare cash when 'our Porto Bello men' came home. Several merchants came from North America; in 1675 a Rhode Islander recorded that New England's coinage was made of silver from Jamaica. The island traded sugar to Virginia and the Carolinas, tobacco to Campeche and Curaçao, and cotton and fustic to New England and New York. Apart from the sugar, most of these commodities must have come from plunder or smuggling – what one resident in the early 1680s called 'many other accidental Commodities brought in from the *Spaniards*'.

Port Royal likewise depended on imports for its existence. Many kinds of foodstuffs, drink, manufactured goods like clothes, tools, or furniture, and other necessaries were brought from outside the island, from Britain and Ireland, or from the farms and fisheries on the North American coast. Residents complained about the high prices. Fresh water had to be ferried across the bay, though other available drinks included Madeira wine, lemonade, punch, and brandy. As well as the fish market by the wharfs, there was another for herbs, fruits, and fowls, and one for meat, including turtle. Even after the town boasted its own craftsmen and began to consume local produce, some raw materials, rare delicacies, and high fashions could only be obtained by trade.

This bustling entrepôt crowded into less than a square mile, within fortifications usually funded by the Crown's cut from buccaneering, while some of the cannon had once graced Spanish battlements. Visitors came ashore at the wharfs and jetties along the north side, plunging along narrow passageways into a jumble of warehouses, homes, and shops of timber and brick. The main streets were unpaved, sandy, and surprisingly broad, 20 feet across or more. Between them lay a labyrinth of buildings, lanes, alleys, and yards. There may have been as many as 2,000 houses by 1691, a tenfold increase in just thirty years.

This teeming throng encompassed wide variations in social status. The fortunate owned their own houses, lavishly furnished for the very wealthy, and dressed in silk or coloured serge with silver and gold thread and buttons. One visitor wrote that 'the merchants and gentrey live here to the hights of splendor, in full ease and plenty, being sumptuously arrayed'. The poorer residents, meanwhile, resided above their shop or lodged with others, sometimes a whole family sharing a room, with a communal brick 'cook-room' in the yard. Indentured servants and other labourers wore drawers and jackets of canvas or coarse linen.

Unsurprisingly, many of the town's professions were linked to the sea. One resident recorded that 'by reson of privateres and debauched wild blades which come hither ... 'tis now more rude and anticque than 'ere was Sodom'. In fact, if the governors' various estimates are correct, buccaneers made up about a quarter of the population. Alongside them could be found shipwrights and chandlers, carpenters and coopers, fishermen and mariners, sailmakers, and watermen. The town also had a number of surgeons, silversmiths, and gunsmiths, all of them connected, in their own way, to the buccaneers' business.

Yet there were other artisans, including butchers, bakers, barber-surgeons, glaziers, gunsmiths, goldsmiths, blacksmiths, pewterers, tailors, hat-, shoe-, and cabinet-makers, ivory-turners whose materials came from West Africa, comb-makers, who worked in tortoiseshell and pipe-makers who used the red clay of the Liguanea Plain across the bay.

Most of the inhabitants, and the buccaneers amusing themselves between voyages, frequented the many taverns, where, D'Oyley wrote, their plunder 'is immediately spent'. At least nineteen received licences in the twenty years after 1665, several with nautical names like the Shipp, the Three Mariners, the Blue Anchor, and the Mermaid. Some were ordinary houses where alcohol could be purchased, but others were bigger establishments. The Feathers, newly built of brick in 1681, boasted a large balcony and a billiard room; another unnamed tavern had a different title for each room, including the 'Vinroome', the Queen's Head, the King's Head, the Nag's Head, and the Rose. One planter grumbled in 1670 about the multiplication of 'tippling houses' in Jamaica – yet when buccaneering was prohibited, it reduced the governments' revenues in liquor taxes, because 'the Privateers made great consumption'.

Nor was alcohol the only entertainment, and richer inhabitants found that the town did not lack 'anything requisit to satisfie, delight, and please their curious appetites'. For the poorer residents, too, Port Royal boasted the varied and often cruel entertainments enjoyed in other seventeenth-century settlements, such as cockfighting and a bear-baiting garden. Exquemelin told fanciful stories of the buccaneers' raucous doings, 'whoring and drinking so long as they have money', spending up to 3,000 *pesos* in one night, even offering one prostitute 500 *pesos* just to see her naked. While only one tavern, operated by John Starr, has been authoritatively identified as a brothel, the existence of what one resident called 'a house of correction for lazie strumpets' and a 'cage for common strumpets' by the turtle market certainly suggests that prostitution was a well-known feature of the town.

Other punitive sites, such as a stocks, a ducking stool, a pillory, and a gallows, show that, despite its reputation, the place was not entirely lawless. A large house between Thames Street and High Street served as a prison until a new one was built by the eastward gate in 1685, beyond which lay the graveyard and the common where townsfolk pastured their livestock. The King's House on Thames Street was nominally the governor's seat, but it fell into a poor condition (one inventory mentioned old yellow curtains) and was rented out by the more fastidious officials. There was a courthouse and a schoolmaster, while in 1670 one John Belfield sold educational books from his shop on High Street.

The town had two Anglican churches and a synagogue; Jewish merchants could be found in most Caribbean colonies, often with connections to other Jewish communities around the Atlantic, although they were also subject to political and legal restrictions, including extra taxes and a bar on public office. Presbyterians and Quakers in Port Royal met in private homes, while Catholics gathered at the house of James Castillo, who arrived in 1684 as the resident agent of the *asiento*, and whose chapel could accommodate 300 people. He was forced out of town in 1687 following a quarrel with the Catholic chaplain of a newly arrived governor. Port Royal seems to have been more tolerant of different faiths than many other places in the British Empire.

Diseases struck Port Royal as they did elsewhere, exacerbated by the crowded and unsanitary conditions, and the distillation of rum in lead pipes may have had a particularly detrimental effect on townspeople's health. However, unlike other colonies, and even other parts of Jamaica, there was an almost equal number of men and women, and a large number of children. Many were indentured servants (the council complained in 1672 that most white labourers were 'malefactors, offenders, and other convict persons'), while about a third of the town's population were enslaved African people.

Port Royal's economy was based on plundering during its early decades, and no doubt there is some basis for Exquemelin's stories and the town's ill fame as 'a very Sodom for wickedness' even if they are exaggerations. During the later seventeenth century, however, the economic focus in Jamaica, and consequently islanders' attitudes towards buccaneers, began to change. The island shifted towards sugar and slavery.

Sugarcane can grow to twice human height, and before mechanisation it had to be harvested by hand, then the juice – as quickly as possible – crushed out, boiled up to six times in six different kettles, crystallised, and washed. Sugar mills have been described as 'agro-industrial' complexes, and the process was enormously labour-intensive and dangerous, which is why its cultivation often involved enslaved labour.

This link between slavery and sugar originated in the medieval Mediterranean on islands like Sardinia, Sicily, and Cyprus. It spread during the fifteenth and sixteenth centuries with Portuguese settlers to Madeira, the Azores and Cape Verde Islands, and São Tomé and Príncipe in the Gulf of Guinea, and with Spanish ones to the Canaries. Spanish landowners initially enslaved the Guanche population but, much like in the Americas later, violence and epidemics scythed through them. Both the Canaries and the Portuguese islands soon turned to the slave trade that already existed within Africa, extending across the Sahara and into the Indian Ocean. In fact, Portuguese involvement in African slavery started during the 1400s as trans-shippers from one part of the continent to another.

Scholars disagree over whether 'slavery' accurately describes these social systems. While conditions varied in different parts of Africa, generally speaking slavery was not inherited, but occurred through capture in war, through legal punishment, or for a debt. Enslaved people could be treated harshly, especially agricultural labourers, but some captives integrated into communities and families and even, in some places, rose to high social rank.

Forms of servitude and unfreedom existed in Indigenous American societies too, but again there is debate over whether this should be called 'slavery'. In Spain and Portugal, meanwhile, captives from the *reconquista* or other Mediterranean conflicts were often enslaved, many of them serving on the royal galleys. One, Estebánico de Dorrantes, came from Azzemour in Morocco and travelled to the Americas, joining an expedition to Florida in 1527 and later reaching what is now New Mexico; he died in 1539 and is remembered in Pueblo folktales.

Slavery quickly characterised European empires in the Americas, too. Columbus sent enslaved Taíno people to Spain, several thousand subsequently travelling east across the Atlantic. Slaving expeditions from the Greater Antilles decimated the populations of the Bahamas, Curaçao, Aruba, and some of the Lesser Antilles. Portuguese settlers in Brazil enslaved Tupi captives, with 40,000 in Pernambuco by 1560.

The transfer of sugar cultivation to the Americas drove the expansion of slavery there, as it had in the Atlantic islands. The first sugar mill reached Brazil in the 1530s, and a century later there were 350 in Bahia alone, with sugar comprising 90 per cent of Brazil's exports. Over the same timeframe, Indigenous populations declined through disease and violence, and imperial governments officially outlawed Indigenous slavery – though continuing forced labour through the *mita* and *ripartimiento* levies, or allowing loopholes for enslavement by a 'just war', on which pretext *bandeirantes* raided into the Brazilian interior.

Indigenous slavery did not disappear, but the slave trade with Africa expanded west. Brazil had a population of 20,000 Europeans and 30,000 Africans or mixed-parentage people in 1570; by 1650 it was 70,000 and 180,000, respectively. African populations in Spanish colonies were smaller, but still in the thousands or tens of thousands, far outnumbering European colonists.

Northern European empires quickly became involved in this trade. Drake and Hawkins started out as slave traders, and the earl of Warwick invested in such voyages, while his raiders often seized Portuguese slave ships, whose captive cargoes they delivered to English colonies. A Dutch ship likewise brought the '20 and odd Negroes' who represent the start of slavery in Virginia in 1619. Enslaved people arrived in Nieuw Amsterdam in 1626 and New England during the 1630s.

These colonists enslaved Indigenous people as well, with perhaps 50,000 Indigenous people captured and sold into slavery in North America between 1670 and 1715. Their status was a subject of some debate; Bermudans disagreed during the 1640s and 1650s over whether some enslaved Indigenous people should in fact be considered 'freeborn'. The island did not, however, reject the 'many Negroes and Indians captured from the Spaniards' brought by William Jackson from his raids on Jamaica and elsewhere.

The middle decades of the century brought a major acceleration as Caribbean islands pivoted to sugar production. There were only a few hundred enslaved people in Barbados in 1640, but by 1705 there were 46,000, while over the same decades the number of European settlers declined from 37,000 to about 12,000. Jamaica experienced a very similar trajectory, as did the French islands: enslaved people made up over half of Guadeloupe's population in 1671, and 81 per cent of Saint-Domingue's by 1713.

The *West Indische Compagnie* shipped about 90,000 captives between 1630 and 1674. Its directors called the slave trade the 'soul' of the *Compagnie*. The Royal African Company, founded in 1672 to replace a previous slave-trading monopoly, transported 100,000 people over its first four decades, with the enthusiastic support of its Stuart patrons, who granted the Company a millennium-long monopoly over African trade, suggesting they were in it for the long haul. James, duke of York, personally invested some £2,000 in slaving voyages.

Dutch and English shippers supplied their own colonies and smuggled enslaved people to Spanish and French colonies, though French companies also participated in this trade. The Royal African Company sold about a quarter of its captives to Spanish colonies in the 1680s, and between a third and a half by 1700. It is telling that, even though the Spanish Empire still did not officially permit trade by foreign ships, an agent for the *asiento* operated in Jamaica from the 1680s onwards.

The total numbers of captives arriving in the Americas rose from 275,000 in the sixteenth century to 1.3 million in the seventeenth (and 5.7 million in the eighteenth). It has been estimated that as many as half of all captives died during capture and imprisonment in Africa or during the horrific conditions of the middle passage. Before the nineteenth century, four out of every five immigrants across the Atlantic was an African captive, and over two thirds were transported to sugar-producing regions.

This enormous economic and demographic shift created a new kind of slavery, and new societies depending on it, though initially the legal status of slavery varied. In some colonies, to begin with, enslaved people were treated much like indentured servants. The Spanish, Portuguese, and French empires, influenced by the Catholic Church and traditions of Roman law, provided some legal protections and forms of manumission, confirmed in judicial codes like the *Ordenações Filipinas*, introduced by Felipe I and Felipe II for Portuguese territories in 1595–1603 and then confirmed by João IV in 1643.

Though enslaved people were not supposed to own property, Spanish laws allowed *coartación*, where enslaved people could buy their freedom. People of mixed parentage might also derive freedom from their European parent: in Guadeloupe before the 1670s, for example, '*mulâtres*' were often freed at the age of 24. In Dutch Suriname, too, military service, usually against escaped *marrons*, could lead to manumission. Free people of colour were most numerous in these empires, though still a minority.

European colonists often ignored these rules in practice, and over time their attitudes hardened through a mixture of prejudice and fear, especially in English and French colonies. Barbados introduced legislation in 1661 that borrowed from martial law, authorising slaveholders to discipline and punish enslaved people. Virginia passed a very similar law the next year, ruling that slavery was inheritable from 'the condition of the mother', while another law of 1669 stated that baptism did not confer freedom. Jamaica enacted similar rules in 1664, 1681, and 1696, South Carolina in 1691, and Antigua in 1697.

The French government introduced the *Code Noir* in 1685, governing all French colonies. While it respected marriage, baptism, and manumission, and included some options of judicial appeal by enslaved people, this code too prohibited legal rights and authorised harsh punishments, as well as banishing Jews from French colonies. Colonial judges, often slaveholders themselves, frequently ignored even these limited protections.

Besides concerns for order and control, these severe and violent laws possessed a cold economic logic. Planters found it most cost-effective to drive their workers to death, and the majority of enslaved people died within a decade of reaching the Americas. This high mortality rate stimulated constant demand for more captives from across the ocean.

Enslaved people resisted their oppression in various ways, sometimes within slavery, through slow working, damaging tools or animals, or taking time where they could for their own socialising. They created their own languages and cultures, mixing diverse African origins – most enslaved people traded to Europeans had already been captured by strangers, travelling far from their homes before they reached the African coast – and fusing these with new influences in the Caribbean. Many died by suicide or ran away, sometimes for a short spell (known as *petit marronage*) and sometimes permanently. Crossing imperial boundaries was one option: Spanish authorities in Santo Domingo and Florida offered freedom to escapees from neighbouring rivals.

Maroon settlements appeared almost everywhere, with substantial communities in Brazil, Jamaica, Martinique, Suriname, and elsewhere. Armed resistance began even on the slave ships, uprisings occurring on one in ten or perhaps even one in five voyages. There were major rebellions in many colonies throughout the sixteenth and seventeenth centuries; in Port Royal, at the time of the earthquake, Thomas Hardwicke recalled that he feared a rebellion by 'those irreconcilable enemies of ours'. Most uprisings ended in the deaths of all the participants.

This resistance had a profound overall effect, challenging slavery as an economic and social system, but in the shorter term slavery in the Americas expanded and, over this period, became increasingly associated with skin colour. The title of the *Code Noir* is no accident. The rules concerning slavery became harsher and the position of free people of colour, or people of mixed parentage, ever more precarious. Both Virginia in the 1690s and French laws of the early 1700s forbade marriages or sexual relations between Europeans and Africans, and the *Code Noir* stipulated that children of enslaved women should remain enslaved regardless of their father's status. People of colour who were born free, or who achieved manumission, often found their freedom in doubt, especially if they had valuable skills or came to the judicial attention of colonial authorities – or were captured by buccaneers.

If anything deserves the title 'Jamaica discipline', it is this new kind of slavery. However vicious the buccaneers were, socially respectable planters inflicted equally vicious, and at the time entirely legal, cruelties on enslaved people.

In fact, buccaneering and slavery were closely intertwined. Some enslaved people escaped to join the buccaneers, but many more were their prisoners and victims. Buccaneering funded the sugar boom. One economic historian has estimated that starting a sugar plantation cost £4,000, sunk for three years with no returns. With little direct investment from England during these decades, much of this capital was provided by smuggling and raiding income. The plunder from Portobelo in 1669 amounted to seven times Jamaica's sugar exports that same year, and two years later Richard White, an Irish double-agent, wrote to the *Consejo* that the only way to make a fortune in Jamaica was 'by robbing Spaniards'.

Yet from the beginning there were also tensions between buccaneering and sugar planting, and these intensified over time. Colonel D'Oyley, when he returned to England, had warned that plunderers made money in the short term, but drew labour away from the plantations. That profit was certainly very useful, but the growth of the sugar-and-slavery economy ultimately changed opinions about buccaneering on the island. Planters like John Styles complained that buccaneers had no interest or stake in the island, though there were exceptions, including Henry Morgan himself. When Ogeron cancelled plundering commissions in 1670, as well as imposing unpopular *Compagnie* taxes, *colons* in Saint-Domingue rebelled – some of them joining Morgan's Panamá voyage. Thomas Lynch complained in 1671 that plundering 'encourages all manner of disorder and dissoluteness' and 'does but enrich the worst sort of people'. He argued that 'privateering and planting are two things absolutely incompatible'.

The government in England had begun to think the same thing.

6

AN HONOURABLE CRIME

L ondon in the summer of 1672 was a tense city. The Third Anglo-
Dutch War began in May, when France, England's ally, invaded
the Netherlands. The French army's initially rapid progress stalled
when the Dutch army flooded key regions. Charles II's alliance with
Louis XIV, which included a secret treaty backing Louis' claim to the
Spanish throne, was unpopular in England. It became even more so after a
combined Anglo-French fleet met defeat at the hands of Michiel de Ruyter
at Solebay on 7 June, for which the French commander Jean d'Estrées was
widely blamed. Fruitless peace negotiations dragged on.

Arriving in July, Henry Morgan learned that Thomas Modyford lay
incarcerated in the Tower. Morgan himself was never imprisoned, perhaps
due to his poor health, but at first the signs did not look good. A petition
on behalf of Modyford, signed by Morgan and around 300 captains, merchants, and planters of Jamaica, had been rejected by the Privy Council
the previous November.

Perhaps the king did not look kindly on those who burned cities in his
name but without his express command. At the same time, it was not clear
that Morgan and the other buccaneers could be classified as pirates. They
posed a significant quandary precisely because they were 'privateers' in
contemporary terms – acting on the borders of, but not entirely outside
of, imperial jurisdiction. Unlike other plunderers, such as those of the *West
Indische Compagnie*, English buccaneers made war during a time of declared
peace, but they did so 'beyond the line', and, at least sometimes, with the
authorisation of colonial governors.

Despite the widespread idea of pirates as 'enemies of all', the laws of
plunder were more complex at this time. Each country had its own laws,
but these influenced and interacted with each other in the early stages of

modern international law. Ideas around piracy, including the buccaneers' raiding voyages, were a key part of that process.

Maritime law as a distinct branch had long antecedents, but developed in Europe especially from the thirteenth and fourteenth centuries. Many rulers began to appoint admirals; the term probably comes from the Arabic *amīr*, a result of Mediterranean interactions. They also established specialised admiralty courts for maritime cases, often with individual jurisdictions for specific provinces or ports.

One area of this law, which came to be known as prize law, dealt particularly with plundering. In fact 'prize', in this sense, appeared in English during the sixteenth century, and 'plunder' is another neologism that arrived in English in the middle of the seventeenth century, from Dutch *plunderen* and German *plündern*. Previous equivalents for these terms included 'spoil', or 'spulzie' in Scotland, and *praeda* or *spolia* in Latin. In another cognate cluster, *būte* in medieval German, originally meaning 'exchange', became *butin* in French during the fourteenth century, 'bottyne' or 'booty' in English by the mid-fifteenth, and *buit* in Dutch in the sixteenth. Once again, etymology illuminates the international connections around, and increasing attention given to, these issues. For simplicity's sake I have stuck to 'prize' and 'plunder', even if these are anachronistic in places.

Prize law *avant la lettre* had been discussed by medieval scholars such as Bartolus de Sassoferrato and sixteenth-century writers like Baltasar Álamos de Barrientos, who encouraged Felipe II to set out warships against *corsarios*, and later Alberico Gentili. Legislation by several European rulers addressed prize law during the sixteenth century – *plakkaten* by the Holy Roman Emperor, which applied to the Burgundian Netherlands, in 1488 and 1540, later adopted by the Dutch Republic; *édits* concerning French admiralty jurisdiction in 1517, 1544, and 1584; English royal proclamations by Henry VIII and Elizabeth I. Renewed study of Roman law during this period also influenced these regulations.

There were three kinds of legal plundering, more or less recognised across all these jurisdictions, as Scottish lawyer William Welwod summarised in his *Abridgement of all Sea-Lawes*, published in 1613. These covered, first, plunder 'taken from Pirates, and sea-thiefes'; second, 'from professed enemies in lawful warfare'; and third, those 'covered with the title of letters of Marque, called *Ius represaliarum*'.

First and simplest, it was legal to plunder and kill pirates. However, pirates did not legally own the goods they had plundered. The captor could keep them only if the original victims lodged no claim.

Second, during a declared war between two sovereigns, their subjects could legally plunder and kill enemies, so long as it was a 'just war' waged for defence, or to revenge an insult or injury, though most rulers tended to believe that all *their* wars were just wars. According to some legal theorists of the day, no bureaucratic court process was necessarily required during such a war and on occasion, as with a proclamation by Henry VIII in 1544, rulers did indeed declare open season on their enemies.

Increasingly, however, rulers forbade armed ships to sail without a formal licence, and treaties ending wars routinely featured agreements to cancel these plundering commissions (and to suppress piracy). Usually, these licences ordered captors to bring prizes into port for approval by admiralty officials before disposing of them. One objective of that was to make sure the prizes were indeed enemy ships or cargoes, but admirals' and sovereigns' desire to secure their share of plunder was at least as important as any concern with preventing injustice.

The third kind of legal plundering, reprisal, was only legitimate, and necessary, during peacetime. When a merchant's ship or goods were seized unlawfully by a foreign vessel, the merchant was supposed to appeal to the captors' sovereign for redress. If this appeal proved unsuccessful, then the merchant's own sovereign could issue a 'letter of reprisal', sometimes, as Welwod noted, called a 'letter of marque', allowing them to seize ships or goods belonging to the offending nationality, on the basis that the owners of these would sort it out with the original malefactors.

In effect these letters granted permission to carry out a limited and private war, although with slightly different conditions to plundering during a public war. Applicants had to prove their losses, to attempt peaceful legal recourse first, they had to bring their plunder for adjudication by an admiralty court, and they could only claim plunder equal to their losses.

Much of the early raiding in the Caribbean was carried out under letters of reprisal, often issued once northern European ships had been seized as *corsarios* by the *guardacostas* – although if perpetual war existed 'beyond the line', as was sometimes claimed, then such letters were not really mandatory. François I gave Jean d'Argo letters of reprisal in 1529, after Portuguese ships attacked him. The Venetian ambassador in Lisbon described the conflict between Portugal and France at sea as a 'silent war'. Francis Drake made similar claims of legitimate revenge after Veracruz in 1568.

The legal situation began to change in the later sixteenth century, with the French wars of religion and the Dutch rebellion. Protestant provinces and towns issued commissions to plunderers that, unsurprisingly, the French and Spanish monarchs did not recognise as legitimate, considering them 'rebels, robbers, and pirates'. It was in response to these plunderers that Spain established the *Armada de Flandes* and a prize court in Dunkirk.

Elizabeth supported both the Dutch Protestants and the French Huguenots, but she did not declare war, even when English troops arrived in Le Havre. Instead, in response to French ships capturing English ones, she issued letters of reprisal, until a treaty in 1564 ended those hostilities. Similarly, when the Spanish government embargoed English and French vessels in 1585, partially in response to attacks on Spanish ships and colonies, Elizabeth willingly answered the clamour from English merchants for letters of reprisal.

Once again she avoided issuing a formal declaration of war, though the letters granted holders authority to act 'in as ample and full manner as if it were in the time of open war', while following the rules of reprisal (only targeting Spanish ships and bringing prizes for adjudication). Increasingly these documents were merely a legal fiction for raiders who had never suffered any personal losses in the first place – and a mechanism to ensure that the Crown and admiral got their cut. On at least one occasion, the admiral provided such a letter to a captain *after* he had already captured a prize.

Sovereigns continued to issue genuine letters of reprisal, or *lettres*, *patentes* or *brieven*, into the seventeenth century, but this use of them to pursue an undeclared public war caused an important change in prize law. A 'letter of marque' came to mean a commission to plunder in wartime, rather than permission for peacetime reprisal. In a technical but significant legal adjustment, possession of a prize was no longer considered to transfer at the moment of capture but was conferred only by adjudication in a prize court, increasing state authority over the rules, if not the practice, of plunder.

The accession of James VI of Scotland as James I in England, and the 1609 truce between the Netherlands and Spain, provided only a temporary hiatus in these developments. From 1621 the Dutch and Spanish governments, and the Huguenots in La Rochelle, resumed issuing commissions for several decades. James may have refused to grant letters of reprisal after 1603, despite pleas from aggrieved merchants, but his son Charles I took the same approach as Elizabeth (indeed, he cited her precedent in diplomatic correspondence). Charles embarked on an undeclared war against Spain and then France during the 1620s through letters of marque, without requiring proof of losses beforehand. Perhaps as many as 950 captains received commissions, and though some were merchant ships taking them as an opportunistic precaution, English ships captured around 1,000 prizes, of which at least 700 went through court adjudication.

By the middle of the century, this new system for letters of marque and prize courts had become the norm. During the British civil wars the king, Parliament, and Irish confederates (who nominally supported Charles I but were largely independent) all issued letters of marque and pursued campaigns of commerce raiding. These new ideas about what constituted a legal plunderer had profound implications for the fourth category of plundering: piracy.

While the contours of legal plundering shifted, the concept of a 'pirate' did not. A pirate was not just someone who plundered without licence, but who did so *without good reason*, for private gain rather than for public purpose, raiding indiscriminately instead of targeting legitimate enemies. Commentators often compared them to bandits and robbers.

Gentili, and numerous other legal authors, adopted the pseudo-Ciceronian language describing pirates as *communes hostes omnium* or *hostis humani generis*, as did legislation in several countries. Hugo Grotius, another extremely influential legal thinker, developed some of these ideas further by analysing honourable and dishonourable plunder. The latter included, alongside pirates, those who attacked before a legitimate war was declared, or who acted under the cover of commissions for their own gain rather than public good.

In fact, the concept was so well established that in maritime laws of the medieval era, and into the sixteenth and seventeenth centuries, piracy informed other aspects of law without requiring a definition. It was illegal to pillage shipwrecks, except if they were pirate ships. Maritime insurance policies (one of the first kinds of insurance, originating in medieval Italy) and the risk-sharing rules of general average both covered piracy from very early on, including them with other 'perils of the sea'.

This concept was accepted without challenge, and the existence of legal plundering did not make rulers indifferent to piracy. The whole point of prize law was to delineate legal from illegal plunder, and European governments regularly prosecuted pirates. Mary, Queen of Scots, gave commissions to captains to hunt down 'pirattis, sey thevis, rubbaris, pilliaris, rebellis and malefactouris upoun the seyis'. Elizabeth executed the famous duo Thomas Walton and Clinton Atkinson in 1583, besides several others. 'Pyrates and Rovers', James VI and I proclaimed, stood 'out of his protection', and could be 'lawfully pursued and punished to the uttermost extremitie'.

However, the other categories of legal plunderer, and even the idea of 'enemies of all', posed certain problems in identifying *who* was a pirate. For example, Scottish merchants complained about the 'piratical wickedness' of Englishmen, while James, in 1590, granted letters of marque against the 'piratt Dunkirkeris'. From a Scottish perspective, these statements were correct: neither English nor Dunkirk ships were legally allowed to attack Scottish ones. Yet both carried licences from their sovereigns.

Not everyone agreed that a captain who broke the terms of their commission, or even one without a commission but who plundered for the right reasons, was a pirate. It might be dishonourable, according to Grotius, but that did not automatically make it illegal. Henry Mainwaring, who did in fact admit that he had been a pirate, went so far as to call his actions *pulchrum scelus*, an honourable crime, because he never plundered English ships but remained 'a dutiful subject preferring the service of my country'.

Therefore, 'piracy' often appeared – as it had with Cicero – as a rhetorical strategy. Those who plundered your ships were, almost invariably, pirates. In 1668, and again in 1684, Charles II published proclamations complaining of 'Piratical Practices, Depredations and Insolencies' committed by foreign ships in English harbours, most of whom were belligerents in their own wars.

Even Gentili wrestled with these problems. In *De Jure Belli*, he argued that some French sailors, fighting on behalf of a candidate for the Portuguese throne, should not have been executed as pirates (which they had been) because they carried licences from the French king, though engaged in no public war or case of reprisal. By contrast, he defended the English Crown's execution of Andrew Barton, a commissioned Scottish raider, as a pirate in 1511. Similarly, when in 1572 Elizabeth ordered 'Sea Rovers, commonly called Frebutters' to depart her harbours, meaning Dutch *watergeuzen* and *vrijbuiten*, she may have carefully avoided using the word 'pirate'.

In his work as an advocate of the High Court of Admiralty, Gentili again tended to interpret the ideas of piracy to suit the interests of his English clients. For example, he argued that the North African regencies of Algiers, Tripoli, and Tunis were *not* legitimate when their corsairs plundered English victims, making these corsairs pirates, but that they *were* legitimate (or, at least, their overlord the Ottoman sultan was) when they provided a market for goods that English plunderers had taken from Venetian ships.

Another example, which I rather like, comes from Francis Drake's circumnavigation of 1577–80. On his return, the lord admiral ordered Drake to return anything 'piratically taken' during the voyage. With a flash of legal inspiration, Drake argued that the plunder had been seized from Spanish smugglers. The king of Spain could hardly complain of piracy if Drake snapped up what was already contraband.

Government approaches to piracy were mostly reactive, since at this time there was little in the way of a police apparatus. The authorities usually took action only when prompted by the complaints of allies or their own subjects. Most regimes were heavily involved in plundering, and often those accused of piracy simultaneously served a ruler – Drake was himself commissioned at one point to apprehend 'pirates, spoilers, malefactors, and robbers at sea', as well as doing civic works in local office, for which he is fondly remembered in Plymouth, and sitting in parliament.

The changes to prize law, by which a licence became a requirement even during wartime, began to move the concept of 'piracy' towards meaning anyone without such a licence. As plundering increased through Elizabeth's reign, so too did problems with English plunderers attacking the wrong ships and, following complaints from many of her allies, she issued proclamations in the 1560s and 1590s that anyone sailing without a licence, or attacking the wrong targets, would be 'reputed and tried as pirats'. The grandly named admiralty judge Julius Caesar advised the queen that she should continue to issue letters of reprisal, otherwise mariners might become 'plaine pirats' (implying that it was the letter that made the difference), or go over to her enemies.

James repeated similar conditions when he made peace with Spain at the start of his reign. He had already dealt with troublesome plunderers in the Hebrides and saw himself as *rex pacificus*, a peacemaker healing a divided Christendom. On one occasion, when an ambassador remarked that his new realm was famous for piracy, James burst out, 'By God I'll hang the pirates with my own hands, and my Lord Admiral as well.'

French laws of the 1500s similarly mandated that ships must acquire a *congé*, or permission, before departure, and Cardinal Richelieu, as *Grand Maître de la Navigation et Commerce*, insisted that anyone who failed to do so would be considered a pirate. A few decades later in 1655, at the conclusion of the First Anglo-Dutch War, the British government cancelled all commissions and declared that offenders would now be 'reputed, and taken as Pirates', and both they and their 'Maintainers, Comforters, Abettors, and Partakers shall suffer death'.

Plunderers could easily acquire commissions from other rulers, though. Martin Frobisher, an Atlantic voyager who was accused of piracy, took

commissions from Willem of Orange and Henri III of Navarre; the earl of
Warwick supplied his captains with paperwork from the Netherlands or
Savoy. Peter Easton, a notorious early seventeenth-century pirate, settled
in Savoy and commanded the duke's fleet. Henry Mainwaring claimed
that Florence, Savoy, Spain, Tunis, and Tuscany had all offered him a job.

Taking foreign commissions was illegal, at least for English subjects,
under Elizabeth. James, too, complained in 1605 that some mariners who
had 'gotten a custome and habite in the time of the Warre to make profite
by Spoile, doe leave their ordinary and honest vocation and Trading in
Merchantly Voyages … [and] betake themselves to the Service of divers
forreine States, under the Title of men of Warre'. Such men were, he
considered, 'no better then Pirats'. Yet the repeated proclamations
recalling mariners from foreign service – five during the 1620s and 1630s,
another eight between 1650 and 1678 – show just how ineffectual those
proclamations were.

These rules concerning commissions were neither continuous nor
concrete. Royal proclamations lapsed on the death of a monarch, unless continued by their heir; the 1655 proclamation by the interregnum government
was, like all its other laws, rendered void by the restoration of Charles II. In
1660, some English merchants published a pamphlet complaining that their
ship had been attacked five years earlier by a French vessel whose crew acted
like 'Notorious Pirates' because, by their own admission, they plundered
without commission, after a peace treaty, and without taking the prize
through adjudication. The merchants went to press because their efforts to
recover their losses through French courts had been entirely unsuccessful.

The uncertainties remained unresolved. While in 1668 Leoline Jenkins,
the admiralty judge, described those 'without any Commission at all' as
pirates and *hostes humani generis*, he distinguished them from a 'lawful man
of war that exceeds his commission'. According to admiralty lawyer William
Oldys, in 1694, there was an important difference between those who acted
in *animo hostili*, the spirit of war, and *animo furandi*, the spirit of theft.

Guess which spirit – and I am not talking about rum – Henry Morgan
and Thomas Modyford would have claimed.

These questions became particularly acute for James VI and I as he struggled to end the plundering that had become such a common occurrence
under Elizabeth. The number of sailors involved in naval or raiding voyages had risen from around 16,000 in the early 1580s to about 50,000 by

the end of the century. When James made peace with Spain, these idle hands continued their old trade, as both Henry Mainwaring and John Smith lamented. The result was a significant spike in English piracy, or at least unauthorised plundering, around 1610.

Coming under greater suspicion and pressure in England, these raiders congregated in two regions: south-west Ireland and Mediterranean North Africa. These places possessed similar characteristics to Jamaica and Tortuga later, being close to Mediterranean and Atlantic shipping routes, with local communities willing to trade with and supply raiders, and political configurations amenable to plundering.

Algiers, Tripoli, and Tunis had all been conquered by Ottoman armies during the 1500s, but were now semi-autonomous regencies. Independent of the sultan's wars or treaties with European states, the regencies licensed their own corsairs, and so too did the Sa'di dynasty ruling the independent kingdom of Morocco, cementing its authority by pursuing *jihād* against occupying Portuguese forces. At the height of the *corso*, the regencies armed about 100 ships at any one time, while the Knights of St John in Malta and the Order of St Stephen in Tuscany set out around 40 vessels.

During the sixteenth century these regencies formed alliances with England and the Netherlands against Spain. Drake stopped off in Morocco in 1577 on his way round the world, and Magharabi ships resupplied in Dutch harbours. Dutch and English ships, sailing more and more often to the Mediterranean, sometimes based themselves in the regencies while preying on Venetian and even Ottoman trade (as did Uskoci raiders in the Adriatic). Aḥmad al-Manṣūr, sultan of Morocco from 1578 onwards, proposed a joint English–Moroccan attack on the Caribbean, though the death of both al-Manṣūr and Elizabeth in 1603 prevented it.

The seventeenth century brought changes, as Istanbul's control over the regencies weakened, while northern European ships became tempting targets. The *corso* often involved captive taking for ransom or slavery, and large numbers of European sailors were seized and taken to the Maghreb. Some converted to Islam and settled there, or joined the corsairs. Algiers became so notorious that its name was, for European writers, synonymous with piracy.

Many of these plunderers floated between the Maghreb and Ireland. The latter was England's first colony: Norman and medieval lords had invaded several times, and English monarchs claimed suzerainty over the island, though in reality controlling only Dublin. During the late sixteenth century, when Ireland remained largely Catholic, English intervention became more direct and violent, as a series of rebellions supported by Spain led to bitter military campaigns in which plunderers like Drake also fought.

Much of Ireland remained under the control of Irish magnates, but their relationship with the English Crown changed. One example is Gráinne Ni Mháille (known in English as Grace O'Malley), often called a 'pirate queen'. The daughter of an aristocratic house, after her husband died in a feud she not only protected his castles but established her own power base on Clare Island, leading attacks on local opponents while resisting the encroachments of the English Crown. In 1593 she travelled to London to plead for the release of two rebel leaders, one her half-brother, and met Elizabeth, promising to support Elizabeth's rule in Ireland in return.

At the same time, Elizabeth's government authorised new Protestant colonisation. A first scheme in Ulster in the 1570s failed, but following a rebellion in Munster the queen granted plots of land to English settlers there in 1597. Several Irish lords held on to their position by making peace with Elizabeth in 1603, like Gráinne Ni Mháille had, but after Aodh Mór Ó Néill and his allies fled the country in 1607 to seek Spanish assistance, James declared them to be traitors and their lands forfeit, paving the way for renewed plantations in Ulster.

Both coastal Irish communities and the new colonists traded with plunderers, continuing into the seventeenth century. Mainwaring called Ireland 'the Nursery and Storehouse of Pirates', noting the 'good entertainment' on offer there and the coastline 'so full of places and Harbours' in which to hide. The 'good store of English, Scottish, and Irish wenches' were also 'strong attractors to draw the common sort of them thither'.

Perhaps as many as 2,000 plunderers and 40 ships operated out of Ireland at this time, though the numbers fluctuated. Several historians have described them as a 'confederacy', although, like *frères de la côte* or the 'Jamaica discipline' for buccaneers, that term exaggerates the unity and coordination of this group. They gathered around particular leaders, including Peter Easton, Richard Bishop, and John Jennings, but their organisation was fluid and fragmentary.

Often they moved seasonally between Ireland, the Mediterranean, and the Atlantic. Mainwaring, for example, mostly sailed from Mamora (now Mehdiya), on the Atlantic coast of Morocco, and spent the summer of 1614 in Newfoundland. That year a Spanish fleet under Luis Fajardo captured and garrisoned Mamora, so in 1615 Mainwaring sailed to Ireland instead.

Munster on the southern coast was particularly well situated for preying on Atlantic trade routes, and Baltimore, the chief town, became known as a hotspot. A 1610 report condemned its 'lewd adulterous women' for their affection towards these plunderers, and, for a few years, the whole region depended on 'the depredation and spoils of pirates'.

Let us run through an exercise I do with my students. Say you are a sovereign in the seventeenth century and, despite all of the legal intricacies outlined so far, you have identified some pirates. Rulers and lawyers certainly thought they knew a pirate when they saw one. You have basically three options.

Option one: you can send out a military expedition to exterminate the pirates, either with your own ships, if you have them, or by commissioning a private vessel. Gentili observed that it was lawful 'to destroy piratical lairs and nests', and most people agreed.

This approach can be risky and costly. Most rulers in the sixteenth and early seventeenth centuries had limited revenues and resources, and were reluctant to expend them, particularly when there was no guarantee of success. It could prove difficult to track down pirates, and even if you did, sometimes their forces outmatched yours.

James tried this option. William Monson sailed with a small expedition to Scotland and western Ireland in 1614, but achieved success only by masquerading as Mainwaring and tricking some pirates. In 1620–21 an English fleet under Robert Mansell went to Algiers, but his blockade proved brief and ineffectual. A Dutch naval force, with James' permission, attacked pirate shipping at Crookhaven in Ireland in 1612 and had more effect. They were supposed to capture the pirates and deliver them to English justice, but the Dutch sailors killed most of those whom they captured, while gathering up a fair bit of *buit*.

Rulers had a possible sub-option here, in that ships attacked by pirates were entitled to defend themselves and, in doing so, destroy their assailants. That happened sometimes, including in the 1610s and 1620s, but it was hardly going to solve piracy by itself, not least because merchant sailors were often reluctant to engage in battle, when pirates might agree to release them for a ransom, or only targeted the ship's cargo but not the possessions of the crew.

In 1664 the English parliament introduced legislation specifically requiring sailors to fight in defence of their ships. It was the only English statute concerning piracy in that whole century, and its reference to 'Turkish Shipps' suggests it was mainly concerned with corsairs and Mediterranean trade. Sailors who captured their assailants would be entitled to any plunder 'as is usually practised in Private Men of War' – a phrase that became 'Privateer' when the statute was reissued in 1671 and 1682.

Option two: you can pardon pirates. Henry Mainwaring took a hypocritically hard line on this question, advising the king to 'put on a constant immutable resolution never to grant any Pardon ... put them all to death, or make slaves of them'. Such a 'resolution' would not have done Mainwaring any good, of course, and pardons were one of the easiest, and possibly the most common, approaches a government could take.

Pardoning pirates made sense, given the valuable maritime and military skills that plunderers often possessed. Mainwaring, a royal advisor and naval officer for the rest of his life, is a case in point, but he was far from the only one. Thomas Fleming voluntarily surrendered himself to the lord admiral in 1588 to help out against the Spanish Armada, for which he was pardoned and rewarded. Government officials would often negotiate with pirates to provide a pardon, and this course appealed to aggrieved merchants too, who were sometimes less interested in seeing justice done than they were in recovering their lost goods. Merchants even interceded for the very pirates who had attacked their ships.

In fact, as Mainwaring wrote, most sailors knew that only captains were likely to need a pardon, since 'the common sort of seamen', as he called them, could claim to be 'Perforst-men', taken aboard against their will. Mainwaring said he had gone through a routine pantomime of forced recruitment to provide willing newcomers with this legal defence, adding that such men, confident in their protection, were 'more violent, headstrong, and mutinous, than any of the old Crew'. On arrival in England, they surrendered to officials, 'complaining of the injury they have received in being so long detained by force, and so they are commonly not molested but relieved'.

The problem with pardons, of course, is that they did not always work. Mainwaring was not unwise to counsel James that pardons might encourage plunderers to continue, knowing they would face no consequences. So it proved in practice. Many of the piratical leaders of the early 1600s, such as Bishop and Jennings, negotiated for pardons, as did other captains. Some of them seem to have been planning an 'exit strategy' throughout their plundering careers, and a few, like Mainwaring, went into naval service. Others, however, returned to piracy (including Jennings, twice), ignored the pardons or, like Easton, accepted a foreign commission instead.

Well then, option three: you can prosecute pirates. In theory, prosecution was unnecessary, because anyone could kill a pirate, but most states followed some judicial process to ensure that the people they were executing were, indeed, pirates.

That approach had its problems too. Most European states followed civil law in maritime cases, derived from Roman law, which set quite high standards of evidence, requiring either a confession or two witnesses, both hard to get in piracy cases. These conditions did not seem to trouble everyone, but in England Henry VIII and parliament introduced a statute in 1536 which bemoaned that 'traytors, pirates, thieves, robbers, murtherers and confederates upon the sea' escaped punishment because of the civil law requirements. The statute therefore granted permission to the admiralty to use common law procedure, with juries and other kinds of evidence, for the prosecution of seaborne crimes. This statute became the basis of piracy prosecutions in England for almost two centuries, and it is important to our story later.

Elizabeth executed Atkinson and Walton under that statute, and it was the basis for increased efforts by the High Court of Admiralty in James' reign to apprehend, interrogate, and execute those involved in piracy. Indeed, it is from the records of these investigations that we know so much about this episode of piracy. Therefore, it is the government's view of these plunderers that has survived, and I wonder whether these men thought of their actions as piracy, or as some kind of lawful plunder, before they were hauled in front of admiralty officials.

In 1608 came the fruits of the court's labours: nineteen men, including Jennings and some who held foreign commissions, were tried. Most of them were condemned and hanged at Execution Dock in Wapping, east London, sending a clear signal concerning the government's position. However, this was a tiny proportion of those involved in marauding at the time.

Indeed, a clear legal procedure does not resolve all difficulties, because you first have to capture the pirates and then you have to ensure that they are tried. One issue here was the various kinds of legal plundering outlined previously, by which defendants might justify their actions; another was local attitudes that were often very sympathetic to plunderers. Regional magnates, like the earl of Orkney in Scotland, the powerful Killigrew family in sixteenth-century Cornwall, or various coastal *seigneurs* in France, not only supported plundering themselves but also used their judicial powers to acquit those accused of piracy. Mayors, local officials, and others in coastal communities – often also possessing close ties to plunderers – did the like, or simply released the accused from jail or connived at their escape.

Rulers tried to stamp this out, but without much success. Elizabeth's proclamations threatened neglectful officers with punishment. In 1582 she suspended local admiralty jurisdictions in a crackdown on piracy, and in 1591 Julius Caesar toured the south coast to bring authorities into line – but he steered clear of Devon and Cornwall, probably to avoid upsetting powerful local interests. Richelieu, as *Grand Maître*, took a similar interest in regional maritime affairs, acquiring for himself the posts of *amiral* of Provence and Brittany, but this was only a temporary concentration of power.

In Ireland during the early 1600s, too, local officials were directly implicated. Thomas Crooke, who received a twenty-one-year lease for Baltimore in 1605, had intended to invest in pilchard fishing but was almost immediately accused of trading with pirates. The deputy vice-admiral of Munster, William Hull, was described as an 'encourager and countenancer of pirates', even welcoming captains who raided East India Company ships.

Officials in England sometimes got into trouble too: Richard Hawkins, son of John Hawkins and vice-admiral of Devon, was fined and imprisoned in 1606 and eventually removed from post two years later on accusations of harbouring pirates. One of Hawkins' accusers, Humphrey Jobson, secretary to the lord admiral, faced similar accusations himself after becoming involved in colonisation in Munster. Unlike Hawkins, though, Jobson – and Crooke and Hull – remained in post, because the Crown relied on them to govern the colony, much like later governors in the Caribbean.

Mariners and maritime communities also took their own view on legal forms of plunder, for example insisting on a customary right of pillage, which permitted the crew to claim anything almost literally not nailed down, or rather, not part of the prize's cargo: things like the captured crew's possessions or the ship's rigging, anchors, and so on. Nor did they always observe the formal process of adjudication before selling off what they had seized.

It is easy to interpret these communities as complicit in piracy and indifferent to law, and probably some of them were. That is how contemporary authorities characterised and mistrusted them, and it is a line historians have often taken, too. More recent scholarship, though, argues that seafarers were very knowledgeable about law, engaging in what one historian calls 'legal posturing', routinely seeking cover or justification for their actions. Moreover, in this transitional phase of prize law, and with inconsistent government policies, it seems likely that in many cases it was unclear whether plundering was piracy or not, until some official made a decision about it. It is also worth noting that most states recognised and respected local and communal customary laws, meaning that seafarers were not just subject to law but also participated in defining it.

Once again, we find that it is not just the act, but the judgement, that makes something into piracy – and it is not only the government that does the judging, in a legal or moral sense.

Mediterranean corsairs, often accused of piracy, continued to attack European shipping throughout the century (hence the 1664 statute), but the episode of English piracy in 1610 ran out of steam fairly quickly. Whether this was a success for James' policies, or resulted from changing behaviours among seafarers themselves, is an open question, though I suspect those two factors were connected.

I have given quite some time to this example because it reveals the complexities of prize and piracy law, and the difficulties for contemporary governments, all of which became even more evident in the Caribbean. Indeed, while James' reign increased attention to piracy, both plundering and colonising got under way once more in the 1620s, and this imperial expansion further afield added another layer of complexity to these legal systems.

The concept of 'no peace beyond the line' in theory rendered all warfare and plundering in the Americas lawful, although that was not always observed in practice. It did not save Walter Ralegh after he attacked a Venezuelan town in 1616, for example. Though he was actually executed for a suspended sentence of treason imposed at the start of James' reign, it was his plundering that breached the suspension, and the protests of the Spanish ambassador that swayed James' decision.

More broadly, new questions arose about who could claim jurisdiction, and where. Spanish and Portuguese assertions of universal empire were predictably unpopular. 'Show me the clause in Adam's will,' François I of France is supposed to have scoffed, 'which gives the king of Spain dominion over half the world.' Elizabeth likewise 'could finde no reason why Spain should hinder her Subjects ... from sayling to the Indies ... [because] the use of the Sea as of the Ayre is common to all'.

In 1602, a Dutch ship in the Indian Ocean seized a Portuguese prize, the *Santa Catarina*, after Portuguese soldiers captured and executed six Dutch sailors. The Amsterdam admiralty court judged the cargo, worth some 2.2 million guilders, lawful prize, and the *Vereenigde Oostindische Compagnie*, the Dutch East India Company, commissioned Huig de Groot, more famously Hugo Grotius, to pen a justification. Grotius was something of a prodigy: scion of an eminent family, a distinguished university scholar in Leiden at 11 years old, a published author by 16. He is often regarded as one of the most important figures in developing international law.

Grotius finished *De Jurae Praedae* (*On the Laws of Prize*), in which he talked about honourable and dishonourable plunder, in 1604. It did not appear in print until the nineteenth century, but one chapter appeared anonymously in 1609 as *Mare Liberum* (*The Free Sea*), probably in a bid to influence truce negotiations between Spain and the Netherlands. Here Grotius compared the Portuguese *Estado da Índia* to pirates, because 'the name of "pirate" is appropriately bestowed upon men who blockade the seas ... worthy objects of universal hatred in that they were harmful to all mankind' – another rhetorical twist of that concept.

Even more controversially, he argued that no ruler could claim ownership of the ocean. That idea upset not only the Spanish–Portuguese monarchy, but also the *doge* of Venice, the king of Sweden, and the newly British king. Where Elizabeth endorsed similar ideas to Grotius – because it suited her war against Spain – James brought his more assertive Scottish interpretation of territorial waters, influenced by competition over North Sea fisheries. Portuguese, English, Scottish, and Italian scholars all leapt to the defence of their various territorial claims.

The English East India Company, meanwhile, commissioned Richard Hakluyt, a vicar and imperial propagandist, to translate *Mare Liberum* into English, and used it in negotiations with the Dutch *Compagnie* about the Indian Ocean. Grotius himself led the delegation that sought to obstruct English trade in some areas, and by this point the authorship of *Mare Liberum* was an open secret, so I like to imagine some devious glee among the negotiators when confronting Grotius with his own writings. Grotius himself was exiled from the Netherlands and entered Swedish diplomatic service, deferentially modifying his position in his 1625 work *De Jure Belli ac Pacis* (*On the Laws of War and Peace*) to respect the views of Gustav II Adolph.

Besides the question of jurisdiction, legal procedure remained a problem, although this seems to have been more pronounced in the English Empire than in others. The Spanish Crown, for example, had granted colonial viceroys and their subordinates the authority to punish *corsarios y piratas* according to the laws of Castille, and to send expeditions against them, early in the seventeenth century. The monumental *Recopilación de las leyes de los Reynos de las Indias*, published in 1680, collected and reiterated this and many other *cédulas* concerning maritime affairs. That included the ban on foreign trade, and the *Recopilación* also reprinted rules by which *guardacostas* could bring in their prizes.

Early French colonies were more disparate, but Louis XIV and Jean Colbert brought all colonial officials under the *Ministère de la Marine* from 1669, establishing *gouverneurs*, *conseils souverains*, and *intendants de la police, justice et finances* in the Antilles and Nouvelle France, just as they did for provinces within France. A new *Ordonnance de la Marine* in 1681 confirmed the authority of admiralty judges to determine piracy cases. In both the French and Spanish empires, then, the same laws concerning piracy applied in Europe and the colonies, and the fact that the *Recopilación* and *Ordonnance* say nothing about either the definition of piracy or court procedure implies that for both empires the civil law already in place was thought sufficient.

The *West Indische Compagnie* also held authority concerning prize law through its charter. Before 1630, the *kapiteins* and *schippers* of the *West Indische Compagnie* were supposed to send prizes back to the Netherlands for adjudication, but afterwards individual governors in the Americas took on this role. From about 1642 onwards, all *Compagnie* ships sailing to the Caribbean received a *hout en zoutbrief*, a licence to trade in logwood and salt, which included permission to capture enemy ships. The *Compagnie* never called its own vessels *commissievaarders*, suggesting a distinction between private ships authorised by one of the five *admiraliteiten* in the Netherlands and those sailing for the *Compagnie* in the Americas, but there was no doubt that the *Compagnie*'s commissions were legal.

In the English Empire there was more uncertainty. The earl of Warwick was himself accused of piracy in 1621, though acquitted, due to his high status. The Providence Island Company commissioned its own raiders from 1626, but some of its captains furnished themselves with Dutch paperwork too. The various 'private' colonies established their own courts, often dealing with maritime affairs. Ireland had different laws, which made it harder to prosecute pirates there, though these were amended by new legislation in 1612 and 1614.

The governors of Virginia and Jamaica both held the office of vice-admiral for their territories, but Colonel D'Oyley, at least, had misgivings about what that meant. He suggested to London that governors should have power to execute 'Piratts and Rovers without Commission' or anyone sailing with foreign commissions. However, when in 1661 he sought to arrest 'henry Morgan, souldier' and others for piracy, he wrote that he was 'loath to bring them to any Triall here, doubting my power'.

D'Oyley lamented the 'customs by which the private men of war here acted formerly when there was no authority in the Indies'. If the absence of authority contributed to the rise of the buccaneers, the rise of the buccaneers created an ever more pressing need, from a European perspective, to introduce some authority.

That did not occur immediately, though. While D'Oyley's successors may have had a clearer remit for their admiralty jurisdiction, they continued to receive mixed signals from London. Lord Windsor was ordered to seek 'a good correspondence and free commerce' with Spanish colonies, but if peaceful persuasion failed – which it did, as did similar French and Dutch attempts – then he should 'endeavour to procure and settle such trade ... by force'.

Modyford too was told, shortly after his arrival in 1664, that the king was displeased about the 'daily complaints of violence and depredations'. He commanded Modyford to 'inflict condign punishment' on the perpetrators, and Modyford duly cancelled all commissions. About a year later, Modyford received Albermarle's permission to issue commissions again and did so, though Morgan did not follow his instructions to the letter (to the delight of his fellow Jamaicans). In 1669 Modyford was told to call in the commissions again.

Meanwhile, the legal status of Jamaica remained an open question. It had been captured by what was considered, after 1660, an illegal regime. Charles decided to keep the island, and the Privy Council similarly approved of Edward Mansfield's capture of Providencia after the fact, perhaps because in 1666 things were going badly with the Second Anglo-Dutch War, plus plague and fire in London. However, the colonists remained anxious about the king's commitment to their wellbeing. There were rumours that he might sell the island to Spain.

The treaty agreed at Madrid in 1667 did not mention Jamaica at all. The *Consejo de las Indias* maintained their claim to the island and throughout the 1660s contemplated several plans for invasion, just as Modyford feared, although none of them went anywhere because of a lack of resources.

When hostilities escalated on both sides during the later 1660s, mutual protests led Charles to dispatch William Godolphin to Madrid, in June 1669, to negotiate a new treaty. The *Consejo* were not impressed by a letter from Modyford at around this time, offering, with some audacity, that the buccaneers might defend Spanish colonies from French aggression, with a thinly veiled threat that such 'good encouragement' would 'prevent their seeking other'. They also failed to tell Godolphin that only two months beforehand the queen had authorised commissions like the one for Manoel Rivero Pardal, or that they continued to consider invasion plans.

The new Treaty of Madrid, signed on 21 July 1670, formally recognised Jamaica as an English colony. The negotiators agreed to ratify it in London by late November, with a further eight months for publication in the Caribbean. Cartagena knew about it by October 1670, and Jamaica by December, when Morgan was assembling his men at the Isla de Vaca – though not by official dispatch.

A letter from Lord Arlington did reach Jamaica telling Modyford to 'forbear all hostilities at land' and, crucially, 'what state soever the privateers are, at the receipt of this letter, you keepe them soe till we have a final answer from Spain'. It was a poor choice of words, since Morgan was already at sea. Modyford instructed him to 'behave with all moderation in carrying on this war'. We know how that turned out.

Godolphin's treaty arrived too late to save Panamá. Cartagena received orders from Madrid to cancel all commissions on the same day that a report of the smouldering ruins arrived. Modyford got formal news of the treaty in June, a week after Morgan handed in his campaign report, and even then it came not from London but the governor of Puerto Rico. Modyford once again wrote to London complaining of the 'fatal doctrine' that governors should wait months for orders from England. London did not agree, and the treaty brought a clearer sense of direction. As Modyford wrote that letter, Thomas Lynch was already on the way to replace him.

Neither Morgan nor Modyford were ever prosecuted, perhaps a result of the legal complexities and the ambiguities of imperial policy over the past decade, or because of the benefits that buccaneers brought to Jamaica in these early years. From here on, though, Charles was more determined to put a stop to buccaneering in Jamaica. Lynch was a suitable choice: a soldier in the civil wars, a colonist, and a slave trader. He had lived in Spain, learning the language and building up contacts, and had been chief justice in Jamaica until Modyford sacked him, when he moved to London, where he was well connected by marriage and through links to Arlington and other courtiers. Modyford had been sent only the ill-fated *Oxford* during his entire tenure, from 1664 to 1671; Lynch sailed with two frigates at his disposal.

At the time of Lynch's appointment, the king, fuming that the island had become a 'Christian Algiers', ordered that all plundering must cease. The buccaneers should be pardoned, given 35 acres each, and 'betake themselves to planting or merchandizing'. It was one thing to write this in London. It was another thing altogether to make it stick in Jamaica.

7

A PRIVATEER FACTION

Thomas Lynch set to with a will. He sent two frigates to Cartagena to organise a mutual declaration of the new treaty and, as Exquemelin noted, ordered that no more 'Roovers' should sail from Jamaica. Lynch offered a general pardon, but intended to prosecute future transgressions. Both Lord Vaughan, who replaced Lynch in 1675, and the earl of Carlisle, Vaughan's successor in 1678, would follow this same official line.

Although the Third Anglo-Dutch War occupied Lynch's early tenure, from 1674 England and its empire were officially at peace until 1688. These fourteen years were the second-longest stretch without international or internecine war during the Stuart dynasty's British rule, which lasted from 1603 to 1714. The longest was the twenty-one years of James VI and I's reign (there was a spell of nine years under Charles I, which ended in civil war, and then two gaps of five years between the three Anglo-Dutch wars).

It is no coincidence that both stretches saw more concerted efforts against piracy, the first in Ireland, the second in the Caribbean. Unfortunately for the governors of Jamaica, it would not prove easy to stop the buccaneers. The Caribbean remained a theatre of war and, like in Ireland, the Crown's desire to suppress marauding was inhibited in Jamaica both by local attitudes and legal uncertainties. By the end of the decade, however, Jamaica's colonial elite, including Henry Morgan, had not only fallen in line: they themselves introduced the first statute against piracy in any English colony.

The first problem, for the governors in Jamaica, was the continuation of hostilities connected to international wars, whether England was directly involved in them or not. The old tensions with Spain had not disappeared, and in November 1671 Lynch reported to London further warnings of an intended invasion. He called a council of war and declared martial law

– though, unlike his predecessor, 'this noise of war makes me more strict in observing the peace'.

The Caribbean remained full of the 'noise of war' across this decade. The Privy Council first warned Lynch to be on guard against a Dutch invasion, though Lynch found it impossible to persuade 'privateers' to cruise against Dutch ships or islands. While the Anglo-Dutch war ended in 1674, France remained at war with the Netherlands until 1678. In 1673 a French attack on Curaçao failed, while Dutch ships struck at both *flibustiers* and French commerce. In May 1676 Jacob Binkes led a Dutch expedition that recaptured Cayenne from French control.

French raiders, and others with commissions from Tortuga, had continued to raid Spanish towns ever since Henry Morgan destroyed the *Armada de Barlovento*. When in 1673 France officially declared war on Spain, as a Dutch ally, it led to another spike in plundering. *Flibustiers* attacked Margarita, Trinidad, Maracaibo, Trujillo, Campeche, and Cuba. French settlers in Hispaniola attacked Spanish towns. It was a bad decade for the *audiencia* of Santo Domingo: in 1669–71 a disease seriously damaged the island's cacao trees, while in 1673 an earthquake struck the city, followed by a hurricane in 1680.

Mariana, at the request of several Spanish governors, renewed her permission for *patentes de corso* in 1673. Spanish authorities soon captured and executed a Captain Thurston and one Diego el Mulato or Diego Grillo (like his namesake from 1629, an escapee from Havana), who had been harassing Spanish shipping. Drawn by this new opportunity, ships from the Bay of Biscay relocated to the Greater Antilles, and in 1674 Lynch wrote to England that Spanish galleons were expected, together with twenty 'Biscayners, Ostenders and Flushingers, which are likely to clear the Indies of all that infests them'.

Lynch tried to avoid offending either party. When the marquis de Maintenon brought a Spanish prize into Port Royal, Lynch refused him permission to sell the ship, but with 'all respect possible'. What Lynch could not avoid was the continuing question of trade with Spanish colonies. The new treaty went no further than allowing English ships in distress to call at Spanish ports. Any hopes that this would provide sufficient cover for regular commerce were quickly disappointed.

The logwood trade from the Yucatán peninsula was a particular source of friction. By the 1670s there were a few hundred men living scattered around the Términos Lagoon. The work was rough, the living conditions rougher, but it was a profitable business and, Jamaicans argued, it should be an open one, since there were no Spanish settlements there. The new treaty's recognition of Jamaica introduced the principle of possession by occupation; Lynch sent an old man to live as 'governor' of the Caymans simply to maintain a claim, and took a similar approach for the Virgin Islands, St Lucia, and Tobago. The government in London was more cautious. Henry Coventry, the secretary of state, advised unhelpfully in 1674 that Jamaican officials should 'neither forbid nor abett' the logwood trade.

Mariana and the *Consejo de las Indias* were not so indecisive. Some of the buccaneers who had scattered after Panamá found their way into Spanish service chasing logwooders (others, like Brasiliano, simply disappeared). Jelles de Lecat and Jan Reyning had sailed to the Caymans after Panamá and seized a *guardacosta* that De Lecat kept, but shortly afterwards they took Spanish commissions, apparently after marooning their English shipmates. Philip Fitzgerald, an Irish sailor, received a commission in Havana and captured several ships during 1672–73, reportedly torturing the crews in revenge for atrocities committed in Ireland by English soldiers during the civil wars two decades before.

In 1674 Charles II issued individual pardons for De Lecat and Fitzgerald as the 'chief instruments' of these depredations, but in the same year Fitzgerald sailed into Havana with English victims hanging from the yardarms. The next year a royal proclamation offered a reward for the head of 'Fitzgerald the Pirate'. What became of him is unknown. Reyning, though apparently catechised as a Catholic, sailed to Curaçao at the outbreak of the Third Anglo-Dutch War and became a local legend for his role in the island's defence. Others took their place, including a new *Armada de Barlovento* of five ships.

Despite the efforts of Jamaican governors to open a peaceful trade, these 'Biscayners' and *guardacostas* continued to seize English ships, and logwooders ashore, throughout the 1670s, with the captives often carried to Havana or Mexico City for execution or imprisonment and hard labour. One English sailor, Jack Hullock, tricked some Spanish soldiers by masquerading as his ship's captain, telling them he and his companions had only come hunting and that he had left his official documents aboard his ship. Hullock was treated with deference, given a horse to ride and chocolate to drink, and after this caper his shipmates always called him Captain Jack.

Some Spanish commanders were less respectful. When one English shipmaster produced a pass from Jamaica, the Spanish vice-admiral who had captured him 'wiped his breech with it and threw it at him again', forcing him to sign a false receipt that he had been paid for his purloined cargo.

Furious protests from Jamaica and the Privy Council received only vague promises of 'just satisfaction'.

Lord Vaughan was authorised to issue letters of reprisal for these outrages, though only after exploring peaceful options first. The threat of such retaliation had little effect, though. Spanish vessels had seized twenty-two English ships, according to a Jamaican report in February 1681, imprisoning many sailors, which 'absolutely ruined our Bay trade'. The report added that the logwood cutters, many of them former buccaneers, were prepared to take matters into their own hands.

Some of them had already done so, since they found ready accommodation outside Jamaica. Exquemelin wrote that after Lynch's arrival several transferred to Tortuga, while William Dampier, who will feature more prominently in our story later, recalled that 'the Privateer-Trade still continued' at Petit-Goâve, 'the Sanctuary and Asylum of all People of desperate Fortunes'. From there they cruised against Spanish shipping.

In 1674, for example, a ship reached Cartagena that had been attacked by an English vessel with a French commission and a crew of English, French,

A buccaneer frigate capturing a Spanish vessel, from Exquemelin's *Zee-roovers*. (Courtesy of the John Carter Brown Library)

Spanish, and Portuguese sailors and at least one '*mulato*'. They seized 6,000 *pesos* and boasted that Morgan would soon sail from England (which was true), bringing 4,000 men to attack Cartagena (which was not). The governor was so unnerved by the report that he asked Peru for help.

Three years later, the Spanish ambassador in London complained that one John Barnett had seized the *Buen Jesus de la Almas* with 46,000 *pesos* aboard. Lynch, then in London, pointed out that Barnett too was sailing with a French commission, and Carlisle later complained that these attacks were 'committed by a sort of man without [i.e., beyond] the reach of government', whereas 'the injuries that we suffer from [the Spanish] are from men in office and public employ', presumably meaning the *Armada de Barlovento* and the *guardacostas*. Such expostulations might preserve a governor's reputation in London, but they did not help to end buccaneering in Jamaica.

Indeed, the threat of war and the hostilities over trade meant that buccaneers' military and seafaring experience remained valuable. Lynch appointed Edward Collier to defend Port Royal and described Lawrence Prince as 'a sober man, very brave and an exact pilot'. John Morris, another old comrade of Morgan's, was sent out to pursue 'stragling privateers', because he was 'a very stout fellow, good pilot, and wee knowe will not turne pyrat'.

William Beeston accompanied Morris, and praised his navigational skills, on a voyage to hunt down De Lecat. They instead captured another experienced raider, Francis Witherborn, sailing together with a *flibustier* called Du Mangles. Peter Beckford, the secretary to the Council of Jamaica, even praised the *flibustiers*, writing 'were not the French from Tortudas daily galling [Spanish colonies] with privateers, we should conclude ourselves in some danger'.

Jamaican attitudes towards the *flibustiers* started to shift a few years later, as an English break with France and alliance with the Netherlands became much more likely when Willem of Orange, Charles II's nephew, married Mary, daughter to the duke of York, in 1677. The earl of Carlisle, who arrived in Jamaica the following year, expected war soon to begin with France. When he reached Port Royal, he reported that buccaneers were gathering there with the same anticipation.

Rumours in London and all along the Lesser Antilles said the same thing, since the *comte* D'Estrées was gathering another fleet for the Caribbean. In

1677 D'Estrées had recaptured Cayenne, before Binkes defeated him at Tobago and D'Estrées returned to France to refit. On the way to Curaçao in 1678 his fleet was wrecked, though D'Estrées himself survived. Michel de Grammont, a *flibustier* accompanying D'Estrées, apparently helped himself to wine, brandy, beef, and pork from the wrecks.

No Anglo-French war occurred, but disquiet persisted. When two French ships sailed near Port Royal in July 1679 and refused the customary salute (perhaps a deliberate insult), the forts and the ships exchanged a few shots. A few days later eight French warships came into sight. The commander, the *comte* d'Evreaux, explained that they simply needed supplies for their onward voyage to Cartagena, but Port Royal remained edgy and on guard.

At the time, in fact, Jacques Neveu de Pouancey, who replaced Bertrand d'Ogeron as *gouverneur* of Saint-Domingue in 1676, took a similar approach to the *flibustiers* to the one Lynch, Vaughan, and Carlisle had been ordered to take with the buccaneers. Pouancey moved the capital from Tortuga to Port-au-Paix on the mainland and encouraged sugar plantations and slavery, bringing Saint-Domingue into the same trends as Jamaica.

Pouancey wrote to Colbert in 1677 that he was making progress, although he estimated that there were still some thousand *flibustiers* living in the colony, particularly at Petit-Goâve. The war between France, the Netherlands, and Spain ended in 1678, with the Treaty of Nijmegen agreed the following year. However, Pouancey's efforts would be interrupted only a few years later when war broke out once more.

In Jamaica, it was local politics and legal questions, as much as warfare, that interfered with the governors' efforts against buccaneering. Lynch, during almost five years as governor, found plenty of opposition among Morgan's old acquaintances. Morgan had friends in London, too, including his relative William Morgan, deputy lieutenant of Monmouth, and the 20-year-old Christopher Monck, now duke of Albemarle after the death of his father George. Morgan got along well in London society: John Gadham, an astronomer, dedicated the fifth edition of his *Jamaica Almanack* to Morgan, and he and Modyford dined with John Evelyn, where they talked of Morgan's 'gallant exploit' at Panamá, as Evelyn described it in his diary.

So well, in fact, that after a year Morgan was invited to prepare a plan for Jamaica's defence, which he then discussed with the king. When, in January 1674, the government decided to recall Lynch and replace him with the earl of Carlisle, they named Morgan deputy governor and around the same time released Modyford from the Tower. He too would return, as chief justice. Carlisle demurred, so the king selected Lord Vaughan instead. Samuel Pepys called Vaughan 'one of the lewdest fellows of the age', which in Restoration London was saying something.

Morgan was also fond of a good time, if the stories of his revelries in Port Royal's taverns hold any truth, but he and Vaughan did not get on. Morgan arrived in Jamaica first and Vaughan was suspicious that Morgan had deliberately stolen a march on him. It did not help that Morgan's ship ran aground on the Isla de Vaca on the way and was rescued by Thomas Rogers, an old comrade now sailing with a French commission.

Morgan's continued connection with buccaneers was the main accusation against him by Vaughan and Lynch, who were soon working closely together. When he heard of Morgan's appointment, Lynch wrote to London of his astonishment that they would 'send the Admirall of the Pryvateers to governe this Island'. Fairly soon after his arrival, Morgan apparently told old friends that they were 'welcome in any harbour', and his brother-in-law Robert Byndloss may have acted as Ogeron's agent, collecting prize shares for him in Jamaica.

Vaughan soon complained that Morgan was trying to 'set up a privateer faction', and in 1676 he removed Morgan from the Council of Jamaica on charges of correspondence with buccaneers in Tortuga, promising them 'abundance of safety' in Jamaica. These letters, written by Morgan's secretary, had in fact been submitted to Vaughan for his approval, so they were hardly indicative of subterfuge, and they never even made it to Tortuga. Both sides sent their stories to London, where very little was done with them.

Perhaps Morgan was indeed in contact with buccaneers, but there were other things going on within this dispute. Lynch probably also resented Morgan's criticism of his time as governor, including that he had failed to pay the admiral's and king's shares for a prize, carrying 544 enslaved people who were sold for some £7,000, brought in by a ship Lynch had commissioned during the last Anglo-Dutch War. Vaughan, meanwhile, antagonised Jamaica's colonial elite by his efforts to impose stricter royal control over the Assembly through legislative procedure, a contest the Assembly eventually won.

Those same colonists who opposed Vaughan praised Morgan for 'his eminent and famed exploits'. Some of them had already begged London to replace Vaughan with Carlisle when, in March 1678, Vaughan abruptly announced that he was leaving, possibly because he had received no funds for some time and had heard that Carlisle would soon be taking over. Morgan stayed on with Carlisle and the two worked effectively together until Carlisle sailed for London in 1680, leaving Morgan in charge once more.

These personal and political wranglings spilled over into, and were exacerbated by, continued uncertainties in colonial maritime law. In 1672 Lynch arrested Peter Johnson, whose ship had run aground and who claimed he had set sail before hearing of Lynch's recent prohibition on plundering. Lynch handed Johnson over to Thomas Modyford junior, who, perhaps angry about his father's arrest and imprisonment in London, instructed a jury to acquit Johnson, despite a full confession. Lynch, furious, presided over a retrial that condemned Johnson, whom he executed, though he reprieved Johnson's crew, sending them to England. Royal officials informed Lynch that they approved his judgement, but not his 'manner of proceeding therein'.

When Beeston and Morris brought in Witherborn and Du Mangles a while later, Port Royal was under martial law, so Lynch tried both 'privateers' (as he called them) at a council of war aboard the *Assistance* frigate. He found Witherborn guilty but, perhaps mindful of the former reprimand, sent him to London, on the same ship as Morgan; once there, Witherborn was impressed into the navy. Charles II himself instructed Lynch to 'try all pirates by the maritime law' in 1673, although his meaning – whether the 1536 statute, the civil law procedure recognised in other countries, or something else – is unclear.

Vaughan was even more irregular than Lynch. He arrested Robert Deane, another old buccaneer who sailed into Port Royal after a long absence, and accused him of seizing an English ship while flying foreign colours, without any lawful commission. Being chief judge as well as governor, Vaughan summarily condemned Deane. Again, his superiors in London concluded that it was 'not warranted by the laws of this Kingdom' and breached the 1536 law on piracy. They ordered Vaughan to release Deane, which he had in fact already done due to a public outcry in which Morgan sided vocally with Deane. Vaughan maintained that merely the threat of execution had led to his 'reclaiming' former buccaneers and done no real harm, though when he tried to persuade John Coxon's crew to hand over their captain in return for a pardon, they refused.

The broader tussle between Vaughan and the Assembly touched on maritime affairs, too, particularly the slave trade and the Royal African Company's monopoly. Before his arrival the Assembly had passed a law allowing 'free importation' (by non-Company interlopers), as well as permitting local admiralty courts to adjudicate prizes. These two issues came together when one court approved a Dutch slave ship captured by the Scottish captain James Browne, again under a French commission. Vaughan overruled the judgement, arguing that the enslaved people had been 'piratically taken' and should be returned to the Dutch shippers; the government in London this time supported Vaughan and cancelled the 'free importation' law.

Browne escaped, but the question of foreign commissions like his had become more pressing. Royal proclamations continued to ban sailors from entering foreign service and in 1674 the Dutch and English governments agreed a treaty that forbade subjects of either state from taking a commission from the other. In 1678 the Treaty of Nijmegen included similar conditions. The *Ordonnance de la Marine* in 1681 stated that any French ship taking a foreign commission, or carrying more than one, or flying the wrong flag, would be punished as pirates. It also declared the goods of enemies, pirates, '*fourbans*', and anyone else at sea without the licence of a prince, state, or sovereign as lawful prize.

This issue reared up again in Jamaica when, in 1677, John Coxon and William Barnes, together with one *Capitaine* Legarde, arrived after sacking Santa Marta, north of Cartagena, bringing away with them the newly appointed bishop of Panamá. They met a cool reception from Vaughan, who released their prisoner. Morgan, with blunt and possibly deliberate irony, presented this honoured guest with some valuable vestments stolen from the cleric's new diocese.

The Assembly hurriedly issued a new ban on any Jamaican serving a foreign sovereign, on pain of death, allowing three months for those who wished to surrender themselves. Several hundred men returned from Tortuga to take up the proffered pardon – among them James Browne. Vaughan immediately had Browne arrested and condemned, though reprieving his men. Browne appealed to the Assembly, who warned Vaughan that 'all our privateers out [at sea] may think this Act a snare ... and so become most dangerous enemies'.

Vaughan, however, had already signed Browne's death warrant and did not think him 'a fit object of mercy'. Vaughan had Browne executed immediately, before either a stay of execution sent by the Assembly or a writ of *habeas corpus* from chief justice Thomas Modyford could arrive. Vaughan also dissolved the Assembly, and left Jamaica a few months afterwards.

In London, the Privy Council refused to approve Jamaica's new law, fearing that the death sentence would scare buccaneers away. Instead they granted Jamaica authority to conduct piracy trials, based on the 1536 statute. The ban on foreign commissions therefore lapsed after two years, as did all Jamaican legislation that did not get London's endorsement. Curiously, it seems that Jamaica's colonial leadership were prepared to go further in prosecuting pirates than the government in London.

Henry Morgan had become a leading figure in that campaign against his erstwhile profession. In 1679, when the ban lapsed, Carlisle appointed Morgan to chair a committee on the matter. They acknowledged that buccaneers 'never want specious protests for irreconcilable hostility' because of the 'horrid butcheries' committed by *guardacostas*. Nevertheless, they concluded that Spanish 'confidence' in Jamaican trade would be greater 'could these ravenous vermin be destroyed'.

Morgan and his fellows advised that the Privy Council should approve the Jamaican laws and send out more frigates. Because the buccaneers remained 'extraordinarily well manned and much better armed', the governor, they thought, 'can do little from want of ships to reduce the privateers and of plain law to punish them'.

They did not exaggerate. Carlisle had sent the *Success* to chase Peter Harris, but this inaccurately named frigate was wrecked pursuing him through the South Cays off Cuba; the shipmaster was court-martialled, flogged, jailed for a year, and barred from royal service. Late in 1679, John Coxon and Bartholomew Sharp arrived in Port Royal with a cargo of indigo captured near Honduras, but were not apprehended and swiftly gathered four other captains. They set out in January 1680, collecting more recruits on the way. We shall follow their story later.

Carlisle sailed for London with the committee's recommendations, to consult the Privy Council. Morgan soon afterwards wrote to London that he had several buccaneers imprisoned awaiting trial, though others 'not daring to enter any of our ports, keep on the wing'. He continued to feel the want of 'plain law'. He got into a long dispute with one Francis Mingham after Morgan, as admiralty judge, condemned Mingham's ship for failing to declare brandy casks to the customs. During the numerous arguments and counter-arguments, in both Port Royal and London, Morgan bemoaned that 'it is hard to find unbiassed juries in Jamaica'. He cited a case where a ship smuggling several cases of Irish soap was acquitted because the jury believed one witness's bold assertion that the cargo consisted of victuals on which you could live for a month.

Despite these hindrances, Morgan boasted to London that he 'spare[d] no care to put down this growing evil'. In London, Carlisle insisted that Jamaica's frigates had captured more pirates than the *Armada de la Barlovento* had, and in 1681 Morgan sent a force of soldiers to arrest the 'powerful and desperate pirate' Jacob Evertson, a *vrijbuiter* who had evaded French and Spanish frigates before anchoring off Jamaica. Evertson and a few others escaped, but six Spanish sailors were sent to Cartagena for trial and an admiralty court condemned sixty-four English mariners to death.

The Assembly decided not to carry out that sentence lest it scare off others who might come in. However, on 2 July 1681 they passed An Act for Restraining and Punishing Privateers and Pirates, explicitly following the 1536 act, and in November proclaimed that all treaties should be 'inviolably kept', repeating the death sentence for those who took a foreign commission. In 1683 the Assembly renewed the piracy law and closed some loopholes. Anyone trading with pirates or privateers was liable to prosecution; officers who refused to pursue a pirate would be fined and informers rewarded; pirates resisting arrest could be lawfully killed.

The reason behind this change of heart for Morgan, and for the colonial leaders who had profited from his voyages, is made clear by another law the Assembly passed the very same day in 1681: an Act for Better Ordering of Slaves. Morgan himself was a substantial planter and slaveholder, with an estate of 6,000 acres and 109 enslaved people at the time of his death. He led military campaigns against maroon communities in Jamaica during the 1670s and 1680s. In 1679–80 he occupied the offices of deputy governor, lieutenant-general, vice-admiral, colonel-commandant of the Port Royal regiment, judge of the admiralty court, justice of the peace, and *custos rotulorum* (public recordkeeper).

In this regard Morgan resembled the Modyfords and Lord Vaughan, who held extensive lands. Lynch owned a whopping 28,000 acres when he died. Lawrence Prince, Edward Collier, John Morris, and Joseph Bradley all purchased Jamaican estates. John Peake, Morgan's secretary during his voyages, became a planter and eventually Speaker of the Assembly.

Nor was such a transition peculiar to the British Empire. A similar figure is the marquis de Maintenon, who first served in naval warships in the Caribbean in 1679–72 and returned in 1674–76 to lead attacks on Margarita, Trinidad, and Cumaná. He became a sugar planter on Marie-Galante and a hunter of *flibustiers* in the early 1680s, then Louis XIV granted him a monopoly over trade with the Spanish mainland, especially Venezuela.

Perhaps it is inaccurate to call these poachers-turned-gamekeepers hypocritical (that other kind of 'enemies of all', according to Bartolus de Sassoferrato). When Morgan and his committee condemned 'the detest-able depredations of some of our nation ... under the colour of French commissions', he probably considered these different to his own actions under English commission.

In any case, with this new legislation, the first in any English colony, the plantation elite sought to put the island's buccaneering era firmly behind it. Except that it was not to be the end. In fact, the buccaneers were about to go global.

II

TURNING TIDES

THE ARABIAN SEA,
YAWM AS-SABT 7 SAFAR 1107
(SATURDAY, 7 SEPTEMBER 1695)

T he ship sailed east, towards the rising sun. It would be among the last to do so that year. The *mawsim al-kaws*, the south-westerly summer winds that propelled ships from Africa and Arabia towards India, would soon cease. Through the winter, the winds reversed, the *rīḥ al-ṣabā* shifting round a half-circle to the north-east. Time then for westward voyages.

These winds were as fickle as any other, falling into a flat calm or blowing so strong and carrying such hard rains that many ports of western India closed in high summer. Nevertheless, the monsoon cycle of winds and currents had, since prehistoric times, shaped the intricate trading world of the Indian Ocean.

The *mawsim al-kaws* carried this ship homewards, after threading the dangerous shoals of the *Bahr Al-Qulzum*, the Red Sea, and passing the even more treacherous strait known as *Bab-el-Mandeb*, the Gate of Grief. It had left the Gulf of Aden and now expected to reach Surat in a little more than a week. Several hundred passengers aboard were returning from the *Hajj*, the annual pilgrimage to Mecca. As they sailed they watched for Girnar, a mountain in north Saurasthra, the common landfall of ships coming to Gujarat from the west. The profile of its twin peaks would tell them whether they were on course.

The ships in this returning fleet had become strung out, but the people aboard the *Ganj-i-Sāwai* were not unduly alarmed. Theirs was the greatest ship of Surat, and heavily armed. In the early seventeenth century an English visitor noted pilgrim ships of 1,600 tons sailing from Surat to Mocha; Portuguese observers described them as floating fortresses. These vessels were well manned, too. Abu'l Fazl, a statesman of the Mughal Empire, listed twelve categories of sailor in his encyclopaedia, including the *nakhuda* who directed the voyage, the *mu'allim* or navigator, the *surhang* or mate, as well as store-keepers, pursers, gunners, and lookouts, besides the mariners (and the *tandil* who commanded them).

Most likely this ship was made of Malabar teak, favoured by shipwrights in the Indian Ocean, stronger than anything in European yards. Its planks may have been sewn with coir ropes, in the traditional manner, although by the end of the seventeenth century European ships were a familiar sight in these waters and shipwrights easily adopted some techniques and styles, including metal nails. *Kotias* built in Gujarat or on the Malabar coast by now resembled galleons, with high, square, ornate sterns.

When they first spied several ships at anchor near a headland, they were probably not too concerned, nor when the lookouts picked out English flags. Only a few years before, the East India Company made war on the Mughal Empire in pursuit of commercial concessions, but that went disastrously for the out-matched Company, forcing them to sue for peace. English ships were once again a familiar sight in Surat and at the Company's castle of Bombay (now Mumbai), a Portuguese stronghold given to Charles II when he married Catarina de Bragança, and by him to the Company.

Perhaps the crew and passengers felt more afraid as these ships hurriedly raised their anchors and sails and set out in pursuit. No doubt the *nakhuda*, *mu'allim*, and other chief officers had a hurried consultation. They knew of pilgrim ships seized in the last few years by European plunderers, and the rumours must have run among everyone else aboard as well. Possibly they recognised one of the ships as a Surat vessel already taken as a prize. The *nakhuda*, Muḥammad Ibrahim, cleared his decks and loaded his guns.

Even the largest of these English ships was much smaller than the *Ganj-i-Sāwai*. They all had a ragged look, as well they might after their long voyage around Africa. Yet they were closing fast. The *Ganj-i-Sāwai*'s cannon thundered and for two hours this firepower kept the attackers at bay, while the passengers huddled below decks, praying desperately for deliverance.

Then disaster struck – a cannon exploded, killing the gun crew and panicking their shipmates. A shot felled the mainmast and the attackers rushed in. Muḥammad Hāshim, a merchant in Gujarat who later wrote a historical narrative under his ennobled title Khāfī Khān, claimed that the ship was so well armed they should easily have resisted this attack. However, according to Hāshim (who admittedly was not present, borrowed heavily from other writers, and invented some of his stories), Ibrahim had already disappeared below decks. Another account claims that he armed some enslaved girls and sent them up to fight. The *Ganj-i-Sāwai* was swiftly captured.

For several days the ships drifted together while the captors pillaged their prize of all its wealth – worth over 5 million *rupees*, about £520,000 at the time – and tortured passengers to reveal their valuable belongings. Hāshim wrote that the assailants spent a week 'stripping the men, and dishonouring the women, both old and young', while one of the attackers himself later admitted that his companions 'Lay with the Indian Women aboard these ships', especially those with 'Habitts and riches in jewells [that] appeared of better quality than the rest'.

An English merchant in India wrote to London soon afterwards that 'the Pyrates ... did so very barbarously by the People of the Gunsway ... to make them confess where their Money was ... and forced several other Women'. The wife and nurse of one eminent man had died by suicide, this correspondent claimed, and Hāshim wrote that many women leapt into the sea or stabbed themselves.

That English merchant acted as an agent for the emperor Muḥī al-Dīn Muḥammad, whose regnal name was ʿĀlamgīr, more commonly remembered as Aurangzeb, an epithet meaning 'Ornament of the Throne'. The *Ganj-i-Sāwai* belonged to Aurangzeb himself, and popular myth states that his daughter or granddaughter was aboard (even if this is untrue, women of the imperial court, and perhaps even royal relatives, may well have been). The merchant added in his letter, 'All this will raise a black cloud at Court, which we wish may not produce a severe storm.'

That is exactly what happened. Riots rocked Surat when the ship limped into port with its survivors, and the governor arrested forty Company employees and all other English residents. These prisoners wrote pleadingly to Bombay, whose governor appealed to Aurangzeb, promising to compensate the losses, by which means he narrowly prevented a besieging army.

Muḥammad Hāshim visited Bombay not long afterwards. Though warned by the Portuguese captain with whom he sailed to be on his guard, Hāshim recorded that he was welcomed courteously by the governor, who asked him why English traders had recently been imprisoned. Hāshim replied, apparently, 'You do not acknowledge that shameful action, worthy of the reprobation of all sensible men, which was perpetrated by your wicked men.'

He then added a curious detail. Several acquaintances aboard the *Ganj-i-Sāwai*, both wealthy and poor, had told Hāshim that among the captors were those 'in the dress and with the looks of Englishmen, and on whose hands and bodies there were marks, wounds and scars'. These scars, they said, came from fighting in the Mughal siege of Bombay during the recent war, and 'to-day the scars have been removed from our hearts'. The governor denied all responsibility. They may once have been Company soldiers, he admitted, but had since joined the '*dingmars*, or *sahanas*, who lay violent hands on ships upon the sea, and with them they are serving as pirates'.

Aurangzeb and his subjects were far from convinced. Unsurprisingly, Asian trading partners suspected that raiders flying European flags acted in concert with official trading companies. Hāshim believed that the commerce of Bombay was insufficient to pay for its garrison, and so the Company made up the shortfall through piracy. He compared the 'reprobate English' to a 'lawless sort of men ... notorious for their piracies' and to the Marathas, longtime enemies of the Mughals. Aurangzeb warned the Company that trade would continue only once the captor of the *Ganj-i-Sāwai*, the notorious Henry Every, was himself caught.

This incident reflects a significant change in the history of piracy in the last two decades of the seventeenth century (or the early twelfth century, in the *al-taqwīm al-hijrī*, or Islamic calendar). As buccaneers expanded their activities into the Pacific and Indian Oceans, they were no longer a useful, if unpredictable, tool for European imperial expansion, as their earlier fellows had been. They were now a direct threat to it.

That made it imperative for European empires to brand these maritime marauders as 'enemies of all', but even more difficult for them to do so. This situation was most threatening to the English Empire: they got the blame in India, while at the same time many of this new generation sailed from the English colonies in North America.

The struggle to define and control piracy that had taken place in Jamaica now played out across the empire. The government's policies collided with legal practices and popular opinions, which still accommodated plundering. A reckoning came with the voyages of two men, Henry Every and William Kidd, who have since become pirate legends. The meaning of piracy, and the future of the empire, hung in the balance.

8

A RETCHLESS CRUE

A new product hit the shelves of Amsterdam's *boekverkopers* in 1678: *De Americaensche Zee-roovers*, by A. O. Exquemelin. Arriving in Tortuga in 1663 as an *engagé*, Exquemelin became a buccaneer a little while later, probably as a surgeon. He may not have participated in all of Henry Morgan's voyages, but he was certainly at Panamá, after which he joined one of the ships raiding along the Mosquito Coast.

By 1674 Exqumemelin was in Amsterdam, where he visited the notary Adraen Lock to draw up a letter of attorney in favour of his uncle, Willem van der Putte, a resident in the city. Exquemelin, who said in this document that he lived at Valenciennes, then in the Spanish Netherlands, was bound outward as chief surgeon on an expedition led by Michiel de Ruyter against the French Caribbean. Exquemelin probably returned to Amsterdam by 1676, when this contract was cancelled, and in 1679 he passed the city's exam to register as a surgeon.

Some scholars have identified Exquemelin with Hendrik Barentszoon Smeeks, from Zwolle, who served the *Vereenigde Oostindische Compagnie*, survived shipwreck and a voyage in an open boat from Australia to Java, then wound up in Tortuga. Smeeks was back in Zwolle and a barber-surgeon by 1680, and died in 1720. However, a marriage certificate in Saint-Malo in 1690 for one Alexandre Ollivier Exquemelin and Julienne le Grand describes him as a native of Honfleur, and this couple baptised two children in Saint-Malo. This Exquemelin probably died before 1711, since he was not a signatory at either of his daughter's two weddings after that date.

If little is known for certain about the author, *Zee-roovers* proved one of the two most impactful books in the history of piracy, alongside the *General History*. Its descriptions of figures like Henry Morgan and François

L'Olonnais, accompanied by engraved illustrations, unsparingly showed the savagery of their attacks on Spanish towns.

The book introduced the stories of these raiders to an international audience. A German translation appeared in 1679, possibly done by Exquemelin himself, a Spanish edition followed in 1681, printed in Cologne, and two English publishers put out versions in 1684, under the title of *Bucaniers of America*. These texts are probably responsible for shifting the meaning of 'buccaneer', in English, away from *boucanier* in French and towards what were still, then, often called 'privateers'. A French version, *Histoire des avanturiers*, appeared in 1686.

Exquemelin, who presumably took his share in the action and the plunder, wrote often in third person about other buccaneers and usually presented his former fellows negatively. Or perhaps the publishers did that to drive sales, as printers were not shy about altering authors' work as they saw fit. The front page of the original edition showed two sword-wielding figures, standing over Indigenous and Spanish victims, various scenes of battle and torture spread above and below them, and between them the title, promising an account of all the '*Onmenselijke Vreetheeden*' – inhuman cruelties – committed by English and French '*Roovers*' (or robbers). A Dutch readership who had gone through three wars against England in the last three decades, and was just finishing six years of war against France, probably recognised this depiction. Perhaps Exquemelin's service with De Ruyter in the war shaped his writing afterwards.

In Dutch, Exquemelin wrote that he named his subjects 'Zee-Roovers, not knowing that they had any other title, as they were supported by no Princes'. In Spanish '*Zee-Roovers*' became '*Piratas de America*', going even further in condemnation of the marauders responsible for so much damage to the empire. The first English translation was taken from this Spanish and included its elaborations, while the second claimed to be 'Made English from the Dutch copy'; both referred to 'Pirates of America'.

Buccaneers and *flibustiers* took their commissions from colonial governors and, as we have seen, were sometimes disowned by the imperial authorities. Yet the word 'pirate' had wider connotations than just the question of legal status, and in this regard *Zee-roovers* drew on, and drove forwards, the swirl of contemporary ideas about what it meant to be a plunderer.

Royal proclamations and legislation concerning piracy did more than just insist on plundering licences or specific procedures for prize law. They also sought to shape the public image of piracy. Elizabeth I's declarations condemned 'lewde and ill disposed ... disordered persons mixt of sundry

The title page of Exquemelin's *Zee-roovers*, showing scenes of buccaneer cruelty and destruction. (Courtesy of the John Carter Brown Library)

nations', who committed 'crimes most hateful to her minde, & scandalous to her peaceable government'. James VI and I described pirates as 'accustomed and habituated to spoile and rapine, insensible and desperate of the peril they draw upon themselves, and the imputation they cast upon the honour of their Soveraigne'. A later proclamation forbidding foreign service, in 1668, took a dim view of those with 'inclinations to Rapine and Licencious courses' rather than 'honest Imployments at home'.

This official line, of pirates (including those who took foreign commissions) as badly behaved, evil men, cut off from society and beyond redemption, was an important ingredient in the concept of 'enemies of all' that shaped both legal discourse and practice and wider culture. Nor was it restricted to government proclamations. Another grimly popular genre of the day comprised narratives of crimes, trials, and executions. Piracy often featured here too.

The execution of several pirates in 1608, for example, prompted an anonymous pamphlet in which some of the biographies were presented as written or recounted by the culprits themselves. As one of these first-person narratives switches to third person halfway through, it seems more likely that an opportunistic printer, perhaps helped by someone from the admiralty court, compiled the pamphlet.

Most of these figures were presented as extravagant, violent, ruthless and dangerous. John Downes was 'cruell and merciles', turning to piracy to pay off debts run up through his 'superfluous expence & retchles [reckless] life'. James Harris (or the narrator) 'blush[ed] to report the rapine that the hands of so fewe did execute on the bodies and substance of many'. Most of the narratives end with a customarily devout repentance by the criminals, before their death.

John Jennings was even worse, of 'meane and low' education, 'bluntly resolved ... to attaine to it then by hooke or by crooks', leading 'a retchles crue' who committed 'many heinous spoyles' only 'to maintaine ryot'. Jennings supposedly admitted that 'his lusts and ryots, [were] the causers of his ruine' and that he 'rejoyced more to heare the Cannons voyce that bid me to fight, then the Church-bell that cald me to prayer'. So great was his disregard for authority and propriety that in one anecdote, during a snowball fight in the yard of the Marshalsea, where admiralty prisoners awaited trial, he was told that Harris had arrived, to which, apparently, he said, 'I love him well, but [if] the hangman himselfe were comming I would throw out my throw first.'

An almost identical picture appeared in a flurry of pamphlets following the trial and execution in 1675 of George Cusack, an Irish captain in French service who plundered in the North Sea and sold his takings in New England before his own capture. One pamphlet called him a 'piratical Caper' (from *kaper*), while another described him as 'the most signal Sea-Robber, that perhaps this age hath known'. He had been 'a grand Mutineer' during his early career in the navy, then seized a ship and went off raiding for fifteen years, supposedly abandoning victims in small boats 'to the mercy of the Ocean', while telling his men, 'I will make you Officers in Hell under me.'

At the trial, Cusack's French commission was considered 'nothing worth', because it was in someone else's name, but even if in his name it would have breached recent treaties and proclamations. Cusack reportedly protested at his trial that the jury were 'Citizens; who did not, he said, understand Marine affairs' and asked to be tried 'by men of our own Trade'. His phrasing was 'understood in another sense [that] made not only the Audience, but his fellow Prisoners to laugh heartily'. Neither the appeal nor the humour saved him.

These accounts lost no opportunity to drive home the point that Cusack's 'Trade' was piracy and that 'amongst all the rapacious violencies practised by wicked Men, there is scarce any more destructive to Society and Commerce then that of Piracy'. Yet again these texts invoked the term '*Humani Generis hostes*, Publique Enemies of Mankind', no better than 'Common vermine'.

Yet not all pirates were equal. Contemporary authors reserved their greatest vilification for North African corsairs. Europeans described these corsairs as 'a sort of outlaws ... that live in enmity with all the world', as William Monson called them, or 'a dissolute and resolute company of Sea-farers and *Pirates*', according to merchant Lewes Roberts. Edward Barlow, a sailor who visited that region several times during the 1660s (though never as a captive), called them 'pirates to all Christian nations'. Many other writers of the time used the same terms.

Even worse than the Magharibi corsairs were the European converts among them. John Smith, who started his own military career fighting against the Ottoman Empire in Hungary, described such a 'runnagado' who 'turned Turke' as 'hatefull to all Christian Princes' in a short comment on 'the bad life, qualities and conditions of Pyrats' which he published in his *True Travels, Adventures and Observations* of 1630. They were the epitome of pirates, Smith thought: 'riotous, quarrellous, treacherous, blasphemous, and villanous ... all they got, they basely consumed it ... so disjoynted, disordered, debawched, and miserable' that 'any wise man would rather live amongst wilde beasts, than them'.

Most notorious of all English renegades was John Ward, who took the name Yusuf Reis after his conversion; his Dutch companion Simon Danseker was also well known. A particular accusation made against some of those executed in 1608 was that they had been 'an arch-pyrate, and formerly a confederate with that famous *Ward*'.

Perhaps capitalising on the attention drawn by that trial, several short accounts of Ward's life were published soon afterwards. These texts hinted at his prior notoriety: one assumed the reader 'hast heard much talke of one captain *Ward*', while another noted how 'so many flying fables, and rumoring tales have beene spread, of the fame, or rather indeede infamie ... of this notorious and arch pirate'.

All these accounts stressed Ward's 'mean' parentage and 'lowe' estate, 'as base in Birth as bad in condition'. He was a fisherman from Kent who joined the navy at the end of Elizabeth's reign, in his fifties, and then led away some similarly disaffected sailors in a stolen bark. They told of the

fabulous riches he plundered from Venetian ships and his rise to promi-
nence through association with the *dey* of Tunis. His actions 'had cleane
taken away the feeling of his wickednes' and he only enjoyed 'the prosecuting of mischiefe'. Ward apparently considered a day wasted 'wherein
he did not triumph in the doing of some notable villany', and he spent his
life in 'a continuall battaile and defiance with Christians'.

One pamphlet told of him living 'in his accustomed riotous and las-
civious manner' in Tunis, while another called him 'a mad rascall, [who]
would sweare well, [and] drinke stiffe ... his successe hath made him
desperate and resolute, his riches have made him proud ... like the *Sea*,
alwaies *unsatisfied*'. None of these accounts mentioned that Ward asked
James VI and I for a pardon and was refused, probably to avoid giving
offence to Venice.

In fact, Ward's most scandalous act was not his piracy but his apostasy, though he was also portrayed as one who, in 'the frantick errours
of his owne wil ... neither feared God nor the devill'. In 1612 the most
famous fictionalisation of Ward appeared in print, Robert Daborne's play
A Christian Turn'd Turk. The play comments briefly on piracy, calling
Ward a 'bloud-thirsty monster', but its dramatic core was a dumb-show
depiction of his conversion, silence being the only style considered safe
for a Christian audience. Danseker also featured as a contrasting 'Dutch
Cavaliere', who told his men 'let's redeeme our honour ... by some worthy
deed' and attempted to destroy Tunis' fleet of 'Pyrats' (Danseker did
indeed free 300 enslaved Europeans, in 1609, and returned to Marseille).

Daborne had Ward repent at the end of the play, in his last dying speech
warning, 'All you that live by theft and Piracies ... heaven is just ... dispaire
attends on bloud and lust.' Such a death was satisfying to contemporary
audiences, but totally inaccurate. Even the pamphlets about him had to
admit that Ward lived out his days 'in a most princely and *magnificent* state',
residing in 'a very stately house, farre more fit for a Prince, then a pirate'.

Ward remained notorious for decades. One sailor imprisoned in Tunis
during the 1650s wrote of seeing an old hulk 'which was said to be [the
ship of] Captain Ward, the great English pirate'. Ballads about Ward
continued to appear throughout the seventeenth century, telling of his
'drunkennesse and letchery'. There were plenty of other piratical ballads
too, including one about Scottish raider Andrew Barton, which survives
in print from the 1630s and which evolved into 'The Lofty Tall Ship', a
staple folk tune today most commonly called 'Henry Martin'.

It did not help Ward's public image that he plundered English ships,
while other contemporaries did not (or so they said). However, the point

I wish to make here is that while the image of a pirate provided in official proclamations evidently circulated more widely, it was, yet again, defined by more than just the act of unauthorised plundering.

The representations of Ward tapped into wider anxieties about Islam in Christian Europe. Captivity narratives set in the Maghreb were another popular genre, circulating in print from the 1580s to the 1790s. The publisher of the first English translation of the Qur'an, in 1649, was thrown in prison. The peculiar revulsion reserved for 'renegadoes', and the focus on Ward's conversion, demonstrates just how much ideas about piracy were influenced by contemporary currents in culture and society.

This particular attention to Mediterranean corsairs also reveals how the legal intricacies I discussed earlier leaked into wider discussions of piracy, because of questions about the status of the Ottoman regencies. Most Christian rulers did not recognise their legitimacy (Gentili doubted it, although selectively). Louis XIV insisted that their representatives should not be treated as the equals of those of sovereign states, and had no qualms about purchasing Algerian captives in Livorno and Genoa to be enslaved in his galleys, despite protests from the *dey* of Algiers that his city and France were at peace. If the regencies were not proper sovereigns, then their corsairs were pirates.

Yet no European state had the military might to destroy the regencies – not for want of trying – and all Christian governments therefore negotiated treaties with them, introducing a system of passes to protect each nation's ships, which consuls often sold on to other nations' ships as well. That implicitly recognised the regencies as legitimate. French officials sometimes provided documents to Algerian and Tunisian corsairs to prove that they were not pirates.

Charles Molloy, an Irish lawyer who worked in London, grappled with some of these issues in *De Jure Maritimo* (*On Maritime Law*), first published in 1676. Molloy repeated the classic '*Hostis humani generis*' reading of piracy, in which he included those with commissions who 'instead of taking prises from the Enemy, turn Pyrats, and spoil the subjects of other Friends'.

However, there are hints of doubt laced throughout the text. For example, he noted that 'a Company of *Pyrats* or *Freebooters* are not a Common-wealth', even if 'they may keep a kind of *equallity* among themselves'. In that assertion he followed Gentili, Grotius, and others. Yet when

Molloy wrote that 'Pyrats and Robbers that make not a Society' should have no 'succour by the Law of Nations', he rather implied that pirates *could* 'make a Society', by which he meant 'such a Society as the Laws of Nations accounts lawful'.

The Magharibi regencies had done exactly that. Molloy described them as 'Pirates that have reduced themselves into a Government of State', which 'makes them not Pirates (enemies of mankind) but gives them the status of enemies (in war)'. Though he called them 'indeed Pirates', he admitted that, 'having acquired the reputation of a Government, they cannot properly be esteemed Pirates', but must be treated as lawful enemies. They were not, in fact, 'enemies of all'.

De Jure Maritimo included chapters on letters of marque and reprisal, and on 'Privateers and Capers', both of which Molloy characterised as recent developments. That these are two separate chapters reflects once again the transitional nature of prize law at this time: Molloy included letters of marque within this discussion of reprisal, rather than as wartime commissions, even though by this time that distinction was dissolving in practice. Moreover, while he assumed that 'privateers' should have commissions, follow proper prize procedures, and suffer death for plundering friends or allies, he also recognised that sovereigns might issue a 'general' commission, permitting all of their subjects to plunder their enemies without requiring an individual licence to do so.

Perhaps Molloy's most interesting comment is this one: 'it were well [privateers] were restrained by consent of all Princes', because 'all good Men account them but one remove from a Pyrat who without any respect to the cause, or having any injury done them ... spoil Men and Goods, making even a trade and calling of it, amidst the calamities of War'. Here, it seems to me, Molloy is using 'privateer' in that wider sense, that communal sense, particularly associated with the buccaneers, and he exhibits a lawyerly disquiet about their tendencies – though he still distinguishes them from pirates.

Molloy's text was not a Latin treatise aimed at other learned theorists (like those of earlier writers), but a handbook, and a very successful one, going through seven editions by 1722 and another three before 1778. These questions of what actually constituted piracy were not considered just in courtrooms or government offices, but in the popular press, which expanded enormously across the seventeenth century. During the 1640s, for example, Parliamentarian writers complained of Royalist 'Arch-Pyrates' who 'with roaving and robberies ... make [Falmouth] a kind of Algier', while Royalist sympathisers replied in kind. One Parliamentarian captain was even accused of being 'a Renegado ... circumcised in the law of Mohammed'.

This nexus between law, politics, and print is especially evident in an intriguing pamphlet called *Lex Talionis* published in 1681 (the title invokes the biblical idea of an eye for an eye). The author, George Carew, appealed to the king and parliament in relation to two ships belonging to William Courten, worth apparently £150,000, which had been seized in the Indian Ocean by Dutch ships almost forty years before. Courten's heirs and co-investors pursued the case in the Netherlands, and during the Second and Third Anglo-Dutch Wars they secured letters of reprisal. The losses had still not been recouped, so in 1680 Courten's creditors pressured Carew, his main heir and administrator, to set forth ships for further reprisal.

Carew did so twice, and on both occasions the crews were arrested, tried, and acquitted for 'not acting with a Fellonious intent, under the colour of that Commission for Reprisals', even though the consortium were not permitted to retain any plunder. In a subsequent Chancery lawsuit the Lord Chancellor declared that Carew's 'Letters of Marque', like all others, had been cancelled by the Treaty of Breda in 1667 (and he moved 'reason of state' as additional justification).

Carew mounted a legal counter-campaign, arguing that the Crown had no right to cancel his letters, because while general commissions were 'an Act of War', particular ones like his were 'a Process at Law'. Carew was unsuccessful in that argument, but the case shows that mariners with erroneous commissions, but not a 'Fellonious intent', might not be considered pirates; that the laws of prize remained debatable, by subjects as well as sovereigns; and that it was not unusual for these debates to appeal to the court of public opinion, as well as the law courts.

While some plunderers were perceived as unequivocally evil and some as, well, just equivocal, others were received with popular adulation. Of these the most famous, in England, was Francis Drake, beginning even in his own lifetime. The queen originally suppressed accounts of his circumnavigation and the participants were sworn to secrecy, to avoid provoking Spain, but a long and rather rambling celebration written by Nicholas Breton the year after the voyage showed that the Drake was out of the bag, so to speak, even if Breton was carefully coy about the details of what Drake had done that deserved such praise.

The first account of that voyage appeared nine years later in the enormous *Principal Navigations*, a collection of ship's journals and travel narratives covering all regions of the world, edited by Richard Hakluyt (who also translated *Mare Liberum* for the East India Company). Individual accounts of Drake's Caribbean voyages appeared at the same time, and in John Stow's *Annales of England* in 1592. On Drake's death four years later a 20-year-old Oxford student, Charles Fitz-Geffrey, who like Drake hailed from the West Country, wrote a paean laden with classical references that may have kickstarted Fitz-Geffrey's literary career.

Some of these accounts acknowledge Drake's less salutary side. William Camden's *Annales*, published in Latin in 1615 and English in 1625, mentioned that during the circumnavigation Drake 'most inhumanely exposed' three African people on a small island in the Banggai archipelago, one a pregnant woman named Maria, whom he presumably captured in Spanish America. This story is corroborated by an anonymous sailor's account surviving in manuscript at the British Library.

Camden also noted that it angered Drake when courtiers refused his gifts of gold and silver, 'as if hee had not lawfully come by it'. However, 'the Commons ... applauded him with all praise and admiration, esteeming, he had purchased no lesse glory in advancing the limits of the *English*, their honour and reputation, than of their Empire'. Later generations more often echoed the latter sentiment, as Drake became the most established model for the plundering hero.

Biographies of Drake, whether reprints or new ones, continued to appear throughout the seventeenth century, tracking closely onto moments of international tension, when patriotic feelings ran high. Two new Drake narratives appeared during war with France and Spain in the later 1620s; one, *Francis Drake Revived*, was based on Drake's own report for the queen and published by his nephew. He was celebrated in other texts of that decade, such as Samuel Purchas' *Purchas his Pilgrimes*, another collection of voyage narratives, also printed as *Hakluytus Posthumus*, continuing Hakluyt's famous work.

Francis Drake Revived reappeared in 1653, and new biographies in 1662 and 1671 – at moments of escalating tension or actual conflict. Two more came out in 1683 and 1687, the latter simply titled *The English Heroe*. Several of these books drew on the earlier ones, and all of them were reprinted throughout the 1690s and into the 1700s.

The 1626 *Francis Drake Revived* called on 'this dull or effeminate age, to folowe his noble steps for golde & silver'. They continued a trend set by Hakluyt, one of the first and most vociferous proponents of empire, who advertised colonisation as an outlet for 'valiant youths, rustinge and hurtfull by lacke of employment'. John Smith's commentary on piracy was informed by similar concerns: in *True Travels* he exhorted soldiers and sailors, 'now regarded for most part, but as the scumme of the world; regaine therefore your wonted reputations, and endevour rather to adventure to those faire plantations of our *English* Nation'. As the buccaneers took up this call (deliberately or not), Drake remained the model. When John Evelyn heard of the attack on Panamá, he wrote that 'such an action had not been done since the famous Drake', whom he described as a 'demigod'.

Many of these texts justified Drake's and others' actions through what has become known as the 'Black Legend' of the Spanish Empire, which did have some basis in fact. Hakluyt and others were particularly inspired by the works of Bartolomé de las Casas, a Dominican friar who travelled in the Americas, excoriated the harsh treatment of Indigenous people, and championed efforts to reform Spanish imperial laws for their protection. His *Brevísima Relación de la Destrucción de las Indias*, published in 1552, was translated into Dutch, French, and English in the 1570s and 1580s, circulating graphic descriptions of torture and abuse.

These ideas became widespread. Walter Ralegh portrayed himself, in his *Discoverie of Guiana* in 1596, promising Indigenous leaders that he would 'deliver them from the tyranny of the Spaniardes'. The anonymous *An Experimentall Discoverie of Spanish Practises* of 1623 condemned their 'cruell, bloudy, and treacherous invasions', borrowing heavily from De Las Casas, as did similar accounts of the Spanish conquest published in the 1650s and 1680s. John Milton's defence of the Western Design insisted that English soldiers would avenge the murders of Indigenous people. The 1683 biography of Drake described how he allied with 'Pedro', leader of the 'Symerons [*cimarrónes*], a Black People, with long hair, who had Revolted from the Spaniards, by reason of their Cruelty'.

Exquemelin picked up on these trends too in *Zee-roovers*. On the title page, the Indigenous victim is subscribed 'INNOCENTER', while the Spanish one suffers 'PRO PECCATIS', 'for sins'. *Zee-roovers* is rather more honest than some of the facetious biographies of Drake in admitting to the violence done against Indigenous and African people by buccaneers and other marauders, though Exquemelin delivers no critique of empire or slavery. Here, as with the condemnations of Magharibi corsairs, and even in the musings of Charles Molloy, we can see how moral and cultural considerations, as much as legal ones, shaped whether someone was identified as a pirate.

Drake's champions would never admit he *was* a pirate, of course, but we can find similar elements shaping the depiction of those who were considered such. For example, the same aspect is clear in several works by the playwright Thomas Heywood that dramatise sea roving.

One of his more famous plays, *The Fair Maid of the West*, has a brave young woman called Bess (a clear homage to Elizabeth I) take to the sea in her own ship after she believes her beloved Spencer is dead. Seizing ships belonging to 'the rich Spaniard, and the barbarous Turke', but sparing Dutch and French vessels, Bess enjoys a joyful reunion with Spencer in Morocco, and a second part to the play features a homeward voyage escaping French pirates.

Fair Maid was published in 1631, but probably the first part was performed at the end of Elizabeth's rule, and the second early in James' reign. It is curious that Bess' plunderings are praised on stage in part one, but piracy appears only as an offstage plot device in part two; also that Mullisheg, the ruler in Morocco, is a more sympathetic figure in the first part than the second, reflecting the growing sense of threat from Magharibi corsairs.

Another of Heywood's plays, *Fortune by Land and Sea*, set during the Elizabethan era but performed in the first decades of the seventeenth century and published in 1655, plays on the contrast between different plunderers even more clearly. The protagonist Young Forrest flees to sea after avenging his brother in a duel, is chosen captain by his crew, leads a successful campaign against Spanish shipping, and eventually captures the two famous pirates Clinton (Atkinson) and Purser (actually Thomas Walton), earning Forrest's own pardon.

Forrest and his men 'dare do any thing that stands with justice, our countries honour, and the reputation of our own names', in contrast to Clinton and Purser, of whom one character says, 'The ocean scarce can bear their outrages, they are so violent, confounding all, and sparing none.' Yet the pair, who admit, 'We know we are Pirates, and profess to rob', still get some sympathy. They share their plunder equally: 'though Out-laws, we keep laws amongst our selves.' Once captured, Clinton declares, 'We bravely liv'd and Ile [I'll] as boldly dye', and as they come to execution they reminisce about their 'golden daies' as 'Lords, nay Kings at Sea, [when] the Ocean was our realm'.

In 1639, after the play was written but before it was printed, Heywood published a prose biography of these two pirates, *A True Relation*. Here he recycled some of the earlier work, again describing their 'irregular & ... illegall lives, as they were notoriously famous, so their deaths and ends were as remarkably infamous'. However, he describes them rather grandly, as 'two Arch Pirats … sitting in Counsell, where they kept a great state … as if they had beene no lesse than two Princes, and rivall Commanders of the maine Ocean'.

Heywood probably took inspiration from a pamphlet published the year they were executed, written as if in their own voice. This text, too, acknowledged their 'due to Death' since they 'abusde our Princes league and law', but it presented them as patriots, no less than Drake: 'I ever wisht my Queene and country well … th'English still I lov'd on Sea and shore'. Atkinson even professed a Robin Hood-esque concern for the poor: 'who holpe the helplesse more … Then Clinton did that came at every call.'

Heywood did not preserve that side of Clinton in *Fortune by Land and Sea*, but something of it appears in *A True Relation*, where, being 'of haughty and ambitious spirits', they chose not to sail 'to benefit and inrich others … it was now high time to be freemen of the Sea, and set up for themselves'. At one point they approached a prize calling out '*Amaine for the Sea*; (a phrase onely used by Pirats)'. 'Amain' was an instruction to lower topsails and permit a ship to be boarded, often used by naval commanders and licensed plunderers. In *A Christian Turn'd Turk*, too, one

The execution of Thomas Walton and Clinton Atkinson, from Thomas Heywood's *True Relation*.

pirate claims, 'We are of the Sea', a phrase that appeared in other popular literature about pirates.

Such language, then, conforms to the idea of pirates as 'enemies of all', as 'Lords, nay Kings at Sea', belonging to no state or ruler but the sea itself, even forming their own 'Common-wealth', as Molloy put it. The choice of that term 'commonwealth' is interesting because, though it could be a neutral legal term (and that is probably how Molloy means it), after the interregnum of the 1650s it could also be interpreted to carry radical, republican overtones. Some of these ideas anticipated, and per- haps inaugurated, popular representations in the 1690s and early 1700s to which I will come later, including elements like 'We are of the Sea'. Already we have the outline of a distinctive piratical genre emerging in the seventeenth century.

At the same time, by describing pirates in exaggerations that deliber- ately and humorously invert the natural order, these authors placed them in a surprisingly powerful position. Heywood praised Clinton and Purser's 'experience and skill in Navigation', and that too is a common theme across these texts. Jennings 'grew to beare the name of a skilfull Marriner' and was 'wholy addicted to martiall courses' from childhood, 'espetially in the manly resolution of seafaringmen'. Danseker was 'a proude (yet we may call him an honest) Pirate'. Cusack, speaking in his own defence at his trial, appeared as 'a Person of a Clear Courage, and good understanding: he pleaded very well for his life'.

For Cusack, though, 'the matter was too foul to be washt off with good words'. All writers in this period condemned, rather than endorsed, pirates, just as the royal proclamations did. On the other hand, in *Fortune by Land and Sea*, Purser (or rather Heywood) described Execution Dock as 'a quick sand that shall swallow many a brave Marine souldier, of whose valour, experience, skil, and Naval discipline, being lost, I wish this land may never have need'.

Heywood was writing at the time of, or just after, James' campaign against plundering, and his words imply concern about the consequent diminution of English maritime and military resources. A few years before *A True Relation*, at Charles I's request, Heywood wrote a poetic description of the king's enormous new flagship, called, with a total lack of subtlety, *Sovereign of the Sea*, which was part of a substantial naval expansion during the 1630s.

That expansion did not put an end to corsair raiding. *A True Relation* in 1639, and the publication of Heywood's earlier plays in the 1650s, might well contain an implicit criticism of current politics, couched in terms of piracy. At the least, like the biographies of Drake, they kept alive a fond (and exaggerated) memory of naval and plundering glory during Elizabeth's reign, and within it the message that plunderers could be a national asset as well as 'enemies of all'.

The response in England to *Zee-roovers*, or *Bucaniers*, tells the same story. Henry Morgan's reputation as the successor to Drake prompted criticism of Exquemelin's unflattering portrait, the *London Gazette* accusing it of 'many false Scandalous and Malitious reflections'. Really, though, Morgan got off lightly compared to L'Olonnais, who was already dead and could not complain.

Morgan could, and did so, after his nephew Charles sent copies of both English editions to his uncle, and he consulted a lawyer. Henry was most furious that Exquemelin described him as arriving in the Caribbean as an indentured servant, which offended his social pretensions. He sued both publishers for £10,000 and sent his lawyer a list of libels by page number. One of the printers settled out of court, while the other fought the case and lost. Morgan only got £200 off each of them, but both had to amend their future editions.

Perhaps his reputation mattered more than the money. Morgan had already begun to present himself as a respectable figure of authority in the London press. The *London Gazette* printed an account of his actions against Jacob Evertson and the *Loyal Protestant* described how he had tried and condemned four men for piracy, executing the 'most notorious' and pardoning the rest.

Morgan paid for a new Anglican church in Port Royal and arranged for the publication of the first sermon preached there. In 1682 another sermon from the church was printed, taking as its text 'Render therefore unto Caesar', signalling dutiful obedience to the Crown. The next year a collection of *The Laws of Jamaica* (including its statute on pirates) appeared in London. Morgan and his allies clearly wanted to challenge their island's reputation as a sink of depravity. *The Present State of Jamaica*, also published in 1683, included copies of Morgan's commissions and instructions, asserting the legality of his plundering expeditions.

A more sympathetic account of Morgan's Panamá raid appeared in 1684, together with a preface trumpeting Morgan's genteel family background, lauding 'the honour of that incomparable soldier and seaman'. Another book in 1686 called itself *Bucaniers of America the second volume*, seizing on the popularity of the first, though it was really nothing of the sort. These new texts, and a genuine second edition of *Bucaniers* in 1684, also included narrative accounts by John Cox, William Dick, and Basil Ringrose of more recent buccaneering voyages that ushered in a new phase of plundering. The fact that they hitched themselves to Morgan's wagon shows not only a loyalty to the buccaneer leader, but also a shrewd attempt to shield themselves with his reflected glory. For these buccaneers had gone in quite a different direction: into the South Sea.

9

GREAT AND HARD
ENTERPRISES

Early in 1680 a fleet gathered at Negril Point, at the western tip of Jamaica. Aboard one of the ships was William Dampier, at 29 years old an experienced rover. This younger son of a prosperous farming family in Somerset had gone to sea at 18, after a little schooling, and sailed to France and Newfoundland, then to India, before serving in the navy during the Third Anglo-Dutch War.

He spent a little time in Jamaica in 1675, on a plantation belonging to his family's landlord. Before departure from England the customs officials discovered a woman aboard, masquerading as the servant of a doctor bound for the same employment. She protested that she was the doctor's wife, they produced a hurriedly forged marriage certificate, and they were allowed to proceed. Within six months, though, the plantation manager complained of these three newcomers as a 'company of wasteful people' and Dampier as 'a self-conceited young man ... who understands little or nothing', though 'something he understands of sailing, which I think his mind hankers after still'.

Dampier was indeed soon back at sea, trading with the logwood cutters in the Yucatán Peninsula. He decided to join them, but in June 1676, after only a few months, a hurricane smashed all that he had. He was forced to 'seek a subsistence in Company of some Privateers' cruising off Campeche. At Alvarado they took only a little plunder, but Dampier was delighted by the many parrots who 'prate very prettily'. He spent another year at logwooding again, then in 1678 went to England, where he married. The following year he returned to Jamaica and he eventually joined one Mr Hobby for a trading voyage to the Miskito people (for whom the Mosquito Coast is named).

Coming to Negril Point, they met a bunch of fearsome captains. John Coxon was already a well-known raider. Bartholomew Sharp had cruised with a commission in the Caribbean during the last Anglo-Dutch war. Later they would join Richard Sawkins, who had been imprisoned in Port Royal only the year before, and Peter Harris, who had evaded the *Success* sent after him. When Hobby's crew went over to these buccaneers, Dampier recalled, 'I was the more easily perswaded to go with them too.'

Among them he encountered Lionel Wafer, a former apothecary's assistant who was around 20 years old. Like Dampier, he had already sailed to India, as an assistant surgeon, and then spent a little time in Jamaica, where he ran into Edmund Cook, also now a shipmate. Cook started out trading to the logwooders during the 1670s and twice his ships were captured, first by Philip Fitzgerald in 1673, and then in 1679, shortly before this voyage. Both times he escaped back to Jamaica and even petitioned Charles II for letters of reprisal, to no avail. Another was Basil Ringrose, from Kent, who like Dampier had some education in England before he came to sea.

Ringrose, Sharp, Dampier, and Wafer all published books about their journeyings, which proved quite unlike any of Morgan's expeditions. They had commissions from the governor of Jamaica to cut logwood in the Bay of Honduras, but that is not where they went. Instead, they joined with others, including *flibustiers* under *capitaines* Jean Bernanos and Jean Rose, totalling some nine ships and almost 500 men, and they began by raiding Portobelo, taking plunder worth around £40 a man. Quickly retreating from a large Spanish counterattack, they set off across the isthmus. They were bound for what Sharp called 'that fair South Sea': the Pacific Ocean.

The western coasts of America promised rich pickings. Lima, the capital of Peru, was as wealthy a city as Mexico, Panamá, Havana, or Cartagena. Founded in 1535, it was the seat of both an *audiencia* and an archbishop, and from 1551 a university. The population rose to more than 25,000 by 1614, about two-fifths African, two-fifths Spanish, and the rest Andean and '*mestizo*'. Its streets housed silversmiths and other artisans, as well as wealthy churches and convents, with some 400 priests, 900 friars, and 1,366 nuns in the city.

The silver and produce that made Lima wealthy travelled north from its port of Callao, or Arica for Potosí, along the coast to Panamá for trans-shipping east. A vital trade route also stretched west. In the first global circumnavigation in 1519–22 Fernão de Magalhães, a Portuguese noble in Spanish service more famously known as Magellan, crossed the Pacific from Mexico, reaching Guam, where he both traded and fought with the Chamorro islanders, and then continuing further west. Only one of the five ships returned to Spain and only one-tenth of the sailors, Magellan himself not among them. Another circumnavigation lasted eleven years. Nevertheless, the path had been opened.

Further expeditions returned during the 1540s and 1560s, claimed and named the Philippines – after Felipe II – and established Manila, on Luzon, in 1571. This major trading centre linked the Americas to Asia. Galleons sailed from Acapulco in Mexico to Manila, taking silver for trade to China, where there was huge demand; Japan, another source of silver, was riven by the internecine wars known as the *sengoku* period.

This voyage was the longest non-stop passage at the time, two or three months westward, with a stop at Guam, while the eastward trip could take six or eight months, following a long northern curve chasing the right winds and currents. More than thirty ships were wrecked or lost in the two and a half centuries that they operated.

During the 1590s, these galleons carried 2 million *pesos* a year westward, and some shiploads exceeded 10 million. Somewhere between a quarter and a half of American silver went through Manila, while tailors in Mexico worked with Chinese silk. Chinese merchants and workers settled in Manila to trade in this and other valuable wares, such as porcelain.

Imperial rule was as brutal here as anywhere else. In 1603 the Spanish authorities massacred Chinese residents and in 1639, aided by Filipino allies, defeated a Chinese rebellion and killed somewhere between 17,000 and 22,000 people. Like in the Atlantic, the Spanish government monopolised trade, officially restricting the Pacific route to just two galleons per year in 1592 and prohibiting direct trade from Peru to Manila in 1631, although such proclamations could not stop regular smuggling.

Northern European raiders soon sniffed out this new opportunity. John Oxenham, a West County seaman who raided Nombre de Diós with Francis Drake in 1572–73, returned to cross the isthmus three years later, once again teaming up with *cimarrónes*. He seized an unsuspecting ship with 60,000 *pesos* of gold and silver aboard, but was soon captured and taken to Lima where, in 1580, the *Inquisícion* prosecuted and hanged him.

Oxenham and his men destroyed and defiled churches, tortured friars, and boasted of a forthcoming invasion of 2,000 Englishmen. That was a lie, but Francis Drake's round-the-world voyage passed the Strait of Magellan early in 1578. He attacked vessels in Arica and Callao, but either never knew about Oxenham or left him to his fate when he heard of a treasure ship that had just departed. Drake first seized a ship carrying 20,000 *pesos*, then hit the *Nuestra Señora de la Concepción*, known more colloquially as *Cagafuego*, 'shit-fire'. Following a fierce battle with this heavily armed vessel, Drake's raiders captured a cargo worth 360,000 *pesos*.

Like Oxenham, Drake tortured some prisoners, but he released others, who commented on the affection with which he treated his men and on his seamanship. He took along painters to record the coast, plundered sea charts from one prize, and forced local pilots to cooperate. Again, like Oxenham, Drake's men targeted churches: at Huatulco, a surviving witness recalled a small, fierce boatswain breaking a crucifix and castigating the Spanish prisoners about their faith.

Drake made a brief stop in California, parlaying with local communities while proclaiming the region 'New Albion', and then headed west, with a captive pilot. The expedition crossed the Pacific and threaded its way through the Indian Ocean, stopping in a few places (and abandoning Maria and her two companions), before reaching England in 1580.

Six years later, Thomas Cavendish led a third English expedition, crossing the isthmus, with some veterans of Drake's voyage in tow. They repeated the iconoclasm at Huatulco – according to popular legend the church's wooden cross miraculously survived the blaze – and, again assisted by a captive pilot, seized the *Santa Ana*, carrying 122,000 *pesos* in gold, silk, and fine textiles. Cavendish too sailed home across the Pacific and through the Indian Ocean, just missing the Spanish Armada in 1588.

These two voyages demonstrated the possibilities for plunder in the South Sea, but few subsequent ones proved so fortunate. Cavendish died during another attempted Pacific trip in 1591 and three years later Richard Hawkins was captured pillaging along the coast of Chile and Peru. These prisoners were unusually lucky: they were transported to Spain and ransomed home (where Hawkins became the vice-admiral of Devon, until his dismissal).

Between the 1590s and the 1640s, five Dutch expeditions set out into the South Sea, looking for plunder and to trade and ally with *cimarrón* and Indigenous communities, such as the Mapuche, who drove the Spanish out of Valdivia in 1599. Most commanders recruited sailors from previous Pacific trips or acquired ship's logs to help guide them, but that did not prevent the incredible difficulties of this arduous journeying. All of them took several years and had a high casualty rate, due to disease as much as battle.

These fleets, ranging from about five ships up to the largest of eleven vessels and 1,630 men, struggled to keep together. Most of them grew unruly, often due to poor victuals and the long passage. More than one commander only told their crews that they were taking the long way round to the Indian Ocean after they were at sea (as Drake had done) and it did not go down well. Some commanders executed officers for treason and one surgeon was accused of witchcraft because he wore a pouch about his neck containing snake anatomy. He confessed, after a ducking from the yardarm, and was also executed.

Some traded in a few places, though this often turned to skirmishing; others blockaded Arica and Callao, again torturing prisoners, especially friars. Their plunder never matched Drake or Cavendish. One commander was tricked by captives who claimed the silver ships had left thirteen (*trece*) rather than three (*tres*) days before. He should have listened to the enslaved sailors he had captured, to whom he promised freedom, who told him the truth. The last Dutch fleet persuaded several hundred Indigenous people from Carelmapu to accompany them to Valdivia, where they established friendly terms with the local *caciques* before sailing for Dutch-controlled Brazil to get reinforcements. Because the war was going badly in Brazil, they never returned.

One effect of these voyages was to intensify Spanish defences in the region, and in the Philippines. As in the Caribbean, the cost was enormous; one squadron disappeared in a hurricane, a new frigate worth 100,000 *pesos* was destroyed in battle, new fortifications at Callao cost 1 million *pesos*, and in 1644 an expedition to retake Valdivia cost 348,000 *pesos*. Still, it would prove much harder in the future to catch the Pacific coast unawares.

So John Narborough found when, in 1670, he captained the first English ship for seven decades to round Cape Horn. On an exploratory mission, Narborough learned much about Patagonia, but spent only a few months on the coast, and just seven days at Valdivia. Most of the men he sent ashore to negotiate were imprisoned.

One of them was a curious figure calling himself Don Carlos, with his servant, Thomas Highway, a 'mulatto' from North Africa, baptised in Spain at the age of 14. He told his Spanish interrogators that he was Carlos Henríque Clerque, 'director' of the expedition, a Catholic in English service, friend to various Peruvian officials, unacknowledged relative of Charles II, and in some way connected to Catarina de Bragança. He may have been linked to London-based Portuguese Jewish merchants. Under torture he claimed to be Olivier Berlin of Saint-Malo in France, but this did not prevent his eventual execution.

Don Carlos was still alive in 1680, as the first wave of buccaneers crossed the isthmus. All Pacific plundering voyages since Cavendish failed to capture any substantial plunder, but the dream of that wealth had not diminished. As Bartholomew Sharp wrote, 'that which often Spurs men on to the undertaking of the most difficult Adventures, is the sacred hunger of Gold; and 'twas Gold was the bait that tempted a Pack of merry Boys of us'. These merry boys would find it a very difficult adventure indeed.

The fleet led by John Coxon first captured a ship sailing from Cartagena to Portobelo, carrying letters warning that buccaneers might soon 'open a door into the *South Seas*'. Perhaps, ironically, that served as their inspiration (though another account says the ship threw all its papers overboard, so this may be pure invention). *Capitaine* Bernanos suggested that they join with the Guna of Darién, though when Andreas, whom the buccaneers called the 'Emperor of Darien', suggested attacking Santa María near the west coast, the *flibustiers* under Bernanos and Rose refused and departed.

Dampier wrote that Andreas and his people had links with buccaneers since, fifteen years earlier, an English captain captured a Guna boy, whom he named John Gret, and who then lived and married among the Miskito before returning to Daríen to negotiate an alliance that 'our Privateers had long coveted'. When Gret disappeared, his community thought he had been captured by Spanish forces, and it was fortunate for the buccaneers that Gret's friends never learned the truth: he was murdered by Englishmen trying to enslave him.

Andreas and two other Guna leaders, one called Antonio and the other known to the buccaneers as Golden Cap for his flashy headwear, led just over 300 men across the mountains, each captain marching with their own flag. Most of the buccaneers carried some combination of pistol, 'hanger' or short sword, and a light musket or 'fuzee' (*fusil* in French, hence fusilier, another term that appeared in French and English during these decades).

They attacked Santa María on 14 April 1680. Here they found that one of Andreas' daughters had been captured by Spanish soldiers, probably why he proposed the attack. She was pregnant, and according to Ringrose the Guna soldiers exacted a bloody revenge on their captives, although the buccaneers sent some prisoners across the isthmus. Then they took their flotilla of canoes and headed for Panamá.

Sharp seized a ship and went off cruising, while the rest encountered a Spanish fleet, first capturing three smaller ships (crewed by 'Biscayners', African sailors, and '*mulatos*') and with those overpowering three larger

vessels and burning two more. Some of the buccaneers also made themselves navigational instruments, a common practice among mariners.

Peter Harris died during this attack and Coxon decided to return over
the isthmus with his men; he later settled, and died, in a Miskito community. The fleet, with Sharp now back among them, chose Sawkins as
the new commander. He exchanged notes with the governor and presents
with the bishop of Panamá (whom Sawkins and Coxon had formerly captured at Santa Marta).

When the governor asked from whom he held a commission, Sawkins
replied that he came to aid the 'King of Darien', whom he called 'the
true lord of Panama'. Similarly, John Cox maintained that they held 'full
Commission' for war against the Spanish Empire from this 'Emperour',
though William Dick's account called it a 'pretended Service ... the real
intent was only to serve our selves with Gold and Silver'. According to
Ringrose, Sawkins even bragged to the governor that he would 'bring our
Commissions on the muzzles of our Guns, at which time he should read
them as plain as the flame of Gunpowder could make them'.

Sawkins never kept that promise, but they captured several Panamá-
bound vessels, including one carrying 50,000 *pesos* for the garrison. When
the 'valiant Commander Captain *Sawkins*' died in an attack on Pueblo
Nuevo, Sharp took over and 'asked our men in full Councel who of them
were willing to go or stay', promising everyone who stayed at least £1,000
in eventual profit. Sixty-three chose to leave.

The South Sea voyages seem to have developed the buccaneers' habits
of consultation and fragmentation to greater levels than their Caribbean
counterparts, perhaps because these fleets were isolated and lacked the
backing of more formal authorities. What some accounts described as open
discussion and shared decisions, others called 'great distraction', 'Fewd' or
even 'mutiny'. Dick commented in his journal that after Sawkins' death
the remaining captains 'were not thought to be Leaders fit for such great,
and hard Enterprises', though he chose to stay. Ringrose considered leaving, already weary of 'hazardous adventures', but feared the crossing of
the isthmus.

Sharp renamed the prize *Trinidad* as the *Trinity* and, with another small
vessel, set sail from Coiba Island on 6 June, heading south. On the way
they missed the Galápagos but stopped at Gorgona, close to the coast
of modern-day Colombia, and at Isla de la Plata, known in English as
Drake's Island.

At each of these stops they revictualled and repaired their vessels –
including careening, a difficult but necessary process where the ship was

heeled over on a beach to scrape the hull clean. Keeping a ship afloat without a proper harbour for as long as these voyagers did was no mean feat. The buccaneers also gambled among themselves for the plunder already taken.

There were a small number of Miskito men among the buccaneers, whose skills in hunting and fishing proved very useful. Dampier later recalled that Miskito companions were 'coveted by all Privateers', describing them as 'tall, well made, raw-boned, lusty, strong, and nimble', able to 'descry a Sail at Sea farther, and see any thing better' than others.

Sailing on, in the Gulf of Guayaquil, they met a small ship with 'a parcel of merry Blades' aboard, *caballeros* who had vowed to hunt down these intruders and who (unfortunately for them) got their wish. The buccaneers shot one of these captives, a friar, and threw him overboard while still alive.

Sharp realised that they had lost the element of surprise, and so it proved, in a series of abortive attacks at Guayaquil in late October and Coquimbo in December (they avoided Lima altogether). In these attacks they seized silver church ornaments and fresh provisions, but little else, and almost lost the *Trinity* at Coquimbo when an Indigenous soldier swam out with a tar-and-brimstone incendiary device, but this was discovered and doused.

Disappointed, the buccaneers retreated to the Juan Fernández Islands to regroup. These islands were named for their discoverer, who, sailing south from Peru in October 1574, had struck out westwards to avoid the prevailing winds and current; he actually named the islands Santa Cecilia. When Fernández arrived in Valparaiso unexpectedly early, he was interrogated by the *Inquisicion* on suspicion of witchcraft, then exonerated and appointed *piloto mayor* of the South Sea.

Abortive attempts to colonise the islands had left behind a population of goats and pigs, so the buccaneers dined on fresh meat, shared out loot, and took to gambling once more. Sharp, presumably happy with his own portion (3,000 *pesos* or £1,000, according to some of his shipmates), suggested returning to the Caribbean, so they replaced him with John Watling, 'an old Privateer' with a reputation as a 'stout Seaman'. Sharp blamed Cox, whom he called a 'dissembling New England man' that Sharp had promoted to vice-admiral for friendship rather than skill.

Tensions always ran high when things went badly, and there was other strife, too. William Cook, servant of Edmund Cook, accused his master of 'buggery' both in England and at sea. Edmund was put in irons; William would be imprisoned later in the same voyage, suspected of collaborating with Spanish prisoners, and died not long afterwards.

The buccaneers left in a hurry in January 1681 when they espied three Spanish sails approaching, accidentally abandoning Will, one of their Miskito companions. Watling led them north again, dodging a Spanish squadron, but an attack on Arica looking for Potosí silver went badly. Of ninety men who went ashore, almost half were lost, including Watling, and three surgeons who got drunk and fell captive.

Sharp resumed command, though Dampier and Wafer voted against him and scoffed at the 'meaner sort' who supported Sharp. Things looked bleak at this point: water was so scarce among them that a pint changed hands for 30 *pesos*. On 17 April, at Isla de la Plata, nearly fifty decided to leave, including Dampier, Wafer, two Miskito men, and a 'Spanish Indian', heading north for the isthmus in a longboat and two canoes.

Sharp, with Ringrose, cruised on, though soon afterwards their interpreter, a *vrijbuiter* named James Marquis, disappeared, suspected of deserting, leaving behind £500 in plunder. Then Sharp's luck began to turn. He captured several prizes, one carrying 40,000 *pesos*. On another they missed 700 pigs of silver, probably worth over £150,000 altogether,

John Watling executes an old man from the island of Iquique, because he could not provide information about Arica. (Courtesy of the John Carter Brown Library)

because they mistook it for lead and took just one pig to make (very shiny?) bullets. Imagine their expressions when, after the voyage, they discovered their mistake. In another prize, the *Santa Rosario*, they captured something else of value, if not with the same price tag: a *derroterro*, a Spanish book of charts. Ringrose recognised it just as the *piloto* tried to throw it overboard.

After an unprofitable landing at Paita, Sharp and the rest decided they had had enough. They rounded Cape Horn just before Christmas and reached Barbados on 28 January 1682. These men feared that the naval frigate stationed there would 'seize us for Pyrateering', so they tried Antigua. There the governor prevented what might otherwise have been a warmer reception, so the buccaneers went their separate ways, giving the ship to seven or eight shipmates who had lost everything in gambling. A few went to Jamaica, some to the northern colonies.

Ringrose, Sharp, and several others sailed for England, arriving in Dartmouth on 26 March 1682. The Spanish ambassador immediately demanded punishment, with testimony from witnesses including a Spanish boy whom Sharp had brought back. They had captured about twenty-five ships, killed around 200 Spanish subjects, and assaulted several towns, as well as costing 200,000 *pesos* for the squadron pursuing them.

These men were acquitted by the admiralty court, however, having presented their strategically valuable *derroterro* to Charles II. Plunderers, even unlicensed ones, could still get away with it if they made themselves useful. Sharp became a naval captain, but 'wasted all his mony ... in good fellowship', purchased a ship and returned to the Caribbean. Ringrose's dealings with the South Sea, meanwhile, were not over.

Those who went north with Dampier and Wafer in April 1681 seized a Spanish merchant ship, sneaking to Gorgona and then towards Panamá. Reaching the isthmus, they negotiated with Indigenous guides to take them across, giving one guide's wife a 'Sky-coloured Petticoat'.

Over this tough terrain Dampier carried his extensive notes rolled up in a bamboo cane, stoppered with wax. One of their companions drowned, Wafer was severely injured in the leg in an accident with gunpowder, and four enslaved men whom they had captured in South America escaped one night, taking Wafer's surgical tools and medicaments with them.

Wafer and some other stragglers recuperated for three months at a Guna settlement ruled by one Lacenta; one of the residents had lived in Panamá and spoke Spanish. They healed Wafer's leg with a herbal poultice, and

Wafer (or so he wrote) cured Lacenta's wife with some careful bleeding, a standard European medical technique of the day. Wafer learned the Guna language and adopted their dress, but in the end he and the others went on to the coast.

There, by curious chance, they met Dampier and their other companions. These men had reached the coast several months earlier, on 24 May 1681, and shipped with a *flibustier* called Jean Tristian, then joined up with their old comrades John Coxon and Jean Row, and others including Peter Wright and the *vrijbuiter* Jan Willems, often known as 'Janke' (or 'Yankey' to the English). Dampier and his fellows joined Wright and, when the fleet split up, cruised towards Cartagena before returning west to the accidental meeting with Wafer – whom they did not recognise at first, dressed and painted as he was in Guna fashion.

Wright, with Wafer and Dampier, joined with Willems for a while, though Dampier noted that Willems had no commission and feared that the *flibustiers* might deprive him of his vessel. They traded with some Spanish towns and French ships, called at Curaçao, and at Tortuga split again.

Dampier and Wright sailed to Caracas and then to Virginia, arriving in July 1682. Dampier left the ship and spent around ten months ashore. In his published account he referred vaguely to 'troubles', which might mean a brush with the law, although he also suffered from a worm infesting his ankle. He paid an enslaved African man for a remedy that he disparaged as powder and 'mumbling', but which worked.

Wafer and another survivor of the first isthmus crossing, John Cook, remained with Willems. Cook took command of a prize but, lacking a commission, was deposed by Willems and Jean Tristian, whom they had run into again. Tristian then carried Cook, Wafer, and others, including one Edward Davis (English, but possibly born in Holland), to Tortuga.

Here, while Tristian was ashore, Cook and his fellows seized his ship and pointedly renamed it *Revenge*. They collected some of their comrades left behind at Isla de Vaca, captured some French prizes, and sailed north for Virginia, where they recruited more men, including Dampier, who seems to have grown tired of life ashore. It was time for another round in the South Sea.

On 23 August 1683 the *Revenge* set sail for Africa, seeking the right winds for Cape Horn. The master, William Ambrosia Cowley, who also kept and published a journal, asserted that he was offered 500 *pesos* to navigate

to Tortuga, only learning the truth at sea. Cowley also claimed that he
had an MA from Cambridge, though his name is absent from *Alumni
Cantabridgiensis*. Dampier believed the quartermaster, Edward Davis, had
more experience than Cowley.

At the Cape Verde Islands the crew got down to business, taking Canary
wine from a Dutch slaver and unsuccessfully attacking another Dutch ship
that turned out to be a heavily armed *Oostindische* vessel. They called at
the River Sherbro and Sierra Leone, trading ashore and seizing a Danish
slaver with sixty African women aboard. They may have sold their captives to the local ruler. A more appalling fate might be implied by the new
name for their prize, *Batchelor's Delight*, when they abandoned the *Revenge*,
though Cowley noted that 'discoursing of women was very unlucky' at
sea. He reported that when they reached Cape Horn on 14 February 1684
they were 'chusing of Valentines' and chatting about 'the Intrigues of
Women' when 'a prodigious Storm' brewed up.

Soon afterwards they met another English ship, commanded by
Thomas Eaton, part of a new expedition led by Charles Swan, a veteran
of Morgan's Panamá raid. Basil Ringrose had persuaded Swan and other
backers to undertake this voyage, with instructions from the duke of York
to trade where they could. Eaton and Swan had lost one another in the
Strait of Magellan, so when Eaton met Cook the two sailed for the Juan
Fernández Islands.

There, on 22 March, they were astonished to discover Will, who after
just over three years alone on the island was joyfully reunited with his
former fellows, especially Robin, a Miskito friend. Here Dampier again
praised 'the sagacity of the *Indians*'. Will had turned his knife blade into a
saw, with which he deconstructed his gun barrel and used it for harpoons,
lances, fishing hooks, and a blade.

Sailing north, they captured a few vessels but had too few men to attack
Arica, so they went instead to the Galápagos, then on towards Realejo,
near modern-day Corinto in Nicaragua. Cook died of an illness and while
burying him ashore they captured three Indigenous scouts working for
the president of Panamá, whom they interrogated.

The men of the *Batchelor's Delight* now chose Edward Davis for captain,
who abandoned the design on Realejo, perhaps due to their prisoners' information, and targeted smaller coastal towns. In some of these they pretended
to be 'Biscayners' and were cautiously accommodated by the Indigenous
officials, although often this precarious situation devolved into bloodshed.

The partnership between the two ships was a struggle. Dampier
wrote that Davis' men looked on Eaton's as 'but young beginners to the

trade', refusing them equal shares. From the Isla de la Plata, Eaton set off across the Pacific, Cowley with him, taking six months to reach Guam, where Eaton pretended to the governor that he was a French explorer. Continuing on to China and the Indian Ocean in April 1686, Cowley and twenty others left Eaton at Timor and reached England by October. Eaton went on to become a naval captain and died in 1698 commanding a frigate.

Davis and the *Batchelor's Delight* continued their coastal raids. The *audiencia* of Peru adopted a scorched earth policy that thwarted the buccaneers, but they met up with Charles Swan, and with him was Peter Harris, nephew of the Peter Harris killed on the previous expedition.

Swan had attempted to trade at Valdivia, as ordered, but he was double-crossed. Only the quick thinking of Ringrose and Josiah Teat, another of the officers, got them out of trouble and back to the ship. This blunder sent warnings racing north along the coast, so Swan sailed for Juan Fernández and from there to the Gulf of Nicoya, north of Panamá. Here he met Harris with a band of buccaneers who had crossed the isthmus, plundering Santa María on the way and taking nuggets from the Spanish gold camps, some of which they used to purchase a barque from Swan and join him.

Running into Davis at Isla de la Plata on 2 October 1684, they all joined forces. Swan depended on Davis for provisions, since he had no resourceful Miskito hunters with him, but he evidently had some misgivings. His instructions were 'neither to give offence to the *Spaniards*, nor to receive any affront from them'. Though the 'affront' at Valdivia could perhaps provide some justification for retaliation, Swan tried to preserve some plunder for his investors and wrote to a contact in October, 'Desire [friends] to do all they can with the King for me, for as soon as I can I shall deliver myself to the King's justice, and I had rather die than live skulking like a vagabond.'

Yet again, the raiders had little success ashore at Plaita and Guayaquil. Off Lima they captured two Spanish vessels, one carrying 1,000 enslaved people, whom the buccaneers imprisoned for their own service. Dampier, who learned from Harris of the gold camps in Darién, was deeply frustrated that none of his fellows shared his vision of establishing a new English mining colony with the forced labour of these 'lusty young men and women'.

Discovering from prisoners that the *galeones* had reached Portobelo, the buccaneers raced north to Panamá Bay to lie in wait for Peruvian silver shipments. In February 1685 they exchanged letters and prisoners with the president of Panamá, pronouncing themselves 'commanders of the whole

South Sea'. Despite their swaggering tone the buccaneers regularly moved anchorage to evade Spanish forces; Swan had brought an astrologer with him, who apparently warned him of impending danger.

Their numbers swelled with more arrivals across the isthmus, parties of French and English raiders from whom they learned that Golden Cap was dead, but his successor Josepho continued the alliance. The *flibustiers* dished out blank petitions from Petit-Goâve, though Swan refused one. Among their many leaders were Jean Rose, François Grogniet, William Knight, Francis Townley, and Laurens de Graaf, and with them was Jacques Ravenau de Lussan, who also published an account of his voyage. They numbered nine ships and around 900 men. Dampier later wrote that the isthmus had 'become a common road for privateers'.

This large band watched for the Lima fleet, but the Spanish commanders knew of the danger. Anxious merchants kept much of the silver in Peru, sending north only half a million *pesos*, guarded by the *Armada del Mar del Sur* in fourteen ships, including two large galleons, much more powerful than any of the buccaneers' vessels.

The two fleets met on 28 May 1685. Holding the advantage of the wind, the buccaneers pressed in, though Grogniet apparently kept back. A running fight dragged into the night, when the Spanish commanders, Tomás Palavicino, Antonio de Vea, and Santiago Pontejos, gave their adversaries the slip by tricking them with false lights. Come morning the buccaneers found themselves outmanoeuvred and disorganised, and the *Armada* easily drove them from the Bay; they fled west to Coiba.

The plunderers had missed their best opportunity yet, though perhaps it was not as good as it seemed, since Palavicino had prudently unloaded all the silver before battle. The English captains blamed Grogniet and 'cashier'd' him, and a combined raid on Pueblo Nuevo then spelt the end of this uneasy alliance, when English raiders offended the *flibustiers* by defiling churches.

Swan and Davis, with most of the English buccaneers, attacked Realejo and marched inland to León. Once again an Indigenous scout warned the garrison, who abandoned the city and harried the buccaneers – Dampier noted that one 84-year-old who had served under Cromwell, John Swan, went down fighting. Failing to negotiate a ransom, the buccaneers burned León, but many men succumbed to typhus on the return march.

This buccaneering fellowship began to disintegrate bit by bit. First, on 25 August 1685, Swan, with Ringrose, Townley, and Dampier, sailed off north, hoping to catch a Pacific galleon. Townley attacked a Lima ship anchored in Acapulco, but his men nearly drowned in a sudden storm. Soon afterwards they plundered a mule train for supplies, with a captured 'mulatto' woman as their guide, whose 'very pretty' son Swan kept, 'a very fine Boy for Wit, Courage, and Dexterity', despite his mother's anguish. After cruising and squabbling for several months, they missed a galleon in January 1686 while gathering provisions ashore.

Swan and Townley separated soon afterwards. Swan led a raid on Sentispac, against the advice of his astrologer, during which he was ambushed and lost fifty men, among them Ringrose. With Dampier's help, Swan persuaded his crew to cross the Pacific in April 1686. We shall pick up their trail later.

Townley stayed on the coast of Mexico, where some of his men were captured, and while plundering in the Gulf of Panamá in August he was injured in battle and died some weeks later. His remaining men, many of them French, now forced an exchange of prisoners with the president of Panamá, by executing some, and following that demanded a ransom of 10,000 *pesos*. The president paid them off.

Davis, meanwhile, still in the *Batchelor's Delight*, had sailed for Peru with Wafer, Harris, Knight, and some *flibustiers*. This group, too, split: Harris left them at Cocos, heading across the Pacific, and later on Knight would lead another group round Cape Horn to the Caribbean – though Knight and his companions stuck around long enough for some share in this last, and most successful, stage of these South Sea voyages.

The *Armada's* voyage north to Panamá had left the southerly coasts more vulnerable. After calling at the Galápagos, Davis struck several towns in Peru in February 1686, capturing 300,000 *pesos* at Chérrepe, ransoming Pisco for 20,000 *pesos* and capturing several prizes, some with enslaved people aboard. Towards the end of the year, following a disappointing attack on Coquimbo, Davis sailed for Juan Fernández, where Knight left him.

With fewer than 100 men left, Davis returned to Peru early in 1687, leaving behind five men who chose to remain on the islands and over several years repelled two Spanish attacks, until they were collected by another English ship in 1690. At Arica, Davis seized a further 40,000 *pesos* and ransomed the *corregidor* of Cañete and his family for another 5,000, before attacking several other towns and destroying a ship of the *Armada*.

The *flibustiers* under Grogniet had also remained in the South Sea since 1685, spending some of 1686 rampaging along the coast of what is now Costa Rica. These groups, too, separated and gathered by turns, before deciding that the *audiencia* of Panamá was too well defended. A Spanish truce with various Indigenous groups had closed the 'common Road for Privateers'. Instead, with some 300 men, they headed for Puná off modern-day Ecuador in April 1687.

The fleet was spotted and the *corregidor* of Guayaquil, Ponce de Léon, put his men on alert, but took no other measures. Guided by an Indigenous pilot and a '*mulato*' called Manuel Boso, the *flibustiers* mounted a three-pronged attack on Guayaquil and seized the town in one morning on 20 April 1687. They found only 10,000 *pesos*, burned half the town and demanded a massive ransom for the rest.

It would have to be brought from Quito or Lima, so in the meantime the *flibustiers* retired to Puná, taking with them captives from Guayaquil, including women and musicians. Grogniet died of injuries on 2 May, succeeded by Pierre le Picard, and two weeks later they were joined by Davis, who had heard about their attack on Guayaquil and decided to let bygones be bygones.

Davis had also intercepted messages showing that the Spanish commanders had no intention of coughing up and were holding out for reinforcements, even though the raiders had executed some prisoners. Fresh demands yielded 42,000 *pesos*, with which the plunderers decided to cut and run, first fighting their way past a squadron of three ships commanded by the experienced Basque *capitáns* Nicolás de Igarza and Dionisio de Artundega, in an indecisive engagement that scattered both fleets.

The marauders regrouped at Punta Santa Elena, where they released their remaining prisoners and shared out all the loot. Apparently it came to 400 *pesos* per man, somewhere in the region of what Morgan's sailors received after Portobelo, albeit taking a considerably longer time and effort to earn. It was still a decent wage for the three years some of them had spent in the South Sea on this voyage, though spread unevenly after all the gambling. Raveneau de Lussan wrote that some, worried about carrying the bulky silver home, traded with friends for more concealable gold and jewels, often paying a markup price.

Now they separated one final time. Le Picard went north to look for a French band who had not joined them at Guayaquil and, after raiding a few more towns, he scuttled his ships in late December and crossed the isthmus, reaching Cape Gracias a Diós two months later. Many, like

Raveneau de Lussan, returned to Tortuga or Petit-Goâve, no doubt clutching their commissions.

Davis took the other route, round Cape Horn, surviving a tsunami off Lima on 20 October 1687 and possibly sighting Rapa Nui on the way. They paused to visit their old shipmates at Juan Fernández and then reached the Atlantic in early 1688, heading for the English colonies. They would have to select their destination rather more carefully.

10

A PIRATICAL AND UNGOVERNED PEOPLE

When some of Bartholomew Sharp's band arrived in Jamaica in the spring of 1682, Henry Morgan, still deputising for the earl of Carlisle, immediately had them arrested. Under the new legislation introduced the previous year they were condemned and hanged. Jamaica had become an inhospitable place for buccaneers, even those who braved the South Sea.

In May 1682 Thomas Lynch returned as governor, after five years away. The Privy Council sent him to replace Morgan after reviewing the case of Francis Mingham, whom Morgan arrested for smuggling brandy. It was not buccaneering that ended Morgan's governorship, but his decisions as an admiralty judge on behalf of royal revenues. Lynch soon removed Morgan from the Council of Jamaica, accusing him and his cronies of 'disorder, passions and miscarriages' around town.

Lynch continued the same policies against buccaneers. He captured several, executed at least one, and encouraged others to turn to peaceful, if not entirely lawful, trade with Spanish colonies. After his death in August 1684, Lynch's successor was his deputy Henry Molesworth, also the local agent for the Royal African Company. Almost immediately Molesworth received more complaints about 'piratical English' who menaced Panamá and Lima, interrupting the silver shipments with which the Company's (illicit) Spanish customers paid for enslaved people.

Unsurprisingly, then, Molesworth took a very similar view to Lynch. When in February 1687 the *Ruby* frigate sailed into Port Royal with four corpses hanging at the yardarm, Molesworth called it 'a spectacle of great satisfaction to all good people and of terror to the favourers of the pirates'. He made sure that it was reported by the *London Gazette*.

Yet other members of Sharp's crew got a different reception in Nevis, where a jury refused to accept witness testimony, even from those of the plunderers who turned king's evidence, and 'God-damned all Indians and Spaniards for a crew of dogs, who should not take away an Englishman's life'. Years later, in 1688, Edward Davis, Lionel Wafer, and their companions were arrested on arrival in the Chesapeake Bay, but after prolonged litigation they were released in 1690 and allowed to return to London. They even kept most of their plunder, apart from £300 taken as a contribution towards founding the College of William and Mary in Virginia.

Jamaica's position was unusual. There were plenty of other places still happy to do business with plunderers – not just in the Caribbean, but in the North American colonies too.

Continued imperial warfare during the 1680s sustained the opportunities for plundering. The Treaty of Nijmegen in 1678, like the Treaty of Madrid in 1670, had not resolved the question of trade, nor recognised the legal existence of Saint-Domingue, which found itself in a very similar position to Jamaica during the 1660s. The fact that Spanish ships called illegally at Tortuga, while colonists on both sides of Hispaniola traded across the border, including members of the *cabildo* and (often unpaid) militia officers, rendered the *Consejo de las Indias* no more accommodating.

Biscayners and *guardacostas* cruised the coasts, provoking repeated complaints from English and French officials about attacks on traders and logwooders, and the torture and execution of prisoners. Lynch wrote bitterly that Spanish ships 'committed barbarous cruelties and injustices ... they are Corsicans, Slavonians, Greeks, mulattoes, a mongrel parcel of thieves and rogues'. Molesworth some years later described similar problems with ships from Cuba, again 'mostly manned by Greeks, but they are of all nations'.

Despite the peace treaties, therefore, *flibustiers*, *vrijbuiters*, and buccaneers continued to gather in Saint-Domingue, perhaps some 2,000 or 3,000 by the middle of the decade, most of them based at Petit-Goâve. Lynch's angry protest that it was 'contrary to international law to grant commissions of war to unknown persons up and down the Indies' went unheeded.

Michel de Grammont, an aristocrat who apparently fled France after killing his sister's suitor in a duel, emerged as a leader. During the last war he had captured a valuable Dutch convoy, escaped the disaster that sank D'Estrées' fleet, and then in 1678 spent six months plundering Maracaibo and Gibraltar in the fashion of L'Olonnais and Morgan. In the next two years he attacked Puerto del Principe, fighting his way out through an ambush, and then La Guaira in Venezuela, along with Thomas Paine and Peter Wright (who would pick up Dampier and Wafer in 1682).

Another war broke out between France and Spain in 1683, lasting only two years this time but provoking another spike of plundering. In March of that year Michiel Andrieszoon, a *vrijbuiter* with a French commission, teamed up with Paine and attacked St Augustine. A couple of months later Andrieszoon joined a large fleet under De Grammont, some thirteen ships and over 1,000 men, including Laurens de Graaf, 'Janke' Willems, Jacob Evertson, and Nicolaes van Hoorn. Meeting at Roatán, they sailed for Veracruz, where they knew two ships from Caracas were soon expected.

De Grammont sailed into the port with Spanish flags flying, was mistaken for the expected ships, got ashore and spent four days plundering the town, as well as ransoming the governor, Luis de Córdova. The plunderers captured some 1,500 enslaved people and the attack yielded around 800 *pesos* per man, among the highest payouts of any Caribbean raid.

This fleet had its rivalries, much like other buccaneering expeditions. De Graaf and Van Hoorn squabbled and when De Graaf wounded Van Hoorn in a duel, of which he later died, De Grammont demoted De Graaf. They went on to sail together again later in 1683, blockading Cartagena for several weeks along with Andrieszoon and Willems. At Cartagena they captured two Spanish ships, one of which De Graaf took for his own.

Danish St Thomas was another plundering haven: William Stapleton, governor of the English Leeward Islands, called St Thomas a 'receptacle of thieves and sea-robbers' under its 'pirate-Governor' Adolf Esmit, himself a former raider. Jean Hamlin, who plundered at least eighteen vessels off Hispaniola in his ship *La Trompeuse* (*The Trickster*), called there in 1683 (Hamlin had taken this ship from some logwooders, who had purchased it from a Huguenot *flibustier*, who had seized it in Cayenne).

At St Thomas, Hamlin ran into Captain Carlisle in the naval frigate *Francis*. Carlisle promptly burned *La Trompeuse*, something of a habit for his crew, as they would also burn Sharp's *Trinity* when it arrived from the Pacific. Esmit rebuked Carlisle, and Hamlin was soon at sea again in *La Nouvelle Trompeuse*, though some of his men were eventually put on trial in St Thomas and Suriname. The so-called 'pirate-Governor' continued to issue commissions until his removal in 1684. Sharp retired to St Thomas in his later years, after a stint as governor of Anguilla, evading English demands for his extradition.

In April 1684 a new *gouverneur* reached Saint-Domingue, Pierre-Paul Tarin de Cussy, with explicit orders from Louis XIV to prosecute pirates; the same month saw a new truce agreed at Regensburg (then called Ratisbon). Officially, Tortuga and Petit-Goâve were now closed to *flibustiers*, although *gouverneurs* continued to support them tacitly, and in any case had limited means to suppress them. The same year that De Cussy came to Saint-Domingue, De Grammont, Andrieszoon, and De Graaf spent six weeks plundering Campeche, though once again De Grammont and De Graaf fell out.

De Grammont led an expedition against St Augustine in 1686, during which his ship sank. De Graaf crossed the isthmus to rendezvous with Edward Davis near Panamá in the summer of 1685, though it was not long before he was back in Saint-Domingue, where De Cussy gave him a government post. These years boosted buccaneering once again. Molesworth worried that 'all people of uncertain fortunes are strangely tempted' by the 'many reports' of the South Sea voyages, and while he captured some, others slipped through his grasp. When Evertson and Willems offered to surrender, Molesworth demanded that they destroy their ships, so they refused and sailed off.

Indeed, buccaneers still found employment with English governors. Thomas Paine, when he joined Andrieszoon at St Augustine, carried a pirate-hunting commission from Lynch, who also employed John Coxon to chase Hamlin. The naval captain George St Lo described James Russell, deputy-governor of Nevis (where Sharp's men had been let off), as 'a great favourer of privateers'. St Lo regularly sparred with Russell and Stapleton, complaining about each other in letters to London, while St Lo was on the Caribbean station.

He particularly disapproved when Stapleton commissioned John Philip Bear in 1684 to cruise against Carib groups and pirates. Bear instead attacked Spanish ships, and the governor of Curaçao sought unsuccessfully to bring him to trial in 1685; in April 1686 Bear attacked Tortola. Yet Russell renewed Bear's commission in July when he turned up in a different ship, and then approved a Spanish prize that Bear brought in, claiming it had attacked him first.

Perhaps St Lo felt vindicated when Bear defected to Havana in 1687, converting to Catholicism. With him went his wife who, in Cuba, claimed a noble background, though Molesworth called her 'a strumpet that he used to carry with him in man's apparel', daughter to 'a rum-punch-woman of Port Royal'. Molesworth sent the *Guernsey* to expose Bear and demand his return, but the Spanish governor refused, and the following year Bear sailed out of Veracruz with a Spanish crew.

Some of these voyages spilled out across the Atlantic too. When Jean Hamlin arrived in St Thomas in 1683, he came from Sierra Leone, where he seized seventeen English and Dutch slavers and gold traders. More than half of his crew were from Africa, though it is unclear whether as captives or volunteers. Nicolaes van Hoorn, too, joined the Veracruz campaign after raiding in West Africa, having originally been commissioned by an *asiento* agent.

If De Grammont's expeditions resembled Morgan's in their coordination and clear targets, others were more random and rather chaotic in nature (just as some earlier buccaneering cruises had been). One very detailed example is recorded in the deposition of Robert Dangerfield, which he gave on 27 September 1684, at the age of 32. He first joined Jeremy Revelle's ship at Negril Point, on a voyage of 'purchase' against Spanish shipping. This trip took him north and then across the Atlantic to the Cape Verde Islands, the River Gambia, Accra, and eventually back across the Atlantic.

None of this was pre-planned. Early in the voyage they were captured by two other plunderers, who then recruited them to attack another ship, but desisted when they realised it was the formidable Van Hoorn. Several times later in the voyage the crew voted about where to go, sometimes with the losers leaving in a splinter group; twice those losers included the former captain, and a new one was chosen. At one point they united with a Newfoundland ship with a mixed French and English crew, burning their old and deteriorating vessel.

Eventually, they sailed for Charleston, where they were shipwrecked on a sandbar. These sailors were arrested (and Dangerfield's testimony written down), but their choice of harbour was revealing, for the northern colonies, no less than some Caribbean islands, regularly welcomed plunderers. Indeed, this arrest was rather unusual. Caribbean governors like Lynch complained bitterly that 'laws against privateers [in Jamaica] neither discourage nor lessen them while they have such retreats as Carolina, New England, and other Colonies'.

European empires dominated the Caribbean islands, but colonies on the north American mainland were confined to the seaboard, a strip east of the Appalachian Mountains. The vast majority of the continent remained Indigenous territory until the nineteenth century.

Louis XIV made extensive claims for Nouvelle France, establishing Louisiana in the later 1600s, while some French travellers, depending on Indigenous assistance, followed the Mississippi River. However, there were only 15,000 *colons* along the St Lawrence and in Acadia by 1700, and far fewer in Louisiana; consequently there were also far fewer *flibustiers* in the north than in the Caribbean islands.

English colonies grew faster, though still within limited territories, and most of them were 'private' colonies. Charles II issued charters for Connecticut in 1662 and Rhode Island in 1663, both already existing for several decades as breakaways from Massachusetts. The latter year he renewed a never-implemented grant of his father's from 1629, for Carolina, throwing in the Bahamas; the new proprietors included courtiers like the earl of Shaftesbury and John Locke, a contemporary philosopher. In 1681 Charles gave Pennsylvania to William Penn to repay a royal debt owed to Penn's father, the admiral who had captured Jamaica in 1655.

Nieuw Nederland also changed hands in 1664 during the Second Anglo-Dutch War, becoming New York, the two Jerseys, and Delaware, confirmed when the Treaty of Breda in 1667 exchanged these colonies for some Dutch and French Caribbean conquests, including Suriname. Three years later the Hudson's Bay Company, begun by two French fur traders, received an English charter.

These colonies were more populous than the French ones: Virginia's inhabitants numbered 40,000 by the 1670s, and New England's almost doubled between 1670 and 1700, to around 100,000. The Chesapeake colonies depended still on tobacco, Virginia's exports rising from 350,000lb to 38 million lb between 1621 and 1700. Enslaved people were most numerous in those staple-producing colonies, but they all embraced the economy of slavery. New England supplied the sugar-producing Caribbean colonies with provisions and other necessaries.

Maritime trade was therefore a lifeline for all of these colonies. In 1676 merchants in old England even complained that New England was supplanting them as 'a great Mart and Staple'. Port towns functioned as vital hubs. Between 1690 and 1740, Boston almost tripled in size (to 17,000 people), while New York and Philadelphia both doubled (to about 9,000 each).

These ports appreciated the benefits of plunder as much as those in the Caribbean. Sometimes it was indirect, such as purchasing silver in Port Royal for coining in New England, which had its own mint from 1652.

From the beginning, though, the northern colonies welcomed plunderers. In Bermuda, for example, Nathaniel Butler had refused to prosecute one John Powell as a 'Pyrate' in the 1620s because he held a Dutch commission and 'so freely and liberally unfurnished himselfe' of his takings. Butler felt a 'fayre warre with the Spaniard' would do wonders for his island, and that people like Powell were especially important because of the 'cutt throate' prices charged by the proprietors. Butler was a former plunderer and by 1639 he took command of Providence Island's raiding fleet and ransomed Trujillo for 16,000 *pesos*.

He was not alone, and many raiding ships found a harbour in these colonies throughout the middle decades of the century. One customs official complained that 'pyratts' were encouraged to bring their silver direct to Boston, where it could be 'coined and conveyed in great parcells undiscovered', a complaint repeated in later decades. Rhode Island, before it even received a charter, issued commissions against Dutch ships during the 1650s, on one occasion to a plunderer who had already captured a prize and who promptly fled to England when the owners sued him. In November 1679, some buccaneers told the earl of Carlisle that if they were unwelcome in Jamaica, they would be 'well entertained' in Rhode Island or the Dutch colonies.

That was no idle boast. After sacking St Augustine in 1683 and calling briefly at New Providence, Thomas Paine made for Rhode Island. A colonial official discovered that Paine had a forged commission describing Lynch as a gentleman of the 'King's Bedchamber', when it should have read 'Privy Chamber' – a minor but telling error. Despite royal orders to the colony to 'exterminate' pirates as 'a race of evildoers and enemies of mankind', which specifically named Paine, he traded freely with merchants, settled in the colony, and within a few years served as a juryman. He was not the only one.

Besides the economic benefits, plunderers also played a military role, as these colonies received few naval resources from Europe and those were concentrated on royal colonies like Virginia, with a naval ship on station in Chesapeake Bay by the middle of the 1680s. That protection probably explains why Virginia was less welcoming to raiders than other regions, coupled with a more dispersed settlement pattern of plantations rather than ports and, on those plantations, a larger enslaved population than other colonies. Unrest occurred in Virginia throughout the 1660s and 1670s, leading to new slavery laws in 1680 and 1682.

Elsewhere, colonists had to find protection where they could. Sometimes, both the need and the solution arose through negotiation and conflict with one another and with Indigenous groups. In the north, *colons* allied with Wendats, but in the middle of the century the Iroquois confederation expanded into the Great Lakes and, over several decades, began to play off English and French colonists against each other. In the last decade of the century an anti-Iroquois alliance, including French settlers, forced them back, and eventually in 1701 they made peace with both French and English empires.

Several English colonies turned to plunderers for protection, despite their tendency to act beyond official control. When John Stone seized several Western Niantic women whom he intended to sell into slavery, it provoked retaliations that escalated into the Pequot War. Stone had been arrested twice for piracy and banished from Boston; he was reputed as an adulterer and even a cannibal. Nor were plunderers easily dissuaded from their own designs. In 1658 Robert Sedgwick gathered forces to attack Nieuw Nederland and, learning that peace had been declared, attacked Acadia instead.

Nevertheless, they were essential to colonial defence, especially when a series of crises erupted in 1675–76, including Nathaniel Bacon's rebellion in Virginia and Maryland, which targeted Indigenous communities, a conspiracy among enslaved people quashed in Barbados in 1676, and a rebellion in the Carolina backcountry the following year. Samuel Mosely, 'an Old Privateer at Jamaica', assembled over 100 men to protect New England during a war against Wampanoags and Narragansetts in 1675–76. Ten or twelve of his men were also 'Privateers', and five of them (one Dutch) were reprieved from piracy sentences for this campaign. Moseley's brutal methods, burning towns and deploying fierce dogs, just as buccaneers did in the Caribbean, earned him criticism from some colonists but praise from others as 'an excellent Souldier ... an undaunted Spirit'.

A decade later, in 1684, Bartholomew Sharp arrived in Bermuda (with a prize in tow) at just the right time to help the governor restore order during an insurrection, which had erupted on news of the death of Charles II and a rebellion against his brother James VII and II by Charles' illegitimate son, the duke of Monmouth. Though Sharp, on this occasion, supported the authorities, a new governor who arrived the next year, himself a former naval officer, asked for 'protection against pirates or other enemy', fearing 'such a man as Sharpe may come again and master the Colony'.

The raiders' military appeal was particularly acute in Carolina and the Bahamas, given the proximity of Spanish Florida. Robert Clarke, governor of the Bahamas from 1680, issued commissions, including to John Coxon, arguing that as governor he had authority 'to attack pirates and savages'. Thomas Lynch protested that Spanish settlements did not belong in either category; many English colonists, perhaps believing in the 'Black Legend', or angry at the conduct of the *guardacostas*, disagreed. Even though he too would later employ Coxon, Lynch sent a copy of Clarke's commission to London, leading to Clarke's replacement by Robert Lilburne, but Lynch could do little more to prevent marauding.

Men from Carolina and the Bahamas joined the 1683 raid on Veracruz. Spanish forces from Havana counterattacked New Providence twice in 1684 and Charleston in 1686. A new governor for Carolina, James Colleton, arrived in 1686 and prevented a planned retaliation, provoking suspicions that he had some secret pact with St Augustine. Colleton was ejected in 1690 when he tried to govern without the colony's General Assembly.

The Bahamas, a chain of 700 scattered islands, were particularly hard to police. Edwyn Stede, lieutenant governor of Barbados, wrote to London in April 1688 with concerning reports that 'a piratical and ungoverned people' had made their own settlements in the Bahamas, although he added, reassuringly, that a naval ship had been there and rounded up those who were suspected of piracy, plus their accomplices.

Plundering was not going to stop any time soon. Within the year these colonies were once more at war.

Even after the latest peace treaties, Louis XIV's territorial ambitions in Europe, together with James VII and II's support for Louis, represented a potential threat to the Netherlands. To forestall it, Willem of Orange invaded Britain and Ireland in 1688, deposing James, his uncle by marriage, with support from English opponents of James' religious and political policies.

Willem became William III of England, and II of Scotland, together with his wife Mary II, and led an Anglo-Dutch alliance with Spain and the Holy Roman Empire against France. The Nine Years' War, also known as the War of the Grand Alliance, or, in the North American colonies, King William's War, lasted from 1688 to 1697 and reached across the Atlantic, Pacific, and Indian Oceans.

By this time the situation in both America and Europe had changed considerably from earlier in the century. Spain controlled the largest territory of any Atlantic empire, but it was surpassed in trade first by the

Netherlands and then Britain and France. By 1686 only 5 per cent of goods sent to the Americas came from Spain, while England's merchant marine had expanded by more than 50 per cent between the 1660s and the 1680s.

In other ways, too, 1688 marked a changing of the guard: in Jamaica, Henry Morgan died on 25 August. The governor, the second duke of Albemarle, hosted a state funeral in Port Royal featuring a 22-gun salute, reportedly with an amnesty for buccaneers to attend, and died himself less than two months later. Molesworth, who resumed his post, died the following year.

This instability left Jamaica vulnerable, as the war brought fresh conflict between and within empires. Jacob Leisler, a German-born colonist in New York, led an uprising there in 1689 against James' representative, and organised a disastrous expedition against Nouvelle France. A new governor sent out by William and Mary in 1691 captured and executed Leisler. William Phips, in Massachusetts, also dispatched soldiers to Port-Royal in Acadia, where they plundered the church and destroyed the settlement. Over the next few years Massachusetts and Montreal sent forces against each other, combined with Iroquois attacks on the French colonies.

The Caribbean witnessed several military campaigns as well. De Cussy attacked Santo Domingo in 1689 and 1690, and in 1691 there was a Spanish counterattack with the *Armada de Barlovento*. The *maestre de campo*, Pedro Morel, was known as 'a great merchant with the French', and his *sargento mayor* accused him of deliberately slowing the attack and releasing prisoners for bribes. Most of the plunder went in Morel's pocket or to Veracruz, and when another campaign began, again under Morel's command, the Santiago militia deserted en masse.

De Cussy also attacked Jamaica in 1689, and his successor Jean-Baptise du Casse, who had commanded a slave ship for the *Compagnie de Sénégal* and mounted raids in West Africa in 1687 and then Suriname in 1689, attacked Jamaica again in 1692 with 26 ships and 1,500 men, coinciding with the earthquake. Former buccaneer and pirate hunter William Beeston, sent to England on legal charges in 1679, returned to Jamaica in 1693 as lieutenant-governor and defeated another attack by Du Casse in 1694, though it damaged many plantations and carried off around 1,300 enslaved people as captives. The following year Commodore Wilmot, together with the *Armada de Barlovento*, captured Cap-Français and Port-de-Paix in Saint-Domingue, but failed to take Petit-Goâve or hold any of these towns for long.

Naval resources were still confined to just a few colonies, so predictably the war brought letters of marque back into fashion. The *flibustiers* had not been out of work for long in any case, while in 1692 parliament passed an act 'for the encouragement of Privateers', which was well received in the colonies. George St Lo, no friend to buccaneers, wrote two pamphlets in which he advocated for commerce raiding, pointing out that French *corsaires* had captured 600 ships, compared with only 60 by the *marine royale*. In 1692–93 English private ships also captured more prizes than the royal navy.

Buccaneers, *flibustiers*, *vrijbuiters*, and Biscayners leapt at the chance. Often they continued their international careers, despite the many treaties and proclamations forbidding foreign service. Huguenot Jean Tristian became a naturalised English subject in Jamaica, although in 1693 a Spanish governor seized and hanged Tristian, despite the alliance, replying to Beeston's protests that Tristian was 'known to be one of the greatest pirates in America'.

Likewise Nathaniel Grubbin, a Jamaica-born buccaneer, sailed with a French commission, as he had before the war. Beeston called him 'chief of these rogues', who, with his knowledge of the island, did 'much mischief' in night raids on lone settlements. Four ships sent out after him were all unsuccessful. In 1694 his French wife fled to Jamaica claiming he 'used her very ill', and in retaliation he warned that he 'would carry off every woman he met with', which he soon did. When Grubbin was captured among several *flibustiers*, Beeston refused Du Casse's demands to exchange him for an English prisoner.

Laurens de Graaf remained in French service too, joining Du Casse in the 1694 attack on Jamaica. His choice was probably influenced by the presence on Tortuga of Marie-Anne Dieu-Le-Veult, the widow of another *flibustier* whom De Graaf married in 1693, supposedly after she threatened to shoot him for insulting her. John Philip Bear, perhaps with his wife, abandoned Cuba when Spain allied with England, and went into Du Casse's service, later attacking Caracas.

In 1697, Du Casse gathered his *flibustiers* and joined a naval fleet of several thousand men commanded by the *sieur* de Pointis. This fleet of nine royal frigates and seven private warships alarmed Beeston in Jamaica, who sent warnings to Portobelo and Havana, while a panicked government in London dispatched a naval squadron. By the time that squadron reached Barbados on 17 April, the French fleet had already struck Cartagena, ransoming it for several million *pesos*. De Pointis sailed directly for France, but the *flibustiers* returned to plunder the city a second time, then made off for Isla de Vaca, though losing their two largest treasure-laden vessels to English ships on the way.

In 1687 some *flibustiers* had remained in the Pacific, led by Franz Rools from Zeeland, also known as *Capitaine* Franco, who over the following two years raided Sentispac, Acaponeta, and Rosario. A prisoner reported that they were 110 strong, of whom twenty were 'blacks who serve for everything' and another twenty 'Indian sailors' taken from a prize. A warship from Acapulco commanded by Antonio de Mendoza kept them away from the Pacific galleons in 1688. Heading south in 1689, Roolz decided to take advantage of the new war, cruising along the Pacific coast for several more years. He returned to France, by way of Cayenne, in 1694, while a splinter group captured more prizes and eventually returned the next year.

An English expedition under John Strong arrived in the South Sea in 1689, hoping to trade and recover Spanish shipwrecks near Guayaquil, inspired by the £300,000 recently salvaged by some Massachusetts ships from such a wreck near Hispaniola. At Valdivia and elsewhere wary defenders fired on Strong, but he managed to trade with a few ships, although the wrecks had already been picked over. Some of his crew, who had sailed with Edward Davis, were captured and executed, again despite the Anglo-Spanish alliance. By February 1691 Strong was back in Barbados.

The war reinvigorated plundering – not exactly a slow business in the early 1680s – and with it the language of piracy. English writers condemned Louis XIV himself as 'a Robber and a Pirate', and his captains as '*hosti Humani Generis*'. Yet there were also concerns that plundering was so well embedded in the social fabric of the North American colonies, which was no secret. The buccaneers, *vrijbuiters*, *flibustiers*, and others in the South Sea and Caribbean continued to target their traditional enemies, even when not sanctioned by a state of war, and that may explain why colonists had few qualms about dealing with them.

These targets, however, were about to change. In a tragic 'novel' printed in 1687, a servant of Lucifer explained to an aristocratic pirate how to use a magic compass. If pursued, he said, 'sail towards the West, and you shall secure your Retreat'. However, 'if you want Booty, sail towards the East, and you shall obtain your Desire'.

During the late 1680s and 1690s, buccaneers from the Americas sailed into the Indian Ocean in large numbers – and this time they went looking for other prey.

MEN OF DESPERATE
FORTUNES

Charles Swan, William Dampier, and their fellows were immensely relieved to sight Guam on 20 May 1686. In their passage from America they had nearly run out of food. Dampier learned from Swan later that the crew had plotted to eat the captain, who joked with Dampier, 'You would have poisoned them, you are too lean.' The governor of Guam accommodated them, partially to help a galleon sneak past on its way to Acapulco, and Swan returned the favour by giving the governor a 'delicate large English Dog', to the chagrin of the crew, 'who had a great value for that Dog'.

This crew tarried for several years in the Indian Ocean. From Guam they went to Mindanao, where Swan befriended the sultan and his brother, who laid on local dancers, while Swan entertained the sultan with his trumpeters, though some of the English sailors were murdered when they 'gave Offence through their general Rogueries and by dallying too familiarly with Women', according to Dampier.

Swan seemingly lost interest in further plundering and, in January 1687, John Read discovered an incriminating diatribe against the crew while perusing Swan's journal. With Josiah Teat, whom Swan had recently punished 'out of jealousy', Read seized their ship and sailed off. Swan later died in Mindanao, possibly killed when trying to escape.

Read, Teat, and the rest, including Dampier, ranged aimlessly for a while. In January 1688 they touched briefly on the north-western shore of Australia, or 'New Holland'. They captured a Spanish ship carrying one Alonso Ramírez, a sailor from the Caribbean who had committed some crime and was banished to the Philippines. Ramirez's account of this captivity was published by Carlos de Siguenza y Góngora as *The Misfortunes of Alonso Ramírez*, although Ramírez did not do so badly out of it: he was eventually released with a prize vessel carrying copper and made his way back to the Yucatán by 1689.

Dampier and several others left the ship at the Nicobar Islands and in May 1688 crossed to Sumatra in an outrigger canoe, enduring a violent storm, aided by some Acehnese sailors whom they had previously captured, who modified the canoe and sailed with them. Dampier then befriended the East India Company's officials in Aceh, sailing in various ships between the Company's trading posts, Melaka, Johor, and Tonkin (now Hanoi) in 1689, and Madras in 1690. At Bengkulu he briefly held a job as gunner at the Company fort, but fell out with the governor and slipped away, taking passage for England, where he arrived on 16 September 1691, twelve years after he departed.

In Madras, Dampier fell in with a trader named Moody, who offered him a job that never materialised but also gave him a 'half share' in two people Moody had acquired in his travels: a man named Giolo or Jeoly, and his mother. Jeoly was, or claimed to be, prince of Miangas, one of the Talaud Islands, where Moody hoped to set up a trading post for the cloves, nutmeg, and gold that Jeoly assured him could be found there.

Jeoly travelled with Dampier to England, but the planned expedition never happened. Dampier sold Jeoly to others in London; he claimed that he was cheated, and spared little sympathy for Jeoly. The new 'owners' exploited this 'painted prince', with his extensive tattoos, and 'exposed [him] to public view every day' at the Blue Boar's Head, Fleet Street. At some time Jeoly died of smallpox in Oxford, a lonely stranger in a strange land.

Dampier's wanderings were characteristic of this first intrusion of the South Sea buccaneers into the Indian Ocean. Most were passing through, or perhaps drifting around in search of new opportunities. When Read reached the Coromandel coast of India, half his crew deserted to join Aurangzeb's armies, but he sailed on for Madagascar, where he swapped to another ship, bound for New York. Teat took command, together with William Knight, perhaps the same Knight who had sailed in the Pacific. We do not know what happened to them, but the location is significant. Madagascar was about to become a notorious pirate haven and a link between two worlds.

Trade across the Indian Ocean went back millennia, as did exchanges between that ocean and the Mediterranean. Arabian, Swahili, Gujarati, Chinese, and Jewish merchants dominated different sections of this commercial world, taking advantage of the monsoon winds for seasonal travel.

A wide range of specialised craft plied these waters, mostly made from teak or coconut wood and bound with coir or reed thread, with sails of reed matting or canvas. These included, in the west, square-rigged Swahili *mitepe* and the double-ended, lateen-rigged Arabian, Indian, and Swahili ships known generically as *dhows*, and further east the similarly catch-all *perahu* or *proa*, referring to outrigger sailing vessels, besides Indonesian *jongs*, with lug-sails and side rudders, and Chinese *junks*, developed from flat-bottomed riverboats.

The rise of Islam in the western sea, with the Abbasid Caliphate ruling Baghdad from the eighth to thirteenth centuries (or the second to seventh centuries in the *al-taqwīm al-hijrī*), and the Tang and Sung dynasties in China over a similar timeframe, provided some stability for trade. Long-distance commerce survived the decline of those dynasties, as shown by the travelogues of Marco Polo in the thirteenth century and Ibn Battutah in the fourteenth, or Aḥmad ibn Mājid's navigational manual in the fifteenth. Valuable commodities like gold, silver, copper, spices, fragrant woods, and silk travelled these routes, and some could only be found here, although they were already reaching Africa and Europe through overland caravan.

Not all such trade was peaceful, of course, and many regions, such as the island of Socotra near Yemen, the Malabar coast of India, and the straits of Melaka, were known to be haunted by raiders. Ibn Mājid described Malabar raiders as a distinct group, 'ruled by their own rulers'; they may have been Mukkuvar fishermen turning their hand to another trade.

Confronting these raiders was one purpose behind a series of voyages mounted by the Ming dynasty in the early 1400s, commanded by Zheng He. At its largest, his fleet comprised 300 ships and nearly 30,000 people, and his longest voyage, reaching East Africa, covered over 12,000 miles, more than four times as far as Columbus sailed. After this monumental effort the dynasty withdrew from maritime investments, partially for ideological reasons, partially because they focused their attention on Mongol raiders to the north.

Europeans traders arrived in the Indian Ocean with the voyage of Vasco da Gama, who rounded the Cape of Good Hope in 1497, leading to the Portuguese *Estado da Índia* in the early 1500s. Northern European competitors followed at the turn of the next century, principally the Dutch *Vereenigde Oostindische Compagnie* and the English East India Company, then the smaller Danish *Ostindisk Kompagni* and French *Compagnie des Indes Orientales* in the later 1600s.

While colonisation here was much less extensive than in the Americas, each of these imperial organisations established bases and formed new trading networks. The *Estado* occupied Mozambique in East Africa, Diu and Goa in western India, and during the sixteenth century also Colombo, in what is now Sri Lanka, and Melaka. The *Vereenigde Oostindische Compagnie* made its headquarters at Batavia (now Jakarta) and seized Ambon, Kochi, Melaka, and Colombo from the *Estado*, as well as displacing them at Nagasaki in Japan. The East India Company had 'factories', meaning trading posts for commercial agents or 'factors', at Surat, Bombay, and Madras (now Chennai) in India, as well as Aceh and Bengkulu in Sumatra.

The Dutch and English trading companies followed the model of several earlier joint-stock trading companies, but also introduced commercial innovations like tradable shares. The Dutch *Compagnie* dealt in coffee, grown in Sri Lanka from the 1650s and introduced to Indonesia in the 1690s, but its most lucrative business was spices. The English Company, unable to compete with the *Compagnie* on spices, focused more on textiles. In 1684 the Company shipped 45 million yards of calico, a brightly coloured and printed fabric, which exceeded the total European imports only a few decades previously and equated to 6 yards *per capita* of the British population. By the 1680s the Company imported £416,828 worth of goods to England on average each year, and during that decade paid dividends of 20 per cent three times, 25 per cent four times, 50 per cent three times, and even 100 per cent on one occasion. Their stock rose 450 per cent between 1681 and 1691.

In exchange for these goods, the Company exported vast amounts of silver, 2 million lb in 1672–79 and 3 million lb in 1680–87; Dutch trade in the Indian Ocean also depended on American silver captured by the *West Indische Compagnie*. There were few European commodities of any value to Asian markets, so these traders could only bring silver – and, of course, violence and protection.

As elsewhere violence went hand in hand with trade. Early Portuguese voyagers allied with Swahili rulers like the *mwenye mui* of Malindi, and with Kochi in India, but also bombarded Calicut (now Khozikode) on several occasions, as well as besieging and then capturing Diu and other cities. The *Estado* also sought to control sea lanes, introducing *cartazes* or passes (local rulers may already have been doing something similar). The *Estado* did not provide any convoys, so the only protection a *cartaz* offered was protection from being seized by the *Estado*.

From the 1590s onwards Dutch ships captured hundreds of Portuguese vessels in these waters, one of them prompting Hugo Grotius' musings on piracy and prize law, and the English Company allied with the Safavid shahs of Persia to drive the *Estado* from Hormuz, at the mouth of the Persian Gulf, in 1622. Dutch, English, and French ships attacked one another during their various wars; the 'Amboyna massacre' in 1623, when Dutch officials tortured and executed twenty-one English employees, became notorious and was often brought up during later wars.

To control the spice trade, meanwhile, the *Compagnie* invaded the Banda archipelago in 1621, known as the Spice Islands, the only place where nutmeg grew. Of some 15,000 Bandanese people only around 1,000 survived this onslaught, now enslaved by the *Compagnie*, which held this monopoly for two centuries, as well as destroying clove production in the Maluku Islands and concentrating it in Ambon, under their control.

For the most part, though, European empires did not capture much territory in the Indian Ocean, and they are best understood as intruders into a complicated political and economic system. They were not the only regional sea powers. During the sixteenth century the Ottoman Empire expanded into the Red Sea, seizing Mecca and Medina, then Basra, Mocha, and Aden. Corsairs like Selman Reis and Hayreddin al-Rumi in the 1520s, and Sefer Reis and Mir Ali Beg later in the century, preyed on Portuguese shipping and raided their ports in East Africa, though the Ottoman Empire had largely withdrawn from the region by the mid-seventeenth century.

In the Persian Gulf, the Yaruubi dynasty rose to power in what is now Oman in the 1620s, driving the *Estado* from Sohar and Muscat and attacking Diu, Mombasa, and Mozambique in the 1660s and 1670s, while drawing revenues from trade and plundering. In the Bay of Bengal, the sultan of Golconda recruited European gunners and sailors for his ships, though Aurangzeb conquered the sultanate in 1687.

Portuguese shippers regularly complained of Malabar raiders preying on their ships in small, fast *paráos*, manned by Muslim sailors linked to Calicut and pursuing *jihād* against the infidels. In the later seventeenth century, raiding on the west coast of India orientated around the rising Mughal and Maratha empires. The Siddis based at Janjira Island allied with the Mughals, as did the East India Company, except for the war in 1688–90, when the Company lost badly. The ensuing peace treaty included permission to set up a new trading base on the Hugli River at the small village of Calcutta in western Bengal – the origins of Kolkata today.

Further south, Shivaji I expanded the Maratha Empire to the west coast in the 1670s, and in 1690 Kanhoji Angria became the Maratha *sarkhel*, or admiral. Kanhoji and his successors rivalled the Company, introducing their own *dastak* or pass and, especially in the early 1700s, capturing many Surat-bound ships. Four separate Company expeditions against the Angrias in 1717–21 all failed to dislodge them.

Both the *Estado* and the *Compagnie* found that strongarm tactics failed in China, too, where the Ming empire allowed only limited trading concessions at Macau. Both Portuguese and Dutch forces therefore allied with *wokuo*, as the smugglers and raiders who broke the imperial ban on trade with Japan were known. One *wokuo* leader, Wang Zhi, was a Chinese salt merchant who moved to Japan and, with the approval of a local *daimyō* or lord, commanded a substantial band of raiders while also trading in guns and ammunition (long known in China but introduced to Japan by Portuguese traders). He was killed in 1559, but another leader, Li Feng, attacked both the Chinese coast and Manila in the 1570s, and may have commanded thousands, including both men and women.

The *Compagnie*, similarly, allied with *wokuo* based in Taiwan, led first by Yan Siqi, known in Dutch sources as Pedro China, who served Li Dan, another Hokkien merchant who had moved to Japan after trading in Manila, being framed by the Spanish authorities, and spending nine years in the galleys. Both Li Dan and Yan Siqi were succeeded by Zheng Zhilong, known to the Portuguese as Nicholas Iquan, who also hailed from Fujian and negotiated on the *Compagnie*'s behalf in China.

Zheng Zhilong built up a force of 30,000 Chinese, Japanese, and European soldiers and sailors, in some 400 ships, and did such damage along the Chinese coast that the Ming empire had no choice but to make him *youji jiangjun* or 'patrolling admiral'. As well as imposing shipping licences, in the form of a large flag bearing the Chinese character 'Zheng', he built a substantial castle at An-peng in Taiwan, with a bodyguard of 300 African soldiers who had escaped slavery in Macau, and a chapel mixing Buddhist and Christian elements.

In 1628, the *Compagnie* seized Zheng Zhilong, forcing him to agree favourable trading conditions, but five years later he attacked and defeated a Dutch fleet, and his son, Zheng Chenggong, known to the Dutch as Koxinga, ejected the *Compagnie* from Taiwan in 1662. The Manchu invaders who toppled the Ming dynasty and established the Qing in the

1640s also killed Zheng Zhilong, but Zheng Chenggong set up a Ming court in exile on Taiwan, with its own bank and coinage minted from Spanish silver. His son continued trading with the English Company until 1681, but a Qing expedition seized the island in 1683.

The European empires did not introduce warfare to the Indian Ocean, nor were they the most powerful forces present. However, the forces of Zheng Zhilong, Kanhoji Angria, and others were not pirates or 'enemies of all', though they were often described as such by European observers. Indeed, Asian ideas and laws around sea raiding did not always match those in Europe.

The European marauders who began to gather at Madagascar during the 1680s and 1690s were not technically pirates either, often carrying commissions from American colonial governors against the enemies of the Nine Years' War. These men, however, did not confine themselves to legitimate targets among European shipping. Their real objectives were the wealthy pilgrim ships plying the Arabian Sea to Mecca, which led to their contemporary title of the 'Red Sea pirates'.

They were not the first to pursue the ships of the *Hajj*. In 1617 a captain supported by the earl of Warwick sailed to the Indian Ocean with commissions from Savoy and Florence. He seized £100,000 on a ship belonging to the Mughal emperor, in a foreshadowing of the *Ganj-i-Sāwai* incident. In Surat, English merchants were blamed as thieves. When the captor returned to England, the captain was imprisoned and Warwick warned to stay out of the Indian Ocean. A few decades later a Dutch ship attacked an Indian merchant vessel bound into Mocha, releasing it for a steep ransom. The city governor attempted to negotiate, but the Dutch and English sailors sank, burned, and looted all the shipping they could.

Those were isolated incidents, however, unlike the explosion of plundering at the end of the century. Besides the same 'sacred hunger of gold' that took buccaneers into the Pacific, religious hostilities provided some justification for these actions, especially in the context of Mediterranean corsairing. The Magharabi corsairs and renegades were threatening on two levels: because of the cultural revulsion towards apostasy, as with John Ward, and because the corsairs genuinely menaced European shipping and sailors throughout the century. European states sent repeated military expeditions: English ones to Salée in Morocco in 1637, Algiers and Tunis in 1654, Bejaia in 1671; a Dutch squadron blockaded Algiers in 1661–63;

French fleets bombarded the city in 1682, 1683, and 1688. Yet none of these, nor the treaties about which Charles Molloy wrote, halted corsairing.

Between 1580 and 1680, an estimated 850,000 European captives arrived in the Maghreb. Raiding parties landed on the coasts of Britain and Ireland, in 1631 attacking Baltimore in Munster, carrying off hundreds of captives (probably including retired English plunderers from the 1610s). While the corsairs are often associated with the late sixteenth and early seventeenth centuries, the numbers of English captives actually climbed in later decades – probably 2,000 in the 1660s, another 3,000 in 1677–82 alone, when England was at war with Algiers. As late as 1695 there were several hundred captives in Algiers and Morocco. Some converted, but many did not, and only the lucky ones were ransomed or escaped.

Sailors and travellers from the American colonies were as likely to experience this captivity as those from anywhere else – more than 100 New Englanders between 1678 and 1684, for example. Several important figures in the colonies experienced captivity in Algiers: Jacob Leisler in 1677; Seth Sothell for four years, captured en route to take up the governorship of Carolina; William Harris, a founder and influential figure in Rhode Island. In 1693 Benjamin Fletcher, the governor of New York, published two letters in Dutch and English asking for contributions towards ransom costs. The Massachusetts preacher Cotton Mather published a *Pastoral Letter to the English Captives, in Africa* in 1698, and his 1692 writings on the Salem witch trial included condemnations of Islam.

These circumstances help to explain why, as an officer of the East India Company reported, 'Some of the old hardened Pirats ... lookt on it as little or no sin to take what they could from such Heathens.' It seems likely that some of these sailors had experienced captivity, or perhaps had sailed on one of the later expeditions sent by European states against the regencies. At least they would have known about it. One group of Red Sea raiders went ashore to blow up a mosque, much as their fellows had desecrated Spanish churches.

Madagascar provided a convenient base to target the pilgrim voyages. The island participated in East African and Arabian trade networks, and from 1641 Dutch ships transported enslaved people from Madagascar to Cape Town, another of the *Compagnie's* bases, and for a while to Batavia as well. Slave traders from English colonies in America began to arrive too, dodging the monopolies of both the Royal African and East India Companies. One from Boston arrived in 1675, and by 1680 the governor of Massachusetts admitted that most of the enslaved people in that colony came from Madagascar.

At the same time, the island, ruled by various competing Malagasy leaders, remained outside the control of any empire. Colonial efforts there, including one by English interlopers William Courten and Thomas Kynnaston in 1644, and another French attempt from the 1660s onwards, failed. A Malagasy attack destroyed the French settlement of Fort-Dauphin in 1674.

In the later 1680s and early 1690s, plunderers began to arrive. Some came by way of the Pacific, others through the service of the East India Company, still others direct from the North American colonies. In 1690 one Adam Baldridge, a former buccaneer, possibly fleeing a murder charge in the Caribbean, sailed there from New York to trade for enslaved people, or kidnap them. Instead he set up a trading post to supply both slave traders and plunderers on the small island of Nosy Boraha, at the time called Île-Sainte-Marie, lying off the north-east coast and offering an excellent natural harbour.

The next year the *Jacob* arrived, from Newport, Rhode Island, fitted out by sailors who had run off with the *Blessed William* (commanded by one William Kidd, of whom we shall hear more presently). Baldridge's trading post and the *Jacob*'s choice of destination suggest that Madagascar was already known as a plunderers' hotspot by this time. At least one other voyage besides the *Jacob* sailed in 1691, the *Batchelor's Delight* under George Raynor, which plundered ships 'belonging to the Moors' before careening at Baldridge's settlement and heading for Carolina.

That was, broadly speaking, the pattern for these voyages, although there are no published accounts written by participants, as there are for Morgan's campaigns and the South Sea raiders. After reaching Madagascar, these ships made for the *Bab-el-Mandeb* or cruised near Surat or Calicut. Some made only one trip, but for others it became a routine: Thomas Tew of Rhode Island made at least three such voyages, returning to the Americas each time.

At the height of this episode, in the last few years of the century, there were probably around 1,500 raiders operating out of Madagascar. Most were English, or from English colonies, but there were French and Danish ships as well. Muḥammad Hāshim was probably right to suppose that many of these men had worked for the Company at one time or another. At least two who arrived on the *Jacob* in 1691, Robert Culliford and William Mason, left the ship at Mangaluru and entered the Company's service as gunners. Only a few years later, in 1696, Culliford joined a mutiny in the Company ship *Josiah*, though that was squashed when a passing ship intervened and dumped the mutineers on a beach in the Nicobar Islands.

Culliford returned to Company service, seemingly unchastened, and mutinied again in the *Mocha* frigate (at least one other Company crew mutinied and turned marauder). The *Mocha*, now called *Resolution*, captured four ships near Melaka, including a Portuguese vessel, before the captain died and Culliford took command. After seizing some Javanese and Chinese prizes, and assaulting but failing to capture a Company ship, they set course for Nosy Boraha. Culliford was later reported to live there with his 'great consort' John Swann, which might suggest a homosexual relationship, although 'consort' at the time referred to close friendships between shipmates and did not automatically imply sexual intimacy.

Mason, unlike Culliford, remained in Company employment, but that did not keep him out of trouble. He was at Calicut in 1693 when a different plundering ship called the *Resolution*, under Richard Chivers, sailed into harbour, seized some ships and demanded £10,000. The Company's officials, thrown in jail, sent Mason out to plead with the crew.

He failed to prevail on any patriotic sentiments, as they told him (as he reported it) that they 'acknowledged no countrymen, they had sold their country and were sure to be hanged if taken'. They intended to 'take no Quarter, and do all the mischief they could'. When several Malabari ships arrived and a fight threatened, the *Resolution* departed with Mason aboard. They dropped Mason off on a beach, from which he made his way back to Calicut, first taking a beating from some irate locals. Other Company employees found themselves arrested by local authorities, suspected of spying for the marauders.

While some of these men, like Tew, returned to the Americas, others remained at Madagascar, selling their plunder to slave-trading ships. Baldridge married the daughter of a Malagasy ruler and built a fortified stockade. His difficulties meeting the demand from slave traders may have encouraged him to deal with what he termed 'privateers', sending his purchases back to the colonies and occasionally arranging passage for plunderers wishing to return home. In 1697, while Baldridge himself was away on a voyage down the coast, a Malagasy attack destroyed his fort, probably provoked by the residents selling some captives to French colonists. Baldridge cut his losses and returned to America, where he settled down 'a sober man and is reputed wealthy'. Not long afterwards, Edward Welch revived the settlement on Nosy Boraha, apparently earning the title of 'Little King'.

Among the survivors of that 1697 attack was Abraham Samuel, a sailor on the *John and Rebecca* who, with his shipmates, moved further down the coast. Samuel, either born in Africa or of African parentage, had escaped from slavery, probably on Martinique, before he joined this crew. Arriving at the ruins of Fort-Dauphin in the south-east, Samuel encountered a local princess or queen mother (accounts differ), who proclaimed him to be her long-lost son by a French colonist who had departed with the rest in 1674, taking the boy with him.

Such a reunion is possible, given the global travels of seafarers in those years, but it would be a staggering coincidence. More likely it was a manoeuvre to maintain the woman's political position. In any case, Samuel established another settlement and styled himself 'Tolinor Rex'. He kept a bodyguard of twenty shipmates and built up an army of 300 men. It was not always a safe place to trade: the *Prophet Daniel*, arriving there to purchase enslaved people, was looted by another ship, whose captain handed the *Daniel* over to Samuel/Tolinor. He sold it on to sailors, who abandoned it in the Caribbean when pursued by a naval vessel. He seems to have held his territory in this region until his death in 1706.

The lure of those plunderers, and their wealth, very quickly caused concern. John Higginson, a minister in Salem, wrote in 1692 to his son Nathaniel, president of the Company's fort at Madras, asking him to put aside money for his younger brother Thomas, who was now in 'Arabia, whither he has gone with privateers, contrary to my mind and his owne promise'. In the letter John Higginson also worried about the witch trials that year. By 1699, the governor of New York reported that 'the temptation is so great to the common seamen in that part of the world ... the seamen have a humour more now than ever to turn pirates'.

The two names most often connected with that 'humour' today are Henry Every and William Kidd – and yet it is possible that both of them 'turned pirates' by accident.

Henry Every was probably the son of John and Anne Evarie, of Newton Ferrers near Plymouth, born in 1659. Some accounts suggest that he spent time in the logwood camps at Campeche and joined the South Sea voyages, but there is no definitive proof.

By 1689 he was a midshipman with Captain Francis Wheeler aboard the naval ship *Rupert*. Every must have been an experienced seafarer, because at the time this rank was reserved for capable mariners who could take command if necessary. He stayed with Wheeler for several years, rising to chief mate and fighting at the Battle of Beachy Head in 1690. According to the ship's paybooks, Every spent little on indulgences like tobacco, regularly consigning his pay to his family.

He then signed on as first mate aboard the *Charles II*, for a private expedition funded by James Houblon, a merchant trading with Spain and deputy governor of the Bank of England (founded in 1694), together with other investors involved in the Bank and similar commerce. The objective was to trade with Spanish colonies, raid French islands, and salvage wrecks, under commander Arturo O'Byrne, an Irish officer with two decades of service in the Spanish navy who secured the support of Carlos II. The flagship's commander, John Strong, had salvaged wrecks near Hispaniola, in 1686–87, probably the same Strong who went hunting wrecks on the Pacific coast.

It seemed like a promising opportunity, but things soon began to go wrong. O'Byrne was arrested and his house searched on suspicion of treason (due to links with the exiled Jacobite court), though he was let off. The ships finally sailed, much delayed, in August 1693, but due to bad weather reached Corunna early in 1694. Here John Strong died while they tarried for several months, awaiting paperwork from the Spanish court.

As was customary, the sailors received a month's wages in advance, but the rest was due after they returned. They had already used up a third of their contracted eighteen months without even leaving Spain, and the prospects of making a big gain dwindled. In March 1694 the men, via their wives at home, petitioned Houblon for six months' back pay, to which he replied (they later claimed) that it was Carlos II's problem. The mood on the ships soured. Houblon later accused the sailors of 'mutiny, Debaucherie and riots on shore', and of refusing to sail at all.

It was apparently at this point that some men proposed an idea to Every: take the *Charles II* for themselves. He began recruiting men in various ships. On 6 May 1694 they went ashore to decide their final plans and the following evening they sprang. The mutiny almost failed from the start when a boat sent to collect fellow conspirators aboard the *James* gave the game away, but Every moved swiftly, cutting the cable and departing, under fire from other ships and the harbour batteries.

Once safely away Every permitted those who were not party to the plan to leave. He even asked the captain, Charles Gibson, to stay aboard in command, but Gibson refused. Some aboard the *Charles II* may have thought they would return to England. Indeed, the crew hardly appear to be a bunch of diehard renegades. Several of them had been in the navy previously, one later claiming he had 'served my King and Countrey this

thirty years', though seafarers moved easily between sectors, so some may
have been more experienced in plundering voyages.

William Dampier, who was present on one of the other ships, did not
join the mutiny. Perhaps he regretted that later. He and others, back in
England, sued Houblon and his partners in the admiralty court for unpaid
wages, but got nowhere with it.

Every, however, seems to have made up his mind fairly quickly. He supposedly told Gibson, 'I am a Man of Fortune, and must seek my Fortune.'
At a general meeting of the remaining eighty-five men, Every persuaded
them to make for the Indian Ocean. They renamed the ship the *Fancy*,
taking down much of the 'upper work' to make it more manoeuvrable.
Off West Africa they raided a few coastal settlements and destroyed two
Danish slave ships.

At Madagascar they stopped for provisions, and then again at Anjouan,
where Every left a note in which he declared himself 'As yet an English
Mans Friend' and gave instructions for how English and Dutch ships could
signal to him to avoid attack. In that he seems to have followed the general pattern of the Red Sea raiders. Between 1689 and 1697 only eight
Company ships were seized, mostly by French *corsaires*.

Shortly afterwards the *Fancy* joined five of these raiders, all of them
from North American ports, and several of them, including Thomas Tew,
holding colonial commissions. The small squadron headed for the *Bab-
el-Mandeb* late in 1695, missing the pilgrim fleet in the night. Pursuing
eastwards, they caught the *Fath Mahmamadi*, which belonged to Abd-ul-
Ghafur, one of the most prominent Gujarati merchants. He had already
lost one ship in 1691, when the Company's officials in Surat were imprisoned for several months and ordered to compensate him 700,000 *rupees*, or
£78,750, until it became known that the culprit was actually Danish. He
had them arrested again in 1692, on the basis that all pirates were English.
Then the five ships seized the *Ganj-i-Sāwai*.

Aurangzeb's fury, when he heard, threatened the Company's very existence in India. The Company officers in Surat found themselves in jail
again, for eleven months. Throughout 1696 letters home complained that
both the forts at Bombay and Calcutta would have been destroyed had
they not been well defended. The Company began to hire out their own
ships to protect the pilgrim fleets, which eventually turned a profit, but in
the short term the future looked very uncertain indeed.

The following year Nathaniel Higginson (whose brother Thomas had
'gone with privateers' a few years before) wrote from Madras that 'our

Portraits of Henry Every: one from the 1725 edition of the *General History*, one from an eighteenth-century engraving.

Servants Lives and our Estates may be in hazard ... by the Pyracies committed in and near the Red Sea ... against all nations without distinction'. Higginson worried that 'so alluring is the gain of piracy; and what it will amount to in a little time, if care be not taken to suppress these villains, God knows'.

Meanwhile, the raiders, including many of Every's crew, went their separate ways. Some of them remained in the Indian Ocean, some leaving at Île Bourbon (now Réunion), others at Nosy Boraha. One was left behind at Anjouan, where he met a Comorian who had previously travelled to London and lived at Bethnal Green. Only a third of Every's men sailed with him across the Atlantic, to the Bahamas, where they arrived in March 1696.

As Every was crossing the Atlantic, in February 1696, the *Adventure Galley* sailed down the Thames, bound out to hunt pirates in the Indian Ocean. The captain, William Kidd, was probably the son of a Presbyterian minister in Greenock, Scotland, born around 1645, but followed a different path to his father and went to sea. By 1689 he sailed aboard a buccaneering ship that, on the outbreak of the Nine Years' War, the Dutch and English sailors in the crew seized from their French shipmates.

Kidd was given command of the renamed *Blessed William* (possibly a nod towards the king, but I like to think maybe a reference to the captain, or possibly evidence of his considerable self-belief). They joined in a successful raid on Marie-Galante. The commander of that squadron later described Kidd as 'a mighty man'.

Mighty, but not lucky, nor a good leader. Shortly afterwards several of the crew ran off with the *William* – and Kidd's share of the loot – to New York, whence they sailed to Madagascar in the *Jacob*. As reward for his service Kidd received another ship in which to pursue them, but they were gone by the time he reached New York.

Instead he helped the new governor, Henry Sloughter, to defeat Leisler's rebellion, and then married a wealthy widow, Sarah Bradley Cox Oort, obtaining the marriage licence just a few days after her previous husband died. Kidd purchased property in the city, though he did not settle down entirely. In 1694 he was reported sailing as a 'privateer', and then in 1695 he embarked on a trading voyage to London.

There he became involved in a new initiative with the help of a fellow Scot, Robert Livingston, a trader and smuggler who had also married into the Dutch mercantile elite in New York. Livingston and Kidd approached Richard Coote, earl of Bellomont, with their idea: a private expedition to Madagascar after pirates, and more importantly, their by-now famous plunder.

Bellomont gathered financial backers, including government ministers as secret partners; the king himself stumped up £3,000. Equally important, Bellomont brought political clout. At this time the admiralty, concerned about naval recruitment, issued only a limited number of letters of marque, despite pressure from merchant groups and the government. Through Bellomont's patronage, Kidd and Livingston managed to get such a letter, on 11 December 1695, and in January 1696 another commission authorising Kidd to pursue Thomas Tew and other named pirates. Eight months later the king signed another warrant allowing the investors to keep any plunder they recovered from pirates, rather than returning it to the original owners, as prize law would normally require; by that time the *Adventure Galley* was already at sea.

It was a new ship, built in December 1695, a manoeuvrable hybrid with both sails and oars, and Kidd recruited seventy men in London before setting sail. The voyage did not have an auspicious start. When Kidd and his crew deliberately insulted a passing royal yacht and then another naval ship, they were detained. It was not until April that they finally set out across the Atlantic.

They captured a French fishing vessel en route to New York, where Kidd recruited another ninety men. Many were mariners, but among them were bakers, vintners, carpenters, and shoemakers, mostly English, a few Dutch, Scottish, French, and at least one African. Some had lived in Jamaica as well as New York, and some had been raiders (one had sailed on both the *Blessed William* and the *Jacob*). Others had different ambitions: Benjamin Franks was a Jewish jeweller who lost everything in the Port Royal earthquake and now wished to get into the diamond market in India.

These 'men of desperate fortunes', as Benjamin Fletcher, still governing New York, described them, set sail on 6 September 1696. They reached Madeira in October and then, in the south Atlantic, ran into a naval squadron commanded by Thomas Warren. He had been escorting East India Company ships, who chose to leave the more cumbersome naval vessels behind.

Kidd sailed with Warren for a while but, when they were becalmed, the *Adventure Galley* rowed away and made straight for the Indian Ocean without calling at the Cape. Kidd probably feared that Warren would impress some of his crew; Warren suspected that, no matter what his paperwork said, Kidd was up to no good. He warned everyone to watch out for this 'old emminant West India privateer', as another traveller through the Cape at this time called Kidd, and soon that warning travelled further east on Company ships.

The subject of those warnings learned about them fairly quickly, because at Madagascar and then the nearby Comoro Islands Kidd encountered ships from the Cape. Low on supplies, Kidd's lack of cash hampered his efforts to trade with them, but he did pick up some runaway crew-members to replace many of his own dying of sickness.

If he wished to prove the rumours about him wrong, Kidd should probably have sailed for Nosy Boraha, where several hundred men could be found, along with their riches. Visitors to the island noted that gambling was a popular pastime here, as it was in the South Sea; stories told of thousands of *pesos* won or lost on a single roll of the dice. Sometimes the entertainment was grimmer, as one account tells of a group pooling their plunder, dividing themselves into two sides and then fighting to the death, with the two survivors taking the winnings.

Instead, Kidd sailed north towards the Red Sea. Kidd's motivations and plans at this point have occasioned much debate. In some of his own accounts, he claimed that he was searching for pirates; in others he ignored this section of the voyage altogether, or claimed that his unruly crew forced him into it.

In any case, his ship spent two weeks in the Gulf of Aden, where they were sighted and warnings ran ahead of them to Mocha. It was unlucky for Kidd that everywhere was on high alert because of Every's voyage the year before, though as Every's men had begun to arrive in the colonies across the summer of 1696, when Kidd was in New York, perhaps he should have expected that.

The *Hajj* ships sailed out under the convoy of several Dutch and English vessels, one of them, the *Sceptre*, commanded by Edward Barlow (who had run into Dampier at Aceh some years earlier, too). Barlow, in his journal, wrote that the *Adventure Galley* flew a red flag, a sure sign of piratical intent, but the *Sceptre* chased Kidd away.

If Kidd was hoping for a quick score and then to escape into obscurity, he was disappointed. His increasingly unhappy ship cruised down the Indian coast. Kidd sailed into various ports, visiting Company officials, denying the rumours and insisting that he was still following his instructions.

At Karwar Kidd met William Mason, another from the *Blessed William* and *Jacob*. Mason commented that Kidd 'carries a very different command from what other pirates use to do'. His royal commission 'procured respect and awe', but still he fought with his men 'on any little occasion, often calling for his pistols and threatening … to knock out their brains, causing them to dread him'. He added that as Kidd, 'by his own strength, [was] a very lusty man', some of the crew were 'very desirous to put off their yoak'. On 30 October 1697 Kidd exchanged words with the gunner William Moore and killed him with a metal-rimmed bucket.

Whatever Kidd told the Company officials, the *Adventure Galley* seized several merchant ships and no pirates. Sometimes they used French flags to trick their victims, in a common *ruse de guerre*, and Kidd was delighted to take a prize by this means on which he found a French pass. Kidd seems to have understood that Company property was off limits, though from one small ship they purloined a few hundred *pesos*, a Portuguese crewman as a 'linguister', and the captain as a pilot.

They touched at the Laccadive Islands, attacking a village after their cooper's throat was cut in retaliation for some of the crew raping women who lived there. In December 1697 they seized a Portuguese ship and then, on 30 January 1698, their most lucrative prize: the *Quedah Merchant*, carrying French passes, but freighted by a Mughal high official. One of the Armenian supercargoes aboard, Coji Babba, tried to persuade Kidd to accept a substantial ransom, without success. At Kayamkulam they sold off some of the valuable cargo, apparently to the tune of several thousand pounds, and in direct contravention of Kidd's orders to bring everything home for adjudication.

Then they sailed for Madagascar, arriving at last at Nosy Boraha in April 1698. Here they met Robert Culliford, whom Kidd reportedly reassured that he had no intention of arresting or attacking anyone. The crew spent months there, dividing up more of the plunder and gambling among themselves. Several trading vessels from the northern American colonies called in during this period, including one whose later arrest has preserved in the admiralty archives some packets of letters between these plunderers and their wives and families back home, a fascinating glimpse into their relationships.

Sarah Horne wrote to her husband, sailing with Kidd, 'We here abundance of flying news concerning you wherfor I should bee very glad to here from you.' Abraham Sasnoya informed his wife that he was 'now in the eastynges' and could be away for years, 'but I am of an honist mind to you still', and signed off 'my love to you and to our Child your ever tru and Constant husband'. Evan Jones similarly told his wife that he had made captain and would be away at least five years. Others sent back plunder to their families, or made wills specifying financial arrangements, though it was often difficult for a widow or heir to actually recover anything.

Some of the seized letters were addressed to Kidd himself. One of his friends told him that 'flying reports' of Bellomont going sour on him were 'false'. Bellomont himself wrote encouraging Kidd to return to New York. Though these copies never reached Kidd, others, sent on different ships, probably did. Perhaps enheartened by such correspondence, Kidd prepared to return, although over 100 of his men chose to remain with Culliford.

At some time in the autumn of 1698, Kidd abandoned the *Adventure Galley* and, with only about twenty men, sailed the still well-stocked *Quedah Merchant*, renamed *Adventure Prize*, for America. Only thirteen of the original crew stuck with him; the rest were new recruits wishing to return from Madagascar.

One was James Kelley, who had sailed on a slave ship to West Africa in 1680, joined Cook on the *Batchelor's Delight* in the South Sea, returned to the Caribbean, seized the *Diamond* and taken it to the Indian Ocean. He joined Culliford in the mutiny on the *Mocha*, and at least twice adopted a new name during his travels. Another was Edward Davis, 'an extraordinary stout man', possibly the Davis who replaced Cook as captain of the *Batchelor's Delight* and was arrested with Wafer in Virginia in 1688.

Kidd and the *Adventure Prize* reached Anguilla early in April 1699. As he had in the Indian Ocean, he found that his fame preceded him. Things had changed while he was away.

12

HANG THEM UP

In 1696 it seemed like the English Empire stood upon the brink of disaster. To the east, the Company quaked before Aurangzeb's displeasure. During the 1690s its average annual imports fell to less than a third of those in the previous decade, disrupted by war and piracy. On 17 July the Lords Justices in England declared Henry Every a 'Common Pirate'. The next month the Privy Council sent out orders to colonial officers to apprehend him and his men. Members of his crew were promised a pardon and £500 for turning him in.

To the west, those same colonies harboured those same pirates, which was doubly embarrassing as the Company tried to deny its complicity. Edward Randolph, the surveyor general of customs for the colonies, who had recently returned to England, submitted to the government a 'Discourse about Pyrates, with Proper Remedies to Suppress Them' on 10 May. He blamed colonial merchants and governors, accusing nearly every colony.

Two years later the political arithmetician Charles Davenant, in his *Discourses on the Publick Revenues*, warned that these colonies might 'erect themselves into Independent Commonwealths, or Pyratical Societies', which, he feared, 'we shall not be able to Master'. Davenant's language evokes that used by Charles Molloy two decades earlier, except where Molloy referred to ideas of 'Common-wealth' and 'Government of state' to discuss the regencies in the Maghreb, Davenant applied it to England's own imperial possessions.

It is tempting to see this crisis as a moment in which the imperial government struggled, and failed, to impose its will on colonists who either disregarded or openly flouted the law; and to find in it, as some scholars have done, overtones of the same disobedience that would erupt just under a century later in the American revolution. Some historians argue that it was this crisis of piracy that truly forged England's empire in the Americas while laying the seeds of its later demise.

There is some truth in this thesis. Randolph and Davenant were both involved in trends towards the rationalisation and coordination of imperial government (at least by contemporary standards). The laws and politics of empire undoubtedly changed as a result of these efforts to deal with piracy.

However, there are three points to bear in mind. The first is that, as ever, piracy was not just about piracy. Davenant's warning comes in a passage much more focused on smuggling and breaches of the Navigation Acts than on acts of plunder. Randolph, too, worried that piracy 'was a great Encouragement to the Irregular Trade'. His report on smuggling to the Privy Council in 1690 had led to his appointment as surveyor general.

The second is that the impetus for these developments came as much from the colonies – or from *some* colonies and colonial officials – as it did from London. There was much rhetoric about the evils of piracy, and no doubt those in power believed in their mission, but government policy on piracy remained essentially responsive, even as that response included a new and more coherent system of law. It is therefore too simplistic to portray this as a conflict between two sides divided by the Atlantic Ocean.

Finally, it is from this crisis, and the paperwork it generated, that most of our evidence for Red Sea marauding, and its colonial entanglements, survives. In that evidence, accusations of 'piracy' once again serve a polemical purpose. The idea of *hostis humani generis* made its appearance yet again, but as jurist and legal writer Matthew Tindal conceded, in 1694, it was 'neither a Definition, or as much as a Description of a Pirat, but a Rhetoricall Invective to shew the Odiousness of that Crime'.

As we shall see, the meaning of plundering, in both legal and moral terms, was still subject to a diversity of opinions, and not everyone agreed that the Red Sea (or the South Sea) raiders were pirates. Indeed, it was the efforts of both colonial officials and Whitehall administrators to impose their definition of piracy that transformed its legal framework and its popular image – and left us the legends of Henry Every and William Kidd.

We can trace this change most clearly by considering the trials related to those two figures; let us start with one and finish with the other. Every himself was never caught, and may have returned, clandestinely, to his wife, who sold wigs on Ratcliff Highway in east London. Six of his men, however, were rounded up in Ireland and elsewhere, and tried in London in October and November 1696. One was captured when a maidservant discovered gold 'quilted up' in his jacket, with £1,045 'in sequins'.

The indictment focused on the *Ganj-i-Sāwai*, and the King's Counsel warned, in his opening remarks, 'Suffer Pirates, and the Commerce of the World must cease.' He enlarged on its dreadful consequences, including 'the Destruction of the innocent *English* in those Countries' and 'the impoverishment of this Kingdom' through 'the total loss of the *Indian* Trade'.

These six men faced trial by the admiralty court, not at its usual location, but at the Old Bailey, the most prominent criminal court in the capital. Alongside admiralty judge Charles Hedges were the Lords Chief Justices of King's Bench, Common Pleas, and the Exchequer. This trial was therefore a stage-managed statement by the dignitaries of English government and justice, to reassure Aurangzeb and others that the Crown did not countenance piracy.

It almost went completely wrong when the jury found the defendants 'not guilty'.

I am a little astonished every time I think about this case. Henry Every was one of the few seventeenth-century plunderers who definitely had no commission and no pretence of a legal justification, since the *Ganj-i-Sāwai* was not even close to being an enemy ship. Indeed, the *Flying Post* reported that 'the Evidence was very full against the Prisoners, in the Opinion of the Court and all the Spectators'.

Perhaps the jury resented the East India Company, or felt that capturing a Muslim ship on the other side of the world was not such a bad crime as to warrant a death sentence. Possibly the fact that Every joined with Tew and others holding colonial commissions introduced some doubts, or the defendants managed to convince the jury that they had been what Henry Mainwaring called 'Perforst-men'. Or maybe the defendants' witnesses, including William Dampier, were especially persuasive about the poor treatment of the sailors at Corunna.

We simply do not know. The incandescent authorities suppressed any records of this first trial and commenced a second one within a couple of days. The new jury were instructed, in no uncertain terms, that a similar verdict was unacceptable. Hedges took charge of this second trial, bringing another indictment against the men for the mutiny on the *Charles II*.

Mutiny was only a felony under martial law, applying in naval ships but usually not others, leading some historians to argue that Hedges focused misleadingly on mutiny to avoid the double jeopardy of trying men twice for piracy, a sign of the government's desperation to get a conviction. However, the proceedings were not quite so shady. The men had been acquitted for one act of piracy and were now tried for another, distinct, act of piracy: the same *type* of crime, but committed on two separate occasions.

Mariners stealing their own ship 'with a felonious Intention' was 'Robbery and Piracy', according to Hedges. He went on that 'Piracy is only a Sea term for Robbery', and 'the King of England hath ... an undoubted Jurisdiction, and Power ... for the Punishment of all Piracies and Robberies at Sea, in the most remote Parts of the World' (perhaps seeking to quiet some qualms arising with the first jury).

Still, there were elements of farce during the second trial. One of the defendants asked to hear the first indictment read out again, but was told sharply 'there is no occasion for that', since they were now dealing with a different 'Fact'. Another protested, 'I am ignorant of these proceedings.' Some of the witnesses admitted that it was so dark during the mutiny that they were not certain who they saw. A witness who did identify the defendants, David Creagh, had been first mate of the *Fancy* and would shortly be on trial himself.

When a defendant complained about Creagh's dubious legal position, appealing, 'I do not understand Law, I hope your lordship will advise us', one of the bench replied, 'I will do you all right.' That judge must have meant that he would ensure due process, as he understood it. The jury dutifully found all six guilty; theft of an English merchant's ship may have concerned them more than attacks on Mughal subjects. The six men were sentenced to death and hanged in Wapping on 25 November 1696.

At the same time, and included in the printed account of this trial, three other men were arraigned for treason, having taken a commission from the *duc* d'Anville on behalf of the exiled James VII and II and plundered English ships. This crew, mostly Irish and French, had been captured early in 1696. Three years before, the English government had resolved to treat anyone with Jacobite commissions as pirates. In 1689 and 1692, the king also replicated earlier proclamations recalling mariners from foreign service.

At a fractious trial of some similar culprits in 1694, the admiralty court advocate, William Oldys (appointed by James in 1686), argued that even deposition or abdication could not erase some of a king's legal powers, including the right to wage war, which would render these plunderers' commissions legitimate. Oldys was promptly removed from that case, but would appear in a similar one in 1697, defending Thomas Vaughan, who claimed to be from Martinique and therefore a French subject. The jury decided he was Irish and guilty of treason, and he was hanged.

In these trials, the government sought to broadcast to the world an uncompromising stance on piracy, and to clarify the boundaries between legal and illegal plunder. On one level, they achieved this, with very public demonstrations at Execution Dock. On another, the trials revealed – in ways that the authorities must have found frustratingly unpredictable – that there were still multiple layers and jurisdictional intricacies to determining who was, or was not, a pirate.

The trial of Every's men drew renewed attention to the connections between the colonies and Madagascar. Two of the witnesses reported that Nicholas Trott, governor of the Bahamas, had accepted large quantities of ivory and *pesos* from them, plus the *Fancy* itself, promising them 'protection and liberty'.

Trott had originally been sent out to replace Cadwallader Jones, who had been accused of 'inviting a notorious company of pirates to make war upon [English] subjects', and he had strict orders to suppress piracy. Instead, when William Beeston sent over orders for the arrest of Every's crew, Trott tipped them off. The one man he did arrest was not only acquitted but provided with a certificate that he produced when later questioned in Boston. Customs surveyor John Graves, who arrived in the Bahamas a little later, found seven of Every's men settled in the islands, some now married.

Nor was this unusual. The Red Sea raiders brought enormous wealth into the American colonies, far exceeding anything gained by the Caribbean buccaneers or the South Sea voyages. Beeston estimated that one ship alone carried £300,000, and another tens of thousands. Beeston claimed that he was offered a bribe of £20,000 to provide a pardon, but resisted the temptation. Thomas Tew reportedly arrived in Newport with gold and silver worth £100,000 in 1694, and boasted about his plundering over drinks.

Several sailors – subsequently caught and questioned, though most were not – admitted taking shares worth thousands of *pesos* and even thousands of pounds, one as much as £10,000. Some were arrested with plunder in their possession, either in coins or in gold, silver, silk, and jewels.

These were fabulous sums, when mariners usually earned a few pounds a month. They explain why, though the mainland colonies produced no silver, they had plenty of silversmiths, much like Port Royal. These precious metals injected liquidity into colonial economies at a time of acute currency crisis and severe economic shocks in England, due to the war. Public debate over these problems intensified, while in 1695–96 John Locke and the mathematician Isaac Newton, master of the royal mint, undertook a massive recoinage programme. Arabian gold joined Spanish silver as the currencies of choice in the colonies. A modern excavation of a naval ship wrecked off the coast of Nova Scotia in 1711 yielded only a handful of English, Spanish, and Dutch coins, but 126 minted in Boston and a whopping 504 from Spanish America.

It was not just the gold and silver, though they were alluring enough. The Company's monopoly, and the restrictions of the Navigation Acts, meant that colonial merchants were supposed to purchase Asian commodities that had been shipped (and taxed) through England first. Like the Caribbean colonies faced with the Spanish Empire's prohibitions, traders in the northern colonies engaged in smuggling and raiding as an alternative. The Red Sea plunderers, whether trading in Madagascar or returning to the colonies, sold those same goods cheap and provided a market for colonial wares as well.

The presence of these raiders shaped colonial societies in similar ways to the Caribbean. Newport had at least twenty taverns, serving a population smaller than Port Royal in its heyday; Charleston introduced licences in 1694, because of a rapid increase in 'Taverns, Tapp Houses, and Punch Houses'. One colonist complained that even Henry Every's crew walked the streets freely and 'brag of [their voyage] publicly over their cups'. James Plaintain remembered being recruited for a Red Sea voyage in a tavern.

However, these men were not just gathering in seedy bars along the quays. Some of them moved in polite society. Adam Baldridge, for example, sailed to Madagascar in the service of Frederick Philipse, one of the wealthiest merchants in New York, who was also a smuggler, clandestinely shifting some of the more questionable cargoes brought back from Madagascar into Europe-bound ships in Delaware Bay. Many of the raiding captains were respectable men, several of them from Rhode Island, where they had wives, families, and social connections in the General Assembly. Carolina's proprietors objected that a decision by that colony's General Assembly in 1693 to permit anyone worth £10 to participate in elections, without any residence requirements, was effectively 'giving every pirate a vote'.

Every's second mate, John Brown, married the daughter of William Markham, governor of Pennsylvania (who himself 'belonged for many years to men-of-war'), and was elected to a seat in that colony's Assembly, possibly because members were exempt from prosecution. Brown was advised not to attend, 'being a Person under some scandalous Reports of Piracy'. Eventually Markham ordered Brown's arrest, then posted bail himself. Customs officer Robert Snead pushed Markham to arrest some of Every's men, but Markham dithered long enough for most of them to escape. Snead wrote scathingly of 'how Arabian gold works with some consciences'.

Many of these captains held commissions, since most colonial governors granted letters of marque throughout the war years, often to protect the colonies against French raiders, but also to Red Sea men. Thomas Tew and Captain Want, another of those who joined Every, both had commissions from Rhode Island; so too did John Hoar (captain of the *John and Rebecca*, with whom sailed Abraham Samuel aka Tolinor Rex) and John Bankes.

John Eaton, the governor of Rhode Island, continued granting commissions even after London told him in 1693 that he had no authority to

A view of New York harbour (originally Nieuw Amsterdam) from around 1670. (From the New York Public Library)

do so, nor to adjudicate prizes, which the General Assembly also carried on doing. Benjamin Fletcher, from 1692 governor of New York and vice-admiral of 'all the seas & coasts about your Government', with military authority over neighbouring colonies, introduced new legislation to prosecute pirates in his own colony and tried to push it on Pennsylvania too. He told the Pennsylvania Council, 'Pirates and privateers may become good men att Last, and the design of that Law is to draw them from their evil courses, and they may become good subjects and inhabit amongst us.' He, too, provided commissions. Tew purchased three, from Bermuda, Rhode Island (for £500), and New York (for £300).

Nor was there any doubt about the destination of these voyages. The registrar in Rhode Island wrote to London that most of the commissions issued in that colony had been given to ships bound for Madagascar, and the deputy collector of customs had to admit that he had known this at the time. In New York, too, Fletcher's commissions purported to be 'against the King's enemies', but the real intention was 'openly declared by the commanders' in order to gather recruits quickly.

After the trial of Every's crew, the government in London removed Nicholas Trott, though he protested that the witnesses against him were 'notorious pirates', one of whom had been executed. The other governors were told to account for themselves. Several of them took the opportunity to protest their innocence. William Stoughton, lieutenant governor in Massachusetts (who presided over the Salem witch trials), insisted that none of Every's men came to his colony.

Others cast stones. Christopher Codrington in the Leeward Islands and Jeremiah Basse in East Jersey pointed the finger at Carolina, though Basse also blamed the Bahamas, New York, and Rhode Island. Markham, himself under some suspicion – not without reason, considering his protection of his son-in-law – wrote to London that Fletcher 'fleeced' these plunderers, 'not by any violence, but blind signs which made them make up a purse of gold for him'. Some of those 'fleeced' would later admit that this was indeed the case.

This outpouring of accusation, and responses to it, provided compelling evidence of the colonies' complicity in these plundering voyages – and, at the same time, it raises questions about whether they were seen as piracy.

What is an empire? That is another question I pose to my students. It is, after all, a word I have been using a lot here. Nowadays, we tend to think of a political unit, with a central authority dominating colonies or peripheries, a view shaped by our own experience of modern empires and nation states, which only really began to appear in the nineteenth century. Most people throughout history did not live in nation states, but in local political communities that were usually part of some larger configuration, such as empires. The fact that the professional discipline of academic history originated at the same time as, and was often deeply involved in, the creation of nation states has done much to colour our understanding of the past.

In the sixteenth, seventeenth, and eighteenth centuries, European ideas of empire were still heavily dominated by Roman legacies, especially the distinction between *dominium*, meaning direct ownership, including of places and people, and *imperium*, meaning jurisdiction or power, but not necessarily control. Contemporary practices of empire were generally much more *imperium* than *dominium*, and indeed in French the word *empire* is still closer to that meaning than 'empire' is in English – although French writers did not often refer to their colonies as an *empire* in any case.

Looking at it another way, an empire is a composite of many different agencies and organisations, each with their own interests and agendas. That is true of all empires, and of modern nation-states and many other organisations too, but there is considerable variation in the degree of alignment expected between these components. It is overly simplistic to place that alignment on a sliding scale from *dominium* to *imperium*, and the two were and are not exclusive, but the broader point is that imperial rulers during this period delegated authority and did not necessarily expect direct control over their 'possessions', even if they probably would not have admitted that fact.

Of course, an empire with no alignment at all will cease to be an empire. There must be a legal and political structure to it, and it does seem that the Stuart realms and colonies had a somewhat different structure to others. That is not to say other empires were harmonious. Dutch and French provinces and Spanish kingdoms – and Ottoman regencies and other imperial subdivisions – jealously guarded their identities and customary privileges. Officials in these empires could hate one another just as easily, as when the *conde* de Lemos imprisoned Juan Perez de Guzmán. After the *flibustier* Trébutor, who had sailed with Morgan, seized a Portuguese ship during a period of peace, the Crown ordered his arrest in 1671. His ship was seized and a dozen of his men condemned at Martinique, but Trébutor and others escaped to Saint-Domingue and Ogeron's protection.

Nevertheless, both the Spanish and French empires had a single hierarchy, through the *Consejo de las Indias* and the *Ministère de la Marine*, while in the Dutch Empire all colonies were subject either to the *West* or *Oostindische Compagnies*. Colonial governments retained a considerable degree of autonomy, and introduced their own laws, but by the 1680s each of these empires had a comprehensive law concerning piracy (as well as others like the *Code Noir*). Louis XIV treated French colonies just like provinces of France, and even today French Guiana, in South America, is legally and politically part of France, sending *députés* to the *Assemblée Nationale*.

There was some hierarchy for the English colonies, with the Stuart monarchy as their recognised head, and their legitimacy derived from royal charter. Governors had to follow the orders of the Privy Council and various courtiers. In 1675 Charles II established the Lords of Trade and Plantations to provide more oversight, and in 1696 – just five days after Randolph submitted his 'Discourse on Piracy' – they were replaced by what is often called the Board of Trade and Plantations, though at times it called itself a Council, and some historians therefore prefer Commissioners as a convenient catch-all. Its members included William Blathwayt, secretary to the former Lords, and John Locke. That body may well represent, as some historians suggest, a march towards greater imperial control, and it quickly embarked on the task of gathering information about the colonies.

Yet every English colony retained its distinct laws and law-making bodies. That included the royal colonies like Virginia, New York, and Jamaica, which is one reason why Lord Vaughan got into so much trouble. Private colonies that became royal ones, as Massachusetts and Maryland did through new charters in the 1680s and 1690s, never relinquished those laws. While acknowledging the king's sovereignty, several of them, especially Massachusetts, openly questioned whether they were subject to English law at all.

I am not arguing for a distinctively insubordinate English character here, since all empires had their share of insubordination. If this structure owes something to English legal and constitutional culture, it was also, I suspect, largely unplanned.

Indeed, in the 1690s the composition of the empire was itself a subject of debate, and not just by the king and queen and their advisors. In 1695, Randolph proposed combining Carolina and the Bahamas and integrating Rhode Island into Massachusetts, to establish royal control along the coastline. Though that scheme was rejected, he was deeply involved in new legislation in 1696 concerning 'abuses' in colonial trade that increased the authority of customs officials and mandated that all colonial governors, including for private colonies, were subject to royal approval. William

Penn believed that Randolph wrote the whole law himself, and, while devising new rules for his own colony, Penn proposed a looser and more permissive union than Randolph's vision. Here we see how the officials carrying out imperial governance were also trying to figure out what it was, or what it should be.

This imperial structure had two important consequences in terms of piracy. The first is that throughout the seventeenth century each colony took its own approach to maritime law and piracy trials. So too did the East India Company, which received a new charter in 1683 that empowered it to establish courts and seize 'Pyrates and Interlopers'. There were also frictions between naval officers and colonial governors, since navy captains answered directly to the admiralty: while some tried to aid colonial authorities, others refused to take any orders.

Prosecutions often did not occur, and where they did, they were not always consistent with English laws. In 1659 a Maryland court banished a pirate crew, but this sentence probably reflected the colony's harrowing experience during the 'plundering time' of the British civil wars, when a Parliamentarian ship captain and his allies in the colony rampaged across several plantations. Some men condemned for piracy in Massachusetts were whipped, others were acquitted; only a few were executed.

The jury in Nevis who protected Bartholomew Sharp's men were not unusual. Colonial juries were notoriously reluctant to condemn those accused as pirates, particularly if the defendant was someone they knew well and had even, as the imperial authorities frequently suspected, done some trade with. Even in Jamaica, with an established piracy law, one man boasted in 1687 of pillaging Spanish churches yet was acquitted through the 'over-nicety of the jury'.

The other consequence is that it fostered inter-colonial rivalries. I am tempted to argue that these rivalries are what really defined the empire, and accusations of piracy became a strategic tool within them. For example, the first ever judgement by the Maryland Assembly in the 1630s was a conviction for piracy, but one that concerned a skirmish between Virginians and Marylanders in Chesapeake Bay. Through that judgement, Maryland proclaimed their own status and territorial rights against their slightly older neighbour. Similarly, a naval captain in Chesapeake Bay in the 1680s found himself accused of piracy because he supported a customs official over local merchants.

The later seventeenth century witnessed some particularly ripe rivalries between colonial officials (not just in English colonies, of course; all empires have their factions). It is from these feuds that many accusations of piracy occur. William Beeston worried about piracy in private colonies because it would 'entice our people away' from Jamaica. As well as wrangling with William Stapleton and James Russell in the Caribbean, George St Lo thought little better of Bermudans, calling them 'a mutinous, turbulent, hypocritical people, wholly averse to kingly government'.

Edward Randolph had few friends and many enemies, though one of those friends was Francis Nicholson, who came from a military background and as lieutenant governor or governor shuttled between New England, Virginia, and Maryland between 1688 and 1705. Randolph described Nicholson as 'really zealous to suppress piracy and illegal trade' and 'very severe to those who were even suspected of countenancing pirates', perhaps because, as Nicholson himself wrote, they might 'debauch the inhabitants [of the colonies] and make them leave planting to follow the same trade'. In 1692 Nicholson sent a ship to pursue plunderers who had arrived in Charleston and later wrote to London condemning pirates as 'profligate men' committing 'barbarous actions ... the disgrace of mankind in general, and of the noble, valiant, generous English in particular'.

Nicholson was not motivated by morals alone. He was deeply suspicious of the private colonies and had a particular animus against Markham in Pennsylvania, accusing him several times of harbouring pirates; Markham described this as 'malice and envy'. When Markham hired one Captain Day and his 'gang of brisk fellows' to protect Pennsylvania from French ships in 1696, Nicholson, suspicious that Day was bound for Madagascar, sent Captain Daniel, with flags flying, to arrest him. Most of Day's men escaped to Philadelphia, at which a furious Daniel challenged Markham to a duel, but was fobbed off. Markham complained of this 'gross affront' from Nicholson, and when the news got to London, William Penn protested that accusations against his governor were 'foul and false', though privately warning Markham of the rumours about him.

Jeremiah Basse was another who, like Randolph and Nicholson, built a career in this fashion. The jeremiads he sent to London as an agent of the West Jersey Society, describing colonial misbehaviour, including piracy, brought him to the attention of William Popple, secretary to the Commissioners for Trade. When Basse visited London in 1697, he promised Popple that he had 'schemes for the suppression of piracy' that required only 'sufficient powers be granted to me'. Basse was sent back across the Atlantic to govern both Jerseys.

In the same year, the earl of Bellomont, Kidd's benefactor, embarked on a similar colonial career as governor of Massachusetts, New York, and New Hampshire, captain general of Rhode Island, and vice admiral. He allied with Jacob Leisler's son, looking to clear his father's name, and with others in the colony who resented Fletcher's governorship. On arrival Bellomont pursued investigations into piracy, and he was particularly interested in anything that discredited Fletcher.

Bellomont was a friend of the so-called 'junto' of ministers then in power in England, leaders of the Whigs, who, along with their opponents the Tories, formed the two main political groupings of this era. Neither was a coherent or coordinated political party in the modern sense, and both these labels were insults used by the opposing side rather than names anyone would call themselves, but these political constellations nevertheless shaped government in England and its colonies. William Blathwayt was also associated with the Whigs.

Another dimension shaping these campaigns was religion. Most of the colonial officials who supported greater royal control, and campaigns against piracy, were committed Anglicans, hostile to the Quaker elites in Pennsylvania, Rhode Island, and West Jersey. Bellomont claimed that many Quakers were 'downright Jacobites' who only feigned Quaker beliefs to avoid swearing oaths. William Penn's friendship with, and support from, James VII and II during his reign fuelled these suspicions.

We have to bear these rivalries in mind when examining the evidence for colonial support of Red Sea plundering – not to say that it did not happen, or that these accusations were entirely confected, but because many people in the colonies probably did not share the accusers' definition of this plundering as piracy. Nicholson, for example, wrote about 'these sort of privateers, or rather pirates' in his accusations, and the Commissioners claimed that 'privateers' was only a 'soft name for pirates'. Nor were such charges confined to the English colonies: Beeston wrote to Cartagena at one point about the seizure of a Charleston ship, which 'looks so like piracy' that he threatened to hang any Spanish sailors he found doing the same, and on occasion he made good that threat.

Their targets disagreed, and said as much in their own correspondence to London. Markham maintained that some who 'went by the name of privateers' had arrived in Pennsylvania, who 'might be pirates for anything I know to the contrary … but if they are pirates or were ever accused as such I never saw nor heard of it'. The General Assembly asserted that their fellow Pennsylvanians were 'sober and industrious and have never advanced their fortunes by illegal trade'. In 1698 the Council of

Pennsylvania wrote to London that the only 'pirates' in the colony were those admitted there by Randolph himself.

Fletcher gave a surprisingly detailed account of his friendship with Tew, whom he described in heroic terms intriguingly similar to the more positive images of plundering captains in popular literature. Tew was 'not only a man of courage and activity, but of the greatest sense and remembrance ... of any seaman'. Fletcher maintained that 'this intimacy proceeded only from the pleasantness of [Tew's] conversation' and Fletcher's 'desire to reclaim Tew from an ill habit he had got of swearing', even providing Tew with reading material for his improvement. Fletcher wrote that such men 'enrich the Charter Governments' and protested, 'It may be my misfortune, but not my crime, if they turn pirates.'

Historians have tended to interpret these protestations in the same way the metropolitan authorities did, as disingenuous excuses by people knowingly embroiled in piracy. Perhaps they were – what else could a governor say to such charges? On the other hand, given the ongoing legal and popular discussions over what constituted piracy and privateering, the contested significance of commissions, or the popular attitudes about plundering religious enemies, I think it is entirely possible that there was a genuine difference of opinion over which voyages were piratical, not just between London and the colonies but between different colonies too.

It is difficult to be sure, because the only evidence we have originated in the context of these arguments and counter-arguments. We do not really know what anyone thought about it before they suddenly found themselves accused of piracy. Nevertheless, I think the comment of some Pennsylvanians to an admiralty judge is potentially significant: 'they do not know them to be pirates till they are convicted'. It is the judgement, not the plundering, that makes a pirate. While the English Empire was not unusually piratical, it may have been especially prone to arguing about piracy – and those arguments have left their mark on our modern understanding of piracy.

Whatever colonists thought, the government in London, stung by the complaints from Randolph, Nicholson, Basse, and others, were not going to let this go. Their approach, throughout the 1680s and early 1690s, was to put pressure on the colonies to individually introduce laws modelled on Jamaica's anti-piracy act, sending orders to this effect first in 1684 and again after Randolph's legislation of 1696, which instituted new vice-admiralty courts in every colony, with judges appointed by the Crown.

Basse and Bellomont were part of this renewed pressure, in 1698 issuing general proclamations against 'vice and profaneness', removing negligent councillors and customs collectors, and rounding up whatever Red Sea sailors they could for interrogation, some of whom they shipped to London, while others they pardoned. Rhode Island acquitted two of Every's men and continued to issue 'defensive commissions', so London gave Bellomont authority to investigate the colony under threat of a *quo warranto* retraction of its charter. Bellomont collected, and forwarded to London, lengthy reports on the governors' conduct and the recent trial, and the colony was forced to pay him a bond for good behaviour.

This pressure did result in colonies introducing new legislation in these decades, and prosecuting and executing some pirates, though many Red Sea men escaped capture – often, it was suspected, with the connivance of local officials. However, these measures ran into several problems. For one thing, colonial assemblies tended to amend the legislation they introduced, stuffing them full of caveats, so that they did not prohibit foreign commissions or give officers sufficient authority in pursuit of pirates.

Rhode Island passed a law that piracy should be tried like criminal offences ashore, with a local jury, and not a single prosecution occurred under this act, which remained in force until 1723. The General Assembly in Pennsylvania in 1697 only criminalised future piracies, as Penn wrote, 'lest honest people might be affected, since many of those reputed pirates had some years ago been permitted to live in this and other Provinces' (again disputing that these 'honest men' were, indeed, pirates). When London demanded to see a written copy of colonial laws, the command was often carefully ignored.

Another issue arose from the status of the 1536 legislation, still the basis of piracy prosecutions in England. In 1684, and again in 1696, the Commissioners consulted with legal advisors, first the King's Counsel and Advocate General and later Charles Hedges, with regard to admiralty jurisdiction in the colonies. The response of these learned lawyers was distinctly unhelpful: they ruled that the statute did not apply outside England. Colonial authorities could arrest pirates, but had to send them to London for trial, and even where local legislation provided a suitable procedure, colonial vice-admiralty courts were restricted to lesser felonies, not capital crimes.

Those lawyerly opinions had a significant impact. Pennsylvania's attorney general, a Quaker, refused to try pirates, and in July 1697 Basse wrote to Popple that there were no courts in his territory with the authority to try pirates, since 'the declared judgment of the Attorney General that we have no Admiral jurisdiction', knowledge of which 'contributes not a little to [pirates'] boldness'. He hoped the new vice-admiralty courts might solve this problem, although both Pennsylvania and Rhode Island made difficulties for the judges; the one in Rhode Island had to hold his court 40 miles out of town.

The alternative would be a single law applying to all colonies, as the French and Spanish empires had, but Charles Hedges hesitated about this idea in 1696, perhaps because it had been attempted before. James VII and II issued a proclamation against 'Pirat or Pirats, Privateer or Privateers' in January 1688, the first for almost eighty years, and the first ever to deal explicitly with the American colonies. Complaining of 'Robberies and Piracies ... daily committed by great numbers of Pirates and Privateers as well on the Seas as on the Land of and in America', James particularly blamed the procedural irregularities by which 'most notorious Pirates' had escaped punishment through the 'facility or partiality of Juries'.

James' solution was to appoint Robert Holmes, an experienced naval officer, to pursue pirates, while encouraging colonial authorities, some of them new men installed by him, to enforce the existing laws. Holmes, however, was suspect because of his close connections with the Spanish ambassador, and even Edward Randolph complained that Holmes did not pursue pirates with sufficient alacrity.

Given the scale of territory Holmes was supposed to cover with only limited resources, this is perhaps not surprising. The many islands and inlets of the coastline, especially around Rhode Island and Carolina, made detection and pursuit of raiders difficult, while the absence of printing presses and newspapers, or other means of public communication, also limited the transmission of accurate information.

Moreover, this proclamation lasted only a few months, until James' deposition. Indignant colonists took that opportunity to remove his officials, not just Leisler in New York, but also Protestants in Maryland, and some in Boston, complaining that these officers had been 'so lavish in their Discourse as to condemn us for *Pirates*'. One of the officers, Edward Randolph, was thrown into jail, from where he wrote scathingly that the town had become 'a new Algiers'. He was not released until the Privy Council ordered it in 1690.

Randolph found himself behind bars again in 1699, this time in Bermuda, where he had arrived to investigate the conduct of the governor, Samuel Day, who had arrested two men who admitted to sailing with

Every and were now local landowners. One had escaped. Day reported to the Commissioners that a jury had convicted Randolph of 'evil and secret practices', and even after he was released nine months later he dared not leave the island for some time, for fear of pirates. Randolph retired soon afterwards, though not before submitting a last report on 'High Crimes and Misdemeanours', and died in Virginia in 1703.

Indeed, the efforts of Randolph, Bellomont, and Basse – and Penn, who arrived in person in 1699 to sort out affairs in his colony – were not doing much to win over hearts and minds. Plunderers from Madagascar continued to return to the Americas, described as 'Every's men' regardless of whether they sailed with him until, from 1699, they became 'Kidd's men', due to the 'flying news' of which Sarah Horne wrote to her husband. New York sent four ships to Madagascar in 1698, though one was snatched by the raiders there and two others were arrested (one of them with Horne's letter aboard). More were expected.

While some of these returners were arrested, often they escaped or were released; officials complained the locals had 'entertained the pirates, conveyed them from place to place, furnished them with provisions and liquors, and given them intelligence and sheltered them from justice'. Those pursuing them were insulted as 'enemies to the country, for disturbing and hindering honest men'.

Some governors continued to issue commissions, even after the Treaty of Rijswijk, on 20 September 1697, ended the Nine Years' War (and formally recognised Saint-Domingue). In the Bahamas, Trott's successor Nicholas Webb appointed former plunderers to official posts, and then his replacement Read Elding did the same, including 'one of the chief of Every's men'. Basse was ejected by the Jersey proprietors in 1699 after offending both the Scottish leaders in East Jersey and the Quakers in West Jersey – prompting him to pen yet another diatribe.

When a customs officer impounded some muslins and calicos, a crowd attacked his house, and in Newark, East Jersey, a 'Rabble' assaulted the courthouse. Bellomont tried to prosecute the master of one New York ship returned from Madagascar, but could find no witnesses. He complained that the inhabitants of Long Island 'have been many of them pirates themselves' and were 'so lawless and desperate' that he could not even collect taxes there.

Into the midst of all of this, in April 1699, sailed William Kidd.

Kidd may already have known that, on 23 November 1698, London had sent out a general order to all the American colonies, declaring him to be a pirate, ordering his arrest, and excluding him from all pardons. After arriving at Anguilla, he made for St Thomas, but the governor refused to protect him against English warships, one of which was already out looking for him.

Instead, Kidd set up shop on the south coast of Hispaniola with the help of Henry Bolton, an old contact from Kidd's Caribbean days and a former customs collector from the Leeward Islands who, after embezzling funds, went into trade in Antigua. With Bolton's help Kidd sold off some of his cargo to ships from Curaçao, again contravening his instructions to bring all his plunder to New York.

Estimates of how much Kidd made vary wildly, but certainly enough to purchase Bolton's sloop, the *St Antonio*, for 3,000 *pesos* and to carry with him 4,200 *pesos* by bills of exchange, collectible in New York, and another 4,000 in gold. Kidd was converting his bulkier, and more incriminating, plunder into transportable wealth, some of which reached his wife and other contacts.

Eventually Kidd sailed north in June 1699, presumably still trusting to Bellomont's promises. He visited his family in New York and sent messengers to his patron, then in Boston, with the two French passes he had taken and promises of a third share of the £30,000 that he claimed still lay in the *Adventure Prize*, as well as some valuable presents for Lady Bellomont. All he wanted was a pardon.

Kidd's crew dispersed. One sent a 'very saucy letter' to the lieutenant governor of New York, from the private colony of Connecticut. James Kelley escaped from jail in New England; he had been identified and charged because of the scar of a forced circumcision, probably done in captivity in North Africa, or elsewhere in the Muslim world.

Bellomont told the Commissioners in May that he believed Kidd's claims of being forced into piracy by his crew, and also delayed issuing the proclamation for his arrest, though it had been published elsewhere. He reassured Kidd that a pardon would be forthcoming and Kidd duly went to Boston for several meetings with the Council of Massachusetts between 3 and 6 July, and some private chats with Bellomont. The Council demanded a written narrative and full accounting, both of which Kidd prepared (probably selectively).

At some point, Bellomont changed his mind. He may have realised that protecting Kidd was incompatible with his public campaign against piracy, or that by arresting Kidd for piracy he stood to gain a larger share of the

plunder than he would as Kidd's partner. In either case, he finally published the proclamation and sent out the constable, who arrested Kidd on
Bellomont's doorstep when he arrived to present the requested documents.

Probably Bellomont had little choice in the end. The clamours from
the Company had not ceased. In 1698 the streets of Surat had filled
again with angry rioters, while Company officials retreated to their fortified quarters and Aurangzeb ordered them to pay compensation or
be expelled. Abd-ul-Ghafur lost another ship in the very next pilgrim
convoy and the Company's trading privileges were suspended again in
1701. Their lobbyists portrayed Madagascar as a fortified pirate haven,
blamed the colonies for supporting raiders, and focused on Kidd as a
suitable scapegoat.

The government had seemingly run out of patience, too, with its efforts
to talk the more recalcitrant colonies round. Charles Hedges began to
consider the possibility of a uniform piracy law with the Commissioners
in 1697, and by 1698, with the war over and complaints still coming from
the colonies, he felt parliament might now accept it. Hedges drafted a new
bill, discussed in parliament between December 1699 and March 1700 and
passed as the Act for the More Effectual Suppression of Piracy.

While this legislation was in process, in February 1700, the
Commissioners ordered governors to follow prosecutions if local laws
and the 'disposition of the people' made it possible, otherwise to send
prisoners to London, which some did. Beeston wrote that it was too costly
to send defendants across the ocean: in Jamaica, he boasted, 'as fast as we
meet them, we try them, and, if good proof against them, hang them up'.

That, in effect, was the point of the new statute, authorising colonial
officials and naval officers anywhere in the world to form a tribunal,
without needing a jury. William Penn protested that few colonial lawyers
understood admiralty law, so they would be reluctant to proceed; even
Beeston was worried, because colonists disliked trying capital offences
without a jury. The East India Company, by contrast, were more enthusiastic and asked for the same authority for their officials.

It was a remarkable, global, assertion of imperial authority. The government issued a pardon for any pirates who surrendered within twelve
months, but they also passed another statute at the same time mandating
punishment, including potential revocation of charters, for colonies that
supported piracy.

Kidd arrived in London about a month after the new act passed,
along with prisoners from the crew of *La Paix*, captured when they
attacked a naval ship in Chesapeake Bay. For a few years now rumours

had been circulating about his plunder, some saying it amounted to £400,000. Parliament debated the voyage and the secretary of state compiled a dossier on it. This seemed a perfect opportunity for Tories to topple Bellomont's high-placed Whig allies, already losing their grip on power. They feared that they might 'appear somewhat rediculous' if the truth came out, but better that than to be implicated in piracy. Kidd would find no assistance there.

He was sick and on his arrival in England wrote desperate letters seeking help. These, with other correspondence from the colonies, the admiralty intercepted and opened, to see whether they contained anything relevant to the case. Bellomont's letters were especially embarrassing. In some he protested Kidd's innocence, in others (intended to remain secret) he admitted that Kidd was probably guilty, but encouraged his associates to find a way to wheedle out as much plunder as they could. He managed to fit in a good deal of vituperation towards his political enemies.

Kidd was interrogated by a committee, who also questioned his two enslaved companions, Dundee and Ventura, although Ventura said little and even Portuguese and Indian interpreters could not communicate with Dundee. Then Kidd was committed to Newgate, rather than the Marshalsea, and probably under the heightened security of solitary confinement. For almost a year he was allowed intermittent visitors, mostly his relatives.

When a new parliament gathered in 1701, now dominated by Tory MPs, they convened a committee on the case. The Company produced witnesses, including Coji Babba, supercargo of the *Quedah Merchant*; Henry Bolton, arrested en route to Africa by a navy ship, was quizzed on Kidd's dealings; Kidd himself appeared on 27 March, followed through the streets by hundreds of curious onlookers.

A bid to impeach certain Whig ministers failed, but Kidd was brought to trial on 8 and 9 May, shortly after James Kelley, who had been recaptured, was tried and executed. Like Every's crew five years earlier, Kidd appeared at the Old Bailey, and this time there were no unexpected surprises.

Kidd pitched his defence on the two French passes he had sent to Bellomont. Several times he and his counsel asked for the passes to be produced, and he maintained that he had only captured ships carrying French documents. 'I am not afraid to dye', he wrote in a letter before the trial, 'but will not be my own Murderer', and he refused to 'admit my selfe a pyrate'. He blamed Bellomont, who (Kidd claimed) had taken the passes and intimated his crew to appear against him. The legality of the voyage was his investors' concern; he was just 'a Tool of their Covetousnesse'.

Now those in power 'would have me dye for Solving their Honor, and others to pacify the Mogull for injuries done by other men'.

He was not entirely wrong about that last bit. It did not save him. Two of his men, both of whom abandoned him for Culliford in Madagascar, appeared as witnesses and received a pardon in return. They gave evidence that he killed William Moore – which Kidd insisted was unintentional, as Moore was fomenting mutiny – and detailed the various ships he plundered. Kidd's own character witnesses confirmed his good service in the Caribbean, but this was dismissed as irrelevant because it occurred before 1695. Kidd was found guilty for both murder and piracy.

The French passes were never produced, though in the twentieth century they were rediscovered in the Commissioners' papers. Government officials commonly held on to documents at this time, so it seems likely that one of them had taken these in hand. It is unclear whether they were deliberately withheld or genuinely mislaid – certainly the former is possible, though it would probably not have made any difference to the trial.

Several others of Kidd's crew, and those of La Paix, were found guilty. Culliford, who also testified on Kidd, was granted the benefit of a pardon he had accepted, in Madagascar, from Thomas Warren, the son of the captain whom Kidd encountered in the Atlantic. The elder Warren had died during the voyage and his son, who was with him, completed his father's mission. Others had heard of the pardon and surrendered to Jeremiah Basse, but the pardon specifically named Warren, so this was disallowed.

The only men let off were those employed on the ship as other men's servants, as the court considered that 'a Pirate is not to be understood to be under Constraint, but a free Agent'. One man, who signed onto a naval ship immediately after the voyage, was not acquitted, but was recommended as potentially suitable for royal mercy.

Awaiting his execution, Kidd made a last-ditch bid for mercy by offering to recover £100,000 stashed in the Caribbean, seeding later legends about his treasure. He had a few visitors, including the widows of two of his crew trying to recover their inheritance, and, surprisingly, Coji Babba, who had entered a compensation claim to the admiralty and wanted Kidd's help. Unfortunately for Babba, when Kidd's goods were sold (for over £6,000) three years later, he lost his lawsuit over it. Some money did go towards purchasing the site that later became the Royal Naval Hospital, then the Royal Naval College, which now hosts the National Maritime Museum and the University of Greenwich.

Eight of Kidd's men died in jail; ten were pardoned, including Culliford, who may have gone into naval service. Bellomont died of an illness before the trial even began, with only a small portion of Kidd's treasure in his hands. Sarah Kidd, whom Bellomont had imprisoned, was released and eventually recovered some of her husband's loot. Two years later she married again and she lived until 1744, raising five children and outlasting four husbands in all.

On 23 May 1701, Kidd and several others came to Execution Dock. One man received a last-minute reprieve, but Kidd and the others were executed before a large crowd. According to the ordinary, the priest who attended to Newgate prisoners, Kidd maintained a 'hard, unmelted heart' in prison and arrived drunk, insisting on his innocence and denouncing those who abandoned him, but after the first rope broke and he fell stunned, he made a somewhat dazed repentance before his death. His body was taken to Tilbury Point and displayed in a gibbet, a warning to the many ships passing on the Thames.

III

BLACK FLAG

CAPE COAST CASTLE, WEST AFRICA
MARCH/APRIL 1722

The sun beat down upon the courtyard. The tropical spring air must have been humid and thick. Perhaps there was some relief in a sea breeze, lifting and flapping the great flag above the castle, a bright blue field bearing the red cross of St George (with its own white outline) over the white cross of St Andrew.

Sounds filtered through from beyond the white battlements, the susurration of the waves beating at the rocky shore just outside the fortress, the bustle from Oguaa, a town clustered not far from the wall, below the line of hills rising inland. Sounds drifted up within, too, through the iron gratings in the courtyard. The clank of chains, faint moans or cries from the hundreds of enslaved people confined in the grim dungeons, awaiting the boats that would take them out to the ships lying offshore. Those that survived their imprisonment.

The next sound must have been the drums of the soldiers as a cluster of captives was marched from the castle down to the beach. These men were Europeans; their sixty-five African shipmates had already been sold back into slavery. For these men the gallows standing before them, between the high and low tidelines, declared their own fate.

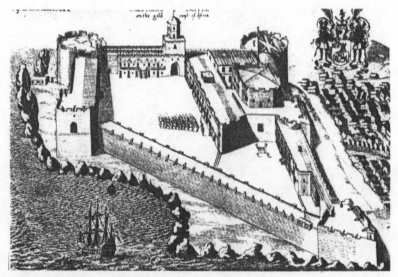

An engraving of Cape Coast Castle, as it looked in the late seventeenth and early eighteenth centuries.

That scene played out again and again throughout late March and early April 1722, as 169 men were cross-examined, accused of being 'traitors, robbers, pirates and common enemies of mankind'. Among them were eighteen French sailors, seven Dutch, and the rest English, Scottish, Irish, Welsh, Manx, from the Channel Islands, or from the Caribbean.

Fifty-two men were hanged, watched by the Royal African Company's soldiers and perhaps the dignitaries who had condemned them. Two were reprieved and seventeen earmarked for transfer to the Marshalsea in London for further investigation, though thirteen died en route, and only three were pardoned. Another twenty were permitted to sign indentures of service to the Company, but all died before their time was out, killed by the perilous diseases that scythed through Europeans in West Africa, while over seventy-four were acquitted. Neither option was offered to the African prisoners.

Those executed here were one of the most prolific crew of pirates ever to sail the Atlantic Ocean. Under Bartholomew Roberts, remembered today as 'Black Bart' (or in his native Welsh *Barti Ddu*), they captured over 400 ships during a rambling journey that lasted nearly three years and crossed the ocean several times. Some of these men had been with Roberts all along, though most had joined later, as captives or volunteers from one of his many prizes.

Roberts' wanderings came to an end when the naval captain Chaloner Ogle, in the *Swallow*, tracked down his ship near Cape Lopez, a headland just south of the equator in modern-day Gabon, on 10 February 1722. Just before, Roberts had defeated two French naval ships sent after him and captured a Company ship named the *Onslow*, which he rechristened the *Fortune*. Roberts had other prizes in tow and his men were reportedly drinking in celebration of another recent capture when the *Swallow* came upon them.

It was a stormy day: the logbooks of the *Swallow*'s officers record thunder, lightning, and a 'small tornado'. Pretending his ship was Portuguese, Ogle lured away one pirate vessel, defeated it and then returned for Roberts himself. The famous captain was probably killed by grapeshot sweeping the *Fortune*'s deck. According to the *General History*, Roberts was snappily dressed for the occasion in a crimson waistcoat and breeches, with a red feather in his hat. After two more hours of fighting, his men surrendered.

Ogle carried them to Cape Coast, the Company headquarters in Africa. There, over four weeks, a tribunal consisting of naval officers and Company officials tried each man, prisoner after prisoner, deciding between life and death. They took statements from witnesses, many of whom had been rescued from the pirates' ships or attacked by them previously.

Those men who could provide persuasive evidence of being coerced into Roberts' crew – who, even if they signed the pirates' articles, had tried to escape, or been beaten by their shipmates, or asked their prisoners for help, even cried tears – were released. Among them were skilled craftsmen, carpenters, tailors, boatswains, and four musicians forced to play for the pirates' amusement. Those who were most active in battle, who swore the most, who took shares in plunder, were convicted and hanged, usually the very next day. One man, a deserter from the naval vessel *Weymouth*, was hanged from that ship's yardarm.

On one level, here was parliament's new legislation, and the rising power of the British Empire, in action. Cape Coast is around 3,000 miles (almost, but not quite, due south) from London, and Cape Lopez is another 800 miles further south-east. The castle was no colony, but an isolated outpost standing on land leased from the local Akan *omanhene*. Yet even here the royal navy and the Royal African Company wielded imperial authority, upon pirates and enslaved people alike. Chaloner Ogle would be knighted as a reward for his service against the famed Roberts, and went on to a prominent naval career in the Caribbean.

At the same time, Roberts' transatlantic operations were emblematic of a final, and in many ways the most extreme, phase of piracy, which occurred during the second and third decades of the eighteenth century. It absolutely was piracy, too, carrying not even the tenuous pretences of legitimacy claimed by earlier raiders, rejecting the political alignments of European empires and their trading partners, ranging randomly, selecting targets opportunistically and even indiscriminately. Its victims included the same colonial merchants who had before supported plundering so keenly.

For once, it seems likely that these pirates thought of themselves as pirates, at least in Roberts' case. While he sometimes used national flags, often to trick victims, Roberts sailed into battle with black flags flying, making no secret of his piracy. These plunderers posed a more immediate threat to imperial commerce than their fellows of previous decades and provoked an even more forceful backlash, although here, as before, the impetus came as much from traders and colonial governors as it did from European throne rooms.

Some of the most famous pirates ever – Roberts, Blackbeard, Anne Bonny, Mary Read – sailed in these years. Even more importantly, they were immortalised in contemporary culture, above all in the *General History* when its first volume appeared in 1724. Drawing on the trends that had developed over previous decades, this book, and others of its time, crystallised the debates over the status of plundering and the nature of pirates. These were the last moments of the 'golden age' pirates, and yet they, more than any other, define the popular image of piracy we still have today.

13

CRUISERS AND CONVOYS

The new law introduced in 1700, and the execution of William Kidd and others in 1701, did not instantly end the problems with plunderers in British colonies. Widespread complaints about piracy continued over these years and afterwards. Jeremiah Basse wrote and published *A Letter … concerning the Suppression of Piracy*, again criticising colonial misdeeds. Virginians still suspected Carolina and Pennsylvania of harbouring raiders. Robert Quarry, the vice-admiralty judge sent to Pennsylvania in 1697, who succeeded Edward Randolph as surveyor general, wrote in 1705 that in Philadelphia the 'Trade of encouraging Pyrates is still carried on as formerly'.

In 1701 the government sent George Larkin, an experienced lawyer, to explain the new legislation, to circulate proclamations enjoining colonial officials to greater efforts, and to collect more information on the colonies themselves. His tour did not go well. At Newfoundland he worried about fishermen indulging in a 'dissolute sort of life' who could only end as 'Rogues and Pyrates'; in New England, 'Pyrates are esteemed very honest men' and still married the daughters of local dignitaries. Larkin was more pleased with New York, where an acquittal at least occurred 'after a full and fair trial', as another official wrote.

Private colonies, though, remained 'a Recepticle or Refuge for pyrates and unlawful Traders'. The East Jersey militia, with a large crowd, broke up a piracy trial and drove the governor from the colony. In Rhode Island, Larkin thought, there was 'scarce a family in three … but some of them have been concerned in privateering'. The Caribbean was a little better: he arrested one of Kidd's men at Barbados, while Christopher Codrington, in the Leeward Islands, was the only one Larkin met who, he felt, 'can be called a good Governour'.

Bermuda was Larkin's downfall, as it had been for Randolph. He got into loggerheads with the governor, Benjamin Bennett, over some pirates languishing unprosecuted in jail. Bennett whipped up a public outcry and then declared Larkin's commission (signed by the recently deceased William III and II) null and void. Bennett had not yet proclaimed Queen Anne, delaying official business, but he *had* replaced the former chief justice and vice-admiralty judge with 'an old harponeer, a poor, illiterate, sorry fellow' who had married a woman and then apparently got both her daughters pregnant. One of Thomas Tew's investors was acquitted in 1702.

Bennett threw Larkin in jail, and both wrote to London, Bennett enclosing sixty-nine depositions, even from 'the common strumpet and the hangman', implicating Larkin in 'several lewd, vicious and debauched practices shamefully and openly committed', including seducing or assaulting enslaved and free women. Larkin was eventually released and went on to replace Codrington in the Leeward Islands, though he died in 1703.

Larkin had a predictably unflattering view of Bermuda, agreeing with Randolph that it should be called 'New Algier, or the Unfortunate Islands' (a sardonic reference to the mythical Fortunate Isles). 'I verily believe,' he wrote to London, 'that some of them don't care if the islands were under the dominion of the Turk, provided that pyracy, and that which they call a Free-Trade, was encouraged.'

He was undoubtedly aggrieved, but Larkin was right that the official views he espoused were not yet shared by everyone in the colonies. William Penn, during his own investigations in Pennsylvania, seems to have developed a somewhat more sophisticated understanding of plundering practice. He recognised that buccaneers had moved from the Caribbean to northern colonies, who supplied Madagascar, and also that plundering was usually just one phase in maritime careers.

Penn wrote that 'something more than hanging ... must cure this deadly poison'. It would take more than royal orders and visiting officials to turn the colonies aways from plundering. It would take another war.

The War of the Spanish Succession began in 1701, just four years after the last major conflict, and it lasted until 1713. Carlos II of Spain died in 1700, with no heir, and his will named Philippe of Anjou, now proclaimed as Felipe V, as his successor. Felipe was the grandson of Louis XIV, but England, the Netherlands, Portugal, Prussia, and Austria supported a rival Austrian Habsburg claim to the throne (in 1702 England agreed a new treaty with Algiers too). When the exiled James VII and II died in September 1701 and Louis officially recognised his son and heir, it was a deliberately provocative act.

The two real issues behind the war were territorial control in Europe – Louis swiftly sent French troops into Sicily, northern Italy, and the Spanish Netherlands – and, perhaps even more importantly, Spanish American trade. That trade had become increasingly international: of eighty-four commercial houses operating in Cádiz in 1702, only twelve were Spanish.

Felipe's succession gave France favourable terms, including the *asiento* contract and access to the Pacific. Jean Beauchesne-Grouin, who first sailed to the South Sea in 1698 on behalf of the recently founded *Compagnie Royale de la Mer Pacifique*, later valued French activities there at £25 million in his published journal (his own first voyage made a loss of 100,000 *livres*, so perhaps he exaggerated).

It was another global war. Europe witnessed major campaigns in northern Italy, the Netherlands, and Bavaria, while English forces seized Gibraltar in 1704, a strategic point for Mediterranean trade. Fighting occurred in St Christopher, Carolina, Florida, Massachusetts, and Acadia. Once again, this war involved Indigenous allies: Yamassee, Talapoosa, Apalachee, and Tuscarora in the south; Iroquois, Algonquian, Abenaki, and Mohawk in the north.

Commerce raiding was another familiar feature. French naval historians have described this period as a shift from *guerre d'escadre* to *guerre de course*. French major warships declined in number from 137 in 1695 to 80 in 1715, while the *corsaires* increased rapidly, led by prominent *capitaines* like *comte* Claude de Forbin and René Duguay-Trouin, and provided with financial and material support by the Crown. French raiders based in Guadeloupe and Martinique captured almost 100 prizes by June 1702. Colonial officials in Jamaica, Montserrat, and Antigua sent back clamorous reports of 'dayly insults by the enemys privateers', even within sight of their islands.

Rio de Janeiro made an appealing target because of a Brazilian gold rush beginning in the 1690s. Jean-François le Clerc, from Guadeloupe, led an expedition that, aided by maroons, landed in Guanabara Bay and attacked the city, but the assault was defeated. Le Clerc himself surrendered and died soon afterwards in uncertain circumstances.

Very quickly a second expedition set out to revenge Le Clerc in 1711, backed by the *comte* of Toulouse and investors from Saint-Malo, and commanded by Duguay-Trouin, who hailed from that town. He had already distinguished himself as a *corsaire* and naval officer, escaping from prison in England and raiding the Irish coast during the previous war. In 1709, having captured sixteen warships and over 300 merchant vessels, he was ennobled by Louis.

With considerable bravado, this newly minted *seigneur* sailed straight into Guanabara Bay and landed 3,000 men, overcoming Portuguese ships and coastal batteries. The governor refused to pay a ransom and evacuated the city, but Duguay-Trouin caught up with him and forced him to hand over 610,000 *cruzados* in gold. One of Duguay-Trouin's treasure ships sank in a storm on the way home, but his investors nevertheless doubled their money and he was fêted as a hero.

In the Caribbean *corsarios*, English allies in the last war, now preyed on English shipping, particularly haunting the Bahamas, where they interdicted the trade routes between the northern and Caribbean colonies; seventeen ships were captured there in 1709 alone. A Spanish force attacked the islands in 1703 and French *corsaires* struck in 1708.

One of the most famous *corsarios* is Amaro Rodríguez-Felipe y Tejera Machado, better known as Amaro Pargo, a folk hero in Tenerife, which English expeditions attacked in 1706 and 1708. From a wealthy landowning and trading family, Pargo probably went to sea in the 1690s, and by 1703 he commanded his own ship on trading voyages to the Americas, including Havana, where he fathered an illegitimate son.

Like many other merchant captains, Pargo took advantage of plundering opportunities. In 1712 he seized the *San Joseph* and sold it in Tenerife, despite the protests of the master that Pargo held no official commission and that the prize was an Irish ship with permission to trade at Cádiz, though his passport had been taken away by a French *corsaire* he encountered earlier. The Spanish authorities found in Pargo's favour.

Pargo's career went on into the 1730s, when he became a merchant and shipowner. He was arrested in Cádiz, in 1719, when he refused to let customs officers aboard the ship, but was released after a personal appeal to the king, and in 1725 he applied for, and was granted, *hidalgo* status. His coat of arms, displayed on his gravestone in the church of Santo Domingo de Guzmán in La Laguna, includes daggers, cannon, and an officer's baton. He donated vast sums to that church and other religious institutions (prompting more legends of lost treasure), and also sacred silverwork decorated with grappling hooks. Pargo was evidently very devout, and neither reticent nor subtle about the sources of his wealth.

British raiders, too, found employment in this war. Proclamations in 1702 and 1703 encouraged 'ships of war and privateers' (another one in 1702 yet again recalled English mariners from foreign service). Several colonies issued commissions freely, not least because naval resources had been reallocated to protect shipping in the Indian Ocean. One report suggested there were 400 plunderers based in New York alone, bringing some £60,000 into the city.

The war did not end the rivalries between colonies, though. Joseph Dudley, governor of Massachusetts, accused his counterpart in Rhode Island, Samuel Cranston, of issuing illegal commissions, because Dudley claimed vice-admiralty jurisdiction over both colonies. The Commissioners for Trade had likewise pointed out, two years earlier, that Rhode Island continued to harbour pirates and smugglers, and had 'erected an Admiralty jurisdiction amongst themselves without any authority'. Dudley maintained that anyone sailing from Newport had 'the face of a Pirate'.

Since these plunderers included some of Kidd's former shipmates, that may have been true, but it was also sour grapes. Dudley's main gripe was that captains carrying his commissions switched to Cranston instead, taking their prize revenue with them. Cranston rode out these charges and was re-elected thirty times, staying in office until 1727, the longest-serving governor of the colony (or its descendant state). Dudley, meanwhile, was himself accused a couple of years later of trading with the enemy and complicity in piracy.

While most English raiders operated in European waters or near their colonial bases, some returned to the Pacific. William Dampier led a South Sea expedition in 1703, investing £200 of his own money and noting in a letter, 'I have not yet written to my wife about [the money] … I know it will not please her.' Dampier had also captained a state-sponsored trip to the Australian coast in 1699–1701, which reached its objective but was marred by infighting between the officers. The ship sank, resulting in a court martial that declared Dampier unfit for naval command. As gifted as he was as a navigator, Dampier made a poor leader, and the same proved true in his next South Sea voyage as well.

Dampier once again fell out with his subordinates, one of whom, Edward Morgan, was another former buccaneer whom Dampier had insisted join them even though he was in prison at the time. Others on the trip claimed that Dampier, Morgan, and another confederate kept everything 'hugger mugger among themselves', rather than consulting the crew, and that in battle Dampier was most concerned with his own safety, protecting himself on the quarterdeck with 'a good Barricado' of rugs and bedding.

Prizes escaped, or were released, allegedly on paying bribes to Dampier; some were never even chased. An attack on Santa María, possibly inspired by Dampier's memory of the gold camps there, went wrong. The two ships on the expedition split up. On the *Cinque Ports* Alexander Selkirk, an experienced Scottish sailor with a record of violence during his youth, but whom Dampier called the best man on the ship, quarrelled with the captain and was deposited on the Juan Fernández Islands. The *Cinque Ports* sank not long after and its survivors were detained in Peru for several years.

Dampier and the *St George*, meanwhile, located a Pacific galleon but were beaten off; the sailors later laid the blame on Dampier, accusing him of drunkenness and indecision. Many of them, including Morgan, now abandoned him – by Dampier's own account one absconder called back, 'Poor *Dampier, thy Case is like King* James, *every Body has left thee.*'

Both parties made their way across the Pacific. Morgan was accused of selling off plunder at Batavia worth £10,000, though probably the sum was much lower. Dampier was imprisoned there for a year as a pirate, his commission having been stolen or gone missing, and finally reached England in 1707, where his investors sued him.

That was not Dampier's last voyage round the world, though. The very next year Woodes Rogers, a prominent Bristol captain, whose father was of the same trade and may have known Dampier, hired him for another trip to the South Sea. Rogers' family lived on the fashionable new Queen's Square in Bristol, and he married the daughter of their near neighbour William Whetstone, a distinguished naval commander.

Even with such connections, Rogers suffered losses during the war and he undertook this Pacific voyage to pay off mounting debts. It was much more strictly organised than Dampier's had been, run by a council chaired by Dr Thomas Dover, a man with no maritime experience but a considerable investor in the voyage. Like in other voyages, the crew only learned of their destination once at sea: one man protested his wife would be fined since he was supposed to serve as parish tithingman that year, but he was 'easily quieted'.

There were still tensions. On several occasions the crew demanded a renegotiation of their shares and asserted their customary right to 'pillage' from any prize, since, as they said, 'there was never any Privateer's Crew hinder'd from Plunder'. It was an international crew, and Rogers called them 'Tinkers, Taylors, Hay-makers, Pedlers, Fidlers', with at least one Black sailor, and 'about ten Boys', a 'mix'd Gang'.

Nevertheless, they held together throughout the voyage. An early mutiny by some crewmembers, discontented that Rogers would not attack a Swedish ship, was swiftly put down. The commanders instituted morning and evening prayers to maintain order and Rogers considered the crew 'more obedient than any Ship's Crews engag'd in the like Undertaking that I ever heard of … modest beyond Example among Privateers'. Of course, he was keen to gild his own reputation, and it was not all obedience and solemnity. In Brazil, Rogers recorded, the musicians with the expedition entertained local dignitaries with '*Hey Boys up go we!* and all manner of noisy paltry Tunes'. 'Hey Boys up go we' is a dancing tune of the time, but many ballads used the melody, including one about a 1692 naval victory, and another describing the various 'wanton Girls of Graves-end Town', a common point of departure on the Thames, who were 'Maintained by the Seamen brave'.

They reached the Pacific at the end of 1709 and collected Selkirk from his solitary life in Juan Fernández – an archaeological excavation has located the very spot on the island where he spent over four years alone. Rogers light-heartedly named him 'Governour' and 'Absolute Monarch of the Island'. Selkirk was soon given command of a prize.

This small fleet took 25,500 *pesos* and £1,000 in plunder at Guayaquil, including, according to Rogers, gold chains that his men had 'modestly' removed from their hiding places around female prisoners' 'Middles, Legs, and Thighs'. That sum was much less than hoped and many men, including Rogers' brother, died of a contagious fever that had recently swept the town. The ships also took enslaved captives, among them women whom Rogers criticised as 'black Nymphs', one of whom was whipped for 'having transgressed this Way', though there is no evidence the man involved was punished.

Sailing north, they captured the first Pacific galleon seized by any English ship since Thomas Cavendish's expedition in 1586. Dampier valued it at £1 million. During the attack Rogers was shot through his face, carrying the musket ball lodged in his jaw for six months, but he survived and in his journal wrote that the scar was 'scarce discernible'. They attacked another galleon, but its teak hull and large, heavily armed crew, among them some Irish and English buccaneers, proved too much and that ship escaped.

With their prizes, the raiders crossed the Pacific and Indian Ocean, calling at Batavia and then Cape Town, where Rogers wrote home with a low reckoning of their plunder at £200,000, while others more optimistically placed it at £3 million. By the time they reached the Netherlands in July 1710, the officers had already begun to send home mutual accusations.

After they reached England, a couple of months later, it took three years to sort and auction the cargo, raising just under £150,000. The East India Company had to be bought off for £6,000 because they claimed Rogers had infringed their monopoly. Few of the crew got more than £70 – not bad for two years at sea, but far below the sailors' expectations. They sued Rogers in Chancery in a sprawling and complicated lawsuit, but the Lord Chancellor disqualified the various new agreements made with the crew during the voyage.

Rogers got a much larger share, £1,500, but most of it went to his creditors. Alexander Selkirk received £800 and some other items, including a silver-hilted sword. Dampier received an uncertain amount in his lifetime, and a balance of just over £1,000 to his cousin, Grace Mercer, after his death a few years later. It was the last of his many long voyages and in combining Dampier with Rogers it provides a bridge, of sorts, from the South Sea men to the next generation of plunderers.

The *corsaires* got the best of this war. Their tally may have exceeded 7,000 prizes, whereas British raiders captured just over 2,000, although those figures are based only on prizes that were legally adjudicated. That discrepancy reflects the considerable growth of British merchant shipping in these decades, meaning there were more targets to plunder, but the pressure from *corsaires* and *corsarios* also brought some important changes.

Merchants called for more protection from the government and, this time, the navy had the resources to provide it, due to the legacy of the Nine Years' War. From 88 ships at the start of that war, the royal navy expanded to 234 at its end, employing 45,906 men. By the end of the War of the Spanish Succession, the British navy exceeded the French, Spanish, and Dutch navies combined.

That expansion created pressing problems of manpower and finance: twelve proclamations concerning recruitment or impressment appeared in 1690–97, eleven in 1702–08, more than ever before, with a lively debate in newspapers and pamphlets as well. Sailors and their families suffered with arrears and unpaid wages, leading to a public outcry and, sometimes, the execution of protesting sailors. The anonymous pamphlet *Piracy Destroy'd*, of 1701, blamed these conditions as a motivation for piracy.

Nevertheless, by the start of the new war the empire's military resources were considerably greater than they had ever been before. The number of smaller ships, most useful for convoying and patrolling, doubled. Convoys had been introduced before during the 1670s and 1680s, and in 1693 a vast British convoy of hundreds of ships sailed to the Mediterranean, accompanied by the Channel fleet, though when it passed the Strait of Gibraltar with only a small squadron it was ambushed and scattered by waiting *corsaires*.

That disaster focused official and commercial attention on the need for more regular protection, which continued into the next war. In 1707 the *West Indische Compagnie* began organising annual convoys to Curaçao and in 1708 the House of Lords considered that while France had 'always endeavoured to infest our Trade by their Privateers ... of late they have had greater Success than ever'. By that point in the war over 1,000 ships had been lost in nearby waters alone, worth at least £170,000.

Parliament's solution was new legislation, the Cruisers and Convoys Act, which appointed forty-three warships for the protection of merchant shipping and set out rules regarding convoys. It also encouraged more commerce raiding, by waiving the Crown's right to any shares in prizes, making it easier to secure a letter of marque, setting regular conditions regarding the division of prizes, and introducing a speedier process for adjudication, which would remain in place for the rest of the century.

This legislation was another step towards a clear line between authorised and unauthorised plundering, and if much of the linguistic flexibility in 'buccaneer' and 'privateer' remained, there may have been trends towards the modern meanings too. John Evelyn, in 1698, called Dampier a 'famous buccaneer' without any sense of condemnation. However, forty-eight women used the term 'Pirates and Buckaneers' when they petitioned the queen in 1708, requesting a pardon for their husbands, still in Madagascar, and promising huge sums in return. In Woodes Rogers' *Cruising Voyage round the World* of 1712, he similarly criticised 'Buccaneers' who 'liv'd without Government', and 'made no distinction between the Captain and the Crew', during 'Revels' in which 'they drank and gam'd till they spent all' – though perhaps he simply wanted to distance himself from such figures.

'Pirate' and 'privateer' remained, to a degree, a matter of perspective. While London newspapers called Kidd a pirate, alongside *flibustiers* like Laurens de Graaf and Nicolaes van Hoorn, colonial merchants continued to use the term 'privateers'. John Campbell, the postmaster of Boston, even used the latter for Kidd's men in his newsletters to various governors, which he began to print in 1699 and which by 1704 became the first colonial newspaper, the imaginatively named *Boston News-Letter*.

One commentator noted that the 'Pyrates' in Madagascar were not 'guilty of any greater Cruelties than what are usual in Common Privateering', while Cotton Mather, in his *Faithful Warnings* of 1704, warned that 'the Privateering Stroke so easily degenerates into the Piratical' and considered that the '*Privateering* Trade' entailed 'so Unchristian a Temper ... [leading to] much Debauchery, and Iniquity'. A Jamaican official feared that trade with the Spanish colonies would be ruined by 'our owne privateers, for under that licence all Nations, French, Dutch, Spanish and English consort together'.

Yet these concerns about the proximity between 'pirates' and 'privateers' reflect, paradoxically, a clearer sense of the distinction between them. Increasingly, commissions were accepted as the distinguishing feature. Jean-Baptiste Labat wrote in 1722 that 'one calls those who cruise at sea without a commission Forbans ... Flibustiers or Corsaires are accustomed to this libertine life during a just War, having Commission from their Sovereign'. Plunderers themselves played their part in these linguistic and conceptual developments. In the 1696 trial of Every's crew, the defendant Joseph Dawson called both himself and the other ships who joined Every 'privateers'. The lord chief justice zeroed in on this: 'You call them Privateers, but were they such Privateers as you were?' he asked. Dawson replied, 'I suppose they had Commissions', though he conceded these 'did not run so far' as the capture of Mughal ships.

William Dampier, in his popular voyage journals, similarly used the term 'privateer', possibly to avoid direct accusations of piracy. Others who published their journals did the same. In an interesting twist, though, George Fisher, the lieutenant who sailed with Dampier to Australia and later hauled him before a court martial, recounted to that court some details of their arguments over piracy and privateering.

Early in the voyage, Fisher claimed, they had argued over whether executing French 'privateers' would have brought a quicker end to the Nine Years' War; Dampier's views on the matter were especially bloodthirsty. Fisher, perhaps deliberately needling Dampier, opined that 'if all nations would give no protection to pirates, but hang them as soon as taken, it would be of good service to all traders abroad'. Dampier 'demanded what he meant by pirates', to which Fisher replied 'such as Every and his men were'. Dampier replied, 'he would not hurt them, nor a hair of their heads', though Fisher pointed out it was his duty as a navy captain.

Dampier proved as good as his word, refusing to take action against some of Every's men whom they found in Brazil. He may have known them personally, given the crossover between South Sea and Red Sea voyages and his own involvement in the *Charles II* voyage. Fisher added that during their arguments, Dampier spoke of 'a pirate's life which my captain called privateer and he said their life was the best of lives'. Dampier retorted, at the court martial, that Fisher had disrespected him, calling him 'that Old Pyrateing Dog'.

These claims and counterclaims are highly suspect, remembered long after the fact and intended to discredit the opposing party. They are nevertheless suggestive of the kinds of discussions occurring in ships' cabins, quayside taverns, colonial parlours, and imperial boardrooms around the Atlantic Ocean and beyond. As the Cruisers and Convoys Act tightened up the regulations, it became more clearly the case that you could only be a 'privateer', and not a pirate, if you held a commission and scrupulously followed the rules.

These conversations meant more than idle chatter over rum punch, as became evident in 1704, with the trial of John Quelch. Lieutenant of a commissioned 'privateer', Quelch took command when the captain fell ill, and in the Caribbean he seized some Portuguese ships that he claimed were Spanish. The *Boston News-Letter* reported in May that Quelch had returned after 'a good Voyage'. However, the ship's owners became suspicious, perhaps because Quelch doctored the ship's log and dispersed his men ashore, and reported him to the authorities, who very quickly ordered Quelch's arrest.

The affair began like previous colonial prosecutions – some of Quelch's contacts helped to hide him and his treasure, and 'the greatest Rogues of them' escaped from jail – but ended very differently. Twenty of the forty-one accused men were rounded up, including one hiding in Rhode Island. Even the captain of another ship who had simply met Quelch at sea was investigated as an accessory. Quelch and six of his men were executed, despite his attorney pointing out various legal irregularities, and Quelch's own protest that '*I am Condemned only upon Circumstances*'.

That Quelch's own merchants handed him over is particularly significant, as it points towards changing attitudes in the colonies. These changes were partially driven by the greater facility with which the new law could try accessories as well as pirates themselves, raising the stakes for merchants' involvement in piracy, but there were other factors too.

One of these was the increasing circulation of information, which made it harder for plunderers to evade detection. The proclamations against

Quelch and his men, and reports on the trial, occupied seven editions of the *Boston News-Letter*. Joseph Dudley published another account of the trial, 'to satisfy and save the clamour of a rude people'. Cotton Mather, who visited the condemned men in prison and preached at the execution, penned an account of their conversations and last speeches. He lamented that in former times the colony's youth had been 'Seduced and Enchanted ... to Piratical Courses', while 'shelter[ing] themselves in the Prosecution of their Piracies'. It was not the first or last time he condemned 'bloody Pyrates'.

For those less concerned with moral issues, there were other factors at work as well. The depredations of the *corsaires* and *corsarios* during the war gave colonial merchants extensive first-hand experience as victims of plunderers, while the growth of British colonial trade during the war, despite the *corsaires* arrayed against it, meant that merchants had more to lose. New legislation encouraged North American trade as a source of naval stores, for example.

London was developing as a more sophisticated financial centre, with the Bank of England established in 1694 and marine insurance businesses booming. In 1692 Edward Lloyd's coffee house in Lombard Street, near the Royal Exchange, began publishing the famous *Lloyd's List*, a journal of weekly shipping movements that is still going today, as is the major insurance market Lloyd's of London.

That growth was not restricted to London, either, as the structure of British trade became less restrictive. Parliament suspended the East India Company's monopoly in 1694, limited the import of Indian textiles to protect domestic production, and permitted an alternative company to be founded in 1698. The contest between the old and new companies was part of the political context surrounding Kidd's trial, since Whigs generally backed the new company, and Tories the old, though some merchants invested in both companies and they were merged in 1708. However, parliament refused the company a perpetual charter, bringing it under review every few years.

When Scottish merchants tried to set up their own Company of Scotland for Atlantic and Indian trade, its immediate impact was disastrous, as an attempt in 1698 to settle a colony at New Caledonia in Darién was a total failure. It folded within two years and only a few hundred of the original 2,500 settlers survived. The involvement of Dampier and Lionel Wafer as consultants raised alarm, among both Spanish and English colonists, that their intent was to 'play the Pyrates ... on the Trades of all Nations'. As Kidd returned to the Americas in 1699, rumours abounded that he would join his compatriots in New Caledonia.

This Company's longer legacy was unexpectedly far-reaching. In 1699 Scotsmen were, for the first time, allowed into the commercial privileges of the Navigation Acts, and the financial disaster in Scotland, together with the impact of *corsaires*, contributed towards the Acts of Union and the creation of the United Kingdom of Great Britain in 1706–07.

The negotiations for that union were so unpopular in Edinburgh that, when the *Worcester* arrived there in the spring of 1705, its captain, Thomas Green, was arrested for piracy, probably because he had worked for the East India Company, which had, the year before, seized a ship belonging to the Company of Scotland. Green was charged with plundering the *Speedy Return*, although the indictment carefully left out the ship's name, many of Green's crew were not permitted as witnesses, and the court denied the legitimacy of his colonial commission. Even when survivors from the *Speedy Return* arrived in England and testified that they had been attacked by Bermudan raider John Bowen, it did not save Green from being hanged on Leith Sands. The case caused a lively debate in print as, once again, piracy became a vehicle for other political arguments.

The Royal African Company also lost its monopoly when in 1697–98 parliament legalised 'separate traders' who paid a 10 per cent levy to cover the cost of Company forts like Cape Coast Castle. Debate over the monopoly continued and the trade was fully deregulated in 1712. British ships transported on average around 3,000 enslaved people annually between 1672 and 1712, a number that quadrupled between 1713 and 1722. William Snelgrave, a merchant who travelled to Africa, reported 33 English ships sailing there in 1712, and 200 in 1726.

By the latter decade, enslaved people formed a two-to-one majority in Carolina (partitioned from 1712 into North and South), where rice, introduced as a foodstuff by enslaved African communities, became the colony's agricultural staple. This growth in slavery brought with it the same concerns about social order as existed in the Caribbean. There were revolts in Virginia in 1706 and 1710, and in New York in 1712. Bermuda banished free Black and Indigenous people in 1705, while New York and New Jersey both introduced slave codes in these years.

The intertwined growth of slavery and trade accelerated after the end of the war. The Treaty of Utrecht in 1713 recognised Felipe V and parcelled out various territories both in Europe and the Americas. It permitted the logwood trade, allowed British ships to resupply at French islands, and transferred the *asiento* to Britain. The South Sea Company, formed in 1711 to help manage the national debt, contracted to ship 4,800 enslaved people per year to Spanish America. French trade also recovered swiftly.

The value of the Canadian fur trade skyrocketed from 260,000 *livres* in 1718 to more than 2 million a decade later, and Saint-Domingue's sugar production would make it the most valuable American colony during the eighteenth century.

The war and its aftermath reorganised international commerce, shifting popular attitudes about maritime raiding. At the same time, the surge in plundering during the war provoked widespread concerns. The vulnerable and thinly populated Bahamas, especially, were feared as 'very ready to succour and trade with Pirates', so that they would 'become a second Madagascar'. Edmund Dummer, postmaster for the Caribbean islands, worried that the war would 'leave to the world a brood of pyrates to infest it'.

That was exactly what happened.

14

UPON THE ACCOUNT

Some time in 1716 Samuel Bellamy went looking for gold and silver 'upon a *Spanish* Wreck', with another captain, Paul (or Paulsgrave) Williams. However, 'not finding their Expectation answered, they ... agreed to go upon the Account, a Term among the Pyrates, which speaks their Profession'. They captured the *Whydah*, carrying ivory and gold from Jamaica to London, probably having acquired this cargo in West Africa, perhaps at Ouidah itself (today known as Glexwe). With 150 'Hands of different Nations', Bellamy and the rest set off on their 'desperate Resolution' to become 'a declared Enemy of Mankind'.

That, at least, is how the *General History* tells it, admitting that little is known of Bellamy's origins. The phrase 'on the account' has become yet another dubious entry in our vocabulary of piracy; 'upon the account of piracy' appears in some contemporary legal documents, but there is little convincing evidence of pirates themselves using it.

In outline, though, this episode captures the circumstances that opened this last phase of plundering, spanning roughly 1716 to 1726, although it is more accurately split into two separate stages, lying either side of 1718 (more or less). The proximate cause of the first stage was the sinking, on 31 July 1715, of the entire Spanish treasure fleet off Cape Canaveral in a terrible hurricane, in which over half the 2,500 crew and passengers perished.

This fleet carried a bumper cargo, too, because the war had delayed sailings. Only one set of *galeones* made it to Portobelo between 1699 and 1713. The fleet in 1715 therefore carried 7 million *pesos* in bullion – one ship alone carried 1,000 chests, each with 3,000 coins in it – plus other American commodities like pearls and emeralds, and spices and porcelain from China. Spanish officials in Cuba swiftly sent out salvage parties and by late October they had gathered 5 million *pesos*. That wealth now lay buried in camps on the coast of Florida.

Cuba was not the only place to hear the news, though, and the timing could not have been worse. The end of war had its predictable effect on maritime industry. The British navy's payroll dropped to less than a quarter of its wartime strength and private plunderers were out of (legal) work. As Spanish soldiers chased logwooders out of the Yucatán, despite the agreements at Utrecht, that added to the numbers of experienced sailors and raiders looking for a job. Spanish governors still impounded even the South Sea Company's licensed ships, partially because these ships often gave cover for Jamaican smuggling.

The wreck-bedecked reefs off Florida's coast acted like a magnet. In Jamaica, a naval captain reported five men deserting every day, the sailors 'all mad to go a wrecking'. The governor, Lord Hamilton, commissioned two ships, under Henry Jennings and John Wills, granting them authority to 'seize pyratical vessels' but with the wrecks as their main target.

Jennings went straight to the largest salvage camp, where the unprepared Spanish soldiers swiftly surrendered. They tried to buy him off with 25,000 *pesos*, but he refused that offer and eventually sailed home with 120,000 instead. Jennings and Wills stopped off at the Bahamas before reaching Jamaica in January 1716. Two months later Jennings set off again to cruise the wrecks, and this time he ran into Bellamy and Williams. A passing observer reported twenty-four English ships picking over the wrecks around this time.

This gathering of opportunistic sailors soon turned to other plundering. Jennings, with Bellamy and Williams, captured a French ship, which they took back to Nassau, on New Providence, and ransacked, before returning to the reefs off Florida. Fernando Hernández, a Black captain who had probably escaped from slavery in a Spanish colony, and who also carried a commission from Hamilton, seized a ship off Cuba carrying 250,000 *pesos*.

The governor in Havana protested and this time the response from London was fairly quick. Hamilton, suspected of Jacobite sympathies, was recalled, though he had refused to meddle with Jennings' plunder when he realised how the captain came by it. Orders for the arrest of Jennings, Wills, and Hernández soon arrived.

It was already too late.

The Bahamas were sparsely populated and weakly governed. In 1701 the inhabitants had imprisoned an unpopular governor and packed him off to London. They also lay close to the shipping routes between North America and the Caribbean. As early as 1714 Henry Pulleine, governor of Bermuda, warned that pirates gathered at the Bahamas, 'haveing riotously and quickly spent, what they as wickedly got'. The next year the *Boston News-Letter* reported two ships based there plundering large sums from Spanish vessels, though there were also rumours in Jamaica of pirates gathering in Darién.

When, in April 1716, Jennings sailed into Nassau, he did not stop at picking over his recent French prize. He and his crew also 'committ[ed] great disorders ... plundering the inhabitants, burning their houses, and ravishing their wives'. Several of the residents fled, one of them, John Vickers, going to Virginia, where he reported to the governor Alexander Spotswood. Vickers added that one Thomas Barrow, former mate of a Jamaican brigantine, had named himself governor of New Providence, expected several hundred more Jamaicans to join him, and intended to 'make it a second Madagascar'.

Spotswood sent Vickers' account of this 'nest of pirates' to London. A correspondent from Jamaica warned the same year that pirates had seized Nassau and its fort, and the naval commander Captain Howard, sent by Spotswood to investigate, reported about 200 men sailing from the Bahamas to the wrecks.

Howard recommended that a couple of frigates would nip this in the bud, but this advice was ignored. Reports from Bermuda and Jamaica in these years told of how 'the pyrates daily increase' and now numbered at least 1,000. Ships bound for Britain, Heywood added, dared not sail without convoy. By 1718, Bennett feared that the pirates might target Bermuda and 'make a new Madagascar' of that, too.

As many as 5,000 men participated in this surge in Atlantic piracy, between 1,000 and 2,000 at any one time. They were mostly young, unmarried, and already experienced in merchant vessels or warships during the last conflict. With the increasing security of naval convoys, merchant crews had decreased in size across the later seventeenth century, making them easier pickings for these much more heavily manned pirate vessels.

While contemporaries thought of Madagascar, a closer comparison, it seems to me, is the much less famous surge of piracy in Ireland a century before. Roughly similar in size (around 2,000 at the peak), in both cases men well versed in wartime plundering moved from their former base, where they were no longer officially permitted, to a location conveniently nearby and conveniently beyond tight political control. Both episodes were also relatively short in duration.

Many of the plunderers in these two episodes continued to target their former enemies, though others were less discriminating. In the 1710s some may have been Jacobites, whether committed or opportunistic, and received commissions from the 'Old Pretender', the son of James VII and II. I suspect that in this first stage they saw themselves as no different to the many other sailors who, in recent decades, had followed their own interpretation of the laws of plunder rather than the narrower dictates of imperial policy. If the label of 'pirate' was very soon applied to them, it is not certain that they took it for themselves quite so quickly.

A few of these plunderers, like previous generations, captured large amounts of silver and gold, but most of their prizes carried everyday cargoes, foodstuffs, textiles, and manufactured goods. As in Munster in Ireland and Madagascar later, the Bahamas became an entrepôt for clandestine trade. Visitors during 1716–18 noticed ships from Boston, Carolina, Virginia, and Port Royal dealing with the plunderers.

Another similarity with previous episodes is the loose and fragmentary organisation of this group. They clustered around particular captains, cooperating at times and separating at others. A merchant captain told the governor of South Carolina in 1717 that there were five leaders: Jennings, Benjamin Hornigold, Josiah Burgess, and Edward Teach, all commanding around 100 men each, and one White, who had only 30.

Some historians have seen this resemblance as evidence of a distinct political tradition reaching back to the first buccaneers, or even earlier. Vickers, in his report to Spotswood, said that those with Jennings 'call themselves the flying gang', another term that has become popular in the piratical lexicon. Whether it was used by all the raiders at this time is unclear, though, and whatever they called themselves, it seems to me more likely that each generation of plunderers simply responded in a practical way to similar circumstances.

Bellamy was only briefly part of this 'Gang'. He had probably served in the navy, and in 1715, at the age of about 26, joined with Williams, a jeweller based in Boston. The chronology of their career is hard to trace: they encountered Jennings off Florida in 1716, though the *General History* elides the moment of their 'desperate Resolution' to 'go upon the Account' with their capture of the *Whydah*, which actually occurred in February 1717.

Just two months later Bellamy sailed north and the *Whydah* sank in a storm off Cape Cod. Over 100 of the crew drowned, including the captain.

By this time Bellamy had plundered more than fifty ships. In 1982–84 archaeologists rediscovered the wreck with plunder aboard worth between £20,000 and £30,000 (prompting some legal wrangles with Massachusetts).

Hornigold soon replaced Barrow as the unofficial leader, telling one Bahamian that 'all pirates were under his protection'. He had sailed from Jamaica with a commission during the war and afterwards continued to target French and Spanish ships. During 1713 he apparently gathered over £13,000 in plunder, and in 1715 he attacked vessels off Cuba, including a Spanish sloop, which he renamed the *Benjamin*. He joined up with Bellamy and Williams, and Olivier Levasseur, the most famous French pirate of this era, pursuing English ships near the Yucatán (possibly against Bellamy's wishes). Vickers reported that Hornigold had captured a Spanish sloop near Florida in 1716 and then made for Nassau.

One of Hornigold's crew, Edward Teach – also rendered Thatch, Titche, Tatch, and Tach in contemporary sources – went on to become the most famous pirate of all time under his 'Cognomen of Black-beard'. He was from Bristol or Jamaica, according to different accounts, and he too served as a commissioned 'privateer' during the war. At some time in 1716, it seems, Teach took command of a captured sloop, staying in company with Hornigold for a while. In the summer of 1717 he cruised off Virginia and Delaware Bay, with the *Boston News-Letter* reporting on his various depredations.

In the autumn Teach teamed up with the curious figure of Stede Bonnet, a wealthy planter in Barbados with no maritime experience who seemingly fitted out his own ship on a whim. Teach offered to take command while Bonnet, again going by the *General History*, loafed about in his 'morning gown' and enjoyed the 'good library' he had aboard.

Soon afterwards they captured *La Concorde*, a French *corsaire* built in Nantes in 1710, which had been converted into a slave ship after the war and was then carrying 516 captives from Ouidah. Teach renamed it *Queen Anne's Revenge*, if not an explicit Jacobite slogan then at least a jibe against the first Hanoverian king, George I, who succeeded Anne in 1714. In this ship, with some 300 men, Teach cruised among the Windward Islands, capturing more prizes, whipping one captain to reveal his money, and burning several ships. One witness noticed the crew eating off silver plate they had stolen, a detail later corroborated by the archaeologists diving the wreck of the *Queen Anne's Revenge* – a rare indulgence for men of their background.

Afterwards they sailed north and, in May 1718, Blackbeard and Bonnet blockaded Charleston harbour. The governor Robert Johnson reported to London that Teach demanded a 'chest of medicins' and he obligingly sent one out, hoping to avoid further trouble. The prevailing theory is that many of Teach's men had contracted syphilis, and indeed the archaeologists later found a metal syringe containing mercury, a common treatment for that venereal disease.

Shortly after the blockade, the *Queen Anne's Revenge* ran aground (lucky for the archaeologists) off North Carolina. Teach encouraged Bonnet to visit Charles Eden, the governor, to secure a royal pardon that had just been offered. While Bonnet was gone, though, Teach sailed off on the one remaining sloop with only twenty or thirty men, leaving some 200 behind; the wrecking seems to have been part of an orchestrated plot to get away with a few hand-picked confederates plus all the loot.

Back in Nassau, meanwhile, pre-eminence seems to have passed from Hornigold to Charles Vane, who acquired a lasting reputation as one of the most brutal pirates. He too had spent time in Port Royal, though he was probably born in England, and may have accompanied Jennings to the wrecks, rising to his own command by the end of 1717.

When news reached Nassau of the same offer of pardon that tempted Bonnet, opinion was divided: some were all for it, but Vane and others were not convinced. In February 1718 the naval officer Captain Pearce reached Nassau in the *Phoenix*, coming on his own initiative to offer pardons. There he found fourteen ships flying Dutch, English, French, and Spanish flags, as well as some wearing the black and red colours associated with piracy.

Pearce chased Vane down at a nearby island and brought him back prisoner, but released him at the entreaty of several 'ringleaders', including Hornigold and Burgess. Probably Pearce did not want to spook his targets, and he collected 209 signatories for the pardon. Two of these 'ringleaders', Francis Leslie and Thomas Nichols, subsequently sailed to Bermuda and appealed to Bennett for clemency instead.

Vane did not change his ways. He plundered a Jamaican ship lying in Nassau harbour, resisting Pearce's efforts to retake it. Some of Pearce's sailors deserted to the pirates, and after Pearce sailed off, convoying five merchant ships, Vane plundered at least twelve more vessels. The survivors of one attack reported that Vane and his men beat and tortured their victims, swearing 'Curse the king and all the higher powers' and toasting 'Damnation to King George'.

According to the *General History*, Vane returned to Nassau and bullied everyone in town, swearing that he would 'suffer no other Governor than himself'. His self-appointed reign would not last long. The empire was preparing to strike back.

Portraits of Stede Bonnet (left) and Charles Vane (right), from the 1725 edition of the *General History*.

If the surge in marauding in 1716–20 resembled previous episodes, so too did the initial response by the authorities. Like previous monarchs, George I also issued a general pardon, on 5 September 1717, which, as noted, achieved some success in the Bahamas and elsewhere. It helped that in 1717 Spain invaded Sicily, prompting a military response from the Quadruple Alliance of England, the Netherlands, Austria, and their erstwhile enemy France, uniting in August 1718 and declaring war in December. Governor Lawes of Jamaica wrote in March 1719 that 'the pirates will now come in, war with Spain being declared, which they have long wisht for'.

Some plunderers took advantage of this war to return to the Pacific. John Clipperton, who had sailed on Dampier's disastrous 1703 voyage, captained the *Prince Eugene* into the South Sea in 1715, plundering some 400,000 *pesos*, but was then captured and imprisoned in New Spain. After his release he led another voyage, accompanied by George Shelvocke. This trip faced problems too, though Clipperton recaptured the *Prince Eugene*. Clipperton and Shelvocke did not get on and split up at least twice;

Clipperton eventually lost his ship in the Indian Ocean. Shelvocke had to dismantle his damaged ship at Juan Fernández to make a replacement and, having sold that at Macau, he was imprisoned for embezzlement and piracy on his return to England.

Even with wartime incentives, though, this general pardon faced the same problems as before, especially the ease with which plunderers returned to their old ways and the reluctance of some to surrender at all. Perhaps this reticence arose as much from mistrust as from commitment to piracy, since at the end of the War of the Spanish Succession the government had threatened to prosecute any colonial governor who pardoned a pirate. The 1717 order permitted pirates to surrender to any colonial governor (without naming specific commissioners), but only authorised those governors to promise a future pardon, which would be granted later – by which time some pardonees had already gone back to plundering. That was rectified by a new order in July 1718, but neither one said anything about what would happen to their plunder.

There were still some concerns about legal process, too, with governor Robert Hunter in New York writing to London that if some of Williams' captured crew came before a jury 'their fate may be doubtfull', because the jury might let them off. The governor of Barbados reported that pirates were unconcerned about naval ships because they still believed they could only be tried in Britain. The new statute of 1700 had expired after seven years, though it was reissued in 1715 and 1719, with some other clarifications to the laws of piracy also introduced in 1717.

If the issues with pardons and judicial process resemble previous episodes, the legislation had now been clarified, and there are two further differences compared with earlier responses to piracy. The first was the naval resources available to the government. The navy now kept warships on station in Jamaica, Barbados, the Leeward Islands, Virginia, New York, and New England, some of these vessels arriving back after wartime service in Mediterranean and Baltic campaigns.

These naval ships had some effect – there are no reports of attacks on Virginian ships after 1717, for example – but it was, as usual, a geographically confined one. The ships on station were small and manoeuvrable compared to the great battleships of the day, but still ill-suited to patrolling a vast and often shallow coastline. They concentrated on the areas of most interest to the central government, the royal colonies, which tended to produce valuable staple crops and were heavily involved in slavery, all of which boosted royal revenues.

Tensions continued between colonial officials and naval captains, too, not least because the Act for Encouragement of Trade to America, in 1708, banned captains from pressing men there. The *American Weekly Mercury* accused naval captains of being too fearful to hazard their ships against 'such desperate Fellows, as the Pirates are reported to be', and Jamaican officials regularly complained that naval captains were more interested in trading for themselves. Three ships sent to the Caribbean expressly to pursue pirates were rerouted to convoy duties when Jamaican merchants complained that those already on station had failed to provide protection. Only one naval captain, Francis Hume, actually captured a pirate ship, at St Croix in the Virgin Islands early in 1717, and many of the sailors aboard got away.

Colonial and commercial authorities therefore took matters into their own hands. It was a petition in May 1717 from merchants in Bristol, complaining that for several months English pirates had been plundering their ships in the Caribbean, that prompted the government's general pardon and increase in naval resources. In 1719 both the East India and Royal African Companies complained about piracy spreading into their territories, and merchant lobbyists interested in sugar, tobacco, and the Newfoundland fisheries protested more vociferously in 1720.

Such an approach is unsurprising given the composite, and fissiparous, structure of the empire that I discussed before. The second feature that distinguishes the 1710s and 1720s is that those colonial authorities who had previously sponsored plunderers now jumped aboard the imperial bandwagon. Trading with plunderers continued, sometimes with the support of a governor willing to offer a pardon, but often in a much more clandestine fashion. If my hunch is correct that most colonists had not seen previous wartime plundering as piracy, then they probably did not find any inconsistency in their new approach, though the developing laws and the changing definition of 'privateers' perhaps made the position clearer.

Spotswood offered a bounty for any pirates captured or killed, continuing Virginia's traditional stance – but so too did Robert Hunter, governor of New York. Rhode Island, where Samuel Cranston was still in charge, sent out expeditions in 1717 and 1722; Pennsylvania dispatched three ships in 1718; South Carolina a couple before 1720; and Massachusetts one in 1726. Jamaica augmented the four naval ships on station with a private vessel to guard the coast.

Captured plunderers could no longer be assured of acquittal or shelter from the law, either. Nine survivors from the wreck of Bellamy's *Whydah*

were immediately put on trial in Boston, of whom six were convicted, on
22 October 1717, and executed less than a month later. Two had been let
off, while a Miskito man called John Julian may have been sold into slavery.
For the others, word of the new general pardon arrived some three weeks
too late, and colonial authorities remained keen to make an example of
those they caught, especially if the defendants had already received a pardon
before returning to piracy.

South Carolina suffered particularly badly in these years, due to its
proximity to the Bahamas, including during Bonnet's and Teach's visit
to Charleston in May 1718. Governor Johnson sent out a ship under local
slave trader William Rhett to chase down Stede Bonnet, who, after being
abandoned by Teach, had cruised off Delaware Bay. Rhett found Bonnet
at anchor in Cape Fear River in September and defeated him in a fierce
fight on a falling tide.

Following his surrender, Bonnet and his men faced trial in Charleston,
only six days after the *Whydah* survivors' trial in Boston. Bonnet's unusual
background attracted attention: the judge described him as 'a gentleman
... [with] the Advantage of a liberal Education ... generally esteemed a
Man of Letters' and his 'piteous Behaviour under Sentence' elicited some
sympathy, but no reprieve. Twenty-nine men from Bonnet's crew were
hanged on 8 November, and Bonnet himself a month later.

Bonnet's former companion Teach likewise found himself targeted by
an expedition, this time a collaboration between Spotswood and some
naval officers, perhaps helped by Spotswood's own military background.
The governor hired two sloops, suitable for inshore sailing, and some
local pilots, while the naval ships in Virginia provided sixty sailors under
Lieutenant Robert Maynard.

On 22 November 1718 Maynard encountered his quarry fraternising
with a local sloop. Having lost the element of surprise, Maynard and Teach
apparently engaged in a shouting match over the water, with Maynard
warning Teach that he intended to take him dead or alive, at which Teach
supposedly demanded a glass of wine and 'swore damnation to himself' if
he offered, or received, quarter. Teach's swivel guns took a heavy toll on
Maynard's crew as the ships closed, but the naval sailors shot away some
of Teach's rigging and sails to prevent him escaping.

As the two ships clashed together, an almost cinematic scene unfolded,
according to various accounts. Maynard and Teach first duelled man to
man as the battle raged around them. Then a Scottish highlander serving with Maynard struck Teach such a blow that it severed his head.
Apparently they found one African sailor below decks preparing to blow

up the ship. This dramatic end to his piratical career did much to embellish Teach's legend afterwards.

Only a few of the crew survived, most of them also African (perhaps some were captives who took no part in the fighting, but that did not save them). Maynard returned to Virginia with Teach's head hanging from the bowsprit – although it was several years before Maynard and his crew received any of Spotswood's promised bounty. Spotswood also sent troops overland, who rounded up several more of Teach's men. On 12 March 1719 sixteen men went on trial. Israel Hands was pardoned for giving testimony, but fourteen men, five of them African, were hanged.

During another trial, of eight men in Massachusetts in 1717, the defendants tried to argue that Queen Anne's proclamations against piracy held no force after her death. Legal intricacies such as these, however, could no longer prevent a 'guilty' verdict. The trial report concluded that pirates 'claim the Protection of no Prince, the privilege of no Country, the benefit of no Law; He is denied common humanity ... [a] wild and savage Beast, which every Man may lawfully destroy'. Walter Moor, captain of a South Sea Company ship, did just that off the coast of Venezuela, when he met what he took to be a pirate ship and preemptively attacked. Others may well have done the same. However they saw themselves, these plunderers were certainly seen, and treated, as 'enemies of all'.

The most consequential anti-piracy expedition of these years was led by Woodes Rogers. After his Pacific voyage failed to yield the riches he anticipated, Rogers was declared bankrupt. He may have separated from his wife, who had moved to live with her father, the retired admiral. She remained in Bristol while Rogers stayed in London, looking for new opportunities.

In 1712 Rogers published a successful account of his Pacific voyage (about which more later) and then sailed to Madagascar in 1713–14, with permission from the East India Company to purchase enslaved people there, whom he transported to Bengkulu. The next year he tried to drum up support for a new settlement on the island, and even wrote to Hans Sloane, the eminent botanist and collector, asking Sloane to furnish him with anything he knew about the place.

Rogers' attention was soon diverted elsewhere, probably through the offices of Samuel Buck, a merchant who, in 1716, sent two ships to trade at the Bahamas, with instructions to find out 'how the pirates might best be dislodged' (one of the ships was captured by them). Buck and Rogers joined forces and, in July 1717, Rogers lobbied the government to be made governor of the islands, promising that he had a ship and a plan of campaign. Fifty-six merchants supported his petition to the king.

The government had no specific plan at all concerning Nassau, so this proposal met with a positive reception. Rogers set sail towards the end of April 1718 with two frigates carrying twenty and thirty guns apiece, and two sloops with six each. With him went 150 sailors, 100 soldiers, and 200 civilian settlers, accompanied by the three naval ships who later ended up on Caribbean convoy duty. This fairly formidable force reached Barbados in July 1718.

Sailing onto Nassau, they found the blackened timbers of some thirty or forty merchant ships lying burned and sunk in the harbour, along with a few trading vessels still afloat, and the pirates' sloops. Charles Vane would not surrender. The second volume of the *General History* printed a letter from Vane to Rogers offering to accept a pardon if he could keep all his plunder, although it is hard to be sure about the authenticity of this document. In any case, they reached no such agreement.

Vane fired on Rogers' ships, and then during the night set his own ship alight and towed it towards the newcomers, making his escape while Rogers' men dealt with the threat. Rogers sent his own two sloops after Vane, who reportedly dropped the English flag he had been flying and put out black colours, 'a signal to intimate that they would neither give or take quarter'. Vane out-sailed his pursuers and got away.

Rogers, meanwhile, landed and proclaimed himself governor over the few hundred inhabitants, bolstered by those arriving with him. Nassau must have stood in a poor state of repair, having been destroyed several times over recent decades, although during its piratical era there was probably some new building by carpenters and others with such skills. Soon after Rogers arrived, an already cracked bastion of the fort collapsed, and in short order eighty-six of his companions died, mainly of sickness. Nevertheless, Nassau was under official control once more.

Rogers issued 200 pardons, established a Council and an Assembly (from which pardoned pirates were excluded), formed three militia companies, and began to repair the fort. Hornigold and Burgess, and John Cockram, a merchant shipmaster who briefly joined the wreck-pillagers and then traded with the 'flying gang' during their occupation of Nassau, had all taken the pardon. Rogers commissioned them as pirate hunters, while Burgess also became judge of the vice-admiralty court and Cockram provided Rogers with an 'indifferently well done' chart of Nassau harbour and the neighbouring islands.

Rogers dispatched Cockram and Hornigold to pursue Vane. They met him off South Carolina, where he had plundered eight vessels together with Charles Years, who then abandoned Vane and went ashore to secure a pardon. The black flag still flew defiantly over Vane's ship. Hornigold and Cockram decided they had too little strength to assault Vane, though they rescued some of his victims' vessels and shepherded them to Nassau. Vane himself wrote to Rogers threatening to come and burn his ships, though he never made good on that promise; we will return to his fate later.

Rogers sent Hornigold and Cockram forth again. This time they captured a sloop near Exuma, south of Nassau, killing three men and bringing back ten captives. Rogers wrote to London extolling Hornigold's transformation, providing 'new proof ... given [to] the world to wipe off the infamous name' that he had formerly acquired.

Though he was initially unsure of his admiralty jurisdiction, the reports of recent executions in South Carolina reassured Rogers and he went ahead with a trial on 9–10 December 1718. The ten defendants were aged between 18 and 45. One had been gunner with Teach, another was a former prize-fighter. Most had accepted a pardon, but 'being instigated and deluded by the Devil' had 'return[ed] to your former unlawful evil courses of robbery and piracy', mutinying aboard their ship and marooning some of the crew, who gave testimony against them.

Only one man, a boatswain forced to join them, was acquitted, while another got a last-minute reprieve. The other eight were hanged outside the fort's walls. One, a former shipmaster in Jamaica, was penitent, but others were sullen, or made a deliberate show, wearing blue and red ribbons at their wrists and knees and in their caps, complaining loudly of the governor's harshness.

Above the gallows was hoisted a black flag – a potent symbol that Nassau's time as a 'new Madagascar' had come to an end. Yet that very recovery would usher in the second and more desperate phase of this final pirate episode.

15

THE CHOICE OF THE PYRATES

On 5 September 1720 Woodes Rogers issued a declaration stating that a sloop, the *William*, had been stolen from New Providence by 'Pirates and Enemies to the Crown'. Hardly an unusual document for its time, but this one was unique. It mentioned 'two Women by Name Ann Fulford alias Bonny, & Mary Read', making it the first surviving evidence to identify the most famous partnership of female pirates in history.

Rogers' colony was struggling. Earlier in 1720, assisted by fortunately timed bad weather, he saw off a Spanish force without a fight, but by autumn things were getting worse. Rogers had dangerously stretched his limited financial resources and relied now on credit.

At least half of those whom he pardoned returned to piracy, 'weary of living under restraint', as he described them, and he no longer had any naval assistance to help him maintain order. The *General History* claimed that though Rogers kept them well supplied with alcohol, 'they began to have such a hankering after their old Trade' that many of them purloined canoes or boats and made night-time escapes.

The theft of the *William* represented just such a relapse. John Rackam, also named in Rogers' proclamation, had sailed first with Charles Vane, became a captain himself, then took a pardon. He is more well known under his sobriquet 'Calico Jack', for his brightly coloured clothes, noted in the *General History*'s second volume (published eight years after his death).

Bonny, Read, Rackam, and some others set sail on 22 August, so it took two weeks for Rogers to officially respond. About a month later his proclamation appeared in the *Boston Gazette*, and only a few weeks after that the pirates themselves were seized off the coast of Jamaica. The proclamation and *Gazette* were not a major factor in the capture: they were never indicted for the theft of the *William*, so perhaps neither version reached the island. Nevertheless, we can see here how colonial authorities, newspapers, and correspondents shared information about piracy.

A trial followed on 16 November, and within a few days, just less than three months after he snuck out of Nassau, Rackam's corpse hung in chains as a warning to others, along with several of his crew. This venture ranks among the shortest of plundering escapades. Rackam in particular appears to have been a rather feckless leader, no matter how dashingly dressed.

Yet the impact of this brief voyage on the history of piracy has been enormous. Bonny and Read became immediately famous. An account of the trial, with their names on the front page, was published in Jamaica the following year. When the first volume of the *General History* appeared three years after that, they were again headline material. These two women were the only individual pirates who were not captains to be named on the title page, feature in their own sections of the book, and be depicted in illustrations. The author and publishers believed that their story would sell well. They have been proved right time and time again.

That story, however, remains an intriguing mystery. We know almost nothing for certain about these two remarkable women. The *General History* embellished the bare facts of the *William* voyage with some personal background that is extremely fanciful. These pages tell us more about the attitudes of the day – not only about pirates but also about gender and sexuality – than they do about the women themselves.

A dual portrait of Anne Bonny and Mary Read from the first edition of the *General History*. (Courtesy of the John Carter Brown Library)

Neither the *General History* nor the trial report preserves their own voices. The *General History* puts imagined words in their mouths; the trial record states only that neither of them offered 'any Thing material' in their defence. Whatever they had to say for themselves, the court clerk, or the pamphlet's editor, did not consider it worthy of note.

The surviving evidence either ventriloquises or silences both of these women. Anne Bonny and Mary Read were undoubtedly bold and unusual, breaking the rules of contemporary society, but their lives were reimagined immediately after their death, and have been ever since. We must distinguish between these sensational caricatures and the women themselves, and examine more closely the realities of women's experiences with piracy.

Let us consider the *General History* first, since its influence on the afterlives of these two women and on ideas about piracy and gender cannot be overstated (I will return to the book's other legacies in another chapter). In fact, their inclusion is probably one reason for the book's success, as the preface yet again drew attention to them, keen to hook readers with the promise of a story that was 'a little Extravagant, yet ... nevertheless true'.

Mary Read, the book says, was born to a sailor's widow, also Mary, in England. Her mother gave birth to a son before her husband was lost at sea and conceived an illegitimate daughter afterwards. The unnamed son died young, so, to escape the opprobrium of bastardy, mother and daughter retired to the country for a few years, until, running short of funds, the elder Mary masqueraded her daughter as her deceased son and prevailed upon her late husband's mother for a regular allowance.

In this disguise the younger Mary entered the service of a French lady, then ran away to the navy, served as a cavalry cadet in Flanders, distinguished herself in combat, and fell for a comrade to whom she revealed her true identity. They married and set up a tavern in Breda, Holland, called the Three Horseshoes.

Domestic bliss was short-lived. Read's husband died, so she went for a soldier again, then as a sailor on a merchant ship. When her ship was captured by pirates, Read volunteered to join them, coming eventually to Nassau, where she met Bonny and Rackam.

Bonny reached New Providence in a different fashion, or so the story goes. Her father was a lawyer in County Cork, Ireland, and her mother was the family maid. The lawyer's wife discovered her husband's philandering through a rather tortuous subplot involving some silver spoons. The maid, now pregnant, was briefly imprisoned for theft, while lawyer and wife separated.

The lawyer disguised Anne as a boy to avoid further scandal, but the news got out, so he, her mother (whose thoughts on all this are never mentioned), and Anne moved to Charleston. It is only there that Anne becomes the focus of the story, growing up with a 'fierce and couragious Temper' after her mother's death. While still young she beat up an acquaintance and would-be rapist so thoroughly that 'he lay ill of it a considerable Time' – a notable role reversal from contemporary expectations of female submissiveness.

Anne married a sailor, who quickly soured on her when the expected dowry failed to materialise because of her father's disapproval of the match. They moved to Nassau, looking for work, and there Bonny met Rackam and started an affair with him. The second volume of the *General History* adds that they 'lived in all Manner of Luxury' on Rackam's takings, while her husband, who is named as James Bonny and described as 'of a sober Life, considering he had been a Pyrate', even agreed to 'resign her [to Rackam] ... by a Writing in Form', in exchange for cash down.

When rumour of this arrangement reached Rogers' ears, the governor summoned Anne Bonny and threatened a whipping over the illegal deal. Furious at this turn of events, Bonny and Rackam 'resolved to run away together, and enjoy it in Spight of all the World', and they gathered eight 'brisk young Fellows ... weary of working on Shore ... [and] all true to the Roguery'. They stole the *William*, apparently from another former pirate, and sailed away.

Apart from the fact that Bonny, Read, and Rackam were all in Nassau by August 1720 and sailed together aboard the *William*, I do not believe any of this.

For one thing, these sections are very light on dates in comparison to other chapters, even for verifiable events like the trial. There are also several plot holes. A brewery called the Three Horseshoes (*De Drie Hoefijzers*) did exist in Breda; the name has been recycled for a twenty-first century redevelopment in the town. Yet it is hard to believe that Mary Read ever had anything to do it with. As told by the *General History*, Read's soldier husband died around the time of the Treaty of Rijswijk, in 1697, more than two decades before her rendezvous with Bonny and Rackam

in Nassau. Even if this is a mistake for the Treaty of Utrecht in 1713, that
still leaves a span of some seven years between Read's supposed departure
from Breda and the *William* voyage.

The first volume also claims that Bonny and Rackam had a child whom
they left ashore in Cuba in an earlier voyage before Rackam took the royal
pardon in Nassau. The second volume, however, suggests that stealing the
William was their first escapade together. Mary Read does not appear at
all in this volume, except as 'Mary Stead' in a paragraph where she is not
only misnamed but obviously mixed up for Bonny. None of this inspires
great confidence in these narratives.

The correspondences between the two stories are even more telling,
and reveal how the author felt that the very existence of these female
pirates required some rationale. Since the book assumes that both women
spent their days at sea disguised as men, their supposed origins outside of
wedlock and consequent early introduction to cross-dressing explains how
they fell into that way of life.

When you compare their chapters with others in the book, this focus
on their supposed journey to becoming pirates appears even more obvious. The first edition gave each woman a subsection of the chapter
on Rackam, marked out by its own title, about eight pages apiece;
several captains, including Rackam himself, got even shorter shrift.
Those other chapters spend a sentence or two, at most a paragraph, on
their subject's life before they became a pirate. In stark contrast, Read
arrives in the Caribbean halfway through her section after several other
adventures, while Anne Bonny is the main character only for the final
two pages of hers, after a lengthy account of her parentage. This unusually detailed attention to their backstories was not accidental and shows
the author's real purpose: to decipher, and to condemn, the apparently
incomprehensible existence of two cross-dressing female pirates.

This obsession with cross-dressing is also a comment on the sexuality
of these two women. The crux of their story in the first volume is the
titillating tension created through the concealment and then revelation
of their gender. In Flanders, Read 'found a way of letting [her future
husband] discover her Sex ... He was much surprized at what he found,
and not a little pleased.' The story of 'two Troopers' marrying caused 'a
great Noise', though their comrades took it well. On the *William*, supposedly, Read became enamoured with a 'young Fellow' who was a coerced
'Artist' – pirate argot for a skilled navigator. Read ingratiated herself to
him by complaining about their lot among the pirates and then, as she had
before, confided in and seduced him.

Perhaps the most sensational aspect for contemporary, and later, audiences is the hint of lesbian attraction. Bonny apparently took a fancy to Read, thinking her 'a handsome young Fellow, and for some Reasons best known to herself, first discovered [i.e. revealed] her Sex to Mary Read ... [but] to the great Disappointment of Ann Bonny, [Read] let her know she was a Woman also'. Despite Bonny's 'disappointment', some historians have found in this passage proof of a homosexual relationship, as their 'Intimacy' made Rackam so jealous that he threatened to kill Read until Bonny 'let him into the Secret'. However deliberate the author's implications, these scenes of the two women in various stages of disguise and undress still captivate audiences, as they did in the eighteenth century.

This account reinforces its message by contrasting the two women's behaviour. Both were certainly unconventional; Read apparently stood in for her 'Artist' lover at a duel. Yet Read also represented contemporary stereotypes of faithfulness and sexual reserve, insisting on marriage, by intent if not always by legal procedure. On trial, says the *General History*, she 'declared that she had never committed Adultery or Fornication with any Man', though the trial record contains no such statement (perhaps it was not 'material' enough to write down).

Bonny appeared as the opposite of Read. Both volumes of the *General History* paint her as entirely lustful, being 'very young, [and] soon turned Libertine' on her arrival in Nassau. James Bonny supposedly found her in a hammock with another man even before she left him for Rackam. The detour where she and Rackam abandon their child in Cuba shows her discarding a conventional maternal role as well as sexual propriety. Then there is her dalliance, consummated or not, with Read.

The deliberate signal of these characterisations is that women – even women who became pirates – could not escape the supposed constraints (as the author saw it) of the female temperament and body. Commenting on Read's infatuation with her 'Artist', the *General History* added that 'Love found her out in this Disguise, and hinder'd her from forgetting her Sex'. The book goes on to say that 'she let him discover her Sex ... by carelessly shewing her Breasts, which were very White. The young Fellow ... had his Curiosity and Desire so rais'd by this Sight, that he never ceas'd importuning her [...] her Passion was no less violent than his'.

At this time, female breasts were becoming more directly associated with both sexuality and motherhood, so the author's fixation on them is associated with these cultural trends as well as casual prurience. Changes to the printed illustrations of the two women in the *General History* fit this trend: they appeared initially as fearsome and well-armed figures in male

Anne Bonny op Jamaica Gevangen.   *Mary Read op Jamaica in de Gevangenisse Overleden.*

Portraits of Anne Bonny and Mary Read from the 1725 Dutch edition of the *General History*. (Courtesy of the John Carter Brown Library)

clothing (in the first edition) but later as temptresses baring their cleavage (in a Dutch translation in 1725). The obsession with cross-dressing and the revelation of 'very White' breasts therefore emphasise the traits of feminine desire and vulnerability in which Bonny, Read, and all women were, according to eighteenth-century patriarchal attitudes, trapped.

Cross-dressing to go to sea was not a total fiction. I came across one such case in the Stadsarchief in Amsterdam: a woman called Elizabeth Watson (or, in the Dutch records, 'Lijsbet Bats' and 'Elisabeth Watssen'). She was born in York, reached Amsterdam at the age of 20 and from there, around 1631, travelled to Brazil aboard a *West Indische Compagnie* ship, dressed as a soldier.

We know about her because she was interrogated two years later in Amsterdam. Asked if she had sailed to Brazil, she answered simply '*Jae*', and only added that she spent some nine weeks '*in mans klederen*'. This questioning proves that her travels in disguise had become public knowledge, but it says nothing about whether her shipmates knew, or whether she was discovered or chose to reveal her identity in transit or in Brazil. When I first read this sensational but sparse record I was torn between delight and frustration.

She did not remain a soldier, but married a surgeon, and the two returned to Holland. Her new husband went to sea again and Watson later heard he had drowned. She was actually interrogated not for cross-dressing but on a charge of adultery with a German *Compagnie* lieutenant, almost twenty years her senior. He claimed she spontaneously seduced him in a tavern; she maintained that he promised to marry her, but had a wife in Germany already. The innkeeper, also questioned, reported that they told him they were married, and Watson's story is considerably more believable.

Watson is not the only example. She was neither prosecuted nor punished, so far as I can tell, and the same is true of others. One particularly interesting case, for our purpose here, is Elizabeth de St Morel, the daughter of a French refugee who joined the Spanish army, under the name Tobias Morello, with a captain called Campo Plantines, whom she then followed into Dutch service.

After the death of her 'protector' (the exact nature of this relationship is unclear), her identity was revealed and William III and II awarded her an annual pension of 200 guilders. De St Morel met and married a man called Weyerman, setting up a soup kitchen in Breda, *De Son* (The Sun). Her son, artist and journalist Jacob Campo Weyerman, born in 1677, spent some time in London in the early 1700s and started a satirical newspaper in Rotterdam.

By curious coincidence another woman, Maria van Antwerpen, served as a soldier and married in Breda, in 1751. Much of the evidence for Van Antwerpen comes from a book written by Franciscus Lievens Kersteman, published in 1769, who claimed to have got the story from Van Antwerpen herself. Kersteman wrote that Van Antwerpen spoke of herself as having the nature of a man in a woman's body, and that she returned to cross-dressing twice after her first marriage, on one occasion marrying another woman while using the name Machiel.

Kersteman might have added a sensational spin here, and we should remember that people at that time did not think about gender in the same way as we do today. Nevertheless, it is an intriguing hint at the way gendered categories could be fluid even in a period of patriarchal, and supposedly very clear, boundaries.

Another example is Hannah Snell, a Worcester woman who, after her sailor husband abandoned her (and was executed for murder), served in the British army and Royal Marines during the 1740s–50s in Europe and India. Like Van Antwerpen, a biography appeared, and though Snell's role in its authorship is unclear, she did go on the stage in her uniform, performing military songs, turning her supposed transgressions into celebrity status.

It is tempting to speculate about the connections between reality and fiction here. Did the author of the *General History* meet Weyerman in London, and was the story of Mary Read inspired by – even a deliberate parody of – Weyerman's background and the experience of Elizabeth de St Morel? Did Van Antwerpen and Snell read that story in the *General History* or its translations and decide to follow its example?

Another connection might be the popular balladry of the later seventeenth and early eighteenth centuries. Only a few women went to sea or to the wars in disguise – Dutch scholars have identified 100 in Britain and Europe, across three centuries – but the idea of cross-dressing 'warrior women' generated a lot of songs. Unlike the real 'warrior women', though, these ballads served to reinforce conventional ideas about gender roles, particularly matrimonial devotion. In most of these songs the woman faithfully follows her lover, remaining undetected (and sometimes indulging in secret romances) until, usually, she switches back into women's clothes and the couple marry. More rebellious female characters, such as one who left her husband and proved 'valiant and bold, / And would not be controll'd', usually came to a bad end in their songs.

However unorthodox their protagonists, these ballads reminded listeners of social expectations about women. Far more common than ballads of warrior women were those where the wife or maiden sweetheart remained at home, faithfully awaiting her man.

A similar polemical purpose in the *General History* is especially obvious because neither Bonny nor Read actually hid their gender during their voyage aboard the *William*. True, they dressed in men's clothes. One witness at the trial, Dorothy Thomas, reported that they 'wore Mens Jackets and long Trouzers, and Handkerchiefs tied about their Heads'. She added that she recognised them as women 'by the largeness of their Breasts'. So far, so *General History*.

Thomas, however, spent only a short spell in their company. Two French witnesses who endured a longer captivity said that 'when they saw any Vessel, gave Chase, or Attacked, they wore Men's Cloaths ... at other Times, they wore Women's Cloaths'.

This evidence contradicts the *General History*'s (and popular culture's) devotion to the idea of Bonny and Read hiding their gender, and suggests that its backstories were pure invention. Possibly one or both women went to sea incognito before 1720; successful efforts would leave no evidence. If, as seems more likely, they met in Nassau and their first voyage together was in the *William*, then everyone aboard, and even Woodes Rogers, knew that they were women from the very start.

There was no clandestine courtship, either of the 'Artist' by Read, or of Read by Bonny, nor is there any need to invoke childhood cross-dressing as an explanation for adult tendencies. The two women probably never wore disguises at all. There is a certain irony, even a poignancy, that this dramatised image has survived and proliferated so successfully, that celebrations of them as trailblazing and feminist figures rely heavily on sources that are not only fictive but decidedly chauvinist.

The *General History* actually played upon this question of veracity. The author insists twice that he heard these stories from reliable sources and that their truth cannot be questioned, being attested by the thousands of witnesses at the trial in Jamaica, who 'heard the Story of their Lives, upon the first discovery of their Sex'. Here, we have a literary sleight of hand. The trial itself unquestionably took place, but we know that their 'Sex' was not 'discovered' there and we cannot prove that 'the Story of their Lives' was recounted there either – or, if it was, that it matches the versions that have since become famous.

Maybe the author even signalled as much when he wrote that if 'their Stories ... [have] a little the Air of a Novel, they are not invented or contrived for that Purpose, it is a Kind of Reading this Author is but little acquainted with', and again 'some may be tempted to think the whole Story no better than a Novel or Romance'. This phrasing is intriguing, since the concept of the 'Novel or Romance' as a distinct genre was coalescing at this time, and authors of the day toyed with the relationship between fact and fiction. Clear distinctions between a 'novel' and a 'history' were not yet drawn.

Daniel Defoe, often considered one of the first novelists, published many of his works anonymously in the style of an autobiography, including *Robinson Crusoe*, which called itself 'a just History of Fact', and its second sequel criticised those who accused the first two volumes of being 'all a Romance'. Did Defoe intend these works to be believed as authentic, did he just enjoy himself by mocking his critics, or did he inhabit his

character's perspective in an entertaining manner that his audience would
have understood as a literary game?

The word 'novel' does not appear in *Crusoe*, but at the time it was more
associated with a short romantic story or 'novella'. In this regard it fits the
General History's sections on Bonny and Read remarkably well, and I think
that in so forcefully *denying* that these sections were a novel, the author
was playing similar games to Defoe. One of the earliest reviews of the
General History, appearing in the *Weekly Journal* a couple of months after
its publication, called these chapters 'a shim-sham Story'. That review, as
we shall see in another chapter, may well have been written by the *General
History*'s author himself.

I doubt the book's protestations of honesty, or the scandalous tales of
Bonny and Read, were ever meant to be believed. Maybe we historians
just missed the joke.

So where does that leave us? If nothing of the *General History*'s account is
true, what can we say about the real Anne Bonny and Mary Read?

Some historians have tried to track down these women. William
Cormac married Mary Brennan in South Carolina in 1694, both Irish-
sounding surnames, and soon afterwards had a daughter called Anne,
whom some identify as Anne Bonny, though little other evidence about
Cormac and his family survives. Young maidservants were vulnerable to
sexual harassment and abuse from their employers, so the circumstances of
Bonny's parentage, while probably fictional, were not unheard of.

I attempted a similar investigation with Mary Read. The name 'Mark'
is sometimes bestowed on her brother (who goes unnamed in the *General
History*), and even on her supposed cross-dressing alter ego at sea. I went looking in parish registers for a Mary Read born around the 1680s–90s with the
right family profile: daughter of a sailor, mother named Mary, brother named
Mark. There are many possible candidates, but none quite fit the bill – often
the son was born *after* the daughter, for example. If Mary Read and Anne
Bonny were both illegitimate, though, they might not even appear in the registers; it would depend on the parents and the variable habits of parish clerks.

More crucially, in pursuing these lines of enquiry we are starting at the
wrong end. We are still trying to fit the historical evidence to the *General
History*. It will not get us anywhere.

In the trial record, Bonny and Read were both introduced as 'late of
the Island of Providence, Spinsters', meaning unmarried adult women

– another point against the *General History*, since if its version was true
Read should have been listed as a widow. It is possible they were born in
New Providence, but several Mary Reads were baptised in Jamaica in the
mid-1680s, and there was a sizeable and wealthy Bonny clan on the island
by the 1720s. Fulford, the other name for Anne given in Rogers' proclamation (and mangled into Fulworth in the second volume of the *General
History*), is found in Barbados and North Carolina during this period. Any
of these could be their origins – or none of them.

One other intriguing possibility exists. Mary Read was the first name
on the 1708 petition seeking a pardon for husbands in Madagascar (the
request was refused, perhaps because it was really a scheme led by one John
Breholt to transfer the fabled plunder from Madagascar to England). Of
course, if Read was her married name then we have no way of identifying her maiden name at all, though again this would not fit her being a
'Spinster' at the trial. Or was the clerk mistaken; was Read associated with
piracy long before she sailed on the *William*?

Another irony of the *General History* is its depiction of women at sea as
unthinkable when, as that 1708 petition shows, women were actually
deeply involved in maritime affairs throughout these centuries. There were
indeed some superstitions about women on ships (as William Ambrosia
Cowley noted when rounding Cape Horn on Valentine's Day in 1684), but
women were actually much more frequent seafarers than you might think.

While European women were a minority in most Atlantic colonies,
women, free and enslaved, nevertheless crossed the ocean in large numbers
during this period. As well as those bound for the Americas, ships carried women to trading settlements in Africa and the Indian Ocean. Some
trace of this appears even in the *General History*: during one of Rackam's
earlier escapades, he supposedly captured a ship from London bound to
the Caribbean with two women aboard.

Those two were far from unusual. European women usually travelled as
passengers, though many a captain's or officer's wife accompanied them to sea.
Some women sailed to join a husband, or to find themselves one, while others
shipped as indentured servants or as convicts condemned to transportation.

One interesting example is Mary Carleton, born Mary Moders, who
travelled in Europe and returned to England claiming to be a down-at-
heel German princess. She was tried for bigamy and acquitted, causing
a pamphlet controversy in which she penned her own defence, and even

appeared on stage, as herself, in an autobiographical play written specifically for her. After arrest for theft she was transported to Port Royal in 1671, but returned to London by 1673, where she was executed on further theft charges. Carleton remained famous after her death: in 1755 a book appeared combining her story with Bonny, Read, and the tales of other scandalous women.

The experiences of these women – at sea and on arrival – depended greatly on social status. An indentured servant or a convict like Carleton faced a far worse time than a *contessa* married to a viceroy. English travellers in Europe also observed national variations, reporting that in Spain and Portugal the middling sorts and aristocracy never allowed women out without a chaperone, while Dutch women acted with a freedom that English observers found unseemly, though many travellers felt that social standards were less rigorously upheld in the colonies. Of course, millions of African women experienced the horrors of the middle passage and life in slavery afterwards.

For many women, their involvement in the maritime world did not begin or end with just one trip across the ocean. Women participated in trade, both as partners with their husbands or relatives and in their own right, ranging from wealthy mercantile transactions down to small-scale trade in local networks. In some African and Asian ports, women played a crucial role as cultural and commercial brokers, including through (often temporary or informal) marriages with visiting European merchants that could, sometimes, enhance the woman's status in her own community.

Women contributed in other ways to the world of shipping, too. Some of these fitted expected female roles of the time, such as hostesses, victuallers and lodging-house keepers – and prostitutes – in sailor town districts. Elizabeth Watson, after her trouble with the lieutenant, said she wanted to have nothing to do with him, but in fact he set her up with a sergeant of the *Vereenigde Oostindische Compagnie*, to whom Watson became engaged. This may have been an arrangement of convenience, because wives and families were entitled to collect their husband's wages while he was away at sea, and the whole arrangement might have been a fraud for this purpose; women were frequently involved in such shady dealings.

Beyond those relationships, women also played a vital role in maritime manufacturing, making canvas, nets, rope, hammocks, flags, and other textiles. Some women even took up trades like blacksmithing, running large workshops, and if these were usually widows who inherited the business, they nonetheless kept those businesses going.

An interesting contemporary contrast to Elizabeth Watson is Jane Hendell of Southwark, who in 1635 was married to a distiller and had previously been married to a shipwright. Her husband's distillery was the site for maritime dealings in which Hendell herself acted as a witness, a broker, and an investor. Such was her knowledge of shipbuilding, and her residential proximity to the dockyards, that shipmasters sometimes asked her to review the work being done on their vessels.

A greater range of opportunities existed in the largest European ports, but women fulfilled similar roles in the many entrepôts of the Atlantic and beyond. In the Americas, most colonists clustered around the coast throughout this period, sea travel being easier in the absence of reliable road networks. For many women in these communities such travel would have been a part of daily life, though in smaller vessels and on shorter trips than the Atlantic crossings. It is very likely, then, that Bonny and Read had some experience of seafaring before they went aboard the *William*; in that at least the *General History* is correct, even if it mischaracterised the nature of that experience.

Dorothy Thomas, the witness who commented on 'the largeness of their Breasts', was captured by them travelling 'in a Canoa at Sea, with some Stock and Provisions, at the North-side of Jamaica', as the trial record noted. Thomas was seemingly alone in her 'Canoa', presumably on some cabotage or other business. She must have been a confident and capable sailor to voyage by herself, and the trial does not give any indication that this was unusual. Women also went to sea on other short trips, in family fishing boats or coastal trading vessels. Women in Indigenous Caribbean communities had long been involved in fishing and turtling voyages, and were even more proficient with 'Canoas'. The sea was not as exclusively a male world as we tend to assume.

Women were as heavily involved in piracy as they were in other maritime activities (again, we can see this in the 1708 petition). The important role that women played in retail trades, especially in second-hand sales and pawnbroking, put them in an advantageous position to handle plundered goods, which they did in the West Country, Ireland, the Caribbean and Americas, Africa, the Indian Ocean – everywhere we have visited so far. Sometimes this was opportunistic theft or bartering, but often it was part of more established communities and networks. Even the notorious renegade John Ward sent money home to his wife, and women often shielded their menfolk from the attentions of the law as well.

We have already witnessed the important role wives, in particular, played in these networks. Plunderers habitually married local women, all over the world. Some Red Sea plunderers corresponded with wives living in the colonies whom they would not see for years, while others – perhaps unintentionally – founded dynasties in Madagascar (as we will see in the next chapter).

Not all of these relations were a model of propriety, of course. While Henry Every may have returned to his own wife after his travels, one of his crew reportedly had a wife in London and another in Dublin. Lord Bellomont was furious when he learned that a chaplain in New York had married the wife of one, living but absent, plunderer to another who was closer to hand. Yet we should not overlook the existence of committed relationships too, as we see in the few surviving letters with their devotion and tenderness. Some wives, like John Philip Bear's 'strumpet'-turned-*contessa*, sailed along on plundering voyages.

At the same time, women were routinely vulnerable to abuse, exploitation, and violence at the hands of pirates. Prostitution was common in places like Port Royal, and the *General History* refers to 'Liberties' which Teach and his crew 'often took with the Wives and Daughters of the Planters' in the Carolinas, though the author makes a joke of not knowing whether any money changed hands. Teach is supposed to have married a 16-year-old girl and forced her to 'prostitute her self' to 'his brutal Companions ... before his Face'. That, again, comes from the *General History*, but Nathaniel Grubbin's wife escaped from abuse and it is likely other women faced similar treatment.

Women captured on prizes, or in buccaneering raids, were unlikely to find themselves protected, however much Henry Morgan or Woodes Rogers protested about the 'modesty' of their men. In 1708 the French Captain Martel stripped, threatened, beat, and tortured an English captain's wife, and her husband, in order to make them reveal their treasure. In the same raid other women, too, were raped and injured. There are plentiful examples of such cruelties in the *General History* and in other plundering episodes, such as in Ireland in the early 1600s.

Indigenous women in the Americas occupied a precarious position: sometimes they acted as guides, in other cases they entered short-term and probably coercive relationships. Exquemelin wrote that when buccaneers traded with local communities on the Mosquito Coast they would often 'buy an Indian woman', sometimes living with the same 'Indian wife' on multiple visits, and while this was common in intercultural trading posts and required the consent of the woman's father, nothing is said about her own choice. Bartholomew Sharp called the women of Daríen 'very handsom ... exceeding loving and free to the Embraces of Strangers', though no doubt this is a self-serving description.

Violence was always a likely outcome, though. Exquemelin wrote of another trip when an Indigenous raid on the buccaneer camp killed two enslaved African women with the buccaneers, possibly targeted in ritual violence. Even peaceful trading between buccaneers and Caribbean groups, Exquemelin added, could lead to fighting when the raiders seized women. Dampier recorded similar encounters in the Pacific and Indian Oceans, though he is usually silent on whether it was assault, prostitution, or something else.

Enslaved women, too, were often targeted, as they were on Woodes Rogers' ships – and then blamed for it. William Snelgrave, a slave trader, recorded in 1718 that in Sierra Leone English traders 'did not scruple to lend their black Wives to the Pirates', in return for 'great Rewards'. In the same region, in 1683, John Cooke, William Dampier, and Edward Davis had named their ship the *Batchelor's Delight*.

Women's connections with piracy, and with the maritime world more broadly, were complex and varied. The *General History*'s efforts to paint Bonny and Read as totally outlandish reflects another form of chauvinism, diminishing the many roles played by women, without whom maritime economies, and of course society in general, could never have functioned. That chauvinism was long perpetuated by historians and has only come under revision in recent decades.

Even against this backdrop, Bonny and Read remain exceptional. They are among the very few women who went to sea not as companions to male rovers but as pirates themselves. That they did not disguise themselves might suggest they were bolder and *more* exceptional than those who did, since Bonny and Read defied even the pretence of male normality at sea. Nor were they daunted by the threats that pirates posed to women.

Let us return to their short and ill-fated voyage. The *William* arrived off Jamaica in August 1720 and, according to the charges against them, on 1 September the crew did 'Solemnly and Wickedly consult' to commit piracy. Throughout the following two months they captured several small fishing vessels and canoes, and plundered at least four merchant ships.

The court estimated their total takings at £1,330 – not a bad haul for two months, had they got away with it.

There is no doubt that Bonny and Read were at the forefront of all these actions. The *General History* declared that 'no Person amongst them was more resolute, or ready to Board [a prize], or undertake any Thing that was hazardous', and this is the only part corroborated by the trial record, from which it was almost certainly copied. Dorothy Thomas reported that 'each of them had a Machet [machete] and Pistol in their Hands, and cursed and swore at the Men', and that they tried to persuade their fellows to kill Thomas 'to prevent her coming against them' in court. As well as wielding a gun herself, Bonny handed gunpowder to her male shipmates during battle, according to other witnesses, who added that Bonny and Read 'were very active, and willing to do any Thing ... both very profligate, cursing and swearing much'.

That readiness and bravery did not save them from capture. The *General History* suggests that news of the plundering reached the Jamaican authorities, whereupon the governor sent out two pirate hunters, including Jonathan Barnet, previously commissioned for the same role in 1715. They chased down and, 'after a very small Dispute', captured the *William*.

The truth is, as ever, a little more prosaic, though the governor, Nicholas Lawes, did commend Barnet for his 'very good piece of service'. A mariner from Port Royal appeared before the court and deposed that two merchant ships, one under Barnet, had been sailing 'on a Trading Voyage' to Cuba, but met a ship that fired upon them, and when hailed declared their captain as 'John Rackam from Cuba'. Rackam not only refused to strike his flag in the king's name but continued to fire, upon which the merchant ships fought back, forcing the pirates to surrender.

The *General History* maintains that only Bonny and Read dared to stay on deck, exhorting their comrades to 'come up and fight like men', even firing down upon them when they failed to do so. In the most famous exchange between Bonny and Rackam, she supposedly told him, on the day of his execution, that 'she was sorry to see him there, but if he had fought like a Man, he need not have been hang'd like a Dog'. This might be more of the *General History*'s exaggeration, but it fits better with the evidence from the trial than most of the other things the book has to say.

Bonny and Read do seem to have chosen poorly when they threw in their lot with Rackam, though most of the evidence about him, too, comes from the *General History*. While we must treat it with the same caution, it suggests an impetuous and unreliable character. Starting out with Charles Vane around 1718, he objected when Vane refrained from attacking a French warship. After 'branding [Vane] with the Name of a Coward', Rackam was elected in Vane's place. The second volume of the *General History* tells a slightly different story: Rackam was made captain of one of Vane's prizes, but the two fell out over the alcohol supply and went their separate ways.

After this separation, incidentally, Vane continued his depredations in the Bay of Honduras, but was wrecked on a small island in a hurricane. An old acquaintance on a passing ship refused to take Vane aboard for fear of him leading a mutiny. Vane managed to talk his way onto a different ship, only to run into the same old acquaintance, who identified Vane and clapped him in irons. He was tried and executed in Jamaica in March 1721.

Before Rackam ended up in New Providence in 1719 or 1720, and took a pardon, he may have had some success roving between Jamaica and Bermuda. A later edition of the *General History* says that he 'kept a little kind of a Family' in Cuba, at which place he and his crew 'staid a considerable Time, living ashore with their Dalilahs', though this was probably before he met Bonny. The trial record, while listing Rackam and most of his crew as from New Providence, like Bonny and Read, does suggest some connection with Cuba, since he announced himself as 'John Rackam from Cuba' to his eventual captors – unless this was merely a ruse.

In Cuba, the *General History* continues, Rackam was once surprised by a *guardacosta* but snuck aboard and stole away with one of the attacker's prizes, which 'enabled them to continue some Time longer in a Way of Life that suited their Depraved Tempers'. Another anecdote, from the second volume, says that Rackam and his crew spent some time on an isolated island until, hearing of the war with Spain, they wrote to Jamaica to seek a pardon and a commission. The governor instead sent out two sloops that caught him unawares and he only narrowly escaped in a small boat.

These stories may be as much of an invention as the romantic backstories I dismissed earlier. Indeed, the appearance of these details in later versions of the *General History* suggests that Rackam generated strong enough interest for further elaboration on his life, interest that probably came from his association with Bonny and Read. Whatever the truth of those tales, when he surrendered to the two merchant ships, he ran out of whatever ingenuity or luck he had. Similarly, whether Bonny and Read were indeed the last to surrender, the testimonies about them in the trial suggest they were at least as audacious as any of their shipmates.

Their trial followed swiftly after the arrest, and was over quickly. Rackam and the other defendants denied any 'Acts of Piracy', maintaining that 'their Design was against the Spaniards', but these 'frivolous and trifling Excuses' were dismissed (since they had plundered English vessels) and the men were condemned to death, as were two more the next day. All were soon executed, some at Kingston, some at Gallows Point near Port Royal. Rackam's corpse and two others were then hung in chains at Plumb Point, Bush Key, and Gun Key, visible to ships visiting the island.

The *General History* spins another cautionary tale about nine men who were simply aboard the *William* for a drink when it was captured, and were nonetheless executed; but there is no mention of this in the trial record. It does, however, include several other documents, such as other trials in Jamaica, as well as some papers exhibited to the court regarding mariners forcibly caught up in piracy, and a full copy of the most recent legislation. Maybe the printer simply padded out the volume with whatever came to hand; or maybe, like the *General History*, and Rogers' proclamation, they wanted to warn off others tempted to follow a piratical path.

Bonny and Read were tried separately, eleven days later, perhaps in implicit recognition that these two women were significantly different to their shipmates, or maybe the court was simply waiting for Dorothy Thomas, who did not appear against Rackam and the others. In either case, Bonny and Read were found guilty and condemned to death.

Now came a last and dramatic announcement from the two women: 'they were both quick with Child, and prayed that Execution of the Sentence might be stayed'. The court ordered 'an Inspection', and as neither woman was executed it must have found that they were indeed pregnant. Given the timeline of the voyage, they might have been pregnant all the time they were pirates.

The *General History* reports that Read's 'Execution was respited, and it is possible she would have found Favour', meaning a longer reprieve, except that she contracted a fever and died. The grave records of Spanish Town's cemetery show that Mary Read was buried on 28 April 1721, six months after her trial.

Bonny, the *General History* goes on, was also 'reprieved from Time to Time' and, with unusual candour, the author admits 'what is become of her since, we cannot tell; only this we know, that she was not executed'. Some have speculated that she returned to Charleston (if you believe her backstory), and South Carolinans claiming to be her descendants assert that she married again, had many children, and lived to a ripe old age. More likely she remained in Jamaica, especially if she was related to the local Bonnys. In 1733 an Anne Bonny was buried in Spanish Town, though whether this was the former pirate is yet again impossible to prove.

At the trial, the *General History* says, Read was asked 'what Pleasure she could have in being concerned in such Enterprizes, where her Life was continually in Danger'. Read is supposed to have replied:

> as to hanging, she thought it no great Hardship, for, were it not for that, every cowardly Fellow would turn Pyrate ... if it were put to the Choice of the Pyrates, they would not have the Punishment less than Death ... [otherwise] the Ocean would be crowded with Rogues ... and no Merchant would venture out; so that the Trade, in a little Time, would not be worth following.

Does this proud speech imply a warning to society concerning the 'Rogues' whom she would rather keep ashore, whom she also accuses of 'cheating the Widows and Orphans, and oppressing their poor Neighbours'? Or was it a wry observation that too many pirates would spoil the market? Does it position pirates as egalitarian 'enemies of all' or as hardheaded thieves?

Of course, Read probably never said these words at all, which sound much like the other fantasies of the *General History*, telling us what people thought about these women, not what Bonny and Read thought of themselves. We do not know whether Read and Bonny saw their time at sea as a refuge from 'Rogues' and other misfortunes, or whether they objected to the mistreatment of widows and orphans. We do not know if they felt death by hanging was just another occupational hazard. We do not know the truth of their childhoods or their love lives. In fact, we know almost nothing about them.

What we do know is that they took 'the Choice of the Pyrates', if not in quite the way meant by the *General History*. That choice inspired the many sensational legends that surround them. We are still listening to its echoes.

16

UTMOST FURY

When Woodes Rogers took over management of the Bahamas in 1718, it did not bring an immediate end to piracy in the Caribbean and Americas, but it did begin to change the direction and nature of this piracy. Plunderers once more spread their operations, especially to the east and west coasts of Africa.

Lacking the connections ashore that had sustained previous marauders, these pirates turned rootless and rambling, more dramatically distinct from contemporary society than previous generations. Some of these men come as close as any in history to being self-declared 'enemies of all'.

Madagascar's legendary status lived on in the decades after the Red Sea plunderers: in 1707, for example, a disaffected servant in Maryland sought, unsuccessfully, to persuade some of his fellows to blow up Annapolis then sail for the island. Nor was it just a legend. English and French ships, including some warships sent to pursue pirates, reported several hundred people, perhaps as many as 830, still present there throughout the first decade of the eighteenth century.

Their numbers declined, with 400 reported in 1708, as attrition seemed to achieve what imperial might could not; it was in that year, too, that one Mary Read and other women petitioned for a pardon for their husbands on the island. Aurangzeb's death in 1707, sparking a war between his three sons, also took some of the former urgency out of the problem. By the time Woodes Rogers visited the island in 1710, 'those miserable wretches, who had made such a Noise in the World, were now dwindled to between 60 and 70', who had become 'very poor and despicable'.

Rogers underestimated some of them, however. One curious consequence of the plunderers' presence in Madagascar was the rise of the Betsimisaraka, a confederation along the eastern coast. Its founding ruler,

Ratsimilaho, claimed to be the son of one 'Tom' or 'Tamo', perhaps even Thomas Tew, while another local leader, who traded with French merchants, called himself Roy Baldridge. Ratsimilaho united several zana-malata groups and fought off a Sakalava attack during the 1730s, later marrying the daughter of a Sakalava ruler. Ratsimilaho's descendants, a fusion of European and Malagasy communities, politics, and culture, ruled the region until the nineteenth century, while on the west coast the Sakalava leaders continued to trade with pirates and enlist their help in warfare into the 1720s.

Different factors drove the spike in piracy on the western coasts of Africa, although still reflecting interactions between European and African communities. The dynamics of trade in West Africa resemble the Indian Ocean more than the Americas, in a number of ways. The Portuguese began establishing *feitorias* (trading posts) in the late fifteenth century and were then challenged by French, Dutch, English, and other northern European traders in the late sixteenth and early seventeenth centuries, who also competed and fought among themselves. Violence was common in these early voyages, but Europeans always depended on alliances with local rulers, and indeed were in an even weaker position here than anywhere else, not least due to the tropical disease environment and the challenging shoreline; African-crewed boats were essential in all ports.

Trade remained under the control of African rulers and merchants, or Eurafrican trading families who emerged in several ports, often descended from *lançados*, Portuguese (and sometimes Jewish) merchants who settled in Africa. Most trading posts were small fortified sites, like Cape Coast Castle, which European trading companies rented from African land-owners. The only colonial territory was Portuguese Angola, established through alliance with the neighbouring *manicongo* of Kongo, who converted to Christianity and entered a rather fractious partnership with Portugal in the 1480s. The *West Indische Compagnie* invaded Angola in the 1640s, joining with local ruler Nzinga Mbande, sister of the previous *ngola*, who succeeded to the throne in 1624 and held off Portuguese conquest long after the *Compagnie* had abandoned their efforts.

The initial objective for most of these traders was gold, which already circulated across the trans-Saharan trading networks of extraordinarily wealthy empires like Mali and Songhay in the fourteenth and fifteenth centuries. Some natural commodities like gum arabic and camwood (the latter another dye ingredient) were also valuable. Over time, however, the demand for enslaved labour in the Americas came to dominate trade, so that enslaved people comprised 90 per cent of Atlantic Africa's exports by 1700.

Historians disagree vigorously over the impact of this commerce in Africa. Some argue that it led to economic under-development, others maintain that its consequences were more limited. Statistics can only be estimated, but it is likely that the continent's population did not decline, though it did stagnate while other global regions increased. Political consequences, too, are debatable. Several powerful empires arose in the late seventeenth and eighteenth centuries that controlled slave-trading routes, such as Asante, Dahomey, and Oyo, originating inland and expanding to the coast, playing European traders off against one another. It is uncertain, however, how much these empires owed their rise to the slave trade or whether it was coincidental with other factors. The importance of European technologies like gunpowder (unreliable in a tropical climate) has been much exaggerated, and probably as many people remained in slavery in Africa as were carried to the coast.

Nevertheless, the growth of this trade reorientated African economics and society in some ways, as the continent developed much closer links to the Americas. It also proved conducive to piracy by the early eighteenth century. The increasingly valuable trade created targets and, in the absence of hegemonic imperial control, both African and European traders were often happy to deal with pirates. John Leadstone, a former buccaneer who served, in turn, English, French, and Portuguese merchants, set up his own trading settlement that the *General History* called 'the best House in the Place', where Leadstone enjoyed 'a jovial Life' with 'his Friends ... the Pyrates'. He was not the only one. Moreover, the particularly harsh conditions of employment in slave ships – though nowhere near as awful as those experienced by enslaved people themselves – probably explain why so many sailors working on these vessels were tempted to turn pirate.

Like other episodes of plundering, it is possible to trace a genealogy of pirate captains and crews during this final phase, emerging out of the initial gathering in the Bahamas. Edward England, despite his name an Irish sailor who, like many others, had previously served with a commission from Jamaica, provides one such link. He was captured in 1716 by Christopher Winter, who brought him into company with Henry Jennings and Charles Vane.

England left the Caribbean in 1718 after Rogers arrived, sailing to the coast of Africa. Off Sierra Leone he captured a slave ship on which one Howell Davis (in his native Welsh, probably Hywel Davies, though no contemporary sources use that version of his name), an experienced sailor, served as chief mate. Davis refused to join England and even said he would rather be shot. Impressed by this bravery, England turned the prize over to Davis and advised him to sell the ship and its captive cargo in Brazil.

Davis' crew, however, refused and sailed to Barbados, where Davis was imprisoned for three months, then released without trial 'as he had been in no Act of Pyracy'. Realising that his reputation was ruined in Barbados, Davis made for the Bahamas, but was disappointed to find it 'newly surrendered' to Rogers. This version of events, from the *General History*, suggests a very tight turnaround if England indeed left the Caribbean because of Rogers, and it is unlikely that the news from the Bahamas had not reached Barbados during that time, though it is not impossible.

In any case, Davis now took service in one of Rogers' own sloops, bound for Cuba with some diplomatic dispatches. Several other members of the crew were recently pardoned pirates, including Thomas Anstis and Walter Kennedy. The latter was born in Wapping, probably to Irish parents, and had served in the navy following an apprenticeship to his anchorsmith father during which, if the *General History* is to be believed, he also dabbled in burglary and pickpocketing. These less-than-reformed pirates seized the sloop, chose Davis as captain, plundered for a while near Martinique and then, perhaps because of Davis' knowledge of the region, sailed for West Africa.

There they teamed up for a while with another ship from the Caribbean, which had been purloined there by William Moody in 1718. Colonial officials reported that both Moody's ship and a companion vessel had large crews with a mix of European and African sailors. Governor Walter Hamilton of the Leeward Islands complained that his one naval ship could do little against 'that vermin'.

When Robert Johnson in South Carolina heard that Moody was expected off his coast, he prepared four ships to pursue him, but Moody had either left early or never been there at all, because these ships captured two other pirates, Richard Worley in the *New York's Revenge*, a reference to his home port, and John Cole in the imaginatively named *New York Revenge's Revenge*. Worley died in the battle, but Cole and several others were captured and hanged in Charleston in November 1718. Aboard their ships were thirty-six female convicts, whom they had captured en route to the colonies; the authorities in Charleston intended to send them to the Bahamas, but they died of starvation before this occurred.

In 1719 Moody sailed for Sierra Leone, where he captured a slave ship commanded by William Snelgrave, who wrote an account of his experiences. Moody ran into difficulties when he abandoned Thomas Cocklyn and some friends ashore after Cocklyn tried to lead a mutiny. The rest of the crew objected and turned Moody, with a few followers, into an open boat, then went to find Cocklyn. Moody, whom Snelgrave described as a 'Gentleman-like Commander', probably made his way back to the Caribbean and accepted a pardon.

This crew now chose Olivier Levasseur as their leader. He was from a bourgeois family in Calais and had served as a *corsaire* in the war, before partnering briefly with Bellamy and Hornigold in 1716. He then took a stolen frigate to cruise off Brazil, where he captured a slave ship and abandoned 240 captives on a small island near Rio. He lost the frigate in a storm, but survived, and was nearly captured by a naval ship in the Caribbean before he joined Moody. He would become the most famous French pirate of this era, under the nickname *La Buse* (The Buzzard) or possibly *La Bouche* (The Mouth). Levasseur and his companions found Cocklyn already back at sea, having overpowered another ship, and both teamed up with Davis, though the partnership did not last long.

We will return to Davis later, but first let us follow Cocklyn and Levasseur around the Cape of Good Hope to the old plunderers' haunt of Madagascar, where they arrived in 1720 – after attacking Ouidah, one of the largest ports for the transatlantic slave trade. Apparently Cocklyn died in Madagascar, though other accounts suggest he was captured and hanged. John Taylor, who sailed with Davis before joining Cocklyn, took command.

Levasseur, meanwhile, ran into and rescued Edward England, who returned to the African coast in 1719, separately to the others, and then sailed into the Indian Ocean but shipwrecked on Anjouan. One of Levasseur's eyes had been scarred many years earlier and was by this time blind, so he wore an eyepatch, the most well-known example of another popular pirate stereotype.

England took command of a Dutch prize, and the trio seized the *Cassandra*, an East India Company ship worth £75,000. When England let the captain, James Macrae, sail off in one of their smaller prizes (he would go on to become governor of Fort St George), Taylor ousted and marooned England, with Jasper Seager taking his place. The three ships continued to cruise for more prizes, though they were driven off by some Bombay ships, raided the Laccadive Islands, and sold their plunder to Dutch merchants.

In 1721 they captured one of the most lucrative prizes ever: the *Nossa Senhora de Cabo*, a Portuguese vessel carrying gold, diamonds, sacred decorations, and other riches – a cargo valued in the millions. The bishop and viceroy of Goa were aboard, whom they eventually released at Île Bourbon, following negotiations with one Edward Congdon. He too had left the Bahamas on Rogers' arrival, sailing first to the Cape Verde Islands and then Brazil. By 1719 he reached Madagascar, recruiting some of the old plunderers there and capturing an Arabian ship that apparently yielded plunder worth £3,000 per man. Congdon traded in Madagascar for a while and then, in 1721, he and some forty others travelled to Bourbon for a pardon. Congdon married the *gouverneur*'s sister-in-law, which is probably why he was called on to treat with Levasseur and the others.

From the *Nossa Senhora* each man supposedly received £50,000, but if that is true, they were not satisfied and kept plundering for a while, alarming the new colonial authorities at Fort-Dauphin when they burned ships with enslaved people aboard. At Mozambique they captured Jacob du Bucquoy, a cartographer working for the *Vereenigde Oostindische Compagnie*, who wrote his own account of this time in their hands.

Afterwards, Levasseur settled for a while in Antongil Bay, acting as a pilot for passing ships, which again suggests that his plunder was not as extravagant as myth makes it. There he may have joined James Plaintain, a Jamaican sailor who accompanied England and then Seager, and perhaps also Congdon, before starting a settlement along similar lines to Baldridge's trading post, apparently styling himself 'King of Ranter Bay', as the region was known to English sailors at the time.

When a British navy squadron arrived in 1722 looking for Taylor and Levasseur, Plaintain told the navy captains his old friends were long gone (and he seems to have escaped any further consequences). Edward England may still have been there, though in much reduced circumstances since his marooning; other accounts suggest he was already dead.

Plaintain may have been covering for his companions, but this piratical band did indeed wind down around this time. Plaintain seems to have joined Kanhoji Angria on the west coast of India by 1728. Taylor, hearing of the naval expedition, had sailed back to the Caribbean by 1723 and there surrendered to the governor of Portobelo, handing over his ship in return for a pardon. He found new employment in the *Armada de Barlovento*, cruising against logwooders.

Levasseur rejected a French amnesty in 1724, apparently because the *gouverneur* of Bourbon would not permit him to keep his treasure. In 1730 he went aboard a passing French ship, was recognised by another old pirate aboard and promptly arrested and taken to Saint-Denis, the capital of Bourbon. There he was summarily convicted and condemned. According to later legend he is supposed to have boasted of his remaining treasure and left a cryptogram with clues to find it. Avid treasure hunters have discovered some evidence of piratical occupation in caves among the Seychelles, but the first mention of the cryptogram came in a book published in 1934, so the whole thing is almost certainly an invention.

Davis had a shorter, and rather less lucrative, career on the coast of West Africa. He seems to have possessed a suave manner, because he persuaded the commander of a Royal African Company fort that he held a legitimate commission and, at a welcoming dinner, seized the hapless officer and ransomed him for £2,000 in gold. When he tried something similar at the Portuguese island of Principe in June 1719, though, he was ambushed and shot.

Before this, Davis had captured another slave ship, from which he forced eight crewmembers to join him, including one Bartholomew Roberts. Born at Casnewydd Bach, a compatriot of Davis' and like him initially reluctant to turn pirate, Roberts was described as tall and dark, though the nickname *Barti Ddu* probably originated in the twentieth century with Welsh poet I.D. Hooson. The crew chose Roberts for captain after Davis' death, probably due to his navigational experience. He vengefully raided Principe, suggesting that he had not taken long to become friends with Davis and get into the piratical spirit.

Roberts then pursued one of the more successful pirate voyages of this era, if you measure success by plundering record, rather than end result. He captured more than 400 ships, the vast majority of them merchant or fishing vessels carrying fairly humdrum cargoes. Early during his long cruise Roberts did capture the *Sagrada Familia*, a Portuguese vessel carrying some 90,000 *moidores*, about £120,000, besides jewellery including a silver-studded cross he apparently wore for the rest of his life. However, soon afterwards Davis left Walter Kennedy in charge of both ship and plunder while he pursued another prize, and Kennedy slipped away with both.

Bartholomew Roberts doodgebleeven.

Portraits of Bartholomew Roberts from the English and Dutch editions of the *General History*.

Not, it must be said, to enjoy the loot for very long. Kennedy made for Ireland, but knowing little of navigation, he reached Scotland instead. He and his men pretended to be shipwrecked mariners, but their riotous behaviour aroused suspicions. Seventeen were arrested, of whom nine were hanged. Kennedy skipped town for London, where he reportedly kept a brothel, until one of the women accused him of theft. Recognised in prison, he was hanged at Wapping on 21 July 1721.

Roberts carried on roving, sometimes in company with the French captain Montigny la Palisse, sailing north to Newfoundland in 1720, where he burnt and sunk twenty-two ships in the harbour of Trepassey, and back to the Caribbean. A few months later, he likewise struck at shipping in the harbour of Basseterre, St Christopher's, with black flags flying. A letter from Roberts himself to the lieutenant general there survives, in which Roberts claimed that he only launched this assault because the official refused to come out and drink a glass of wine with him, and warned him 'hereafter not to expect anything from our hands but what belongs to a pirate'. According to some of Roberts' captives, his men boasted of plans to assault Marie-Galante and take revenge on Antigua and Barbados. One report early in 1721 even said a 'John Roberts' had captured and hanged the incoming governor of Martinique, though that was probably no more than a rumour.

By the summer of 1721 he was back on the West African coast, apparently hoping to purchase gold on the cheap. If this crew were thinking towards retirement, though, they were in no hurry, spending six months on the coast doing so much damage that, in response to Company complaints, two naval ships sailed from England on 5 February 1721, the *Swallow*, under Chaloner Ogle, and the *Weymouth*. On the latter served Alexander Selkirk as mate, but this was his last voyage. He, and somewhere between 200 and 300 others (accounts differ), succumbed to disease during the voyage. Back in England, two women claimed to be Selkirk's wife and went to court over his remaining possessions.

Ogle made up his numbers by impressing men from the Company forts and by purchasing enslaved people. On 10 January 1722 he received word of two pirate ships terrorising vessels at Ouidah and set off to pursue Roberts, meeting him at Cape Lopez a month later in the battle, and the ensuing trials and executions, that I have already described.

The last act of this last act occurred on the coast of the Americas. Walter Kennedy was not the only one of Roberts' crew to break away; Thomas Anstis, another old Bahamian, chose to remain in the Caribbean in 1721 when Roberts sailed for Africa. With him were Brigstock Weaver, whom Roberts had forcibly recruited, now given command of a prize, and John Phillips, a ship carpenter whom Anstis captured near Newfoundland in the spring of 1721.

Anstis wrote to Jamaica for a pardon, camping on the coast of Cuba for nine months awaiting a reply, which came in the form of two naval ships under Admiral John Flowers. They captured some of the pirates, though the leaders escaped and cruised on to Honduras and the Bahamas. Weaver, going solo for a while, looted more than fifty vessels before he rejoined the others. Admiral Flowers caught up with them in 1723, careening their ships in Tobago. Again the leaders escaped, but Anstis was murdered by some of his men, who sailed for Curaçao, where they received a pardon and handed over some shipmates to be hanged.

Weaver and Phillips both went to Bristol, where Weaver was recognised by a captain he had pillaged, who, when Weaver could not make good the losses, had him arrested, along with some others of Anstis' crew. Those men were executed, though Weaver was pardoned in 1725 on the basis that he had been forced.

Phillips, fearing arrest, skipped town for Newfoundland, then in 1723 seized a schooner and cruised down the American coast. One of their prisoners was John Fillmore, great-grandfather to a future president of the USA, who later wrote an account of his time in their hands. At Tobago they picked up an old friend, Pedro, a Black survivor of Anstis' crew, and made for Nova Scotia, pillaging fifty-three ships in less than eight months, until one targeted ship overpowered them in April 1724 and carried four prisoners to Boston, all of whom were executed on 2 June.

Other plunderers also roamed the Americas in these years. Louis Serville was a free person of colour from Guadeloupe who commanded a Spanish ship, with a crew of French, Martinican, Spanish, English, African, and Indigenous sailors – these last especially feared for their poisoned arrows. Serville was eventually captured in Guadeloupe and condemned to the royal galleys.

Several more, like Davis and Roberts, came to piracy by way of the slave trade. George Lowther was a second mate on a slave ship who led a mutiny and then, falling out with some of his fellows, made for the Carolinas and the Caymans in 1721. He spent even longer at sea than Roberts and in 1722 he was joined by another band led by Edward Low.

According to the *General History*, Low was born into poverty in Westminster and took to thieving from a young age. He moved to Boston around 1710 and became a sailmaker, marrying Eliza Marble in 1714. Their first son died, and Eliza too died giving birth to a daughter, all of which seems to have taken a toll on Low; later reports said he often spoke of the daughter he left ashore.

Low joined a Honduras-bound merchant ship, then deserted with some others and stole another vessel near Rhode Island. They met Lowther in the Caymans, then Low made for New England and Nova Scotia, and the Cape Verdes and Brazil, gathering several crews under his command and apparently naming himself a commodore. In January 1723 he captured a Portuguese ship carrying 11,000 *moidores* and sailed for the Azores, then Carolina, where a naval ship pursued him, capturing some of his followers, who were tried and executed in Newport.

Low continued along the American coast, meeting Lowther and Francis Spriggs (who had deserted with Low at the start). They sailed for Africa, where they captured a ship named *Merry Christmas* which Low took for his own, until one of his crew, Richard Shipton, ousted him. What became of Low is unknown: he may have sailed to Brazil, while other reports, of varying reliability, suggest he was killed by Miskito near Roátan or served as a gunner in Portobelo.

Lowther and Spriggs had already abandoned Low and then split up. Time ran out for Lowther when, in February 1724, he ran into the naval ship *Eagle*. Four men escaped, one of them Lowther, but he was found dead ashore, having shot himself, according to newspaper reports in England. Twenty of his men were taken for trial, though many claimed to have been coerced.

Meanwhile, Shipton and the *Merry Christmas* rejoined Spriggs and they plundered in the Caribbean, sometimes recruiting new companions, such as Philip Lyne, who had formerly been acquitted on a piracy charge in 1718 in Philadelphia, and sometimes losing splinter groups, again one being Lyne, who went off in 1725 and was captured by pirate-hunting sloops. Shipton and Spriggs themselves encountered the naval ship *Diamond* in August 1724 and escaped; the next year they met the *Diamond* again, when Shipton was captured, though Spriggs eluded pursuit. The *Post-Boy* of 25 June 1726 described him being marooned among the Miskito (along with Low, apparently). Another piratical fellowship had come to an end.

Some scholars have found in the febrile mixing, joining, and splitting of pirate crews across these years evidence of a shared culture, a communal identity, and mutual recognition. I would interpret it differently, showing an even greater tendency towards instability and fragmentation than among the buccaneers or the South Sea and Red Sea raiders. That quality makes it difficult to trace the careers of individual pirates, especially when conflicting accounts exist: all the short biographies I have offered here are subject to that caveat.

Perhaps more importantly, it suggests a great deal of contingency, always a feature of maritime life but even more so in this period, especially regarding who was recruited into piracy. If some men deliberately sought out a piratical career during this last phase, it seems that many more entered piracy only because their ship encountered pirates. While some who claimed to be coerced into piracy were not telling the whole truth, it does seem that a much greater number were genuinely forced into piracy during these years, unlike the charades of 'perforstmen' described by Henry Mainwaring a century earlier.

The same contingency affected how these voyages played out, making them seemingly more random than earlier plundering efforts. Many of the voyages of the buccaneers, and into the South Sea and Red Sea, followed a loose pattern and purpose. If some of those earlier voyages were directionless, that seems to have become a more dominant quality of the transatlantic criss-crossings in the 1720s.

Perhaps that was due to the lack of a safe harbour, more so in the Atlantic than at Madagascar. Even the ships these pirates sailed were temporary homes, regularly replaced by new prizes, as they had no resources for extensive repairs. It also implies that if some of these raiders were still looking for a quick jackpot and retirement, for others the purpose of piracy was simply to sustain their piracy. The absence of a clear objective and of a guaranteed safe haven may explain why pirates increasingly had to coerce men to join them.

The encrustation of myths around these pirates makes it difficult to be sure what their motivations and objectives were. Many of their more famous characteristics, such as piratical flags and codes, are closely bound up with the *General History*; I will discuss them with that book in the next chapter.

The names they took for their ships, though, may be significant. A large number chose some variation on *Revenge*, indicating perhaps animosity towards the authorities ranged against them. It is intriguing that at least two, England and Low, both called their ships the *Fancy*, probably an homage to Henry Every. Roberts favoured some form of *Fortune* for several of his ships: did that describe what he hoped to attain, or hint at an impulsive, even fatalistic, approach to pirate life?

Others imply Jacobite leanings, such as *Queen Anne's Revenge*, Levasseur's *Windham Galley* and Cocklyn's *Duke of Ormond* (both Tory lords with known Jacobite leanings), and Davis' *Royal James*. The exiled Jacobite court considered an alliance with these pirates, but whether these names bespeak a genuine commitment to the Stuart cause, or a more opportunistic alignment, is impossible to say.

Another aspect supported by various evidence is a peculiarly extreme kind of violence. Previous plunderers were hardly gentle, but the 1720s seem to have brought a more deliberate level of cruelty. Snelgrave wrote that Cocklyn beat his own men and tortured his prisoners, and that the crew chose Cocklyn over Moody precisely because of this 'Brutality'. Congdon reportedly cut off victims' noses, and Low apparently forced one captain to eat his own broiled lips, burned a French cook alive, and massacred Spanish prisoners – though he would never force married men to join his crew and allowed women to return to port unharmed, because of his daughter.

Though some of these stories come from the *General History*, other evidence, like trial records, makes clear that such violence was commonplace. One of Low's crew, John Russell, who was probably Portuguese, shared his captain's proclivities. Philip Ashton, one of their prisoners who escaped, described how 'with outragious Cursing and Swearing [Russell] clapt his Pistol to my Head', though it misfired. When he suspected Ashton of helping two boys to escape, Russell 'in the utmost fury, drew his Cutlash, and fell upon me with it', but Ashton escaped into the hold. Roberts, too, was renowned for slaughtering crews who resisted: when one ship refused to pay a toll, he set it alight, with eighty enslaved people still aboard. There were exceptions – Snelgrave called Davis 'a most generous humane Person' who protected him from Cocklyn's worst excesses – but they seem to have been notably, well, exceptional.

Historians have interpreted these tendencies in different ways. One economist, who compares piracy to other forms of organised crime, suggests that these were cost-saving or risk-managing measures: victims terrified by cruelty are less likely to fight back. There may be some truth in this, but I am not convinced that piracy can be explained entirely in terms of rational choice theory.

Another explanation is that this violence specifically targeted shipmasters who mistreated their men. Snelgrave wrote that pirates would consult their prisoners on this subject (and he was saved by having treated his own crew well). Philip Lyne claimed to have killed thirty-seven shipmasters. One of Anstis' crew, at his execution, blamed both drinking and brutal merchant captains for his descent into piracy. William Fly, who led a mutiny in 1726 but spent just two months at sea before his capture and trial, also declared at his execution that the captain and mate of his ship had 'used us Barbarously' and 'poor men can't have Justice … let them never so much abuse us, and use us like Dogs'. Perhaps that is why so many pirate ships were named *Revenge*.

At the same time, there is plenty of evidence for brutality towards fellow pirates and low-ranking sailors too, which rather throws into question the idea that pirates really pursued social justice. If many crewmembers were forced, as they claimed in court, then violence probably served a simple coercive purpose. Much of the violence seems compulsive, vindictive, or even habitual. Most of these men had fought in a war that lasted more than a decade before they even became pirates; during that time their violence, in the service of the same empires that now hunted them down, had been construed as heroism.

This wave of piracy was one of the most intense, and one of the shortest. By 1724 there were only 500 or so pirates active in the Atlantic, about a quarter of the peak a few years before; after another two years, it was around 200. By that time, all the captains mentioned in the *General History*, and most of those named in contemporary newspapers, were dead or had ceased sailing.

The imperial authorities still had some problems. Woodes Rogers, for example, sailed to Charleston in 1720 to sort out his woeful financial affairs, where he duelled with a naval captain with whom he had already quarrelled at the Bahamas. The Assembly there had written to the king with thanks for sending Rogers out, rescuing them from 'pirates the worst of enemies', but that captain was not the only one to find Rogers overbearing. Even a lieutenant Rogers sent to London to get help instead disparaged him to their superiors.

Unsurprisingly, the Commissioners for Trade decided to replace Rogers. Back in London he declared bankruptcy yet again in 1724, spending some time in debtors' prison (as Daniel Defoe also did, three times), and complaining to the king in July 1726 that his expedition to the Bahamas cost him vast sums. In 1728, backed up by Hans Sloane, Benjamin Bennet, Alexander Spotswood, and rising political star Robert Walpole, Rogers appealed to the new king, George II, to be reinstated as governor.

He got his wish, and it was around this time that he had his only surviving portrait, a family scene, painted by William Hogarth. Rogers' replacement, George Phenney, had not done much better. His wife interfered in the local court, bullying both judge and jury, and set her own prices in trade. When Rogers arrived in Nassau again, late in 1729, Phenney asked Rogers to keep his wife in Nassau while he slipped away to England for a divorce, but she found out and put a stop to it. Nor would Rogers have an easy time afterwards. Two experienced merchants he brought out to help him run the colony fell out with him, leading to acrimonious disputes. Rogers died in July 1732.

These years also witnessed two spectacular market crashes, both linked to colonial trade. The first occurred in Paris, where Scottish financier John Law, in service to Louis XV, had tried to build a new economic edifice through a *Banque Générale Privée* in 1716, and the merger of several trading companies into a *Compagnie Perpétuelle des Indes* in 1719. Law exaggerated the profitability of Mississippi, driving up speculation, and the bubble burst in 1720. That triggered a very similar crash in London, where the South Sea Company held a similar role in national debt. The duke of Marlborough made money from this crash, but the king lost £56,000, and his physician £80,000.

If these market crashes reveal the precarity of finance and trade in this era, they also demonstrate its increasing sophistication, which not even piracy had halted. Naval protection seems to have improved, especially after legislative amendments in 1722 prohibited naval officers from engaging in trade themselves and mandated that accessories would be tried as pirates (an element of former royal proclamations now made into statute law). In 1724, the navy offered a bounty for anyone who captured a pirate, with a sliding scale depending on the captive's rank, and those who deserted from pirate crews would be permitted to keep their plunder.

Piracy trials continued apace. The prosecution of thirty-six pirates in Rhode Island, who had sailed with Low, was one of the largest of the time (though not quite on the scale of Roberts' crew in Cape Coast Castle). Twenty-eight were convicted and hanged. Five pirates were hanged in Antigua in 1723, two more in Boston in 1724, and eleven, who had been with Lowther, in St Christopher. Another sixteen were tried in Massachusetts in 1726, of whom four were convicted, the rest judged to be unwitting acquaintances.

Somewhere between 400 and 600 pirates were executed between 1716 and 1726. Going by the estimates of total numbers, this represents only one in ten, although some died in battle or in some other manner at sea. Many who sailed in pirate ships were pardoned or acquitted or simply never came to trial. Nevertheless, this is a much higher proportion than at any other time, signalling a new persistence by the imperial authorities. During these years, pirates' bodies hanging in chains became a familiar sight, and warning, in many Atlantic harbours.

Despite the short duration of this episode and the determination of empires to suppress it – indeed, perhaps because of those factors – these men have had an enduring legacy. They, and the stories told about them, changed the way we think about piracy forever.

17

WE ARE OF THE SEA

A General History of the Robberies and Murders of the Most Notorious Pyrates first appeared in the bookshop owned by Charles Rivington at the Bible and Crown in St Paul's Churchyard, London, on 14 May 1724. Rivington was a major publisher who focused mainly on religious and educational literature, but evidently he knew a good deal when he saw one. The *General History* was an immediate sensation.

This first edition was also sold by James Lacy at the Ship near Temple Gate, and J. Stone near the Crown coffee house. A second edition, 'with considerable additions', was rushed out the same year by Thomas Warner, at the sign of the 'Black-Boy' on Paternoster Row. This edition commented on its forerunner's 'Success by the Publick, [which] occasioned a very earnest Demand for a second' and added that 'there have been some other Pyrates … [whose] Adventures are as extravagant and full of Mischief', promising another volume 'If the Publick gives [the author] Encouragement'.

Warner brought out a third edition the following year, modifying the title to *A General History of the Pyrates*. Abridged versions under various names appeared the same year in London and Dublin, and by 1726 there were translations in Dutch, French, and German. Thomas Woodward, at the Half-Moon in Fleet Street, produced a fourth edition of the first volume that year, and at some time between 1726 and 1728 added the promised second volume, called *The History of the Pyrates*.

Such a rapid flurry of publishing activity was rare. In all some twenty-five versions of the book are listed before 1801 in the English Short Title Catalogue maintained by the British Library, from the 1730s onwards often merging with sensational stories about highwaymen, murderers, and other criminals.

A GENERAL

HISTORY

OF THE

PYRATES,

FROM

Their firſt RISE and SETTLEMENT in the Iſland of
Providence, to the preſent Time.

With the remarkable Actions and Adventures of the two Female Pyrates

MARY READ and ANNE BONNY;

Contain'd in the following Chapters,

To which is added,

A ſhort ABSTRACT of the Statute and Civil
Law, in Relation to Pyracy.

The ſecond EDITION, with conſiderable ADDITIONS

By Captain CHARLES JOHNSON.

LONDON:

Printed for, and ſold by *T. Warner*, at the *Black-Boy* in *Pater-
Noſter-Row*, 1724.

The front page of the expanded second edition of the *General History*.

It is a complex and problematic text, attributed to Captain Charles Johnson, a pseudonym whose owner has never been identified. Attribution to Daniel Defoe, first made by a literary scholar in the 1930s, has now generally gone out of fashion, though Defoe was indeed a prolific writer of the time and produced several other stories about pirates, and many websites and catalogues still list the book under his name.

A more likely candidate is Nathaniel Mist, a Jacobite controversialist who worked with Defoe at times, and who got into regular trouble with the law for his forthright opinions about the Georgian monarchy. He fled to France in 1727, though he was permitted to return before his death in 1737. The fact that the first two (favourable) reviews of the *General History* appeared in the *Weekly Journal* in May and June 1724, the newspaper that Mist himself edited, supports this view.

Whoever the author was, they had done their homework, gathering information from newspapers and published trial records. They probably had some access to official government papers too. The author admitted that 'some Parts ... may not be so exact' but called on readers to send in any 'Correction or Addition', and the later editions and the second volume amended some details and exhibited correspondence from colonial contacts. Woodes Rogers may have been involved, since he was in London between 1721 and 1729, and the book casts him in a favourable light. The second volume described it as 'an Undertaking of great Length and Variety' and emphasised 'the Pains we have been at, to collect Matters for the composing a genuine History ... the great Care we have taken to deliver nothing but the Truth'.

As I mentioned in a previous chapter, that may have been a playful claim. The author interlaced their gathered facts, not always entirely reliable, with fanciful and eye-catching elaborations, each edition introducing another layer of these, which probably goes some way to explaining the book's considerable and continuing success. While the first volume only deals with real people, inventing some stories about them, the second includes several fictional characters, without distinguishing between them and the real ones.

This book drew on ideas from previous literature on pirates, but took those ideas much further in forging the image that still, more than any other, defines our picture of pirates today. The *General History* is a puzzle, one that has fascinated historians and fired imaginations for three centuries.

The official line on pirates had not changed since the early seventeenth century, and with the legislation and executions from the 1690s onwards the government continued to present this line in print as well. They contracted the respectable publisher John Everingham, one of the largest booksellers in London, to publish a record of the trial of Henry Every's crew in 1696 – carefully excising any details about the first jury's verdict.

Another pamphlet of that year covered the executions of the Jacobite plunderers Vaughan and Murphy, alongside five of Every's crew, condemned for their 'crying and bloody Cruelties', recounting how these 'Barbarous and Inhumane Wretches' had stolen the *Charles II* and 'immediately set out as *Pyrates*'. This text may be the origin of the story about Aurangzeb's daughter, since it luridly describes them 'Ravishing and Deflowering the Virgins and Women, and then turning them out naked, to starve upon shore ... [they] most inhumanely Ravisht a Young Princess, and the rest of her Female Train'.

Captain Kidd also became a character in print, 'the famous, or rather Infamous, Pirate', as the *Post-Boy* described him in August 1699, while he was still at sea. Five accounts of his trial quickly appeared, the most 'official' by the ordinary, or chaplain, of Newgate, who had a regular sideline in publishing accounts of confessions, trials, and executions, and who even took out newspaper advertisements warning that only his was a 'true account', unlike the 'sham papers' of his competitors.

Many more trial pamphlets came in subsequent decades, including those of John Quelch, Stede Bonnet, and Bartholomew Roberts' men. Cotton Mather published descriptions of his efforts to reclaim piratical souls among the crews of Edward Low, with *Useful Remarks* in 1723, and of William Fly in *The Vial Poured out upon the Sea* in 1726. He noted in his diary, with some satisfaction, that pirates forced their captives to curse his name. As late as 1769 one enterprising printer brought out a pamphlet claiming to be the dying speeches of pirates executed at Newport in 1726.

Newspapers regularly reported on piracy, as well as advertising the trial records and other books on the subject. One of Benjamin Franklin's earliest publications was 'The Downfall of Piracy', a lyrical description of Maynard's battle with Teach, which Franklin later dismissed as 'wretched-stuff, in the Grub-street-ballad style', though it 'sold wonderfully'. The *Boston News-Letter* featured thirty-one stories about piracy in 1718 alone, and in 1720 a Boston paper recounted how the *Winchelsea*, on the coast of Africa, hanged 150 pirates and 'hoped soon to clear the Seas of those Vermin'. A couple of years later readers received weekly updates on Edward Low. The regular comments on Black pirates aboard these ships reveal the crews' diverse make-up, but also the perennial anxieties in colonial society about slavery and social order.

These publications reinforced the image of villainous pirates and emphasised the new laws. Nicholas Trott, who presided over Stede Bonnet's trial, offered an erudite discussion of admiralty jurisdiction and the laws on piracy, printed with the trial record in 1719. He went on to publish the first general compilation of British colonial laws and received doctorates from Oxford and Aberdeen. James Menzies, judge at the trial of some of Low's crew, condemned pirates as pursuing 'a perpetual War with every Individual, with every State ... they have no Country, but by the nature of their Guilt, separate themselves, renouncing the benefit of lawful Society'. Menzies had earlier defended Quelch, while Trott's uncle had welcomed Henry Every to the Bahamas. Their actions and statements as judges show how the position of colonial elites had changed.

As part of this shift, the terms 'privateer' and 'pirate' became even more polarised, though still fundamentally polemical. Henry Barham, who wrote an unpublished history of Jamaica in 1722, included Henry Morgan's commissions and instructions, and maintained that there was a 'Great Deal of Difference between a Privateer or a Buccaneer, or a Freebooter', mainly a commission, those lacking one being 'no Better than Pyrates'. Barham criticised Exquemelin for failing to understand this distinction; it did not occur to Barham that things might have changed since Exquemelin's day. Bryan Edwards, another Jamaican writer towards the end of the eighteenth century, similarly insisted that privateers were not the 'piratical plunderers and public robbers which they are commonly represented', because they were 'furnished with letters of marque and reprisal'.

Not everyone was quite so certain, it must be said. Alexander Justice, in his legal handbook *A General Treatise of the Dominion and Law of the Sea* of 1705, refused to 'enter into Enquiries of [privateers] being lawful by the Law of Nations, for if War is lawful, Privateers are certainly so', and added that 'Our Laws take not much Notice of these Privateers, because the Manner of such Warring is new, and not very honourable'. Justice did, however, note that privateers carried a legal commission, and he was considerably more down on pirates, who were 'always reckoned *Hostis Humani Generis* ... common Sea-Rovers ... [who] acknowledge no Sovereign nor no Law ... ravenous Beasts ... Traytors to God and Man ... the Common Plague and Disturbers of the Peace of the Universe'. Their 'total Extirpation', he considered, was 'the Duty of all Princes, Potentates and People'.

Justice then used that definition to condemn French *corsaires* who were, at the time of his writing, capturing thousands of British ships. Ignoring that they were commissioned, he described their 'Piratical Wars ... the Dilligence of our Enemies in this Piratical way', characterised by 'Barbarity ... Rage and Insolence'. France, Justice thought, had 'entred into Treaties and divided the Plunder with these common Enemies of Mankind' – unlike England, who 'to their everlasting Glory, have always been at a considerable Charge for the Reduction of those Inhuman Wretches', an exaggerated boast even in 1705. Justice's text, which included recent laws like the Anglo-Dutch Treaty of 1674 (prohibiting torture of prisoners), the Piracy Act of 1700, and the Cruisers and Convoys Act of 1708, seems to have found a receptive audience, going through three editions by 1724.

These distinctions made their way into the *General History*, along with some of the old stereotypes, for example that 'the Way of Life of a successful *Jamaica* Privateer ... is not an Example of the greatest Sobriety and Oeconomy'. The author noted that 'in War Time there is no room for any [pirates], because all those of a roving advent'rous Disposition find Employment in Privateers', and described the ease with which these lawful plunderers, 'when an honest Livlyhood is not easily had ... run into one so like their own ... when the War is over ... they too readily engage in Acts of Pyracy ... mak[ing] very little Distinction betwixt the Lawfulness of one, and the Unlawfulness of the other'. Yet if privateers did not make that 'Distinction', the law certainly did. A curious dimension here is that, with one or two exceptions, the *General History* uses 'privateer' mainly to describe a ship or as a verb ('to go a privateering'), reflecting how its meaning had shifted away from a social group, as Thomas Modyford, Thomas Lynch, Henry Morgan, and others had used it, and towards the legal status of the vessels they sailed in.

The government and the lawyers did not control all popular discussion of pirates, of course, just like in the seventeenth century. Several of these famous figures – including Henry Every and William Kidd – became the subject of ballads, and while many of these reinforced the idea of repentant criminals lamenting their evil ways, not all did.

The most curious of these is *A Copy of Verses, composed by Henry Every*, first published in 1694, even before he captured the *Ganj-i-Sāwai*. It is unlikely that these verses were indeed penned by Every himself. James

Houblon submitted a copy to the Privy Council as evidence of Every's 'Piraticall Design', but this seems a cynical manipulation. Variations of the ballad reappeared in newspapers in 1696, coinciding with the trial of Every's crew, and the slight differences between the versions suggest it circulated by oral transmission at the time.

The ballad opens with an exhortation to 'brave Boys, whose Courage is Bold' to join Every, in what may be a deliberate reference to *The Trumpet of Fame*, a 1595 ballad in which Francis Drake encouraged 'Gallants bold' to accompany him. Some lyrics play on Every's piratical status: 'My Commission is large and I made it my self,' he boasts, 'and the Capston will stretch it full larger by half.' Yet there is a nationalistic streak too, for Every 'Honour[s] St *George*, and his Colours I were [i.e. wear]'. Indeed, Every appears as an aristocrat deprived of his ancestral lands near Plymouth, condemning the 'false-hearted Nation' that deserted him, but which he had not deserted.

One verse highlights Every's globe-trotting travel to remote and exotic places, leaving 'this Climate and temperate Zone' for 'one thats more torrid ... to the *South-Seas* and to *Persia* I'll go'. That aspect became one of the more prominent elements of Every's afterlife in print, chiming with a broader shift in depictions of piracy, in response to the expansion of buccaneers into the Pacific and Indian Oceans from the 1680s onward.

This change was driven by the writings of buccaneers themselves. After Bartholomew Sharp and Basil Ringrose published their voyaging accounts in the 1680s, it set a precedent that many other Pacific buccaneers followed, including Jacques Raveneau de Lussan's *Journal du Voyage fait à la Mer du Sud avec les Flibustiers de l'Amérique*, published in 1689. New editions and translations of these texts, sometimes merged with Exquemelin's *Zee-roovers*, continued to appear into the 1690s and 1700s, and other plunderers got in on the act as well. Jean-Baptise du Casse published an account of his expedition against Cartagena.

William Dampier's *A New Voyage Round the World*, which appeared in 1697, was particularly successful, although some of the credit should probably go to his publisher, James Knapton, who also printed Dampier's other works, as well as a 1699 collection including Sharp's and Cowley's South Sea journals, and Lionel Wafer's *A New Voyage and Description of the Isthmus of America*. Rather enterprisingly, as well as Dampier's account of his difficult voyage to Australia, Knapton also published critical accounts of Dampier's captaincy from other officers on the same voyage. That might explain why Dampier's rejoinder was published by a different and less prolific printer, Mary Edwards of Fetter Lane.

A little later, Edward Cooke raced to publish his *A Voyage to the South Sea, and Round the World* in March 1712 after he returned from voyaging with Woodes Rogers – a copy of which found its way aboard the *Queen Anne's Revenge*. Rogers' own *A Cruising Voyage round the World* came out a few months later, while George Shelvocke also wrote a narrative, *A Voyage round the World*, which appeared in 1726.

All of these authors were careful to portray themselves as 'privateers', and their purpose may have been a public defence of their reputations, hence why Ringrose and Sharp were so protective of Morgan as well. Dampier's original manuscript journal survives and illustrates how much he modified that text for publication – fashioning himself as a genteel natural philosopher, and minimising the plundering and violence that characterised his travels.

Others had previously included comments on geography or natural history, like Richard Hawkins, who was captured in Peru in 1594 and published an account in 1622. However, Dampier took this much further, with vivid descriptions of flora and fauna, producing the first descriptions of many plants and animals to appear in English. Dampier dedicated *A New Voyage* to the president of the Royal Society, a group of gentlemen and aristocrats interested in scientific inquiry to whom Charles II had granted a charter in 1662, and a positive review of the book duly appeared in the Society's *Philosophical Transactions*. The history of science and the history of plundering are more closely connected than you might expect.

The history of literature, too. Cooke and Rogers mentioned Alexander Selkirk's time on Juan Fernández – Cooke very briefly in his first volume, hastily expanded in his second, while Rogers depicted Selkirk as a devout hermit. Richard Steele, a friend of Cooke's, also interviewed Selkirk and wrote about him in *The Englishman*. This moment of celebrity for the former buccaneer probably inspired *Robinson Crusoe*, although there are other candidate castaways too. *Crusoe* was even more successful than the *General History*: first published in April 1719, it went through four editions and a sequel in the same year. Its popularity is a testament to the appeal of exotic travelling yarns (although Crusoe's early travels, in which he is captured in North Africa and then becomes a slave trader in Brazil, have received less attention than his long isolation).

These same themes appeared in later depictions of Every. An anonymous biography, *The Life and Adventures of Captain John Avery*, appeared in 1709, praising his 'good Genius ... superior to his evil' and depicting him as 'Raised from a Cabbin-Boy, to a King' by the election of his men at Nosy Boraha. Four years later a play written by Charles Johnson (a different one), *The Successful Pyrate*, featured the pirate-king 'Arverigus'.

In both versions, Every/Arverigus marries a Mughal princess and encourages his men to settle down and marry in Madagascar, a scene played for laughs in *The Successful Pyrate* when one sailor protests he already has multiple wives, and another says he would rather marry a can of sack (a kind of sweet wine). Defoe wrote another biography, *The King of Pirates*, in 1719, and his fictional *Captain Singleton* of 1720 was inspired by the same story. Of course, if anyone can claim to be the 'pirate king' of Madagascar it is Abraham Samuel, aka Tolinor Rex, not Henry Every.

One critic condemned *The Successful Pyrate*, a theatrical hit, calling Every 'the most detestable Villain that ever the Sun or Moon beheld, banish'd not only from his own but from all Countries, declar'd the Pest of all Human Society', no doubt now 'lolling at *Madagascar* with some drunken sun-burnt Whore over a Can of Flip'. Yet others found it appealing – Edward Butler, in 1699, encouraged his shipmates to mutiny and sail to 'Capt[ain] Avery's protection at Madagascar', even though Every was long gone. Walter Kennedy was apparently inspired by Every's exploits. There was a two-way relationship between piratical fiction and real-life plundering.

The *General History* aimed, according to its second volume, to provide 'a distinct Relation of every Pyrate who has made any Figure'. In this rogues' gallery, beginning in the first volume with Every, it fused those pre-existing themes, the criminal and the exotic. Every, it noted, had caused 'a Noise in the World … as one that had raised himself to the Dignity of a King' – but the *General History* insisted that 'these were no more than false Rumours', and that Every died in poverty, a similar ending to the one Defoe gave in his biography.

That moral purpose is evident elsewhere too. When narrating Walter Kennedy's life, the author of the *General History* paused to reflect 'what a disastrous Fate ever attends the Wicked, and how rarely they escape the Punishment due to their Crimes'. They worried about 'giv[ing] too much Encouragement to the Profession' and cautioned 'Maritime Readers' that 'the far greater Part of these Rovers are cut short in the Pursuit'. Indeed, 'to a trading Nation, nothing can be so Destructive as Pyracy, or call for more exemplary Punishment'.

Most of the pirates presented here are 'enemies of all'. Howell Davis made 'a Declaration of War against the whole World', while John Bowen, with a crew 'of all Nations', committed 'Pyracies ... upon Ships of all Nations'. Many of them were preordained for villainy: 'Nature seem'd to have designed [Edward Low] for a Pyrate from his Childhood', for he fell into crime early, 'rav'd like a Fury, [and] swore a thousand Oaths ... a base cowardly Villain'. John Walden was 'known among the Pyrates ... by the Nick-Name of Miss Nanney (ironically its presumed from the Hardness of his Temper)'. William Fly, Walter Kennedy, Philip Roche, John Taylor, Charles Vane, and others are all presented in a similar manner.

Yet there is some recognition of the conditions that encouraged piracy, too, not just the 'many uninhabited little Islands and Keys' in the Caribbean, which made pursuit difficult, or 'the great Commerce thither', but also that 'Privateers in Time of War are a Nursery for Pyrates against a Peace'. The author blames Spanish governors for issuing commissions 'on Pretence of preventing an interloping Trade', with twenty-two English ships seized in 1716. Economic circumstances, once again, were key: 'I have not so much as heard of a Dutch Pyrate', the author wrote, because Dutch mariners could find employment in their North Sea fisheries. The author even recommended that 'our Legislators' ought to 'put some of the Pyrates into Authority ... according to the Proverb, set a Thief to catch a Thief', which is exactly what Woodes Rogers had done with Benjamin Hornigold and others.

Some of the book's characters emerge from this somewhat more complex milieu. Stede Bonnet was 'a Gentleman of good Reputation' at Barbados, 'Master of a plentiful Fortune, and had the Advantage of a liberal Education', and turned pirate 'from a Disorder in his Mind ... occasioned by some Discomforts he found in a married State'. At times he suffered 'Melancholy' because of his 'Folly'. Henry Jennings was 'a Man of good Understanding, and good Estate'; Samuel Burgess 'had a good Education'; and Captain Lewis 'had a great Aptitude for Languages'.

Others were noted for their behaviour rather than background. Thomas Tew 'in Point of Gallantry, was inferior to none', while Captain Halsey 'was brave in his Person, courteous to all his Prisoners, lived beloved, and died regretted by his own People'. Edward England, too, objected to the 'ill Usage' of prisoners and possessed 'a great deal of good Nature, and did not want for Courage; he was not avaritious' – for all of which he was marooned. John Halsey had 'an heroick Spirit' and even William Kidd 'first meant well'.

None of those characteristics redeemed these individuals; none of them were heroes in the mould of Francis Drake or Henry Morgan. Edward England, despite his 'good nature', remained 'engaged in that abominable

Society ... obliged to be a Partner in all their vile Actions'. Rather, like the earlier accounts of Thomas Walton and Clinton Atkinson, these descriptions recognise the implicit value of seafaring plunderers, while lamenting the misuse of those skills in the wrong way. The author defended 'giving the Name of a History to the following Sheets, though they contain nothing but the Actions of a Parcel of Robbers', because 'it is Bravery and Stratagem in War which make Actions worthy of Record; in which Sense the Adventures, here related will be thought deserving that Name'.

Where the *General History* departs most momentously from previous accounts of piracy is by imagining a pirate 'commonwealth'. Charles Molloy used that idea to analyse the status of Magharibi regencies and Charles Davenant did so to warn about errant colonists, but in the *General History* we get a fully fledged independent community of pirates, serving only themselves. The second volume, for example, describing the height of piratical activity in the Bahamas, has them 'advancing their Power, and maintaining their Sovereignty, not over the Seas only, but to stretch their Dominions to the Plantations themselves ... [they] never endeavour'd to conceal their Names, or Habitations, as if they had been Inhabitants of a legal Commonwealth, and were resolved to treat with all the World on the Foot of a free State'.

Pirates recognised one another as 'one of the Fraternity', as 'Confederates and Brethren in Iniquity'. The *General History* refers to 'the Pyrates Laws', maintaining that 'the principal Customs, and Government, of this roguish Common-Wealth ... are pretty near the same with all Pyrates'. When hailed with the customary inquiry about their ports of origin and destination, pirate ships would supposedly reply 'from the Seas', renouncing any terrestrial loyalties. That phrase was associated with Walton and Atkinson too, and earlier authors had commented on the distinct rules and customs of the buccaneers as a so-called 'brethren of the coast', but never anything quite so extreme as this.

One element of this community was their humorously outlandish conduct, again more extreme than in Exquemelin's *Zee-roovers*. Among them 'Liquor was as plenty as Water' and 'Sobriety brought a Man under a Suspicion of being in a Plot against the Commonwealth'. They spent their time in 'unheard of Debaucheries, with drinking, swearing and rioting ... there seemed to be a kind of Emulation among them, resembling rather Devils than Men, striving who should out do one another in new invented Oaths and Execrations'. In one particularly memorable, and distinctly unlikely, scene, Francis Spriggs' crew captured a cargo of horses and 'rid them about the Deck backwards and forwards a full Gallop, like Madmen at *New-Market*, cursing, swearing, and hallowing'.

The cruelty I discussed in the last chapter is also much commented on, and irreligion, too, was a prominent feature. During a storm Bellamy's crew, rather than praying, gave out 'Blasphemies, Oaths, and horrid Imprecations' and the captain himself 'swore he was sorry he could not run out his Guns to return the Salute, meaning the Thunder, that he fancied the Gods had got drunk over their Tipple, and were gone together by the Ears'. When one of Roberts' captured crew spent his time in prayer, another swore at him and asked *'what he proposed by so much Noise and Devotion ... did you ever hear of any Pyrates going thither* [to heaven]? *Give me H-ll, it's a merrier Place'*.

Yet the image presented here is not merely ridiculous. The *General History* is the main, and sometimes the only, source for most popular myths about piracy today. For one, it mentions the famous 'Jolly Roger', the 'Name they give their black Flag', and describes, in the text and in illustrations, a range of variations on that shared aesthetic.

Another aspect repeated in popular culture and academic scholarship alike is a distinctively egalitarian political structure, including elections for captains: 'they only permit [someone] to be Captain, on Condition, that they may be Captain over him.' The captain, as 'military officer', had authority in chase and battle, but 'in all other Matters whatsoever, he is governed by a Majority'. The crew who elected Roberts considered that *'all good Governments had (like theirs) the supream Power lodged with the Community'*.

Various chapters also mention the role of quartermaster, which Dampier had described as 'the second place in the Ship, according to the Law of Privateers'. The *General History* took this idea much further, though, calling the quartermaster 'an humble Imitation of the *Roman* Tribune of the People', who 'acts as a sort of a civil Magistrate on Board a Pyrate Ship'. The second volume even describes an investiture ceremony where, following 'an unanimous Consent, or by a Majority of Suffrages', the quartermaster hands the captain a sword while saying, *'This is the Commission under which you are to act, may you prove fortunate to your self and us.'*

These rules were enshrined in pirate codes, which appear throughout all versions of the *General History* and which, while distinct to each ship or captain, follow a general pattern not dissimilar to the articles agreed by

Henry Morgan and other buccaneers, governing areas like shares, rewards and punishments, and remuneration for injuries. Perhaps the most famous is Bartholomew Roberts' code, whose first rule, '*Every Man has a Vote in Affairs of Moment*', plus '*equal Title*' to provisions and liquor, embodies the supposed egalitarian ethos of the 'commonwealth'.

That ethos appears, too, in the idea of Edward Congden's 'Administration of Justice', in which he punished merchant shipmasters who treated their men badly, and in the much-quoted speeches placed in the mouths of certain captains. Samuel Bellamy is said to have criticised a merchant shipmaster in these terms: 'you are a sneaking Puppy, and so are all those who will submit to be governed by Laws which rich Men have made for their own Security ... there is only this Difference, they rob the Poor under the Cover of Law, forsooth, and we plunder the Rich under the Protection of our own Courage.' Roberts, too, supposedly became a pirate because of the 'disagreeable Superiority' of shipmasters. '*In an honest Service, says he, there is thin Commons, low Wages, and hard Labour; in this, Plenty and Satiety, Pleasure and Ease, Liberty and Power ...* A merry Life and a short one, *shall be my Motto.*'

That is the picture of a pirate that, I suspect, you carry around in your head (at least until you started reading this book). Yet, like the backstories for Anne Bonny and Mary Read, I find most of this very hard to believe once you start to look more closely.

While all the chapters of the first volume deal with figures from the 1710s and 1720s, apart from Every, the second volume mixes in real and fictional figures from the 1690s and 1700s as well, without distinguishing between them or even giving dates. Some, like Thomas Tew, were never formally charged for piracy: here the book erases the debates and differing opinions over the status of plundering that had rumbled through previous decades. Curiously, it is only those based in Madagascar during the 1690s and 1700s – *not* those from the Bahamian 'Commonwealth' – who announce themselves as 'from the Seas', including several fictional figures in the second volume.

Another example I'm rather fond of is an apparent account of walking the plank: pirates extended 'the Ladder of the Ship' and forced a prisoner to step along it into the sea. However, this comes from an introductory section discussing Cilician raiders during the Roman era. Likewise, the islands of the Caribbean were 'the hiding Places for their Riches, and

often Times a Shelter for themselves', but this occurred 'in buccaneering
pyratical Times' and only 'till their Friends on the Main, had found Means
to obtain Indemnity for their Crimes'. Few pirates would (intentionally)
leave their treasure heaped in caves or buried on islands for very long, and
there is no mention at all of treasure maps marked with an 'X'.

The idea of pirates 'administering justice' does not really hold up either,
at least not as a consistent practice, though there is independent evidence
of something like it happening, such as in William Snelgrave's account.
John Evans supposedly interrupted his men's efforts, haranguing his crew,
'*What have we to do to turn Reformers, 'tis Money we want*'. Captain Lewis
punished a merchant captain for 'betraying the Trust' of his shipowners
by allowing his ship to be captured and revealing where the treasure was
hidden. At other times, the *General History* noted, 'the Gentry', meaning
pirates, 'are provok'd to sudden Fits of Loyalty' to the British monarchy,
'by the Expectation of an Act of Grace'.

The 'Jolly Roger', too, may be somewhat fanciful. The first edition
of the *General History* only mentioned a 'pyratical Black-Flag', 'black
Colours', a 'black Ensign', and sometimes a 'red Ensign' or a 'bloody Flag',
which seems to have been the more longstanding tradition; trial records
often mention black or red flags as well. The detailed descriptions of specific pirates' flags arrive only with the expanded second edition.

There is some other evidence for these flags; the trial of Stede Bonnet's
crew even mentioned 'a large black Flag, with a Death's Head and Bones
a-cross'. Two accounts of the trial of Low's crew described a black or
'deep Blew Flagg', bearing 'the Poutrature of Death' or 'an Anatomy' and
'having an Hour-Glass in one Hand, and a Dart in the other, at the end of
which was the Form of a Heart with three Drops of Blood falling from it'.
The fact that the *General History* ascribes that design to both Roberts and
Spriggs suggests, to me, that the author was simply making it up based on
whatever came to hand.

We can say the same with pirate codes. Trials often mentioned signing
articles – it was a key piece of evidence to determine guilt or innocence
– and newspapers also sometimes printed copies of these, as with Low's
crew. That does not mean we can trust the *General History*, though. The
author admits that Roberts' crew 'had taken Care to throw over-board the
Original they had sign'd and sworn to', leaving 'a great deal of Room to
suspect, the remainder contained something too horrid to be disclosed' –
or to suspect that the whole thing was an invention.

Certainly, the code presented in the *General History* does not add up
with the evidence from the trial at Cape Coast Castle. It seems unlikely

that the many coerced crewmembers had '*a Vote in Affairs of Moment*', and there is plenty of evidence for brutal, tyrannical, and coercive pirate leaders. The code's prohibition on fighting aboard ship, with all disputes settled by duelling ashore, is contradicted by the beatings and fighting mentioned by witnesses. The *General History* itself undermines the code, by describing how Roberts formed 'a sort of Privy-Council of half a Dozen of the greatest Bullies' (no quartermasters here) and himself killed a man who insulted him 'on the Spot', which 'put the whole Company in an Uproar ... like to have ensued a general Battle'.

Scholars keen to believe in Roberts' code usually fail to mention that the author of the *General History* included a satirical comment on each of the articles. On the rule that '*No Boy or Woman to be allowed amongst them*', also noted by William Snelgrave, the author of the *General History* adds 'they put a Centinel immediately over [any female prisoner] to prevent ill Consequences', but in fact 'they contend who shall be Centinel, which happens generally to one of the greatest Bullies, who, to secure the Lady's Virtue, will let none lye with her but himself'. The whole point of this passage is not to celebrate the principled life of pirates, but to entertainingly expose their hypocrisy – making them, to go back to Bartolus de Sassoferrato, doubly 'enemies of all'.

The *General History*'s picture of pirates is satirical rather than authentic, and it is satirical with a purpose. That is especially evident in the most famous example of politically radical piracy in the book, the description of Libertalia (sometimes printed in the book as Libertatia). This supposed pirate utopia in Madagascar appears in the chapters of the second volume concerning Captain Misson and Thomas Tew.

The story goes as follows: Misson started out as a *corsaire*, then moved into piracy, joined up with Tew and eventually established a Madagascan base. Misson and his men 'unanimously resolved to seize upon and defend their Liberty', opposing slavery and freeing enslaved people. He named his followers the *Liberi*, 'desiring in that might be drown'd the distinguish'd [i.e. separate] Names of *French, English, Dutch, Africans*, &c.' These *Liberi* adopted a 'Form of Government' in 'Democratical Form, where the People were themselves the Makers and Judges of their own Laws', with an elected assembly meeting yearly, a Lord Conservator elected every three years, 'Treasure and Cattle ... equally divided', and 'a great many wholesome Laws'.

Yet another pirate commonwealth, and another one that never existed. Misson is fictional (linking him to Tew is another clever sleight of hand by the author). Even those historians inclined towards a radical interpretation of piracy acknowledge this fact, seeing it instead as an inspiring dream of liberty originating among the political culture of pirates.

I know I sound like a broken record here, but I am unconvinced. The *General History* was not written by pirates, and the *Liberi* deny being pirates, too. When deciding about flags, the boatswain advises 'Black as the most terrifying', but Misson's companion Caraccioli objects 'they were no Pyrates', even if others might 'brand this generous Crew with [that] invidious Name'. Instead, Caraccioli suggests a 'a white Ensign, with Liberty painted in the Fly, and ... *a Deo a Libertate*, for God and Liberty'.

Indeed, the political ideology in this chapter comes from Caraccioli, 'a lewd Priest' and Misson's confessor, 'as ambitious as he was irreligious'. It is Caraccioli who turns Misson towards atheism and then critiques social inequality – but his idealised solution is a pre-monarchist 'paternal Government, [where] every Father was the Head, the Prince and Monarch of his Family'. Caraccioli even argues that 'Obedience to Governors was necessary', so long as they acted as 'a real Father ... with the equal and impartial Justice of a Parent' and not with 'immeasurable Avarice and Tyranny'. When the *Liberi* elect their first Lord Conservator, it is no surprise that they choose Misson, with Caraccioli as secretary of state and Tew as admiral. I do not think it is a coincidence that scholars advocating for radical pirates as a historical thesis rarely mention Caraccioli.

Nor is this tale a sympathetic rendering of Libertalia's fictional political experiment. It ends abruptly following a Malagasy attack, with Tew and Misson choosing to return to America and Europe with their riches (and no apparent regrets). Misson then sinks in a storm. Before that, Tew visits a splinter group of *Liberi* who have set up their own, even more anarchistic, government, led by a quartermaster. He protests 'it would be Madness again to subject themselves to any Government, which, however mild, still exerted some Power ... 'tis ridiculous to think we will become Subjects to greater Rogues than our selves'. That quartermaster does, however, urge Tew to get 'a Commission for the settling a Colony', and elsewhere the author gushes over Madagascar's colonial potential, not least as 'a Curb on Pyrates'.

Libertalia, then, is a mishmash of the previous tales about pirates in Madagascar, and elsewhere in the book descriptions of a 'pirate commonwealth' share the same purpose as the account of Roberts' code: humour through an exaggerated and grandiose tone, and satire. The 'commonwealth', or more accurately commonwealths, rarely last long. When

Edward Lowther and John Massey cooperated, 'as all Constitutions grow old, and thereby shake and totter, so did our Commonwealth in about a Month of its Age, feel Commotions and intestine Disturbances'. After Vane and Rackam's falling out, 'the Empire of these Pyrates had not been long thus divided before they had like to have fallen into a civil War'.

Nor do they all share Misson's (or Caraccioli's) vision. One of Samuel Bellamy's crew, formerly a 'Stroler' or strolling player, encouraged his captain to 'lay the Foundation of a New Kingdom' on the Caribbean coast, offering to be secretary of state (having been a 'Servitor' or serv-ant at Oxford), and *'by the squeezing your Subjects (whom under the specious Pretence of Liberty, I will keep in abject Slavery) drain such Sums as shall ever keep them poor'*.

Significantly, the 'Stroler' adds, *'it was thus the greatest Empires of the World were founded'*. Here is a clue to what is really going on in the *General History*. The author's purpose, especially in the second volume but also, I think, in the first, was not only to give 'a distinct Relation of every Pyrate', but through them to develop a commentary on government (and the Church) in contemporary Britain, much as Thomas Heywood may have done in his writings on Walton and Atkinson.

We find the same purpose in the description of supposed mock trials held by pirates. Among pirates, writes the author, there 'was no feeing of Council, [or] bribing of Witnesses ... no packing of Juries, no tortur-ing and wresting the Sense of the Law ... no puzzling or perplexing the Cause with unintelligible canting Terms, and useless Distinctions'. In one of these trials, the pirate sitting as judge asks, 'What have we to do with Reason? ... we don't sit here to hear Reason; – we go according to Law.'

Pirates may indeed have held such mock courts to ridicule authority, but I doubt the author of the *General History* cared whether they did or not. The law itself is the real target here. That play-acting judge passes a pretend death sentence on the basis that 'it is not fit I should sit here as Judge, and no Body be hang'd ... you must be hang'd, because you have a damn'd hanging Look ... and 'tis a Custom, that whenever the Judge's Dinner is ready before the Tryal is over, the Prisoner is to be hang'd'. In the 1720s Britain had begun to expand the death penalty to a range of crimes against property, and it is perhaps to this new harshness that the author gestures.

One last example: the author describes John Taylor and his men enjoy-ing their ill-gotten gains in Portobelo, 'without the least Remorse or Compunction, satisfying their Conscience ... that other People would have done as much, had they the like Opportunities'. The author adds, pointedly, 'If they had known what was doing ... by the *South-Sea* [Company] Directors ... they would certainly have had this Reflection for their Consolation ... *That what ever Robberies they had committed, they might be pretty sure they were not the greatest Villains then living in the World.*'

If the author of the *General History* was Nathaniel Mist, or someone like him, then he was probably motivated by animosity towards the Hanoverian dynasty and the Whigs who largely controlled government throughout the 1720s and 1730s. His descriptions of pirates served not only to remind readers of the failings of that government, but also to lampoon the government itself through unflattering comparison.

One of the reviews published in Mist's own *Weekly Journal* gleefully imagines a Whiggish reader of the *General History* growing ever more apoplectic at the allusions and imputations, recognising in each piratical figure – even Bonny and Read – a specific contemporary politician (though sadly not naming any). The author describes pirate ships as 'good Governments', as an egalitarian and enfranchised 'commonwealth', not to praise pirates for their political tendencies, but to condemn certain political tendencies by association with piracy. Piracy is, once again, not just about piracy.

The colourful depictions of this piratical 'commonwealth' have survived, and thrived, in popular culture, and among historians eager – like the original author – to make their own political point. The purpose and context that generated those depictions are too often forgotten.

I wonder what the author, whoever he was, would have thought about it all.

AFTERWORD

The *General History of the Pyrates* was not the only popular text about pirates published in the 1720s or thereabouts. Besides his book on Every and *Captain Singleton*, Daniel Defoe alone wrote at least four other novels featuring pirates. Figures like Walter Kennedy found their way into compendiums of criminal biographies that circulated in these and subsequent decades.

The *General History* had the most clout and staying power, though. Besides its own continued circulation, it provided the basis for later representations. Writers, and then film-makers and computer game developers, have repeatedly gone back to its pages for inspiration. Countless historians have mined it for evidence, perhaps with a little too much credulity.

We can trace a series of steps from the *General History* to modern culture, each reinforcing the same pirate image. Robert Louis Stevenson drew on it for his *Treasure Island*, which appeared as a serial in 1881–82 and a book the following year. In the early twentieth century J.M. Barrie's *Peter Pan*, performed in 1904 and published in 1911, and Rafael Sabatini's novels of the 1910s and 1920s, like *Captain Blood* and *The Sea Hawk*, again evoked the style of the *General History*, though Sabatini modelled Captain Blood on Henry Morgan as well.

The arrival of cinema brought another strand to this image of pirates. Pirate films have appeared in every decade since the 1900s. The so-called 'golden age of Hollywood' saw a flood of swashbucklers in the middle of the twentieth century. In the twenty-first century came the *Pirates of the Caribbean* franchise, beginning in 2003, while computer games such as *Sid Meier's Pirates!* (released in 1987 with a remake in 2004) and more recently *Assassin's Creed IV: Black Flag* (2013) offer players a more interactive imagination of piracy.

Increasingly, this multimedia genre has responded to itself more than anything else. *Treasure Island* spawned at least thirty-five film and TV adaptations, at least twenty-four stage productions, plus radio versions and computer games – probably more than any actual pirate. Part of its enduring appeal, I suspect, is Long John Silver, both a threatening murderer and a sympathetic and protective friend to the young hero Jim Hawkins. Like many real plunderers did, Silver escapes at the end of the novel with a portion of the treasure in his hands.

Nor was *Treasure Island* the only novel to make it to the screen. Several Hollywood blockbusters, including *Captain Blood* (1935) and *The Sea Hawk* (1940), were adapted from Sabatini's popular novels. The *Pirates of the Caribbean* franchise deliberately invoked the visual styles of those earlier Hollywood films, to the point of copying some scenes very closely indeed.

These novels, films, and games are artefacts with their own histories and, rather like the *General History*, they reinterpret pirates to fit their own social context. The swashbucklers of the 1940s–50s had plucky heroes (often Dutch and English) standing up to tyrants (often Spanish), and usually the protagonists turned out to be government agents or ultimately reconciled with imperial authorities – where they commit any piracies, even if these are not fully legal, they are always morally justified.

In the *Pirates of the Caribbean* franchise, by contrast, pirates are more ambiguous, both protagonists and antagonists; the British imperial authorities, meanwhile, are simultaneously upright and ridiculous. Over the course of the initial trilogy, the originally villainous pirates morph into freedom-loving rebels against the greedy and brutal East India Company. There is a certain irony in Disney taking such a square aim at one of the first truly global corporations.

From the *General History*, Blackbeard and Anne Bonny have proven the most popular characters to revisit – and if differences between films of the mid-twentieth and early twenty-first centuries reveal a shift in attitudes concerning imperial politics, they show a rather more depressing continuity on gender and sexuality. Anne Bonny as a 'Libertine' is the figure that still draws most attention, often with cross-dressing as a key plot point.

The Spanish Main (1945), *Anne of the Indies* (1951), and *Against All Flags* (1952) depicted Bonny as a violent and promiscuous temptress, usually besotted with the male hero. Sometimes she is a tragic figure who sacrifices herself for the object of her affections, ensuring that he and his more respectable love interest get their happily-ever-after. In *Pirates of the Caribbean: On Stranger Tides*, released in 2011, a döppelganger of the fictional Jack Sparrow turns out to be his old flame Angelica. The moment of revelation occurs when Sparrow kisses Angelica and, moments later, pulls open her shirt to reveal her cleavage. Later in the film, Angelica appeals to Sparrow by telling him (with implied dishonesty) that she is pregnant.

The humour comes partially from Angelica's ability to impersonate the deliberately camp Sparrow – an unanticipated characterisation that apparently caused some concern among Disney executives. Sparrow subverts the conventionally hypermasculine pirate image, though some scholars have argued that cultural representations of piracy in the eighteenth century and earlier often evoked sexually transgressive tropes of the time, including homosexuality.

Perhaps the character of Angelica is a deliberate homage to scenes in the *General History*, but if so, it is an uncomfortable one. Likewise, in the original trilogy the explicitly feminist Elizabeth Swan rises to the rank of a pirate king, but still ends up ashore, with a child, awaiting the return of her man. These films raise questions about how much conventional attitudes regarding female bodies have really changed since 1724.

It is the *General History*'s stories about these two women that live on. In the game *Assassin's Creed*, Bonny is presented more sympathetically, but still in a male disguise until she reveals her identity, while in the TV show *Black Sails* (2014–17) she is a cold and calculating character. *Hellcats*, a fiction podcast from 2020, focused on the idea of a love affair between Bonny and Read. A statue of the couple was displayed temporarily on the riverside in Wapping, though the town for which the statue was intended as a permanent display actually rejected it, unwilling to celebrate pirates.

One other aspect of these representations of piracy is worth commenting on: the absence of piracy itself, in the sense of robbery at sea. An exception is games like *Sid Meier's Pirates!*, where plundering makes up a substantial part of the gameplay, but even there you can purchase a letter of marque or go off on side quests like looking for buried treasure and trying to marry a governor's daughter. Of course, some of those are things that plunderers actually did.

Elsewhere, piracy has receded in the representation of pirates. Even if these figures are still implicitly and vaguely threatening, they are also safely historical, in setting if not in accuracy, and often ridiculous. It is no coincidence that the vast majority of pirate media is marketed at children. I have not got space here to go into the legion of pirate books I have read, or toys I have encountered, in recent years.

Around the turn of the millennium, it seemed as if piracy was *only* for children: major films like *Hook* (1991), *Muppet Treasure Island* (1996), and *Treasure Planet* (2002) all catered to a younger market – all based on

Stevenson or Barrie. Curiously, the *Pirates of the Caribbean* moved in a more 'grown-up' direction, and likewise both *Black Sails*, a dark and gritty prequel to *Treasure Island*, and the charmingly silly, but often quite explicit, *Our Flag Means Death* (2022). These too have gone back to the same image of pirates, and are still rarely concerned very much with acts of piracy.

I confess to mixed feelings about this genre. It works only because of that image, which, as I hope I have shown, deserves a robust critique. At the same time, it is hard to avoid indulging in something that most of us encounter in childhood. I am sure it has helped recruitment on my undergraduate course. I have become rather fond of *Swashbuckle*, a BBC children's gameshow. I have watched quite a lot of it.

Just last night – the night before I wrote these words – I read the first two chapters of *Treasure Island* to my son. He tells me I do a passable pirate voice. I hope he will enjoy the story as much as I do.

The idea of a pirate has become fixed through this genre as an entertaining historical character. The practice of maritime raiding has never ceased.

Even as piracy declined in the later 1720s, plundering remained a feature of maritime life. Some *guardacostas*, like Augustin Blanco, Simon Mascarino, and Matthew Luke, had teamed up with English pirates earlier in the decade, and *guardacostas* continued to target English shipping, despite a new treaty in 1729. British and colonial newspapers complained about their 'pyratical Courses'. One prominent *capitán* was formerly enslaved Miguel Enríquez Cavallero de la Real Effigea; others included Christopher Winter and Nicholas Brown, who left the Bahamas at Rogers' arrival and went into Spanish service, as did John Taylor with the *Cassandra*. Nicholas Lawes, in Jamaica, protested that these men were traitors, but Spanish officials protected them, so far as they could.

Brown was eventually captured by John Drudge in 1726, apparently an old schoolfriend, which did not prevent Drudge from decapitating Brown and pickling his head in rum in order to collect a £500 bounty. Matthew Luke, a Genoese captain with a Spanish commission, was also captured in 1722 and fifty-eight of his crew were tried and executed, despite Spanish protests. Not that these prosecutions stopped the *guardacostas*: their actions caused another war in 1739.

Privateering, in the modern sense of licensed raiding, continued for another century or so. During the 1740s George Anson led a circumnavigation that captured a Spanish treasure galleon, while in 1739 Edward

Vernon sacked Portobelo with a mixed naval and private force. Both men had been naval officers in the 1720s and 1730s, in North America and the Caribbean, pursuing pirates and presiding over their trials. Private sea raiding was not formally abolished until the Treaty of Paris in 1856, at the end of the Crimean War between Russia on one side and Britain, France, and the Ottoman Empire on the other – and not everyone immediately agreed with the treaty's signatories.

That treaty reflected a broader continuation of the dynamic begun in the late seventeenth century, by which European empires exercised increasing control over maritime violence, not only condemning unauthorised raiders as pirates, but also using the language and law of piracy to extend their imperial jurisdiction and to target those who opposed them. When interconnected revolutions in South and Central America during the early 1800s prompted another burst of raiding in the Caribbean, it was again declared piracy, and the USA sent a naval squadron to police it in 1821. As the USA's trade with the Mediterranean expanded rapidly, they also sent an expedition to blockade Algiers, Tunis, and Tripoli in 1815, while Britain bombarded Algiers in 1816 and France invaded the region just over a decade later.

Similar patterns played out in the Indian Ocean – Kanhoji Angria was already called 'a famous *Indian* Pyrate' in the *General History*, and in other published accounts of the East India Company's conflict with the Marathas. The Company seized the last Angria stronghold in 1756 and thereafter positioned itself as the 'Moghuls' admiral', trying to control what it called the 'Piratical Ports' of the region and criticising their inhabitants as 'Banditti'.

Both the language and the practice intensified into the nineteenth century, combining expanded imperial power with racial and religious prejudices. The Company responded to the rise of Qawasim raiders in the Persian Gulf by allying with Oman and sending in a military expedition in 1819. In 1825 legislation offered a bounty to naval sailors for each 'piratical Person' they captured, originally intended to deal with the Caribbean but soon extended to the Indian Ocean as well.

British officials in Malaysia complained that 'piracy is now an evil so extensive and formidable', adding that 'from the earliest times ... piracy has been a distinguishing feature' of the region, reflecting an assumption that certain groups were inherently piratical and, therefore, conveniently suitable for conquest or extirpation. British officials pursued such policies in the 1820s, and so too did the Dutch Empire in the Malukus. Piracy provided a similar justification for increasing French intervention, and ultimately invasion, in northern Vietnam from the 1860s to the 1880s, though Emperor Tu Duc accused the French themselves of being pirates. A group of Sulu sailors, condemned to death in Singapore in 1841, responded to their sentence: 'If we had *not* been pirates, our own chiefs would have killed us; and, because we *are* pirates, you kill us ... either way: we die.'

Debate over the legal status of maritime raiding, and whether it qualifies as piracy, has continued apace into the twentieth and twenty-first centuries. The 1958 Geneva Convention on the High Seas and the 1982 United Nations Convention on the Law of the Sea set a legal definition of piracy as violence or theft committed for private purpose, on the 'high seas' (outside individual jurisdictions), and involving one ship or vessel attacking another. While these are a seemingly simple set of terms, not every nation has ratified them and the definition still runs into problems – especially the question of purpose. On several occasions, the USA has sought to define an action as piracy when it was carried out for political purposes by a terrorist group, or by a government the USA did not officially recognise.

During the early 2000s, an intense episode of piracy occurred off the coast of Somalia. In the second decade of a civil war, foreign ships were overfishing and dumping waste, including nuclear materials, lead, and heavy metals like cadmium and mercury, in Somalia's unpoliced territorial waters. Local fishermen, their livelihoods collapsing, began to capture vessels passing in one of the busiest shipping lanes in the world, usually ransoming the crews and cargo, increasingly with the involvement of international criminal networks. These attacks rose to around 200 per year by 2010, more than half of all such incidents worldwide, and estimates of the value of this piracy suggest $30 million in 2006 and $150 million in 2009.

Legally, other nations could not enter Somalia's territorial waters. The United Nations Security Council passed a series of resolutions permitting them to do so, but very specifically defined the geographical boundaries and temporary period for this, clearly worried about setting precedents. Prosecutions presented another problem: Britain and the USA made an agreement with Kenya to carry out prosecutions there, but Kenya withdrew from it in 2010, dissatisfied with the additional strain placed on its legal system.

None of these episodes, from the eighteenth to the twenty-first century, dislodged the popular image of pirates. Depictions of Somali piracy, such as the film *Captain Phillips* in 2013, are starkly different in tone to the more conventional representations of seventeenth- and eighteenth-century pirates. Yet the two dimensions may have interacted. The concept of pirates as 'enemies of all' certainly supported imperial campaigns of the nineteenth century. It is tempting to speculate that media coverage of Somali piracy in the early 2000s had something to do with the renewed interest in 'golden age' piracy in films, TV, and games, and perhaps even in historical and legal scholarship too.

If nothing else, the continued political and legal campaigns during the nineteenth century, the international discussions during the twentieth and twenty-first centuries (dealing with many unresolved problems faced by officials 300 years ago), and the celebration of pirates in popular culture all circle around the point with which I began this book. Maritime violence and raiding are very real, but *piracy* is still a question of interpretation – of the stories that we tell.

Let us finish with one more story, from *De Civitate Dei* (*The City of God*), written in the early fifth century by theologian and philosopher St Augustine, who lived in what is now eastern Algeria, later moving to Rome.

According to Augustine, Alexander the Great captured a pirate (*pirata*) and demanded what he meant by infesting the sea. The pirate answered 'with bold pride' by asking Alexander what *he* meant by seizing the whole globe. 'I do it with a small ship, I am called a thief; you, with a great army, are called an emperor.'

This story is, again, apocryphal, since Augustine wrote many centuries after Alexander's time. Yet, like so many other stories about pirates, it has lived on. It appeared in John Gower's fourteenth-century poem *Confessio Amantis* (where Alexander decides to employ the pirate, just as some later rulers would). Alberico Gentili cited it, critically, in his sixteenth-century writings. Noam Chomsky used it as a title for a 1986 book on terrorism.

It even appears in the *General History*. When Samuel Bellamy called himself '*a free prince* ... [with] *as much authority to make war on the whole world as he who has a hundred sail of ships at sea*', it may be an oblique reference. More directly, the 'Stroler' who accompanied Bellamy supposedly put on a play for his fellows, called the *Royal Pirate*. It turned from 'Farce into Tragedy' when the ship's drunken gunner, witnessing a scene of Alexander judging a captured pirate and thinking that his shipmate was genuinely in for it, started a fight and nearly blew up the ship.

Augustine's story fits neatly with one more etymological nugget: the words 'pirate' and 'empire' both stem from the same root in Greek. In fact, it is all a little too neat. I do not believe that pirates ever placed themselves on par with emperors or rejected imperial authority. Most plunderers operated in concert with that authority. Others probably knew that they acted beyond imperial laws, but I am not sure they really challenged the ideological principles of those laws. I am open to the idea that some pirates were politically sophisticated; to assume otherwise is to accept the judgemental prejudices of imperial officials. Even so, I do not see the *General History* as convincing evidence.

Still, Augustine's story raises a crucial point. Empire, too, is a business of plunder and of slavery, and much of what people now call piracy was committed with imperial backing. Even the laws against piracy were a way for empires to distinguish between their own violence and the violence that they considered unacceptable. Condemning some plunderers as 'pirates', claiming they were 'enemies of all' and therefore outside politics, is itself a political move.

Without pirates there would have been no empires, and without empires there would have been no pirates.

If you take anything away with you from this book, I'd really like you to take two things. The first is that, when you next see a pirate film, or a toy, or any of the other seemingly endless iterations of this image, you will know a bit more about where this all comes from, about what pirates were really like, and about the broader impact they had on history.

The second is that, at that moment, you will ask yourself two questions.

Who is calling whom a pirate?

Why?

ACKNOWLEDGEMENTS
AND SOURCES

I have incurred many debts in writing this book and it is a pleasure to acknowledge them here. I am grateful to Tom Killingbeck for the conversations that kicked it all off; to Kate Williams, for her very kind advice and assistance early on; and to Robert Kirby, Georgina Le Grice, Alex Stephens, and Kate Walsh at United Agents for representing me.

I am most grateful to QGIS and Natural Earth for making open source mapping possible, and to the Archivo del Museo Naval, Birmingham Museums, the John Carter Brown Library, the Library of Congress, New York Public Library and the Rijksmuseum for making their materials available in the public domain. Beatrice Okoro at Royal Museums Greenwich and Lee Curran at Alamy offered very helpful assistance with images from their respective collections.

The last couple of decades have witnessed a flourishing of scholarship on the history of piracy. I am deeply indebted to the scholars listed in the 'Further Reading' section for their work. Particular thanks are due to Nathan Jopling, Graham Moore, and Luke Walters for their comments on drafts. For valuable conversations on matters piratical, maritime, imperial or otherwise over the years, I would like to thank Catia Antunes, Lauren Benton, Amanda Bevan, Matthew Conway, James Davey, Joël Félix, Oliver Finnegan, Maria Fusaro, Christos Giannatos, Mark Hanna, Jean-Marc Hill, Claire Jowitt, Miranda Kaufmann, Graham Kerr, Daniel Lange, Simon Layton, Margarette Lincoln, Elaine Murphy, Erik Odegard, Ismini Pells, Rebecca Simon, David L. Smith, Edmond Smith, Nicholas Rodger, Ben Weddell, Mark Williams, Nikki Williams, and David Wilson. I am grateful to my colleagues at the University of Reading for making it such a congenial place to be a historian.

This book is dedicated to all my students, past, present, and future. I have benefited from opportunities to study this topic with them on my undergraduate course on the history of piracy and by supervising undergraduate and postgraduate dissertations. It is no exaggeration to say that without those students this book would not exist.

Finally, I would like to thank my family for their continued support and tolerance with my historical enthusiasms, especially my parents, who first kindled my love of history and of the sea. I owe more to my wife Rachael than I can ever say. Ben, I hope you will read and enjoy this book one day (and thank you for sharing your own interest in pirates with me). Sam, we miss you every day.

FURTHER READING

This section does not aim to be a complete list of the secondary works I consulted in writing this book. My intention here is to provide guidance for general readers on the most influential or up-to-date academic research and to highlight some of the scholarship I have discussed in certain chapters. For more information, please consult my webpages at the University of Reading website.

I highly recommend Kris Lane's 'Piracy' bibliography in the Oxford Bibliographies series on Atlantic history (oxfordbibliographies.com), which provides excellent introductions to that now vast scholarly field. Good overviews include Douglas Egerton, Alison Games, James G. Landers, Kris Lane, and Donald R. Wright, *The Atlantic World: A History, 1400–1888* (2007); Thomas Benjamin, *The Atlantic World* (2009); and D'Maris Coffman, Adrian Leonard, and William O'Reilly, eds, *The Atlantic World* (2015). K.N. Chaudhuri's *Trade and Civilisation in the Indian Ocean* (1993) and Edward Alpers' *The Indian Ocean in World History* (2014) are excellent introductions to the history of that region.

For works on piracy covering the entire chronology discussed here, I have found the most useful to be Kris E. Lane's *Pillaging the Empire* (1998); Peter Earle's *The Pirate Wars* (2003); John C. Appleby's *Women and English Piracy* (2013); and Mark Hanna's *Pirate Nests* (2015). Philip Gosse's *The Pirates' Who's Who* (1924) and David Marley's *Pirates and Privateers of America* (1994) offer biographical dictionaries. Margarette Lincoln's *British Pirates and Society* (2014) covers 1680–1730 and gives particular attention to print culture, while Virginia Lunsford's *Piracy and Privateering in the Golden Age Netherlands* (2005) is an excellent discussion of Dutch piracy.

Important collections of academic essays by multiple authors include C.R. Pennell, ed., *Bandits at Sea* (2001); Claire Jowitt, ed., *Pirates? The*

Politics of Plunder (2007); Stefan Eklöf Amirell and Leos Müller, eds, *Persistent Piracy* (2014); David Head, ed., *The Golden Age of Piracy* (2018); and Stefan Eklöf Amirell, Bruce Buchan, and Hans Hägerdal, eds, *Piracy in World History* (2021); also the two volumes on archaeology edited by Russell K. Skowrownek and Charles Robin Ewin, *X Marks the Spot* (2006) and *Pieces of Eight* (2016).

On sixteenth-century Atlantic raiding, the best overview remains K.R. Andrews, *The Spanish Caribbean* (1978), besides his numerous other works; also Paul Hoffman's *The Spanish Crown and the Defense of the Caribbean, 1535–1585* (1980). John C. Appleby's *Under the Bloody Flag* (2011) is a general discussion of Tudor piracy, and he has also written on piracy in Ireland, on which see also Connie Kelleher's *The Alliance of Pirates* (2020), and for the Maghreb, Adrian Tinniswood, *Pirates of Barbary* (2011), and Gillian Lew Weiss, *Captives and Corsairs* (2011). Claire Jowitt's *The Culture of Piracy* (2010) discusses literature from the late sixteenth and early seventeenth centuries.

Dudley Pope's *Harry Morgan's Way* (1977) is a detailed biography of Morgan, while Peter Earle's *The Sack of Panamá* (1981) makes extensive use of Spanish sources. On the *flibustiers*, see Jacques Ducoin, *Bertrand d'Ogeron* (2013). On the social and economic development of Port Royal and buccaneering, see Nuala Zahedieh's many articles, especially 'Trade, Plunder, and Economic Development', *Economic History Review*, 39 (1986) and 'A Frugal, Prudential, and Hopeful Trade', *Journal of Imperial and Commonwealth History*, 18 (1990); Michael Pawson and Davis Buisseret, *Port Royal* (2000); and Carla Gardina Pestana, 'Early English Jamaica', *William & Mary Quarterly*, 71 (2014). On banjos, see Laurent Dubois, *The Banjo* (2016). Arne Bialuschewski's *Raiders and Natives* (2022) is a detailed discussion on Indigenous communities and buccaneers.

For the South Sea voyagers, the best general account is Peter T. Bradley, *The Lure of Peru* (1989). Anton Gill, *The Devil's Mariner* (1997) and Diana and Michael Preston, *A Pirate of Exquisite Mind* (2005) offer good biographies of Dampier, with a more general account of those voyages. On the Red Sea raiders, the classic work remains Robert C. Ritchie, *Captain Kidd and the War against the Pirates* (1986), and more recently Rebecca Simon, *Why We Love Pirates: The Hunt for Captain Kidd* (2020); on Every see Joel H. Baer, '"Captain John Avery"', *Eighteenth Century Life*, 18 (1994). Douglas Burgess, *The Politics of Piracy* (2014) and Kevin P. McDonald, *Pirates, Merchants, Settlers, and Slaves* (2015) both examine the colonial links and politics of Red Sea voyages.

Sebastian Prange, 'A Trade of No Dishonor', *American Historical Review*, 116 (2011) and Patricia Risso, 'Cross-Cultural Perceptions of Piracy',

Journal of World History, 12 (2001) both discuss the longer history of plundering in the Indian Ocean (and I have drawn on Risso's article for linguistic terms in the foreword). On pirates and Malagasy communities, see Arne Bialuschewski, 'Pirates, Slavers, and the Indigenous Population in Madagascar', *International Journal of African Historical Studies*, 38 (2005); Jane Hooper, 'Pirates and Kings', *Journal of World History*, 22 (2011); and Ryan Holroyd, 'Whatever Happened to those Villains of the Indian Seas?', *International Journal of Maritime History*, 29 (2017).

For the 'Black flag' era, David Cordingly's *Spanish Gold* (2011) is a biography of Woodes Rogers that also covers the wider subject. Marcus Rediker's *Villains of All Nations* (2012) is among the more influential books on the subject and, with his many other works, has most forcefully argued for politically radical pirates. David Wilson's *Suppressing Piracy in the Early Eighteenth Century* (2021) is a recent, very detailed analysis of this period; see also Arne Bialuschewski's 'Between Newfoundland and the Malacca Strait', *Mariner's Mirror*, 90 (2004). The most recent biography of Anne Bonny and Mary Read is Rebecca Simon, *Pirate Queens* (2022).

Concerning Exquemelin's *Zee-roovers*, see Richard Frohock's 'Exquemelin's Buccaneers', *Eighteenth-Century Life*, 34 (2010) and 'Common Mischaracterisations of Early English Translations of Exquemelin's Buccaneers', *Notes & Queries*, 57 (2010); Jason Payton, 'Alexander Oliver Exquemelin's "The Buccaneers of America"', *Early American Literature*, 48 (2013); and Joseph Gibbs, '"A Certain False, Malicious, Scandalous and Famous Libel"', *International Journal of Maritime History*, 30 (2018). Concerning the *General History*, see Arne Bialuschewski, 'Daniel Defoe, Nathaniel Mist, and the "General History"', *Papers of the Bibliographical Society of America*, 98 (2004) and Richard Frohock, 'Satire and Civil Governance in "A General History"', *Eighteenth Century*, 56 (2015). On the representation of Bonny and Read see Sally O'Driscoll, 'The Pirate's Breasts', *Eighteenth Century*, 53 (2012), and for the broader context of female cross-dressing, Rudolf Dekker and Lotte van de Pol, *The Tradition of Female Transvestism in Early Modern Europe* (1988). On pirates, gender, and sexuality in literature more generally, see Hans Turley, *Rum, Sodomy, and the Lash* (1999).

On piracy, law, and empire, the most influential work is Lauren Benton's *A Search for Sovereignty* (2010), and she has written much else besides on this subject. Janice Thomson's *Mercenaries, Pirates, and Sovereigns* (1994) is another good general overview. J.D. Ford's *The Emergence of Privateering* (2023) gives an extremely detailed account of prize law up to the mid-seventeenth century, including discussions of Gentili and Grotius. Also useful are Michael Kempe's articles 'Beyond the Law: The Image of Piracy in the Legal Writings of Hugo Grotius', *Grotiana* (1980) and '"Even in the Remotest Corners of the World": Globalized Piracy and International Law', *Journal of Global History*, 5 (2010), and N.A.M. Rodger, 'The Law and Language of Private Naval Warfare', *Mariner's Mirror*, 100 (2014).

Different perspectives on pirate economics can be found in Peter T. Leeson's *The Invisible Hook* (2009) and his various other works, applying rational choice theory; and in J.L. Anderson, 'Piracy and World History', *Journal of World History*, 6 (1995), and David J. Starkey, 'Pirates and Markets', in C.R. Pennell, ed., *Bandits at Sea*, both discussing the relationship between 'pirate cycles' and market forces.

For the afterword, I have relied on Simon Layton, 'Discourses of Piracy', *Itinerario*, 35 (2011) and 'Hydras and Leviathans', *International Journal of Maritime History*, 25 (2013); also Stefan Eklöf Amirell, *Pirates of Empire* (2019). Omer Direk *et al.*, 'Somalia and the Problem of Piracy', *Uluslararası Stratejik Araştırmalar Kurumu*, 6 (2010) is an excellent discussion of modern piracy law. Michael D. High's 'Pirates without Piracy', *Jump Cut* (www.ejumpcut.org) contrasts mid-twentieth- and twenty-first-century pirate films.

Primary Sources

All quotations are from primary sources, the majority of which have been consulted in the originals. Several of the pamphlets cited in the text, including many trial records, are reprinted in Joel Baer's four-volume *British Piracy in the Golden Age* (2007). E.T. Fox's *Pirates in their Own Words* (2014) reproduces manuscript sources including testimonies by plunderers and witnesses. Another useful anthology is Kris E. Lane and Arne Bialuschewski, eds, *Piracy in the Early Modern Era* (2019).

I must also mention the following works that have been of help: Benjamin, *Atlantic World*; Burgess, *Politics of Piracy*; Cordingly, *Spanish Gold*; Earle, *Sack of Panamá*; Gill, *Devil's Mariner*; Hanna, *Pirate Nests*; Lane, *Pillaging the Empire*; Pawson and Buisseret, *Port Royal*; and Ritchie, *Captain Kidd*.

Manuscript Collections

Archives Municipales du Havre: Famille Boivin (49Z)
Archives Nationales d'Outre-Mer, Aix-en-Provence: Fonds ministériels, premier empire colonial/Secrétariat d'Etat à la Marine (COL C8-9, F3)

British Museum, London: Additional MSS; Harley MSS; India Office
  Records; Sloane MSS
National Maritime Museum, Greenwich: Journals and Diaries (JOD);
  Gosse (GOS)
Stadsarchief Amsterdam: Archieven van de Schout en Schepenen (5061)
The National Archives, Kew: Admiralty (ADM), Colonial Office (CO), High
  Court of Admiralty (HCA)

Printed Sources

Anne, *Declaration for the Incouragement of ... Ships of War and Privateers*
  (24th. 1702)
—— *Declaration for the Further Encouragement of ... Ships of War and
  Privateers* (1703)
Anon, *Clinton, Purser & Arnold, to their Countreymen Wheresoeuer* (1583)
—— *An Experimentall Discoverie of Spanish Practices* (1623)
—— *A True Relation of the Life and Death of Sir Andrew Barton* (1630)
—— *The Sea-mans Protestation Renewed, Confirmed, and Enlarged* (1643)
—— *The Seamans Song of Captain Ward the Famous Pyrate of the World* (1658)
—— *A Remonstrance or Narrative by Way of Complaint* (1660)
—— *A Farewel to Graves-End* (1671–1702?)
—— *News from Sea or, the Takeing of the Cruel Pirate* (1674)
—— *An Exact Narrative of the Tryals of the Pyrates* (1675)
—— *The Present State of New-England* (1676)
—— *The Present State of Jamaica* (1683)
—— *The Voyages of the Ever Renowned Sr. Francis Drake into the West
  Indies* (1683)
—— *The Voyages and Travels of that Renowned Captain, Sir Francis Drake* (1683)
—— *Cynthia* (1687)
—— *An Appeal to the Men of New-England* (1689)
—— *The Woman Warrier* (1690)
—— *A Country Dialogue between William and James* (1692)
—— *A Full Account of the Late Dreadful Earth-quake at Port-Royal* (1692)
—— *A New Ballad on the Great Victory at Sea* (1692)
—— *A True and Perfect Relation of that Most Sad and Terrible Earthquake, at
  Port-Royal* (1692)
—— *The Truest and Largest Account of the Late Earthquake in Jamaica* (1693)
—— *A Copy of Verses, Composed by Captain Henry Every* (1696)
—— *The Last Dying Speech and Behaviour of Capt. Thomas Vaughan* (1696)

—— *The Proceedings ... for Several Felonies and Piracies* (1697)

—— *A Collection of Original Voyages* (1699)

—— *An Account of the Behaviour and Last Dying Speeches of the Six Pirates* (1704)

—— *The Life and Dangerous Voyages of Sir Francis Drake* (1708)

—— *The Lives and Adventures of the German Princess, Mary Read, Anne Bonny [and others]* (1755)

—— *An Account of the Pirates* (1769)

—— *Interesting Tracts, relating to the Island of Jamaica* (1800)

Atkins, John, *A Voyage to Guinea* (1735)

Augustine of Hippo, *The City of God*, ed. Demetrius B. Zema and Gerald G. Walsh (2008)

Barker, Andrew, *A True and Certaine Report of ... Ward and Danseker* (1609)

Barlow, Edward, *Barlow's Journal of his Life at Sea*, ed. Basil Lubbock (1934)

Barnard, John, *Ashton's Memorial* (1725)

Beverley, Thomas, *Evangelical Repentance [...] upon the Solemn Occasion of the Late Dreadful Earthquake in Jamaica* (1693)

Bigges, Walter, *A Summarie and True Discourse of Sir Francis Drakes West-Indian Voyage* (1652)

Blount, Thomas, *Glossographia* (1668)

—— *Nomo-lexikon* (1670)

—— *A World of Errors Discovered in the New World of Words* (1673)

Botero, Giovanni, *Le Relationi Universali* (1596)

B., R., *The English Heroe* (1687)

—— *The English Empire in America* (1698)

Breton, Nicholas, *A Discourse in Commendation of ... Frauncis Drake* (1581)

Broeck, Adrian Van., *The Life and Adventures of Capt. John Avery* (1709)

Calendar of State Papers, America and West Indies, ed. W. Noel Sainsbury *et al* (1860–1969)

Calendar of State Papers Domestic: Edward VI, Mary and Elizabeth, 1547–80, ed. Robert Lemon and Mary Anne Everett Green (1867–72)

Calendar of State Papers Domestic: James I, ed. Mary Anne Everett Green (1857–59)

Calendar of State Papers, Ireland, 1608–1610, ed. C.W. Russel and John P. Prendergast (1874)

Calendar of State Papers Relating to English Affairs in the Archives of Venice, volume 10, 1603–1607, ed. Horatio F. Brown (1900)

Camden, William, *Annales the True and Royall History of the Famous Empresse Elizabeth* (1625)

Carew, George, *Lex Talionis: or the Law of Marque or Reprizals* (1682)

Casas, Bartolomé De Las, *In Defense of The Indians*, ed. Stafford Poole (1992)

Casse, Jean-Baptiste du, *Relation Fidèle de l'Expédition de Cartagène* (1699)

Cervantes Saavedra, Miguel De, *The History of the Most Renowned Don Quixote of Mancha* (1687)

Charles II, *A Proclamation Whereas the Safeguard and Protection* (1668)

—— *A Proclamation for the Discovery and Apprehension of Captain Don Philip Hellen, alias Fitz-Gerald* (1675)

Charlevoix, Pierre-François-Xavier de, *Histoire de l'Isle Espagnole ou de S Domingue* (1730–3)

Child, Josiah, *A New Discourse of Trade* (1693)

Cicero, M. Tullius, *De Officiis. With an English Translation*, ed. Walter Miller (1913)

—— *The Verrine Orations with an English Translation*, ed. L.H.G. Greenwood (1928)

Clarke, Samuel, *The Life & Death of ... Francis Drake* (1671)

Coles, Elisha, *An English Dictionary* (1676)

Cooke, Edward, *A Voyage to the South Sea* (1712)

Cowell, John, and Thomas Manley, *Nomothetēs* (1672)

Coxere, Edward, *Adventures by Sea of Edward Coxere*, ed. Edward Harry William Meyerstein (1945)

Cromwell, Oliver, *A Proclamation ... [concerning] Letters of Marque, or Reprisal* (1655)

Daborne, Robert, *A Christian Turn'd Turke* (1612)

Dampier, William, *A New Voyage Round the World* (1697)

—— *Voyages and Descriptions* (1699)

—— *A Voyage to New Holland* (1703)

—— *Capt. Dampier's Vindication* (1707)

Davenant, Charles, *Discourses on the Publick Revenue* (1698)

Davenant, William, *The History of Sir Francis Drake* (1660)

Dee, John, *John Dee: The Limits of The British Empire*, ed. Ken MacMillan and Jennifer Abeles (2004)

Defoe, Daniel, *The Life, and Strange Surprizing Adventures of Robeson Cruso* (1719)

—— *The Farther Adventures of Robinson Crusoe* (1719)

—— *The King of Pirates* (1719)

—— *Serious Reflections during the Life and Surprising Adventures of Robinson Crusoe* (1720)

—— *The Life, Adventures, and Pyracies, Of the Famous Captain Singleton* (1720)

Dennis, John, *Original Letters, Familiar, Moral and Critical* (1721)

Doolittle, Thomas, *Earthquakes Explained and Practically Improved* (1693)

Downing, Clement, *A Compendious History of the Indian Wars* (1737)

Elizabeth I, *The Fourme of the Proclamations to be Published in the Port Townes* (1572)

—— *Proclamation, Declaring Her Princelie Intention to Inhibit Her Subiects upon Most Extreme Paines, from Offending on the Seas* (1591)

—— *A Proclamation to Represse all Piracies and Depredations vpon the Sea* (1602)

Evelyn, John, *The Diary of John Evelyn*, ed. William Bray (1901)

Exquemelin, Alexandre, *De Americaensche Zee-roovers* (1678)

—— *Die Americanische See-räuber* (1679)

—— *Piratas de la America* (1681)

—— *Bucaniers of America* (1684)

—— *Bucaniers of America ... the Second Edition, Corrected, and Inlarged* (1684)

—— *The History of the Bucaniers* (1684)

—— *Histoire des Avanturiers* (1686)

—— *The History of the Bucaniers of America ... This Second Edition* (1695)

—— *The History of the Bucaniers of America from their First Original down to This Time* (1699)

Fitz-Geffry, Charles, *Sir Francis Drake his Honorable Lifes Commendation* (1596)

Fletcher, Francis, *The World Encompassed by Sir Francis Drake* (1628)

Fuller, Thomas, *The History of the Worthies of England* (1662)

Funnell, William, *A Voyage Round the World* (1707)

Grotius, Hugo, *Commentary on the Law of Prize and Booty*, ed. Martine Julia van Ittersum (2006)

Gupta, J.N. Das, ed., *India in the Seventeenth Century as Depicted by European Travellers* (1916)

Hakluyt, Richard, *The Principall Navigations* (1589)

—— *A Discourse Concerning Western Planting*, ed. Leonard Woods and Charles Deane (1877)

Harlow, Vincent T., ed., *The Voyages of Captain William Jackson (1642–1645)* (1923)

Heath, Emmanuel, *A Full Account of the Late Dreadful Earth-quake at Port-Royal* (1692)

Heylyn, Peter, and John Birkenhead, eds, *Mercurius Aulicus* (1643–45)

Heywood, Thomas, *The Fair Maid of the West* (1631)

—— *A True Description of His Majesties Royall Ship* (1637)

—— *A True Relation, of the Lives and Deaths of ... Purser, and Clinton* (1639)

—— *Fortune by Land and Sea* (1655)

Hickeringill, Edmund, *Jamaica Viewed [...] by E. H.* (1661)

Jamaican Assembly, *The Laws of Jamaica, passed by the Assembly* (1683)

James I, *A Proclamation to Represse all Piracies and Depredations vpon the Sea* (1603)

—— *A Proclamation for Revocation of Mariners from Forreine Seruices* (1605)

—— *Whereas the Kings Majestie hath Always bene Ready to Imbrace and Cherish such a Perfect Amitie vetweene Him and the King of Spaine* (1605)

James II, *A Proclamation for the More Effectual Reducing and Suppressing of Pirates and Privateers in America* (1688)

Johnson, Charles, *The Successful Pyrate* (1713)

—— *A General History of the Robberies and Murders of the Most Notorious Pyrates* (1724)

—— *A General History of the Pyrates ... the Second Edition* (1724)

—— *The History of the Pyrates* (1728)

Justice, Alexander, *A General Treatise of the Dominion and Laws of the Sea* (1705)

Kingsbury, Susan M., ed., *The Records of the Virginia Company of London, Volume I: The Court Book* (1906)

Labat, Jean-Baptiste, *Nouveau Voyage aux Isles de l'Amerique* (1722)

Ligon, Richard, *A True & Exact History of the Island of Barbados* (1657)

Lords Justices, *A Proclamation ... that One Henry Every ... Committed Several Acts of Piracy* (1696)

Louis XIV, *Ordonnance ... touchant la Marine* (1681)

Mainwaring, Henry, *The Life and Works of Sir Henry Mainwaring*, ed. G.E. Manwaring (1920–22)

Marsden, Reginald Godfrey, *Documents Relating to Law and Custom of the Sea* (1915)

Mather, Cotton, *Faithful Warnings to Prevent Fearful Judgments* (1704)

—— *Useful Remarks* (1723)

—— *The Vial Poured Out upon the Sea* (1726)

—— *Selected Letters of Cotton Mather*, ed. Kenneth Silverman (1971)

Molloy, Charles, *De Jure Maritimo et Navali* (1676)

Monson, William, *The Naval Tracts of Sir William Monson*, ed. M. Oppenheim (1902–14)

Nichols, Philip, *Sir Francis Drake Revived* (1626)

Parliament, *An Act for Preventing Injuries and Wrongs done to Merchants at Sea* (1650)

Parliament, *An Act for Calling Home Sea-men and Mariners* (1652)

Pepys, Samuel, *The Diary of Samuel Pepys*, ed. Henry B. Wheatley (1893)

Pereira, Antonio de León Pinelo, and Juan de Solórzano, ed., *Recopilación de Leyes de los Reynos de las Indias* (1680)

Pulido, Daniel García, *et al*, eds, *Amaro Pargo: Documentos de una Vida* (2017–19)

Purchas, Samuel, *Purchas His Pilgrimes* (1625)

Raithby, John, ed., *Statutes of the Realm* (1810–25)

Ralegh, Walter, *The Discoverie of ... Guiana* (1596)

Ramírez, Alonso, *The Misfortunes of Alonso Ramírez*, ed. Fabio López Lázaro (2012)

Raveneau de Lussan, Jacques, *Journal du Voyage fait à la Mer du Sud* (1689)

Raveneau de Lussan, Jacques, *A Journal of a Voyage Made Into the South Sea* (1698)

Raynal, Abbé, *L'Histoire Philosophique et Politique* (1770)

Ringrose, Basil, *Bucaniers of America* (1685)

Robert, Henry, *The Trumpet of Fame* (1595)

Roberts, Lewes, *The Merchants Mappe of Commerce* (1638)

Rogers, Woodes, *A Cruising Voyage round the World* (1712)

Sánchez, Manuel A. de Paz et al, eds, *El Corsario de Dios: Documentos sobre Amaro Rodríguez Felipe (1678–1747)* (2015)

Shelvocke, George, *A Voyage round the World* (1726)

Sloane, Hans, *Voyage to the Islands* (1707)

Smith, John, *The Generall Historie of Virginia* (1624)

—— *An Accidence ... for all Young Sea-men* (1626)

—— *The True Travels, Adventures, and Observations of Captaine John Smith* (1630)

Smith, William, *Several Letters of Great Importance, and Good Successe* (1643)

Snelgrave, William, *A New Account of Some Parts of Guinea* (1734)

Steele, Robert, ed., *Tudor and Stuart Proclamations 1485–1714* (1910)

St Lo, George, *England's Safety: Or, a Bridle to the French King* (1693)

—— *Britannia Triumphans* (1694)

Stow, John, *The Annales of England* (1592)

Taylor, John, *Jamaica in 1687: The Taylor Manuscript at the National Library of Jamaica*, ed. D. Buisseret (2008)

Tertre, Jean-Baptiste Du, *Histoire Générale des Isles de S. Christophe, de la Guadeloupe, de la Martinique, et Autres dans l'Amérique* (1654)

—— *Histoire Générale des Antilles Habitées par les François* (1667)

Thornton, H.P., ed., 'The Modyfords and Morgan: Letters from Sir James Modyford on the Affairs of Jamaica, 1667–1672, in the Muniments of Westminster Abbey', *Jamaican Historical Review*, 2 (1952)

Tindal, Matthew, *An Essay Concerning the Laws of Nations* (1694)

Trott, Nicholas, *The Laws of the British Plantations in America* (1721)

Voltaire, *Essai sur l'Histoire Générale* (1761–3)

Wafer, Lionel, *A New Voyage and Description of the Isthmus of America* (1699)

Welbe, John, *An Answer to Captain Dampier's Vindication* (1707)

Welwod, William, *An Abridgement of all Sea-lawes* (1613)

Wynne, William, ed., *The Life of Sir Leoline Jenkins* (1724)

INDEX

Note: *italicised* page references indicate illustrations

Silver *pesos de ocho*, or pieces of eight, coined by hand in Mexico in 1729–33, recovered from the Dutch shipwreck *'t Vliegend Hart*. These coins circulated globally and often became degraded as they did so. (Rijksmuseum, Amsterdam)

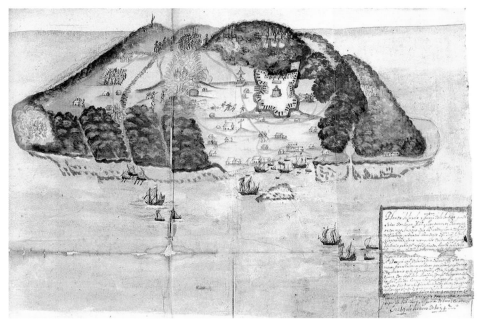

Plan of the island and fortifications of Tortuga, showing an attack by Spanish troops in 1654. (España. Ministerio de Defensa, Archivo Histórico de la Armada Juan Sebastián de Elcano, AHA 0595 Ms 1841)

This sketch, by merchant sailor Edward Barlow, captures the cramped conditions in Port Royal. Barlow visited Jamaica several times in the later seventeenth century. (© National Maritime Museum, Greenwich, London)

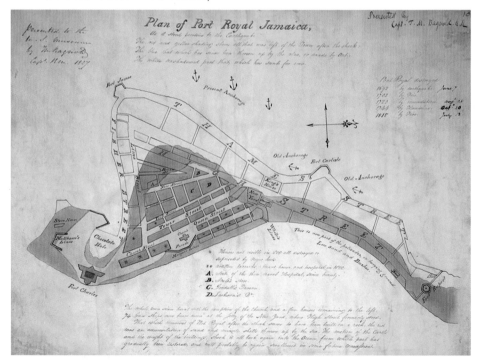

A nineteenth-century plan, showing Port Royal's street layout before the earthquake, and the extent of destruction in 1692. (Courtesy of the British Library Board)

A nineteenth-century engraving of Nassau harbour; the obelisk on the right was a later memorial to those who died in a storm. (Colin Waters/Alamy Stock Photo)

A chart of Charleston from 1777, which shows the sandbars and islands at the entrance to the harbour, and with a profile of the town. (© National Maritime Museum, Greenwich, London)

A late seventeenth-century chart of Madagascar, by Robert Morden; Nosy Boraha (Île-Sainte-Marie) and Antongil Bay are marked at the north-eastern corner of the island, with Anjouan (Joanna) in the Comoro Islands to the north-west. (Chronicle/Alamy Stock Photo)

Johan Teyler's painting, from 1688–98, shows a Dutch frigate to the right and a *jacht* to the left, with a similar fore-and-aft sail plan to the one used on Jamaican and Bermudan sloops. (Rijksmuseum, Amsterdam)